ERNEST SOSA

AND HIS CRITICS

PHILOSOPHERS AND THEIR CRITICS
General Editor: Ernest Lepore

Philosophy is an interactive enterprise. Much of it is carried out in dialogue as theories and ideas are presented and subsequently refined in the crucible of close scrutiny. The purpose of this series is to reconstruct this vital interplay among thinkers. Each book consists of a temporary assessment of an important living philosopher's work. A collection of essays written by an interdisciplinary group of critics addressing the substantial theses of the philosopher's corpus opens each volume. In the last section, the philosopher responds to his or her critics, clarifies crucial points of the discussion, or updates his or her doctrines.

1. Dretske and His Critics
   Edited by Brian McLaughlin

2. John Searle and His Critics
   Edited by Ernest Lepore and Robert van Gulick

3. Meaning in Mind: Fodor and His Critics
   Edited by Barry Loewer and Georges Rey

4. Dennett and His Critics
   Edited by Bo Dahlbom

5. Danto and His Critics
   Edited by Mark Rollins

6. Perspectives on Quine
   Edited by Robert B. Barrett and Roger F. Gibson

7. The Churchlands and Their Critics
   Edited by Robert N. McCauley

8. Singer and His Critics
   Edited by Dale Jamieson

9. Rorty and His Critics
   Edited by Robert B. Brandom

10. Chomsky and His Critics
    Edited by Louise M. Antony and Norbert Hornstein

11. Dworkin and His Critics
    Edited by Justine Burley

12. Ernest Sosa and His Critics
    Edited by John Greco

ERNEST SOSA

AND HIS CRITICS

Edited by

John Greco

Blackwell
Publishing

© 2004 by Blackwell Publishing Ltd
except for editorial material and organization © 2004 by John Greco.
Michael Williams, "Mythology of the Given: Sosa, Sellars, and the Task of Epistemology,"
PASS, vol. LXXVII (2003) and Ernest Sosa, "Reply to Williams," *PASS*, vol. LXXVII (2003).
Reprinted by courtesy of the Editor of the Aristotelian Society © 2004

BLACKWELL PUBLISHING
350 Main Street, Malden, MA 02148-5020, USA
108 Cowley Road, Oxford OX4 1JF, UK
550 Swanston Street, Carlton, Victoria 3053, Australia

The right of John Greco to be identified as the Author of the Editorial Material in this Work
has been asserted in accordance with the UK Copyright, Designs, and Patents Act 1988.

All rights reserved. No part of this publication may be reproduced, stored in a
retrieval system, or transmitted, in any form or by any means, electronic,
mechanical, photocopying, recording or otherwise, except as permitted by the UK
Copyright, Designs, and Patents Act 1988, without the prior permission of the publisher.

First published 2004 by Blackwell Publishing Ltd

Library of Congress Cataloging-in-Publication Data

Ernest Sosa and his critics / edited by John Greco.
    p. cm. – (Philosophers and their critics; 12)
    Includes bibliographical references and index.
    ISBN 0-631-21798-3 (hardcover : alk. paper) – ISBN 0-631-21799-1 (pbk. : alk. paper)
  1. Sosa, Ernest. 2. Knowledge, Theory of. I. Greco, John. II. Series.
B945.S7274E76 2004
191–dc22
2003026676

A catalogue record for this title is available from the British Library.

Set in 10/12pt Ehrhardt
by Graphicraft Limited, Hong Kong
Printed and bound in the United Kingdom
by TJ International, Padstow, Cornwall

The publisher's policy is to use permanent paper from mills that operate a sustainable
forestry policy, and which has been manufactured from pulp processed using acid-free
and elementary chlorine-free practices. Furthermore, the publisher ensures that the text
paper and cover board used have met acceptable environmental accreditation standards.

For further information on
Blackwell Publishing, visit our website:
http://www.blackwellpublishing.com

Contents

Notes on Contributors   viii

Cited Works by Ernest Sosa   x

Preface   xii

Introduction: Motivations for Sosa's Epistemology   xv

Part I   Critical Essays: Epistemology   1

1. Intellectual Virtue and Epistemic Power   3
   ROBERT AUDI

2. Structure and Connection: Comments on Sosa's Epistemology   17
   STEWART COHEN

3. Sosa, Safety, Sensitivity, and Skeptical Hypotheses   22
   KEITH DEROSE

4. Foundational Justification   42
   RICHARD FELDMAN

5. A Trial Separation between the Theory of Knowledge and the Theory of Justified Belief   59
   RICHARD FOLEY

6. Achieving Epistemic Ascent   72
   RICHARD FUMERTON

7	Sosa on Reflective Knowledge and Virtue Perspectivism ALVIN GOLDMAN	86
8	How to Preserve Your Virtue while Losing Your Perspective JOHN GRECO	96
9	Sosa on Circularity and Coherence ALLEN HABIB AND KEITH LEHRER	106
10	Skepticism: Ascent and Assent? PETER KLEIN	112
11	Sosa on Human and Animal Knowledge HILARY KORNBLITH	126
12	Skepticism Undone? PAUL MOSER	135
13	Sosa and Epistemic Justification NICHOLAS RESCHER	145
14	Perceptual Knowledge and Epistemological Satisfaction BARRY STROUD	165
15	Mythology of the Given: Sosa, Sellars, and the Task of Epistemology MICHAEL WILLIAMS	174
16	Epistemic Value Monism LINDA ZAGZEBSKI	190
Part II	**Critical Essays: Metaphysics**	**199**
17	Sosa on Realism WILLIAM P. ALSTON	201
18	Reference and Subjectivity BILL BREWER	215
19	Sosa's Existential Relativism ELI HIRSCH	224
20	Sosa on Internal Realism and Conceptual Relativity HILARY PUTNAM	233

| 21 | On What There Is Now: Sosa on Two Forms of Relativity
JAMES VAN CLEVE | 249 |
| 22 | Sosa on Abilities, Concepts, and Externalism
TIMOTHY WILLIAMSON | 263 |

Part III   Replies   273

| 23 | Replies
ERNEST SOSA | 275 |

    Index   327

Notes on Contributors

WILLIAM P. ALSTON is Professor Emeritus of Philosophy at Syracuse University, New York.

ROBERT AUDI is Professor of Philosophy and David E. Gallo Professor of Business Ethics at the University of Notre Dame, Indiana.

BILL BREWER is CUF Lecturer in Philosophy and Tutorial Fellow of St. Catherine's College, Oxford.

STEWART COHEN is Professor of Philosophy at Arizona State University.

KEITH DEROSE is Professor of Philosophy at Yale University.

RICHARD FELDMAN is Professor of Philosophy at the University of Rochester, New York.

RICHARD FOLEY is Dean of the Faculty of Arts and Sciences and Professor of Philosophy at New York University.

RICHARD FUMERTON is F. Wendell Miller Professor of Philosophy at the University of Iowa.

ALVIN GOLDMAN is Board of Governors Professor of Philosophy at Rutgers University.

JOHN GRECO is Associate Professor of Philosophy at Fordham University, New York.

ALLEN HABIB is a doctoral student at the University of Arizona.

ELI HIRSCH is Professor of Philosophy at Brandeis University, Massachusetts.

PETER KLEIN is Professor of Philosophy at Rutgers University.

NOTES ON CONTRIBUTORS

HILARY KORNBLITH is Professor of Philosophy at the University of Massachusetts, Amherst.

KEITH LEHRER is Regents Professor of Philosophy at the University of Arizona.

PAUL MOSER is Professor and Chairperson of Philosophy at Loyola University of Chicago.

HILARY PUTNAM is Cogan University Professor Emeritus of Philosophy at Harvard University.

NICHOLAS RESCHER is University Professor of Philosophy at the University of Pittsburgh.

ERNEST SOSA is Romeo Elton Professor of Natural Theology and Professor of Philosophy at Brown University, Rhode Island, and Distinguished Visiting Professor at Rutgers University, New Jersey.

BARRY STROUD is Mills Professor of Metaphysics and Epistemology at the University of California, Berkeley.

JAMES VAN CLEVE is Professor of Philosophy at Brown University, Rhode Island.

MICHAEL WILLIAMS is Krieger-Eisenhower Professor of Philosophy at the Johns Hopkins University, Baltimore.

TIMOTHY WILLIAMSON is Wykeham Professor of Logic at the University of Oxford.

LINDA ZAGZEBSKI is Kingfisher College Chair of the Philosophy of Religion and Ethics at the University of Oklahoma.

Cited Works by Ernest Sosa

ACE   "Abilities, Concepts, and Externalism," in J. Heil and A. Mele, eds., *Mental Causation* (Oxford: Clarendon Press, 1993).

BIF   "Beyond Internal Foundations to External Virtues," in Laurence BonJour and Ernest Sosa, *Epistemic Justification: Internalism vs. Externalism, Foundations vs. Virtues* (Malden, MA: Blackwell Publishing, 2003).

BSB   "Beyond Skepticism, to the Best of our Knowledge," *Mind* 97 (1988): 153–89.

CEP   "Circularity and Epistemic Priority," in R. Schantz, ed., *The Externalist Challenge: New Studies in Cognition and Intentionality* (de Gruyter, forthcoming).

CSP   "Consciousness of the Self and of the Present," in James E. Tomberlin, ed., *Agent, Language, and the Structure of the World* (Indianapolis, IN: Hackett, 1983).

ER   "Existential Relativity," in Peter French et al., eds., *Midwest Studies in Philosophy*, 22: *New Directions in Philosophy* (Minneapolis, MN: University of Minnesota Press, 1999).

FLT   "For the Love of Truth," in Abrol Fairweather and Linda Zagzebski, eds., *Virtue Epistemology: Essays on Epistemic Virtue and Responsibility* (Oxford and New York: Oxford University Press, 2001).

FR   "Fregean Reference Defended," *Philosophical Issues* 6 (1995).

HDOM   "How to Defeat Opposition to Moore," in James Tomberlin, ed., *Philosophical Perspectives*, 13: *Epistemology* (Atascadero, CA: Ridgeview Publishing, 1999): 141–53.

HRPP   "How to Resolve the Pyrrhonian Problematic: A Lesson from Descartes," *Philosophical Studies* 85 (1997).

KCSD   "Knowledge in Context, Skepticism in Doubt," in James Tomberlin, ed., *Philosophical Perspectives*, 2: *Epistemology* (Atascadero, CA: Ridgeview Publishing, 1988).

KP   *Knowledge in Perspective: Selected Essays in Epistemology* (Cambridge and New York: Cambridge University Press, 1991).

MG   "Mythology of the Given," *History of Philosophy Quarterly* 14, 3 (July 1997): 275–86.

PA   "Privileged Access," in Quintin Smith, ed., *Consciousness: New Philosophical Essays* (Oxford: Oxford University Press, forthcoming).
PIA   "Propositions and Indexical Attitudes," in Herman Parret, ed., *On Believing* (Berlin: de Gruyter, 1983).
PPR   "Putnam's Pragmatic Realism," *Journal of Philosophy* 90 (1993): 63–84. Extracts reprinted with permission of the publisher.
PSEC   "Philosophical Scepticism and Epistemic Circularity," *Proceedings of the Aristotelian Society*, supp. vol. 68 (1994): 263–90.
PSPF   "Postscript to 'Proper Functionalism and Virtue Epistemology,'" in Jonathan Kvanvig, ed., *Warrant in Contemporary Epistemology* (Lanham, MD: Rowman and Littlefield, 1996).
PT   "The Place of Truth in Epistemology," in Michael DePaul and Linda Zagzebski, eds., *Intellectual Virtue: Perspectives from Ethics and Epistemology* (New York and Oxford: Oxford University Press, 2003).
PVE   "Perspectives in Virtue Epistemology: A Reply to Dancy and BonJour," *Philosophical Studies* 78 (1995): 221–35. Reprinted in Guy Axtell, ed., *Knowledge, Belief, and Character: Readings in Virtue Epistemology* (Lanham, MD: Rowman and Littlefield, 2000).
RA   "Relevant Alternatives, Contextualism Included," forthcoming in *Philosophical Studies*.
RK   "Reflective Knowledge in the Best Circles," *Journal of Philosophy* 94 (1997): 410–30.
RK2   "Reflective Knowledge in the Best Circles." Reprinted in Ernest Sosa and Jaegwon Kim, eds., *Epistemology* (Malden, MA: Blackwell Publishing, 2000).
RP   "The Raft and the Pyramid: Coherence versus Foundations in the Theory of Knowledge," in Peter French et al., eds., *Midwest Studies in Philosophy*, 5: *Studies in Epistemology* (Minneapolis, MN: University of Minnesota Press, 1980).
RP2   "The Raft and the Pyramid: Coherence versus Foundations in the Theory of Knowledge." Reprinted in Ernest Sosa and Jaegwon Kim, eds., *Epistemology* (Malden, MA: Blackwell Publishing, 2000).
S&C   "Skepticism and Contextualism," *Philosophical Issues* 10 (2000): 1–18.
SI   "Skepticism and the Internal/External Divide," in John Greco and Ernest Sosa, eds., *Blackwell Guide to Epistemology* (Oxford: Blackwell Publishing, 1999).
STB   "The Status of Temporal Becoming: What is Happening Now?" *Journal of Philosophy* 76 (1979): 26–42.
TCK   "Tracking, Competence, and Knowledge," in Paul Moser, ed., *The Oxford Handbook of Epistemology* (Oxford: Oxford University Press, 2002).
TFD   "Two False Dichotomies: Internalism/Externalism and Foundationalism/Coherentism," in Walter Sinnott-Armstrong, ed., *Pyrrhonian Skepticism* (Oxford: Oxford University Press, 2003).
TR   "Thomas Reid" (co-authored with James Van Cleve), in Steven Emmanuel, ed., *The Modern Philosophers: From Descartes to Nietzsche* (Oxford: Blackwell Publishing, 2000).
VE   "Virtue Epistemology," unpublished manuscript.
VP   "Virtue Pespectivism: A Response to Foley and Fumerton," *Philosophical Issues* 5 (1994): 29–50.

Preface

This book is a volume in Blackwell's "Philosophers and Their Critics" series. As such, it follows the usual format of the series: the book is composed of several critical essays addressing the work of Ernest Sosa (our philosopher), with a reply by Sosa. The book also has a few special features that are worth mentioning.

First, Sosa's replies are limited to those critical essays that deal with some aspect of his work in epistemology. This was decided in order to limit the length of the "Replies" and to expedite the publication of the book – a reply to the broad range of issues raised in the "Metaphysics" section of the volume would have required more words and more time than seemed desirable. Also, this allowed a more coherent and self-contained approach to the "Replies" essay. Rather than answering critics point by point, Sosa has written an essay divided among several themes of current interest in epistemology. We agreed that this would be the most valuable and most readable approach.

Second, the book handles references to Sosa's work in a way that is intended to be especially reader-friendly. In particular, each essay contains full references to each of Sosa's works cited in that essay. After a full citation, further references to the work are abbreviated and appear parenthetically in the text. For example, a reference to page 214 of *Knowledge in Perspective* would appear as (*KP*, 214). In addition to the references within each essay, a list of all cited works by Sosa, with abbreviations and in alphabetical order, appears at the beginning of the volume. Thus there are two ways to check the full reference information for an abbreviated citation: one can either go to the first citation of the work within a particular essay or go to the list of cited works at the beginning of the volume.

Finally, my introductory essay to the book does not try to summarize the critical essays or to otherwise summarize the contents of the volume. Rather, I thought it more helpful to provide a kind of introduction to Sosa's epistemology and to Sosa's approach to epistemology. Sosa's work in this area is rich and complex, and sometimes difficult. It is also divided among several essays, in various places, and across several years. Accordingly, it is not always easy to appreciate how the various parts of the system fit together, what is the motivation for a particular position, etc. The introduction is intended to help in this respect, by providing an overview and a context for some of Sosa's most influential views in epistemology.

I would like to thank Ernest Sosa and all of our contributors for their participation in the project. Thanks also to Ernest LePore, the editor of the series, and to Daniel Breyer, who was a great help with various aspects of the book, including the index. It has been a pleasure working with such an outstanding group of philosophers.

Volumes such as this one are always a kind of tribute to the philosopher under discussion – it goes without saying that not everyone's work merits or receives this sort of attention. This volume turned out to be a tribute to Ernest Sosa the person, as well. I say this on the basis of the wonderful response by our contributors. I can't imagine that it has ever been so easy to bring together such an outstanding group of philosophers, so eager to participate in the project and so generous in their efforts. This has been a great celebration of Ernie and his work.

Introduction: Motivations for Sosa's Epistemology

Over the last four decades, Ernest Sosa has defended a complex and penetrating theory of knowledge – one that has consequences for every important issue raised in recent epistemology, and for many related issues as well. The essays in this volume, for example, address Sosa's positions regarding the nature of knowledge, internalism and externalism about justification, skepticism, foundationalism and coherentism, and the nature of intellectual virtue, but also his positions regarding realism, internalism and externalism about mental states, and the nature of reference.

I will not try to summarize Sosa's views here, or to otherwise give them adequate treatment. This I leave to the volume's capable contributors, who provide both useful summaries and critical discussions of many aspects of Sosa's work in their essays. Rather, in this introduction I will reconstruct what, it seems to me, are some of the most important arguments motivating Sosa's general position in epistemology. I take this general position to be "externalist," in that it makes positive epistemic status depend on factors relevantly external to the knower. Furthermore, Sosa's general view is correctly characterized as a virtue theory, in that it adopts a distinctive direction of analysis. Specifically, it defines the evaluative properties of beliefs in terms of the evaluative properties (or virtues) of believers. Finally, Sosa's view places central importance on the notion of an epistemic perspective, where this is understood as a set of second-order beliefs about one's first-order beliefs and the reliability of their sources. Hence the label "virtue perspectivism" for Sosa's view.

1 Three Options in Epistemology

It is fair to say that Sosa sees three broad options available in epistemology – not in the sense that these are the only ones logically possible, but in the sense that these are the ones deemed most plausible by those, past and present, who have thought carefully about relevant matters. The options are these:

Classical foundationalism. The central idea is that one knows only what is obvious and what can be deductively proved from the obvious. Descartes's rationalism is an example, since "he concludes that we know only what we intuit or deduce: that our acceptance of a true proposition can have the epistemic justification (authority, warrant, status, call it what you will) required for knowledge only if it is either itself a rational intuition or the outcome of a logical deduction from nothing but rational intuitions as ultimate premises."[1] Hume's theory also counts, however, since he accepts as knowledge only what can be proved "on the basis of what is obvious at any given moment through reason or experience" (*KP*, 166–7).

Coherentism. The coherentist rejects the idea of foundational knowledge, or knowledge that is not dependent on further knowledge for its evidence. The central idea is that all knowledge (justified belief, warranted belief) depends on further beliefs for its status as such. More specifically, a belief qualifies as knowledge in virtue of its membership in a sufficiently coherent and comprehensive system of beliefs.

Reliabilism. A belief qualifies as knowledge (justified, warranted) in virtue of its deriving from a reliable (truth-conducive) process. Since some reliable processes depend on further beliefs for their inputs and some do not, there is no bar in principle to foundational knowledge. In fact, reliabilism is best understood as a kind of foundationalism. "Every bit of knowledge still lies atop a pyramid of knowledge. But the building requirements for pyramids are now less stringent. A belief may now join the base not only through perfectly reliable rational intuition but also through introspection, perception, or memory. And one may now erect a superstructure on such a basis not only by deduction but also by induction, both enumerative and hypothetical or explanatory" (*KP*, 89).

Sosa levels several objections against the first two options, some of them quite traditional. For example, classical foundationalism is criticized for allowing too narrow a foundation to preserve the bulk of ordinary knowledge, and coherentism is criticized for failing to assign a proper role to experience in the justification of belief. Such objections can be both powerful and instructive, especially in the versions that Sosa formulates. I will ignore these here, however, and instead focus on a different series of objections raised by Sosa. These latter are aimed not so much at technical flaws or theoretical lacunae, but at the very motivations for the two positions. Properly understood, I believe, these objections help us to recognize, and to some extent reconceive, what is at issue in the dispute among competing options in epistemology.

2 Against the Argumentative Account of Justification

Standing behind various arguments for coherentism, and behind various objections to foundationalism, is what Sosa calls the "argumentative account of justification" (*KP*, 253). According to Donald Davidson, "What distinguishes a coherence theory is simply the claim that nothing can count as a reason for holding a belief except another belief. Its partisan rejects as unintelligible the request for a ground or source of justification of another ilk."[2] According to Richard Rorty, "nothing counts as justification unless by reference to what we already accept, and there is no way to get outside our beliefs and our language so as to find some test other than coherence."[3] Such reasoning at once makes foundational beliefs absurd and coherentism the only live option in sight. Right behind such reasoning, Sosa suggests, is the following argumentative conception of justification (AJ):

(a) that for a belief to be justified is for the believer to justify it or to have justified it; and
(b) that for one to justify a belief (really, successfully) is for one correctly and seriously to use considerations or reasons in its favor.

But why accept (AJ)? Of course one can point to common usage, and insist that to justify is to bring reasons in favor. And if that does not work, one can simply stipulate accordingly. However, Sosa points out, neither of these strategies will give the coherentist what he wants. For in that case it remains possible that some knowledge is not justified, and so nothing so far counts against foundationalism or in favor of coherentism. The substantive issue is raised again by talking about epistemic authority (or warrant, or aptness), and by asking whether all epistemic authority requires argumentative justification.

Moreover, Sosa argues, the argumentative account is in trouble as an account of epistemic authority in general. For to "correctly" use reasons in favor is surely to use *justified* reasons in favor, and in that case we are faced with a vicious regress. If a belief is knowledge only by being justified, and if being justified requires being based on further justified reasons, then there will be no end to the process of justifying.

A natural response by the coherentist is to say that justification ends in coherence: that ultimately a belief is justified not by further reasons brought in its favor, but by its membership in a coherent system of reasons. An alternative response is to say that justification ends with what our peers let us say: that ultimately a belief is justified because it meets the standards that society plus context fix in place. But either response gives up the argumentative account of justification, and the idea that epistemic authority is always won by virtue of giving reasons. On the contrary, each response specifies an alternative basis for justification (coherence or social standards), and in doing so enters into a dispute with the foundationalist on equal footing. In other words, each response claims that something else, not justified reasons, is the ultimate source of epistemic authority.

3 Supervenience and Normative Epistemology

The issues above are brought into clear focus by another important theme in Sosa's work: that of the supervenience of the evaluative. In general, Sosa thinks, we should accept the thesis that the evaluative supervenes on the non-evaluative. In other words, we should accept the idea that a thing has its evaluative properties in virtue of its non-evaluative properties.

For example, suppose we think that a particular car is a good one. Surely this must be in virtue of other properties that the car has, for example the mileage that it gets, its ability to accelerate, its look, etc. To deny this would be to accept that two cars could be alike in all their non-evaluative properties (both intrinsic and relational) and yet differ in their evaluative ones. But this seems absurd. The same reasoning holds for epistemically evaluative properties.

> Suppose S and Twin-S live lives indistinguishable physically or psychologically, indistinguishable both intrinsically and contextually, on Earth and Twin-Earth respectively. Surely there can then be no belief of S epistemically justified without a matching belief held by Twin-S with equal epistemic justification. Epistemic justification must accordingly supervene upon or derive from physical or psychological properties of the subject of belief, properties either intrinsic or contextual. (*KP*, 110)

An important aim of epistemology, Sosa reasons, is to specify the non-evaluative basis of supervenience, thus allowing a special sort of insight into the nature of justification and knowledge. In this respect, coherentists and foundationalists share a common goal: to specify such a basis in relatively simple and complete terms.

It is from this perspective that the argumentative account of justification seems clearly hopeless. According to (AJ), for one to justify a belief is for one "correctly and seriously to use considerations or reasons in its favor." But again, how are we to understand "correctly"? The most obvious way is in terms of some epistemically evaluative property. Alternatively, "considerations or reasons" will have to be understood that way. And therefore the argumentative account fails to get beyond the epistemically evaluative. What is required for that, as we saw above, is that something else be considered more ultimate.

Also from this perspective, certain arguments against foundationalism can be seen in a new light. For example, "doxastic ascent" arguments charge that there can be no property F in virtue of which belief B is foundationally justified, unless one is justified in believing that B has F. But then B is not foundational at all, since its justification depends on B′: the belief that B has F. But this line of reasoning, Sosa argues, would implicate all of substantive epistemology with foundationalism, coherentism included. For anyone who accepts it would have to accept the following as well:

> that a belief B is justified in virtue of membership in a coherent system only if one is justified in believing that it has such membership.

And more generally,

> that a belief B is justified in virtue of *any property* X only if one is justified in believing that B has X.

Clearly, such commitments entail an infinite regress of justified beliefs. More importantly from the present perspective, however, they are inconsistent with the supervenience of the epistemically evaluative. No matter what we specify as a non-epistemic source of justification, coherence included, such commitments require that something else is needed; *viz.*, another justified belief. This "would then preclude the possibility of supervenience, since it would entail that the source of justification *always* includes an *epistemic* component" (*KP*, 183).

4 Against Internalism

Considerations about supervenience throw light on another important issue: the dispute between internalism and externalism about justification. In effect, the internalist claims that justification (or warrant, or aptness) supervenes entirely on factors that are in some sense internal to the knower. From the point of view of coherentism, this includes only the knower's beliefs, and perhaps relevant relations among them. From the point of view of classical foundationalism, this includes other psychological states as well, including sensory experience and other relevant aspects of conscious awareness. If internalism is correct, then it is not possible for believers to be equal in these internal respects and yet different in their epistemically evaluative properties. But that seems wrong, as several thought experiments show.

Consider first the victim of a Cartesian deceiver. Such a victim might be your psychological counterpart, with a system of beliefs as coherent as your own. Now suppose some few of these beliefs are true. Surely they do not amount to knowledge, even though they are both true and coherent. The moral of the story, Sosa suggests, is that knowledge requires some epistemic excellence other than coherence.

Notice, however, that the same reasoning applies if we broaden our conception of the internal. For we can imagine that the demon victim is like you in *all* internal respects, including those deemed important by classical foundationalism. Hence we can imagine a victim who shares not only your beliefs, but also your sensory experience, and all other aspects of your conscious awareness. Again, the victim's beliefs are not knowledge even when true, and therefore something epistemically significant is lacking in his predicament. What might that be?

> Compare this: Mary and Jane arrive at conclusion C, Mary through a brilliant proof, Jane through a tissue of fallacies. At present, however, they both have forgotten the relevant stretches of their respective reasonings, and each takes herself to have established her conclusion validly.... No doubt we normally would grant Mary justification and withhold it from Jane. Would we not judge Jane's belief unjustified since based essentially on fallacies?[4]

Sosa's point in the above passage is that aetiology matters for epistemic justification; i.e., it matters how a belief comes about, even if this is lost on the believer. But of course aetiology is an external matter. A belief's causal history is not something "internal" in any relevant sense.

> Second case: You remember having oatmeal for breakfast, because you did experience having it, and have retained that bit of information through your excellent memory. Your counterpart self-attributes having had oatmeal for breakfast, and may self-attribute remembering that to be so (as presumably do you), but his beliefs are radically wide of the mark, as are an army of affiliated beliefs, since your counterpart was created just moments ago, complete with all of those beliefs and relevant current experiences. Are you two on a par in respect of epistemic justification? (SI, 153–4)

Clearly you are on a par in *some* senses of "justification"; for example, any sense that depends only on factors internal to the believing subject. Presumably you are also on a par in respect to doing your epistemic duty, believing with epistemic responsibility, and believing according to your own deepest standards. But all of these senses of justification, Sosa argues, fail to capture aspects of epistemic excellence that are important to knowledge. Most importantly, they fail to capture any involved in being appropriately related to the truth.

> Knowledge requires coherence, true enough, but it often requires more: e.g., that one be adequately related, causally or counterfactually, to the objects of one's knowledge, to one's environment or surroundings, which is not necessarily ensured by the mere coherence of one's beliefs, no matter how comprehensively coherent they may be.... Knowledge requires not only internal justification or coherence or rationality, but also external warrant or aptness. We must be *both* in good internal order and in appropriate external relation to our surrounding world.[5]

The epistemically evaluative supervenes on states internal to the knower, such as her beliefs and experiences, but also on states broader than these, including external relations to the object known and to the wider environment. Internalism with respect to the epistemic justification, or the kind of justification involved in knowledge, is false.

5 Virtue Epistemology

Let us take stock of what we have so far: The argumentative account of justification motivates coherentism, while internalism motivates both coherentism and classical foundationalism. But considerations about the supervenience of the evaluative tell against both the argumentative account and internalism. Coherentism and classical foundationalism, therefore, are importantly undermined.

One might consider internalism to be inessential to classical foundationalism, however. For example, one might accept Sosa's characterization of rationalism as a limiting case of reliabilism, where the reliability that is required is infallibility. Still, there are problems with classical foundationalism other than internalism. We have already seen one such problem: the foundations that classical foundationalism proposes are too narrow to account for all of our knowledge. In this section I will introduce another as well. These problems are important to consider, because Sosa thinks that turning to a virtue epistemology solves them.

According to classical foundationalism, foundational knowledge is through intuition and introspection. A broader foundationalism allows observation as well. But how are we to understand these sources of knowledge? According to Sosa, there is an important problem here.

> What is a rational intuition? Is it a true belief, without inference, in something logically necessary? Not necessarily, for such a belief can arise and be sustained by guessing or by superstition or brainwashing – and, in any of these cases, even if one believes something logically necessary, this does not imply that one knows what one believes. The question remains: What is a rational intuition?[6]

Similar questions arise with regard to introspection and observation.

> The observer sees the white dodecagon and has two thoughts. He thinks, first, that his visual experience has a certain character, that of being a visual experience as if he saw a white dodecagon. And he thinks, further, that in fact he sees a white dodecagon a certain distance away. Although he is twice right, however, he is right only by chance, for he lacks

the capacity to distinguish dodecagons with a high probability of success – indeed he often
confuses dodecagons with decagons. (BIF, 117–19)

The foundationalist might try to account for introspective knowledge by invoking the idea of direct awareness. But there is an ambiguity in the essential notion of awareness. In one sense, all conscious states are objects of awareness. In this sense, it is possible to be "aware" of something without taking note of it, as happens when we fail to attend to some aspect of our conscious experience. In another sense, however, awareness implies that the object of awareness is *noticed* – that it is the object of one's conscious *attention*. Sosa calls the first kind of awareness "experiential awareness" (or e-awareness) and he calls the second "noticing awareness" (or n-awareness). The latter notion will not do in an account of introspective knowledge, however, since it is already epistemically evaluative. As Sosa notes, to be n-aware of something already implies a kind of positive epistemic status. If the notion of direct awareness is to explain the evaluative in terms of the non-evaluative, therefore, awareness will have to be understood as e-awareness.

But that puts us back where we started: How are we to explain the *lack* of introspective knowledge regarding the dodecagon, if introspection involves belief based on direct e-awareness, and if the observer has such awareness of the dodecagon quality of his experience?

As Sosa notes, the problem here is analogous to Chisholm's "Problem of the Speckled Hen." The classical foundationalist wants to say that we can have introspective knowledge of certain features of our conscious experience. But clearly not *all* features of our experience can be known by introspection – for example, we cannot know by introspection that the image of a hen has forty-eight speckles. So which features are the ones that we *can* know by introspection? And of course similar questions arise for rational intuition and observation: Which necessary truths are the ones we can know just by intuiting them? Which features of things can we know just by observing them?

Sosa concludes that to answer these questions we must invoke the notion of an intellectual virtue.

How will the classical foundationalist specify which features belong on which side of that divide? It is hard to see how this could be done without appealing to intellectual virtues or faculties seated in the subject. For example, an attribution of a feature to an experience or thought is perhaps foundationally justified only when it derives from the operation of a reliable virtue or faculty. (BIF, 134–5)

According to Sosa, an intellectual virtue is a truth-conducive disposition in the subject. It is a competence or power to reliably arrive at truth and avoid falsehood in a relevant field, when in relevant circumstances. It is with reference to such dispositions, he argues, that we can solve the Problem of the Speckled Hen, as well as the analogous problems for rational intuition and observation.

How then would one distinguish

(i) an *unjustified* 'introspective' judgment, say that one's image has 48 speckles, when it is a true judgment, and one issued in full view of the image with that specific character, from

(ii) a *justified* 'introspective' judgment, say that one's image has 3 speckles?

> The relevant distinction is that the latter judgment is both (a) *safe* and (b) *virtuous*, or so I wish to suggest. It is 'safe' because in the circumstances not easily *would* one believe as one does without being right. It is 'virtuous' because one's belief derives from a way of forming beliefs that is an intellectual virtue, one that in our normal situation for forming such beliefs would tend strongly enough to give us beliefs that are safe. (BIF, 138–9)

Finally, we may return to the problem of narrow foundations. By understanding knowledge in terms of intellectual virtue, Sosa argues, we can solve this problem as well. Because they are reliable, faculties such as rational intuition and introspection count as intellectual virtues, and thereby give rise to epistemic justification for their respective products. But so is memory reliable, as are various modes of sensory observation. Similarly, various faculties of inductive reasoning, including coherence-seeking reason, reliably take one from true belief to further true belief, and hence count as virtues in their own right. By defining epistemic justification in terms of intellectual virtue, we get a unified account of all the sources of justification recognized by classical foundationalism, and more besides.

6 A Kinder, Gentler Externalism

So far our discussion has left out a central theme of Sosa's epistemology: that fully human knowledge requires an epistemic perspective, or a perspective on one's beliefs as deriving from intellectual virtues. Such a requirement is needed, Sosa argues, to accommodate persistent internalist intuitions regarding knowledge and justification. Internalism is false, Sosa thinks, as the arguments above show. Nevertheless, "Such intuitions reflect a long tradition and still demand their due."[7]

Such intuitions are brought out by two related problems.

> *The New Evil Demon Problem.* Suppose that S is your cognitive twin, sharing an identical mental life, but in a possible world where his beliefs are in massive error due to the influence of a Cartesian deceiver. It seems wrong to say that S's beliefs are in no sense justified, even if they are not reliably formed.
>
> *The Meta-incoherence Problem.* Suppose that S's belief is produced by a perfectly reliable faculty of clairvoyance. Suppose also, however, that S has no evidence in favor of the belief, or even has evidence against it. It seems wrong to say that S's belief is justified, even if it is reliably formed.

These are problems for externalism in general and for reliabilism in particular, since they suggest that justification is indeed an internal matter.

Sosa addresses the two problems by noting that intellectual virtue, and hence justification, is relative to an environment and to an epistemic group. Accordingly, we may say that a belief is justified relative to an environment E and group G, only if it is produced by what is an intellectual virtue (i.e., a reliable cognitive faculty) relative to E and G.

Usually E and G will refer to a normal environment and normal human beings, although E and/or G could be different depending on context.

Regarding the New Evil Demon Problem, we can say that S's beliefs are justified relative to our normal G and E, since they are produced by cognitive faculties that are intellectual virtues relative to normal human beings situated in the actual world. Sosa reasons that "the victim of the evil demon is virtuous and internally justified in every relevant respect... for the victim is supposed to be just like an arbitrarily selected normal human in all cognitively relevant internal respects. Therefore, the internal structure and goings on in the victim must be at least up to par, in respect of how virtuous all of that internal nature makes the victim, relative to a normal one of us in our usual environment for considering whether we have a fire before us or the like" (*KP*, 143).

The same considerations, Sosa argues, solve the Meta-incoherence Problem as well. For justification requires that the subject be as internally virtuous as a "normal one of us," and this means, according to Sosa, that "the subject must attain some minimum of coherent perspective on her own situation in the relevant environment, and on her modes of reliable access to information about that environment" (*KP*, 143). This is what the clairvoyant lacks, and that is why his belief is not justified on the present account.

Sosa develops the above strategy by drawing two distinctions: (a) that between aptness and justification, and (b) that between animal knowledge and reflective (or fully human) knowledge. First, a belief is *apt* only if it is produced by what is, relative to the environment, an intellectual virtue. A belief is *justified* only if it fits within a coherent set of beliefs, including a perspective on one's first-order belief as deriving from an intellectual virtue. Second, a belief qualifies as *animal knowledge* so long as it is true and apt. A belief qualifies as *reflective knowledge* only if, in addition to this, it is justified as well; that is, only if it fits within the coherent perspective of the believer (*KP*, 144–5).

Here is Sosa on the value of such coherence:

> Yet coherence is, of course, valued not only by philosophers but by the reflective more generally. One also wants faculties and virtues beyond reflective, coherence-seeking reason: perception, for example, and memory. Equally, internal coherence goes beyond such faculties, and requires reason, which counts for a lot in its own right. (RK, 421)

The resulting position, Sosa thinks, respects the internalist's intuitions about justification, while at the same time preserving both internalist and externalist insights about knowledge.

By way of concluding, I should stress that in this essay I have presented only some of the motivating arguments for Sosa's position.[8] Moreover, I have presented that position only in broad strokes – in actuality it is far more detailed and subtle, as are the arguments that Sosa brings in favor of it. All this will be apparent in the essays that follow, and in Sosa's replies to them. Nevertheless, I believe that the arguments above are some of the most important in shaping Sosa's epistemology, and in shaping contemporary epistemology as well.

John Greco

Notes

1 *Knowledge in Perspective: Selected Essays in Epistemology* (Cambridge: Cambridge University Press, 1991) (cited as *KP*), p. 88.
2 Sosa quotes Davidson's "A Coherence Theory of Truth and Knowledge," in Ernest LePore, ed., *Truth and Interpretation: Perspectives on the Philosophy of Donald Davidson* (Oxford: Basil Blackwell, 1992). Quoted in *KP*, p. 108.
3 Sosa quotes Rorty's *Philosophy and the Mirror of Nature* (Princeton, NJ: Princeton University Press, 1979). Quoted in *KP*, p. 108.
4 "Skepticism and the Internal/External Divide," in John Greco and Ernest Sosa, eds., *Blackwell Guide to Epistemology* (Oxford: Blackwell, 1999) (cited as SI), pp. 152–3.
5 "Reflective Knowledge in the Best Circles," *The Journal of Philosophy* 94 (1997): 410–30 (cited as RK), p. 430.
6 "Beyond Internal Foundations to External Virtues," in Laurence BonJour and Ernest Sosa, *Epistemic Justification: Internalism vs. Externalism, Foundations vs. Virtues* (Malden, MA: Blackwell, 2003) (cited as BIF), pp. 117–19.
7 "Virtue Epistemology," unpublished manuscript.
8 For example, Sosa argues that a distinction between reflective and animal knowledge, and hence the notion of an epistemic perspective, are needed to address a certain line of skeptical argument. See his "How to Resolve the Pyrrhonian Problematic: A Lesson from Descartes," *Philosophical Studies* 85 (1997). He also thinks that the notion of an epistemic perspective yields a solution to the generality problem for reliabilism. See *KP*, esp. pp. 278 and 281–4.

Part I

Critical Essays: Epistemology

1

Intellectual Virtue and Epistemic Power

ROBERT AUDI

Virtue ethics is an old and venerable orientation in ethical theory. Virtue epistemology is a recent approach. Each is a kind of trait theory, by contrast with a rule theory. Virtue ethics construes moral action as action from moral virtue and has implications for the entire realm of practical reason, including rational action as the most general case in the domain of behavior.[1] Virtue epistemology, in the form in which it is closest to virtue ethics, construes both justified belief and knowledge as belief from intellectual virtue – as true belief in the case of knowledge. The theory has implications for the entire realm of theoretical reason, including rational belief as the most general case in the domain of cognition. There are now many philosophers developing one or another kind of virtue epistemology,[2] but the earliest epistemologically sophisticated statements of the position, and certainly as well-developed a version of it as there is now, have been constructed in a series of works by Ernest Sosa.[3] His virtue epistemology, moreover, is informed by numerous connections with other kinds and aspects of epistemology and by decades of cutting-edge research in the general field. There is much to be learned from his recent writings in virtue epistemology. They illuminate both the elements and explanatory power of virtue epistemology itself and some central epistemological problems. My aim here is to explore this orientation as we find it in some of his major works and to bring out some of its distinctive features and some of the problems it raises for the tasks of general epistemology.

1 Some Major Elements in Virtue Perspectivism

The overall epistemological view developed by Sosa in recent years is *virtue perspectivism*. It will soon be plain why it represents not only a virtue epistemology but also a perspectival theory. If any single notion is central in the position, it is that of intellectual virtue. In an early statement of what constitutes such virtue, he said that "[a]n intellectual virtue is a quality bound to help maximize one's surplus of truth over error," to which he immediately added a forecast of theoretical elements to come and a qualification: "or so let us assume for now, though a more just conception may include as desiderata also generality, coherence, and explanatory power, unless the value of these is itself explained as derivative from the character of their contribution precisely to one's surplus of truth over error."[4]

This opening characterization, forecast, and qualification are quite important for the development of the overall theory. The characterization is highly refined and extensively developed; the forecast proves, on analysis, to be correct at least for well-developed intellectual virtues; and the qualification gestures toward a major question that we must still address in order to understand Sosa's virtue epistemology: the extent to which the notion of intellectual virtue is externalist and reliabilist.

Later in the same paper he indicates the importance of justification for the notion of intellectual virtue. Of a man who, by good luck, is correct as a result of believing his horoscope, Sosa says:

> S does not know in such a case. What S lacks, I suggest, is *justification*. His reason for trusting the horoscope is not adequate – to put it kindly. What is such justification?
> A being of epistemic kind K is prima facie justified in believing P if and only if his belief of P manifests what, relative to K beings, is an intellectual virtue, a faculty that enhances their differential of truth over error.[5] (*KP*, 239)

We now find that justification as well as knowledge is to be conceived as grounded at least in part in intellectual virtue. This in turn is conceived as a faculty, which is roughly an ability or power (*KP*, 234) or, better, a "virtue or a *competence*," and virtue lies "in the general family of dispositions" (*KP*, 274).

The horoscopic belief, lacking as it does justification as well as reliable grounding, is not a candidate for knowledge even of the weaker of the two main kinds Sosa countenances. To see what the weaker kind is in contrast to the stronger kind, we must consider a distinction introduced late in this paper and figuring importantly in his subsequent work:

> One has *animal knowledge* about one's environment, one's past, and one's own experience if one's judgments and beliefs about these are direct responses to their impact – e.g., through perception or memory – with little or no benefit of reflection or understanding.
> One has *reflective knowledge* if one's judgment or belief manifests not only such direct response to the fact known but also understanding of its place in a wider whole that includes one's belief and knowledge of it and how these come about. (*KP*, 240)

Clearly, it is reflective knowledge to which we should aspire for much of our outlook on the world and which is crucial for the successful exercise of intellectual virtue. One way we achieve it (given favorable conditions) is quite natural: "A reason-endowed being automatically monitors his background information and his sensory input for contrary evidence and automatically opts for the most coherent hypothesis even when he responds most directly to sensory stimuli" (*KP*, 240).

In his later, major statement of virtue perspectivism, published in *Knowledge in Perspective*, Sosa develops the ideas we have been sketching. One major element is an aretaic (i.e., virtue-theoretic) conception of knowledge:

> We have reached the view that knowledge is true belief out of intellectual virtue, belief that turns out right by reason of the virtue and not just by coincidence. For reflective knowledge you need moreover an epistemic perspective that licenses your belief by its source in some virtue or faculty of your own. (*KP*, 277)

If this conception of knowledge is even roughly correct, then we can achieve a good epistemological understanding of the concept of knowledge if we can provide, as a basis for it, an illuminating account of intellectual virtue. This is precisely what Sosa goes on to do in this paper and subsequent work. Later in the paper we are given the following account of *having* an intellectual virtue:

> S has an intellectual virtue V(C, F) relative to environment E if and only if S has an inner nature I such that
>
> if   (i)   S is in E and has I,
>   (ii) P is a proposition in the field F, and
>   (iii) S is in conditions C with respect to P,
> then, (iv) S is very likely to believe correctly with respect to P, (*KP*, 286)

where F is the appropriate field (such as the realm of observables relative to a proposition ascribing color), C is the set of relevant conditions (for instance, normal lighting relative to a proposition ascribing visible properties at a distance), and believing correctly may be a matter not only of believing, but also of disbelieving or simply not believing. (Believing correctly with respect to P is not equivalent to believing P *truly*; the correct thing may be to disbelieve it or to withhold judgment.)

We are now in a position to see what it is to believe *out of* intellectual virtue:

> S believes P out of intellectual virtue V(C, F) iff
>
> (a) S is in an environment E such that S has intellectual virtue V(C, F) relative to E,
> (b) P is a proposition in F,
> (c) S is in C with respect to P, and
> (d) S believes P.[6] (*KP*, 287)

Since knowledge is true belief out of intellectual virtue, we can account for it by adding truth to these conditions and specifying that the virtue is "sufficient," in the sense that the ratio of true to false beliefs based on it is at least "up near the average" for the relevant reference group, such as human beings (*KP*, 287–8). In this way, intellectual virtue is relative. Visual acuity for human beings need not, for instance, be as great as for birds, and our virtue in forming visual beliefs may reflect this. Such *species-relativity* is not, however, the only kind for which Sosa's position allows. The reference group in question can, for instance, be a sub-species as well.

From the case of horoscopically based belief, we can already see that the inner nature appropriate to achieving knowledge cannot be possessed by people who, upon believing in accordance with their nature, are not likely to be correct. There the believer, if correct, is simply lucky; the person's norm would not be to believe truths in the relevant domain. Sosa uses the contrast between an ordinarily near-sighted person aware of the limitation and Magoo, who is comparably near-sighted but unaware of it, to bring out other elements in the notion of intellectual virtue. Perceivers of the former kind have an inner nature (perhaps as a matter of having achieved epistemic balance and caution) that determines them (at least for the most part) to believe, on the basis of vision, only those propositions that meet the conditions in question: roughly speaking, they believe, on the basis of visual sensations, only in appropriate environments and within the limits of their visual acuity.

There is an important distinction central for understanding Sosa's epistemology here. It is needed to account for the broadly "internalist" intuition that, epistemically, one might be highly responsible yet, in a world controlled by a Cartesian demon, likely to be incorrect in a majority of one's beliefs. Here it is crucial, for Sosa, to distinguish justification from aptness:

> The "justification" of a belief B requires that B have a basis in its inference or coherence relations to other beliefs in the believer's mind – as in the "justification" of a belief derived from deeper principles. (*KP*, 289)

By contrast,

> The "aptness" of a belief B relative to an environment E requires that B derive from what relative to E is an intellectual virtue, i.e., a way of arriving at belief that yields an appropriate preponderance of truth over error. (*KP*, 289)

Summarizing the former point, Sosa says that "'justification' amounts to a sort of inner coherence, something that the demon's victims can have despite their cognitively hostile environment" (*KP*, 289). Aptness is quite different: "Justification of a belief that *p* requires the (implicit or explicit) use of reasons. A belief can be apt, however, without being thus justified" (*KP*, 290). Indeed, aptness is exhibited by "animal knowledge," which need not be constituted by justified belief, and "[v]irtue perspectivism accepts a sort of reliabilism with respect to animal knowledge, and with respect to unreflective knowledge generally" (*KP*, 291).

For reflective knowledge, by contrast, more is required than reliabilism demands as a constitutive condition for knowledge: "For the exercise of virtue to yield [reflective] knowledge, one must have some awareness of one's belief and its source, and of the virtue of that source both in general and in the specific instance" (*KP*, 292). In his later "Reflective Knowledge in the Best Circles,"[7] the same distinction is stressed, with a similar willingness to allow that reliabilism, as opposed to virtue perspectivism, may account for some animal knowledge. Here Sosa holds that

> (a) our broad coherence is necessary for the kind of reflective knowledge traditionally desired; and (b) such broadly coherent knowledge is desirable because in our actual world it helps us approach the truth and avoid error. This is not to deny that there is a kind of "animal knowledge" untouched by broad coherence. It is rather only to affirm that beyond "animal knowledge" there is better knowledge. This reflective knowledge does require coherence, including one's ability to place one's first-level knowledge in epistemic perspective. (RK, 67)

The distinction between animal and reflective knowledge is, in this later work, paired with Descartes's distinction between *cognitio* and *scientia*, but freed of the theological dependency of the Cartesian distinction and its associated infallibilism (RK, 71).

Sosa's epistemic perspectivism, then, combines elements from reliabilist externalism, epistemic internalism, Cartesian higher-level foundationalism, and the epistemological analogue of virtue ethics. The result is an account of knowledge that roots it in traits of the knowing subject and distinguishes the natural, animal cognitions that come with our elemental responsiveness to the world from the higher-order beliefs we form when, as in achieving scientific knowledge, we believe what we do in the light of suitable self-understanding. I want to explore this epistemology mainly in relation to two questions: Why is intellectual virtue as Sosa conceives it *virtue*, and, assuming that reflective knowledge is indeed knowledge from virtue, is the ideal it indicates too demanding for normal knowers?

2 Virtue and Power

In the works I have discussed so far, Sosa does not devote much space to the general notion of a virtue operative in ethical literature and in everyday appraisals of persons. He does, however, cite two passages from Aristotle's *Nicomachean Ethics*. In the first, Aristotle says that "[When] thought is concerned with study, not with action or production, its good or bad state consists [simply] in being true or false. For truth is the function of whatever thinks (1139a27–30).[8] In the second he says, "Hence the function of each of the understanding parts is truth; and so the virtue of each part will be the state that makes that part grasp the truth most of all" (1139b11–13). Here, however, Aristotle is speaking of the virtue of "parts" of the mind, not – or not directly – of the virtue of a person or of overall character. Compare some passages in which he is describing overall virtue:

> Virtues, by contrast [with the senses] we acquire, just as we acquire crafts by having previously activated them ... we become just by doing just actions, temperate by doing temperate actions, brave by doing brave actions. (1103a31–1103b2)
>
> If it were not so, no teacher would be needed, but everyone would be born a good or a bad craftsman. (1103b11–13)
>
> To sum up, then, in a single account. A state [of character] arises from [the repetition of] similar activities. Hence we must display the right activities, since differences in these imply corresponding differences in the state. (1103b21–3)

None of these claims of Aristotle's is inconsistent with construing what Sosa calls intellectual virtue as virtue in Aristotle's sense, but there are at least two points of apparent contrast. I take them in turn.

First, contrary to the picture we have in Sosa's work, the notion of virtue in Aristotle seems *historical*: it appears (in at least some passages from Aristotle) to be part of the concept of a virtue that it is acquired by repetition. This applies even to intellectual virtue: "Virtue of thought arises mostly from teaching" (1103a15). For Sosa (as for most contemporary epistemologists, I think), the notion of a virtue is not essentially historical, however commonly virtues are acquired in the way Aristotle described. The second point is related to the first: in part because, for Aristotle, virtues are conceived as acquired by proper habituation or by internalization of standards or practices one is taught (or from both), the Aristotelian virtues all seem to be the sorts of things for which one deserves praise. This may be mainly because having them reflects success in what is normally a series of effortful activities. Another reason may be that they constitute a source of desirable conduct. For Sosa, presumably a duplicate of me created at an instant would have whatever intellectual virtues I do at the time; and similarly, a being with certain powers to acquire true beliefs would have such virtues whether any credit is due for their possession or not. In "Virtue Epistemology," for instance, he contrasts his own view with a historical version of reliabilism and stresses, in characterizing virtue, not its developmental history but its stability.[9] That is not essentially a historical characteristic.

It may be, however, that the contrast with Aristotle here is not deep. Perhaps Aristotle can be read, not as conceiving the very notion of a virtue as historical, but as not clearly distinguishing his genetic account of virtue from his conceptual one. If we then distinguish retrospective praiseworthiness – roughly praiseworthiness for *acquiring* the virtue in which a belief is grounded – from contemporaneous praiseworthiness, which is roughly praiseworthiness for *having* this trait, Sosa's view can account for both, nor need he deny that Aristotle is right about the normal path to acquisition of (at least many) virtues. To be sure, contemporaneous praiseworthiness may be essentially *forward-looking*, since one ascribes it partly in anticipation of good conduct in the future; but it could be possessed at the last moment of a life when no such future conduct is in prospect.

Whatever we say about the extent of the suggested contrasts, there seems to be a distinction between a virtue and a *power*. The former is perhaps a species of the latter, but not every power, even to do or achieve something desirable, is a virtue. In the intellectual domain, this can be seen by noting that someone could have the power to come to know the weather upon simply considering what it will be tomorrow without thereby having a virtue – or at least, in saying that one of the person's "virtues" is an ability to foretell tomorrow's weather just by considering the matter, we would be using 'virtue' in a sense that does not imply any praise for an accomplishment or any positive attitude toward one's character as distinct from the set of one's characteristics. The person might have no idea how the belief arises or why it should be true, and may be puzzled by holding it.[10]

Sosa's perspectivism has a resource for dealing with this kind of case without unduly stretching the notion of a virtue. The kind of characteristic in question (a kind of epistemic power) can be considered a capacity for animal knowledge and hence taken not to be a virtue. If this line is the solution, however, then (as Sosa realizes) knowledge in general cannot be considered to be true belief grounded in virtue – unless perhaps we distinguish what might be called *animal virtue*, which would be a kind of epistemic power, from *reflective virtue*, which would be a trait for which one merits a measure of praise.

That there might be something plausibly called animal virtue is consonant with an idea Sosa has put forward in arguing that knowledge entails "credit" for true belief.[11] Credit is not the same as praise, but it is a positive attribution that shares with praise at least a presupposition that the action or other element in virtue of which a person merits credit is non-accidental. We might then say that virtues are creditable characteristics, but allow that there are creditable powers that are not virtues – even if we also allow that some of these are animal virtues. We might certainly allow that there can be epistemic credit for a belief that is not strictly grounded in an epistemic virtue. If we think in Aristotelian terms, we might add that in the normal course of developing virtue, creditable responses come first. It is only when one has achieved a *pattern* of credits that bespeaks a virtue of character – whether epistemic or moral or of some other normatively important kind – that one may be said to have a virtue.

So far, I have been mainly exploring Sosa's virtue epistemology and how, in the light of a conception of intellectual virtue, it accounts for one or another kind of knowledge or justification of interest to him. It is also instructive to consider what, independently of the theory, seem intuitively to count as intellectual virtues and to explore Sosa's resources for accounting for them so conceived. The paradigms are traits whose successful exercise issues in knowledge of certain kinds, for instance, perceptiveness, insightfulness, discernment, imagination, and rigor. Some of these are, to be sure, more "methodological," others more substantive, and all can be limited, as where one is insightful in psychological matters but not in philosophical ones.

Some of these traits overlap Aristotelian "productive" virtues; for instance, imagination can lead to creating artworks as well as to arriving at knowledge through framing intuitively plausible hypotheses that one then establishes. But consider being critical. This might lead to withholding belief as often as to forming it in a certain way. Being logical, moreover, might be possible for someone who is very poor at finding true premises from which to draw logically valid inferences. This deficiency could thus lead to multiplication of falsehoods more often than to finding truth or avoiding error. It is only when we have truth to begin with that using good logic guarantees our arriving at truths.

Sosa's epistemology has resources to provide an account of these cases. For one thing, he has distinguished between traits that produce true belief and traits that simply lead to believing appropriately, where this may entail withholding belief. He can thus applaud critical habits of mind that often lead to suspending judgment, provided they do not lead to overzealous skepticism. He can also note that some virtues, such as logicality, require as one of the conditions for their proper operation, combination with other virtues that give them appropriate *inputs*. His theory is in no way epistemically *atomistic*; it can be developed in an aretaically holistic direction. This does not imply a version of the Aristotelian thesis of the unity of the virtues. To say that some virtues operate only, or best, in combination or interaction with others is not to imply that having any of them entails having them all.

There are, however, at least two problems we should consider here. First, there is some question of how to conceive the environment appropriate to explicating the notion of believing "out of intellectual virtue" (characterized by Sosa in the quotation from *KP*, 287). Second, some of what Sosa says concerning epistemic virtue leaves open how internal the notion is on his view. Let us take these in turn.

On a quite natural understanding of the notion of an environment in which one believes something, the environment is roughly the physical surroundings of the believer. But this notion will not do justice to what Sosa has in mind (indeed, his notion is not sharply separable from that of the conditions appropriate to believing the kind of proposition in question from the virtue, as he indicates on *KP*, 284–5). For one thing, in a given physical environment one has many beliefs, and for many of them, such as many that are stored in memory, one's physical environment is irrelevant. Recall the case of Magoo; here we are focusing on a visual belief, to which his physical surroundings are relevant, not on an arithmetic belief, to which they are not. Indeed, I would speculate that in characterizing intellectual virtue, Sosa has in mind mainly features of one's physical *or* psychological surroundings pertinent to one's justification for or reliability in believing, the proposition in question.

One might now wonder why, for very simple arithmetic beliefs, environment is relevant at all: if the propositions in question are self-evident, why should environment matter? I have two suggestions. First, if it does not, the environmental condition can be deemed to be trivially satisfied, in the sense that any environment will do. Second, Sosa treats a demon world as a special kind of (epistemically hostile) environment (see, e.g., *KP*, 289, where he speaks of a "demonic environment"). This environment would matter for whatever beliefs are grounded in a way that makes them epistemically vulnerable. True perceptual beliefs would not, for instance, count as knowledge (though they might still be justified, for reasons suggested above and extended below); but the relevant virtue is not "designed" to operate in a demon environment, whereas a belief of a self-evident proposition might remain untouched. The matter of how internal the notion of a virtue is is more difficult to deal with. In "Virtue Epistemology" he sympathetically explores the idea that

> If it is believed of a certain process that it would yield a high enough preponderance of truth over falsity in the actual world when employed, that process is allowed into the list of virtues, and if it is believed that it would yield a low enough ratio of truth over falsity, then it is placed on the list of vices. (VE)

He has in mind such processes as forming beliefs on the basis of perceptual experience, and I take it that the corresponding virtue is the related stable disposition to form beliefs given appropriate visual experiences in the right kind of environments (and with the other restrictions quoted from *Knowledge in Perspective*). The formulation is qualified in the succeeding pages, but Sosa does not specify that the processes in question or the grounds of beliefs formed through those processes are internally accessible: roughly, of a kind the person can be conscious of through introspection or reflection. Suppose we discover a process of belief formation that operates on the basis of exposure to surrounding air and is such that the person in question always forms a true belief about the percentage of carbon dioxide content, but has no idea why the belief arises (and later forgets forming it, so that there is no memory of a track record that might yield inductive justification). Do we want to speak of an epistemic virtue here? I think not, and if Sosa were to countenance knowledge here, I believe that he would rightly consider it "animal knowledge."

There is no reason, however, why he cannot make use of a distinction suggested earlier, between an intellectual virtue and a mere intellectual power. He could then treat the notion of intellectual virtue just cited as capturing a concept of virtue as power and build in an internalist requirement to capture the more ordinary notion of intellectual virtue. Making the suggested kind of distinction between virtue and power indeed comports well with his emphasis on reflective knowledge as the proper goal of intellectual activity so far as the grasp of truth is concerned. In suggesting we make use of this distinction, I am not implying that powers as such cannot be admirable; the point is that not every epistemically good power is happily considered a virtue. It seems intrinsic to a virtue as opposed to a power that the *person* is in some way admirable, even praiseworthy, on account of possessing it. If one wants to retain a generic notion of virtue in the intellectual domain that encompasses mere epistemic powers as well as traits we intuitively consider intellectual virtues, I suggest that the technical term 'epistemic virtue' might serve for this purpose. For the connection with knowledge that it implies does not obviously entail (and I think does not entail at all) the element of merited praise for the subject that is commonly implicit in 'virtue.' The same would hold, of course, for what I suggested could be called an "animal virtue."

We can better understand Sosa's epistemology and can also see some problems it raises for any epistemology if we consider reflective knowledge in relation to intellectual virtue. This will be the main task of the next section.

3 Reflective Knowledge, Intellectual Virtue, and Skepticism

A natural hypothesis to pursue given the distinction between an intellectual virtue and a mere intellectual power is that the former is largely or perhaps wholly constituted by the latter together with the kind of second-order understanding Sosa requires for reflective knowledge. There are, however, different formulations of this requirement in Sosa's work. In one passage quoted above from *Knowledge in Perspective*, he speaks of reflective knowledge as embodying "understanding of its place [the place of that knowledge, I take it] in a wider whole that includes one's belief and knowledge of it and how these come about."[12] In "Reflective Knowledge" he says that "reflective knowledge does require coherence, including one's ability to see one's first-level knowledge in epistemic perspective." These conditions may be plausibly considered different. The first seems stronger, especially if we take it to include (as it seems to) detailed causal knowledge. The second emphasizes cognitive ability rather than possession of actual knowledge. On that score, at least, it seems to me preferable.[13] Neither actually specifies *reflection*, in the standard sense requiring a temporally extended consideration of some of the elements in question. That is important, since plainly Sosa does not take actual reflection to be a requirement for achieving reflective knowledge. If this were required, one could not acquire it instantaneously no matter how good an understanding one had of the relevant variables.

If, however, the later conception of reflective knowledge is modest in not requiring a process of reflection or any detailed causal knowledge, it seems strong in requiring an "awareness of *how* one knows, in a way that precludes the unreliability of one's faculties" (RK, 426). Perhaps we can easily be aware of whether our knowledge is, say, visual or inductive or *a priori* – at least where we intuitively deserve credit for "reflective knowledge." But what does it take to be aware of this in a *way* that rules out the unreliability of the relevant faculties? I do not see how to answer this question *a priori*. But I also cannot see any bar to there being something in the way in which we are aware of how we know, in such "reflective" cases, that rules out the unreliability of the faculties in question. We could, for instance, be simply built this way by God or evolution (the 'or' is of course inclusive). Our awareness of how we know might be connected in a lawlike way with the reliability of the relevant faculties.

It should be stressed that a way of being aware of how one knows that "precludes the unreliability of one's faculties" does not entail an awareness of how this way of knowing does that. This point should help to make Sosa's requirement appear satisfiable in the kinds of cases where it is plausible to attribute knowledge in a full-blooded sense. Still, granting that this higher-order cognitive requirement *can* be met, we might ask whether it *need* be, either for genuine knowledge or for knowledge conceived as resulting from an exercise in intellectual virtue. One motivation is plain in Sosa's earlier apparent sympathy, regarding reflective knowledge at least, with a "principle of exclusion": "If one is to know that *p* then one must exclude . . . [i.e., know not to be the case] every possibility that one knows to be incompatible with one's knowing that *p*" (RK, 425). Clearly the knowing is characteristically dispositional here: one need not have in mind or bring to mind all of the competing propositions (even supposing one actually could). One need only have dispositional beliefs constituting the relevant kind of knowledge.[14] This condition may seem to invite skepticism, since many of us know that our present perceptual knowledge is incompatible with a certain kind of deception by a Cartesian demon, but seem not to know that there is no such demon. However, some philosophers think we do know that; others hold that we do not need to know it.[15]

I cannot pursue this difficult issue here. Skepticism and even the narrower question of the status of closure principles important for it are very large topics. I prefer to pursue two questions more pertinent to virtue epistemology as such. First, does knowledge grounded in intellectual virtue require such second-order knowledge? Second, is the cognitive state constituted by overall reflective knowledge a unitary kind of knowledge at all?

On the first question, I have already noted that Sosa grants that a kind of justification is immune to the deception that a Cartesian demon can induce in our framework of beliefs. I have also pointed out the element of praiseworthiness appropriate to virtues in general as admirable traits of persons. Sosa himself speaks of "praise" in connection with virtues and aptitudes, and says that "[t]o praise a performance as skillful or an action as right, or a judgment as wise or apt, accordingly, is to assess not only the action or the judgment but also the reflected aptitude or character or intelligence" (RK, 420). Now granting that there are intellectual success terms like 'perceive' and 'intuit' that, in some of their uses, require true belief or knowledge, it is surely possible for a person who is intellectually rigorous to achieve justified belief, to construct imaginative theories, and to frame rigorous arguments, without achieving even first-order knowledge, much less the kind of second-order knowledge required for what Sosa counts as reflective knowledge. If one is hallucinating in a situation in which one has no way of figuring this out, and on that veridical-seeming sensory basis one comes up with an ingenious plausible explanation of phenomena one seems to see, this can be a case in which one has justified belief grounded in the kind of faculty that would, under "normal" conditions, yield knowledge. Consistently with hallucinating, one might even take steps to see that one is not doing so, but be fooled there too! Another person in the same situation might come up with nothing but foolish conjectures. Might we not find intellectual virtue in the first case – ill-fated, to be sure – and intellectual laxity in the other case?

Some intellectual virtues, by contrast, seem external in a way that precludes this internally grounded possession, where unavoidable falsehood in a belief manifesting them is compatible with that same belief's having a kind of intellectual merit; but surely some intellectual virtues are internal, or largely so.[16] It is true that *perceptive* people must have an appropriate proportion of true beliefs in the right situation; and *logical* people must make valid inferences and at least be disposed to know, within a certain range, which are valid and which not. But (intellectually) *imaginative* people can be factually mistaken in a great proportion of their beliefs. I suggest, then, that Sosa's framework might be extended to accommodate the contrast between external and internal intellectual virtues. Both may be essentially connected with truth, but the kinds of connections in question seem to be different in the two cases, and there may also be differences in the kind of reflective understanding required. Perceptiveness may require less in this respect than, say, analytical rigor.

However the framework might take account of the contrast between what it seems natural to call internal as opposed to external virtues, our second question remains: Is reflective knowledge unitary, in the intuitive sense in which it is if knowledge that p is constituted by a certain kind of well-grounded true belief of that proposition? Or is reflective knowledge more nearly a compound consisting of knowledge together with – indeed integrated with – other elements, perhaps including, but not limited to animal knowledge?

One might agree with Sosa that reflective knowledge is needed if the skeptical threat is as serious as it seems to many to be and is to be met. It does not follow – and I do not think he is suggesting that it does – that reflective knowledge is unitary, in virtue of being constituted by a certain kind of well-grounded true belief. Much of what he says, however, creates the impression that it is unitary, for instance the characterization of knowledge as true belief out of intellectual virtue, and his use of the standard way of referring to knowledge as if it is constituted by belief of the proposition said to be known. It appears to me that reflective knowledge "that p" is not unitary in this sense, but is better conceived as knowledge both of and *regarding p*. It consists of knowledge that p, *together with* appropriate second-order capacities, including dispositional beliefs that themselves constitute knowledge (or at least of knowledge together with suitably grounded dispositions to believe, where the beliefs that would be formed will at least normally constitute knowledge).

So viewed, reflective knowledge seems both to occur quite commonly and, at least some of the time, to bespeak intellectual virtue. But if we can find a way to rebut (even if not refute) the principle of exclusion, we need not hold that such knowledge is required to manifest intellectual virtue (perhaps we need not hold that in any case). It would seem that intellectual virtue can be manifested when, despite our making every critical effort that can be expected of us in seeking evidence in the situation, we lack the knowledge needed to guarantee the reliability of our faculties, i.e., knowledge whose content, or at least existence, guarantees this (which is not to say we know that it does so). Indeed, unless some internal requirements are imposed on the second-order components (as I think Sosa intends to do for at least some cases), I do not see that their presence is sufficient to render an instance of knowledge an exercise of intellectual virtue either. Logically speaking, we could be gifted with animal knowledge having the right higher-order content just as easily as cursed by the deceptions of a Cartesian demon. We might, to be sure (as I suggested earlier) distinguish between ordinary and animal virtue, much as we distinguish reflective and animal knowledge. If, on the other hand, satisfactory internal requirements are imposed, then even if skepticism remains a threat to the common-sense view that we have knowledge of the external world, Sosa could cogently claim that external world beliefs out of intellectual virtue can be amply justified. Justification might be, as it were, largely up to nurture even if knowledge is largely up to nature.

Despite the brevity of this sketch of Sosa's virtue epistemology, we can discern some of its major features. It makes use of a series of essential distinctions – among kinds of trait, between internal and external criteria of justification, between justification and aptness, and between kinds of knowledge. Its explication of knowledge as true belief out of intellectual virtue is well developed; it incorporates the ideas of a faculty, of its field of application, and of conditions of its operation. The treatment of skepticism is resourceful and represents a reconstruction of what is best in Descartes's higher-order approach to dealing with the possibility of error. Sosa captures the elements of internalism, of reflexivity, of reliabilism, and of epistemic responsibilism in Descartes's epistemology without endorsing the elements of infallibilism, deductivism, skepticism, or voluntarism that we also find in parts of Descartes's writings. I have stressed a distinction between intellectual virtue and epistemic power, argued for what seems a stronger internalist conception of intellectual virtue than the dominant conception one finds in Sosa's works, and suggested that skepticism may be resistible without the exclusion principle. These points might perhaps be adapted to Sosa's virtue perspectivism without radical changes on either side; but even if we incorporate them into a quite different virtue epistemology, we will have to use the kinds of basic conceptual materials he has provided and explicated. Anyone wanting to develop a virtue epistemology must take careful account of his contribution.[17]

Notes

1 I have provided a detailed account of action from virtue, with special attention to the character of the 'from', in "Acting from Virtue," *Mind* 104 (1995): 449–71.
2 For a variety of approaches to virtue epistemology, see, e.g., Jonathan Kvanvig, *The Intellectual Virtues and the Life of the Mind* (Lanham, MD: Rowman and Littlefield, 1992), James A. Montmarquet, *Epistemic Virtue and Doxastic Responsibility* (Lanham, MD: Rowman and Littlefield, 1993), Linda Zagzebski, *Virtues of the Mind* (Cambridge and New York: Cambridge University Press, 1996), and John Greco, *Putting Skeptics in Their Place* (Cambridge and New York: Cambridge University Press, 2000). For an approach premised on the idea that "[t]he focus of our 'epistemic lives' is the activity of *inquiry*," see Christopher Hookway, "Cognitive Virtues and Epistemic Evaluations," *International Journal of Philosophical Studies* 2 (1994). These approaches differ much from one another, as well as in the extent to which they take moral virtue as a model for epistemic virtue and in how they do so.
3 A number of Sosa's writings will be cited below, and many further references to his voluminous works in epistemology will be listed in this volume. There are also volumes appearing that contain many papers discussing his work in virtue epistemology. See, e.g., Guy Axtell, ed., *Knowledge, Belief, and Character: Readings in Virtue Epistemology* (Lanham, MD: Rowman and Littlefield, 2000), Michael DePaul and Linda Zagzebski, *Intellectual Virtue: Perspectives from Ethics and Epistemology* (Oxford: Oxford University Press, 2003), and Abrol Fairweather and Linda Zagzebski, eds., *Virtue Epistemology: Essays on Epistemic Virtue and Responsibility* (Oxford and New York: Oxford University Press, 2001). All of these volumes contain work by Sosa himself, and in one of the papers in Axtell's collection (pp. 99–110) Sosa replies to criticism by Laurence BonJour and Jonathan Dancy.
4 "Knowledge and Intellectual Virtue," originally published in *The Monist* (1985), reprinted in Ernest Sosa, *Knowledge in Perspective: Selected Essays in Epistemology* (Cambridge and New York: Cambridge University Press, 1991) (cited as *KP*), p. 225. Page references to this paper and, unless otherwise specified, to others of Sosa's writings, will hereinafter be parenthetically included in the text.

5   The notion of the differential of truth over error is not meant to be merely quantitative, referring simply to a favorable proportion of true to false beliefs. One dimension of intellectual virtue is a kind of wisdom regarding what truths are, in the way appropriate to the person and context in question, important. Sosa discusses the nature of such importance in more than one place; for a valuable detailed treatment see his "For the Love of Truth" in Fairweather and Zagzebski, eds., *Virtue Epistemology*.

6   This formulation contains no element that clearly captures the causal character of 'out of', but much that Sosa says in this and other papers indicates that he intends that character to be reflected in his conception of believing out of intellectual virtue.

7   "Reflective Knowledge in the Best Circles," *The Journal of Philosophy* 94 (1997): 422 (cited as RK). In *Knowledge in Focus, Skepticism Resolved* (Princeton University Press, forthcoming), which Sosa has kindly given me for a fuller perspective, the same range of issues is considered in more detail in ways that – in the May, 1999, version, at least – are compatible with the approach attributed to Sosa here.

8   The translation is by Terence Irwin (Indianapolis: Hackett, 1985). Other citations of Aristotle are also to this edition.

9   "Virtue Epistemology," unpublished manuscript (cited as VE).

10 That such non-inferential, apparently "wired in" knowledge is possible is argued in ch. 7 of my *Epistemology* (London and New York: Routledge, 1998).

11 See Ernest Sosa, "Beyond Skepticism, to the Best of our Knowledge," *Mind* 97 (1988). The idea that knowledge entails credit for the belief in question is developed and defended by John Greco in "Knowledge as Credit for True Belief," in DePaul and Zagzebski, *Intellectual Virtue*.

12 To avoid an apparently vicious regress, Sosa would presumably not require that the needed higher-order knowledge is reflective. How plausible is it, however, to conceive it as animal knowledge? This is perhaps a contingent matter; the answer, I suppose, depends on how we are built, particularly on how much self-understanding is a natural, "direct" response to our belief formation processes and other epistemically relevant elements of our cognitive system. I assume that higher-order knowledge can in any case be construed as a kind of knowledge that can become reflective, whereas animal knowledge *need* not meet that condition.

13 Still another interesting passage in which Sosa discusses the requirement in question occurs in a reply to BonJour, in which he says,

> VP [virtue perspectivism] requires that one's first order beliefs be placed in "epistemic perspective," where one takes note of the sources of one's beliefs (or the first order ones, at a minimum) and of how reliable these are. Thus one's epistemic perspective would classify a typical perceptual belief as a perceptual belief of some relevant sort, and would combine that with an assessment of the reliability of beliefs of that sort."

See "Perspectives in Virtue Epistemology: A Reply to Dancy and BonJour," in Axtell, *Knowledge, Belief, and Character*, p. 103. What is required to take note of such a thing? In the minimal case, surely no reflection is needed. A telling phrase here is 'one's epistemic perspective would classify,' which suggests to me that the process can be automatic and may indeed be accomplished through the acquisition of dispositions to believe as opposed to the formation of beliefs or – especially – that of classificatory thoughts.

14 John Greco makes a plausible case that only dispositions to believe, which are not themselves beliefs, as opposed to dispositional beliefs, need be posited by Sosa here. See *Putting Skeptics in Their Place*, pp. 187–90 (this book contains much discussion of Sosa's position and a well-developed, complementary alternative, which Greco calls "agent reliabilism"). I have developed this distinction in "Dispositional Beliefs and Dispositions to Believe," *Nous* 28 (1994), but have been assuming here that Sosa intends to include what I prefer to call dispositions to

believe under his term "implicit belief." If that is his intention, then the suggested revision can be made without major substantive change in his theory.

15 Peter D. Klein's *Certainty: A Refutation of Scepticism* (Minneapolis: University of Minnesota Press, 1981) makes a case for our knowing such skeptical hypotheses false; Fred Dretske, in, e.g., "Epistemic Operators," *The Journal of Philosophy* 67 (1970) has argued that we do not need to. For my own case that we do not need to see, e.g., *Epistemology*, ch. 6.

16 This is argued in my "Epistemic Virtue and Justified Belief," in Zagzebski and Fairweather, *Virtue Epistemology*.

17 This paper is dedicated to Ernest Sosa, from whom I have learned a great deal over many years. There are many aspects of his epistemology which it has been impossible even to begin to address here, and I am well aware that even his virtue perspectivist theory may have undergone major developments by the time this essay appears. For helpful comments on an earlier version I thank John Greco.

2

Structure and Connection: Comments on Sosa's Epistemology

STEWART COHEN

Ernie Sosa has been a major force in Epistemology at least since I first became interested in the topic 25 years ago. He has had illuminating and influential things to say about virtually every topic in epistemology and I have learned much from his writings. It is with great pleasure and gratitude that I contribute to this collection of essays on his work.

I would like to make some comments about work in which he describes in detail his most recent views.[1] My comments concern two central topics in his work – the structure of knowledge, and the nature of the epistemic mind–world connection.

The Structure of Knowledge

For Sosa, there are two kinds of knowledge – animal knowledge (*cognitio*) and reflective knowledge (*scientia*). Animal knowledge is a matter of being reliably connected to the world – having one's belief be safe. Reflective knowledge is derived from animal knowledge, by putting such knowledge in proper perspective:

> reflective knowledge, while building on animal knowledge [secured by reliable, apt faculties], goes beyond it precisely in the respect of integrating one's beliefs into a more coherent framework. This it does especially through attaining an epistemic perspective within which the object-level animal beliefs may be seen as reliably based. (TR, 72)

According to Sosa, if one has epistemically virtuous faculties – faculties that produce, apt, reliable, beliefs – then one can come to know things via

> perception and introspection, along with intuition, as well as inductive and abductive reasoning, along with . . . deductive reasoning. . . . By use of such faculties . . . one attains . . . a broad view of oneself and one's environing world. And, if all goes well, then in terms of this epistemic perspective one can feel confident about the reliability of one's full complement of one's faculties. (RK, 102)

So the picture that emerges is this: One first acquires animal knowledge without benefit of any knowledge of the reliability of one's faculties. After acquiring such knowledge, one uses it to gain a perspective from which one can learn of the reliability of the faculties in virtue of which one's initial animal knowlege was acquired. Presumably, once one knows one's beliefs are reliably based, one can come to know that one's beliefs constitute knowledge, i.e., one can come to know one knows.

In a certain respect the kind of knowledge structure Sosa endorses is circular: it allows one to use the deliverances of a cognitive faculty as a basis for establishing the reliability of that very faculty. But Sosa argues that the circularity is not vicious and indeed provides a solution to the problem of the criterion.

This problem arises because a natural intuition (pretheoretically, anyway) is that a potential knowledge source, e.g., sense perception, cannot deliver knowledge unless we know the source is reliable. But surely our knowledge that sense perception is reliable will be based on knowledge we have about the workings of the world. And surely that knowledge will be acquired by sense perception. So it looks as if we are in the impossible situation of needing sensory knowledge prior to acquiring it. Similar considerations apply to other sources of knowledge like memory and induction. Skepticism threatens.

On Sosa's view, we can acquire animal knowledge prior to knowing anything about the reliability of our cognitive processes. Once we gain enough animal knowledge, we acquire a perspective – "a broad view of oneself and one's environing world" – from which we can see that our cognitive processes are reliable. And this enables us to ascend to reflective knowledge.

Sosa's view provides an ingenious way to circumvent the problem of the criterion. But I have two concerns. The first concerns the details of this circular structure. Sosa views the kind of circularity he defends as Cartesian. And he argues that G. E. Moore's famous anti-skeptical reasoning can be viewed in the same non-viciously circular way (RK, 417).

1 Datum: I know with a high degree of certainty that here is a hand.
2 I can see and feel that here is a hand, and that is the only, or anyhow the best explanation of the source of my knowledge that here is a hand.
3 So my perception that here is a hand is what explains why or how it is that I know (with certainty) that here is a hand.
4 But my perception could not serve as a source of that degree of justified certainty if it were not a reliable faculty.
5 So, finally, my perception must be reliable faculty.

But this Moorean structure looks very different from the structure described in the earlier quotations. There one begins with one's first-order knowledge and, on that basis, acquires knowledge of the reliability of one's faculties. From there, I supposed, one could acquire second-order knowledge – knowledge that one knows. But in the Moorean structure, one *begins* with second-order knowledge – I know that I have a hand – and from there, acquires knowledge of the reliability of one's faculties. But this inference to reliability of one's faculties follows straightforwardly from the necessary truth that one's faculties cannot deliver knowledge unless they are reliable.

Now my question is this: What role does animal knowledge play in the acquisition of reliability knowledge on the Moorean model? The only possibility seems to be that it plays a role in one's acquiring one's second-order knowledge, e.g., Moore's knowledge that here is a hand. So first one acquires animal knowledge. Then on the basis of one's animal knowledge, one comes to know that one knows. And then one infers, from the fact that one knows, that one's faculties are reliable. The problem I have with this account is that it's puzzling how one's animal knowledge could lead to knowing that one knows without first leading to knowledge of the reliability of one's faculties. That is, it would seem that one gets to second-order knowledge via one's animal knowledge by one's animal knowledge leading to knowledge of reliability. But according to the Moorean picture, one acquires one's second-order knowledge prior to acquiring one's reliability knowledge.

However the details are to be worked out, it's clear that Sosa intends that reflective knowledge is built up from animal knowledge. This provides the basis for his treatment of the problem of the criterion. My second concern is that Sosa's view faces what I have called "the problem of easy knowledge."[2] As Sosa envisions it, gaining knowledge of the reliability of one's faculties is a significant cognitive achievement. Such knowledge comes only after putting a substantial amount of animal knowledge into perspective. This is as it should be. The problem is that there seems to be nothing to prevent one from using one's animal knowledge to acquire reliability knowledge in ways that, intuitively, are too easy.

The problem of easy knowledge arises in two ways. The first exploits the deductive closure principle. On Sosa's view, I can come to know, e.g., that the table is red simply on the basis of my belief being safe. I do not need to know that the circumstances are not such that my color vision is unreliable. I do not need to know, e.g., that it is not the case that the table is white with red lights shining on it. (It's enough for it to be unlikely in the context.) But once I know the table is red, it follows from closure (provided that I see the entailment) that I know it is not white with red lights shining on it. And similarly for any alternative to the table being red, I can come to know that alternative is false in this trivial way. But if one has no prior knowledge that there are no red lights shining on the table, it seems counterintuitive that one could acquire it subsequently in this way.

Imagine my 7-year-old son asks me: "Daddy but what if the (seemingly red) table is white with red lights shining on it?" I reply, "Well – look, the table is red." According to Sosa, this is something I can know, provided my belief is safe. So I can appeal to it in reasoning. So I continue: "But since it's red, it can't be white with red lights shining on it. See?" I take it that this reasoning is unacceptable. But I don't see how Sosa can avoid sanctioning it without giving up closure.

The second way the problem of easy knowledge arises has been pointed out by Jonathan Vogel and Richard Fumerton. Suppose my perceptual faculties produce the safe belief that there is a red table before me. Again, I can have this knowledge even if I do not know my perceptual faculties are reliable, or indeed even if I do not have any evidence for their reliability. Now suppose my introspective faculties produce the safe belief that it looks to me as if there is a table before me. Putting these two beliefs together, I would seem to have acquired some evidence that my perceptual faculties are reliable. But clearly if I did not have such evidence prior to my acquiring these beliefs, I cannot in this way acquire such evidence. Moreover, it is not clear why I could not in this way manage to produce enough evidence to come to know that my perceptual faculties are reliable. But intuitively, at least by my lights, one cannot, in this way, come to know one's perceptual faculties are reliable. But I do not see how, on Sosa's view, it can be prevented.

Safety

Central to Sosa's epistemology is the notion that belief must be reliably connected to the world in order to constitute knowledge. Sosa proposes to replace the Dretske/Nozick notion of tracking or sensitivity with his own notion of safety:

> [S's] ... belief is *safe* iff S would not have held it without it being true. (S&C, 14)

As Sosa notes, safety avoids many of the problems of sensitivity. But it seems to result in the failure of deductive closure for knowledge. We can illustrate this with Kripke's (unpublished) red barn case.

> Suppose there is a region where there exist barns along with barn replicas visually indistinguishable from actual barns. The residents of the region picked out all the sites and at each one flipped a coin to determine whether they would put up a real barn or a replica. As it turns out all the replicas are green. S is unaware of the replicas and seeing an actual red barn, comes to believe that there is a red barn before him.

Does S know there is a red barn before him? The safety condition seems to allow that S does know. Because all of the replicas are green, S would not believe there was a red barn before him unless there was. Does S know there is a barn before him? Here, safety rules out knowledge. S would believe there was a barn before him if there were a green replica before him. So deductive closure fails.

Sosa recognized this problem and proposes a more sophisticated formulation designed to avoid the problem:

> A belief is safe iff it is based on a reliable indication.

A reliable indication is a deliverance that would occur only if the delivered proposition were true. Deliverances occur when you ostensibly perceive, or remember, or deduce something. And a proposition is delivered when the ostensible perception, etc., inclines you to believe it (TCK, 270).

Sosa does not spell out how this reformulation of safety avoids closure failure. But I think I see how it is supposed to work. In the Kripke example, the original version of safety yields the result that S knows there is a red barn before him without knowing there is a barn before him. But revised safety avoids this result. S's belief that there is a barn before him is based on the deliverance of a red barn. And *that* deliverance would only occur if there were a barn before him. So revised safety does not yield the result that S fails to know he sees a barn and closure is saved.

Though revised safety avoids closure failure, it does so only at the cost of producing strongly counterintuitive results. Kripke's red barn case is a variant of a case Goldman introduced into the literature as, among other things, a counterexample to the causal theory of knowing.[3] On that view, being causally related to the fact that p is sufficient for a belief that p to be knowledge. But Goldman notes that even if I see a barn, and so my belief that there is a barn before me is causally related to the fact of there being such a barn, I still fail to know there is a barn before me if unbeknown to me there are barn replicas in the vicinity. Most people share that intuition, especially if the case is specified so the barn replicas are abundant and very close by. In the Kripke version of the case, original safety produces closure failure by allowing that S knows he sees a red barn while failing to know he sees a barn. Revised safety avoids this problem by allowing that S can know there is a barn before him as well. But that result runs counter to the robust intuition that S fails to know in such cases. If S sees a barn in a region with perceptually indistinguishable barn replicas, he does not know there is a barn before him.[4] So it looks as if revised safety avoids closure failure at the cost of producing a counterintuitive result for this case.

Notes

1 "Reflective Knowledge in the Best Circles," *The Journal of Philosophy* 94 (1997): 410–30 (cited as RK); "Thomas Reid" (co-authored with James Van Cleve), in Steven Emmanuel, ed., *The Modern Philosophers: From Descartes to Nietzsche* (Oxford: Blackwell, 2000) (cited as TR); "Skepticism and Contextualism," *Philosophical Issues* 10 (2000): 1–18 (cited as S&C); and "Tracking, Competence, and Knowledge," in *The Oxford Handbook of Epistemology* (Oxford: Oxford University Press, 2002) (cited as TCK).
2 "Basic Knowledge and the Problem of Easy Knowledge," Rutgers Epistemology Conference 2001, in *Philosophy and Phenomenological Research* (September 2003).
3 "Discrimination and Perceptual Knowledge," *The Journal of Philosophy* 73 (1975). Goldman credits Carl Ginet for the original example.
4 Here I am indebted to discussions with Jonathan Vogel.

3

Sosa, Safety, Sensitivity, and Skeptical Hypotheses

KEITH DeROSE

Fortunately for those of us who work on the topic, Ernie Sosa has devoted much of his (seemingly inexhaustible) intellectual energy to the problem of philosophical skepticism. And to great effect. With the three exceptions of Peter Unger, whose *Ignorance: A Case for Scepticism* (1975) is a grossly underappreciated classic of epistemology; Timothy Williamson, whose *Knowledge and its Limits* (2000) is, I hope, on its way to being a less underappreciated classic; and Thomas Reid, I have benefited more from Sosa's wrestlings with skepticism than from anyone else's work on the topic.

Though I am an advocate of a particular kind of "contextualist Moorean" response to skepticism, I still have strong sympathies with "straightforwardly Moorean" responses of the type Sosa favors. If I were forced to abandon the contextualist approach, I would myself adopt a straightforwardly Moorean position. Sosa's work, then, represents an exploration of what, for me, is the path not taken. I am very happy to have such an expert traveler exploring that path so fruitfully.

In two recent papers, Sosa spends considerable space explicitly comparing his solution to the skeptical problem with contextualist solutions in general, and with mine in particular.[1] I will here continue that conversation. Sosa has not convinced me to change paths, nor do I expect to convince him (though I will claim that in certain ways our approaches are very similar, and perhaps more similar than Sosa thinks). Nevertheless, I welcome the opportunity to compare notes. To properly keep the focus on Sosa's work, I will avoid as much as possible spelling out the details of my own and other alternative approaches, and will endeavor to explain them only so far as is needed to make the comparative points I will argue for.

Key to Sosa's recent efforts is his advocacy of a "safety" approach to knowledge and skepticism. Fred Dretske, Robert Nozick, and (in a quite different way) I make use of the concept of the "sensitivity" of beliefs in our response to skepticism. Sosa admits the "undeniable intuitive attractiveness" of such sensitivity approaches, but claims to be able to co-opt its benefits by means of his substitute notion of safety, which he claims is easily confused with sensitivity, but which produces much better results when applied to the problem of skepticism (HDOM, 143). But it turns out that Sosa, too, uses the notion of sensitivity in his account in a way that renders his account as susceptible to the main problems he raises as is my account – and perhaps as susceptible as are the other sensitivity accounts. Or so I will argue. For this and other reasons, I will dispute Sosa's claim to have produced a superior account.

1 Sensitivity Accounts – Direct and Indirect

A variety of cases elicit from us a strong and surprising intuitive pull toward saying that the subjects of the case don't know the propositions in question. Thus, in the relevant familiar cases, there is a strong pull toward saying that I do *not* know that

(E1) I've lost the lottery.
(E2) My newspaper isn't mistaken about whether the Cubs won yesterday.
(E3) Those animals are not just cleverly painted mules.
(E4) I'm not a BIV.

Sosa points out (HDOM, 147), and I agree, that it isn't nearly as intuitively clear as some would make it out to be that there is no knowledge of things like (E4) – and I'd say the same about our other Es. (More on this in section 9, below.) Indeed, it is my position that, in an important way, I in fact do know all of the above in the relevant cases.[2] Nevertheless, as I trust even those who sympathize with that position of mine will agree, there is at least a strong intuitive pull toward the verdict that I don't know each of the above. Of course, there are many propositions which I intuitively seem not to know. What's surprising about the above? Well, each of the above Es can be paired with another proposition, which we'll in each case label "O" about which there are powerful intuitions to the effect that (a) I *do* know that O and, (b) If I don't know that E, then I don't know that O. Consider these Os, which can each be paired with the similarly numbered E, above:

(O1) I won't be able to repay my loan by the end of the year.
(O2) The Cubs won yesterday.
(O3) Those animals are zebras.
(O4) I have hands.

In the case of (E2)/(O2), we suppose that my only source of information about the result of the game is my newspaper, which didn't carry a story about the game, but just listed the score under "Yesterday's Results." Intuitively, if the newspaper is a normally reliable one, and, of course, if the Cubs did in fact win, it seems that I know that they won. Yet, in the imagined circumstances (my newspaper is my only source of information about this game), this conditional also seems intuitively correct: If I don't know that my paper isn't mistaken about whether the Cubs won yesterday, then I don't know that they won – if I don't know that (E2), then I don't know that (O2). These two fairly strong intuitions, if correct, would seem to point to the conclusion that I know that (E2). That's why it's surprising that there's such a strong intuitive pull toward saying that I *don't* know (E2). Similar points would apply to our other case pairs. What accounts for this intuitive pull toward saying that the likes of (E1)–(E4) are not known?

It's here that many appeal to the notion of sensitivity. Roughly, a subject S's true belief that *p* is sensitive iff *p* were not the case, then S would not have believed that *p*. Given the natural understanding of the relevant cases, (E1)–(E4) seem *not* to be sensitive beliefs, while (O1)–(O4) do seem to be sensitive. (Thus, to continue using the (E2)/(O2) pair, *If the Cubs had not won, I would not believe that they had won* seems true, while *If my paper had been mistaken about yesterday's game, I would not believe it wasn't mistaken* does not seem true – it seems that if my paper were mistaken, I'd have believed as strongly as I in fact do that it wasn't.) Sensitivity explanations appeal to this insensitivity of beliefs (E1)–(E4) to explain why they seem not to constitute knowledge.

The *direct* way to do this is to follow Dretske and Nozick in supposing that sensitivity is a necessary condition for knowledge. If our concept of knowledge were simply that of true, sensitive belief, it would be no surprise that we tend to judge that insensitive beliefs are not knowledge. And, of course, that point will hold also for more complicated theories of knowledge, so long as they make sensitivity a condition for knowledge.

I also appeal to the insensitivity of (E1)–(E4) to explain why those beliefs can seem not to be pieces of knowledge, but I do not take the above direct approach. Mine is an *indirect sensitivity* account – one that appeals to the insensitivity of (E1)–(E4) in explaining why they seem not to be knowledge, but does not do so by building a sensitivity condition (or anything like a sensitivity condition) into the very concept of knowledge.

Both direct and indirect sensitivity accounts appeal to the insensitivity of (E1)–(E4) in their explanations of why these beliefs seem not to be knowledge. Both types of accounts then seem to depend on some claim to the effect that we have at least a fairly general – though not necessarily exceptionless – tendency to judge that insensitive beliefs are not knowledge. Without some such assumption, the insensitivity of (E1)–(E4) would not do the explanatory work assigned to it. So both types of account utilize what in "Solving the Skeptical Problem" (hereafter referred to as SSP)[3] I called the "Subjunctive Conditionals Account" (SCA) – in the relevant cases, they explain why S seems not to know that *p* by means of the following two claims:

SCA
1. S's belief that *p* is insensitive; and
2. We have some at least fairly general – though perhaps not exceptionless – tendency to judge that insensitive beliefs are not knowledge.

Where direct and indirect sensitivity accounts diverge is in their further account of *why* (2) holds. *Direct* sensitivity accounts hold that this is so because:

(a) Sensitivity is a necessary condition for knowledge.

Indirect sensitivity accounts, then, utilize SCA, but have some explanation other than the one based on (a) for why (2) holds. (In section 4, below, I'll mention a type of sensitivity account – a "modest direct sensitivity account" – that uses a variant of (a) that's nonetheless close enough to (a) that the account should still be labeled "direct".)

2 The Attack by Counterexample on Sensitivity Accounts – And Why SCA Seems on the Right Track Nonetheless

As I've noted, Sosa hopes to advance his own safety account as preferable to sensitivity accounts. What's wrong with the sensitivity accounts? Sosa's main attack – at least the main attack that is not limited to targeting only direct sensitivity accounts (Sosa and I seem to be in agreement about what's wrong with direct sensitivity approaches) – is one of counterexamples: he presents cases in which we intuitively judge that a subject knows that p, despite the fact that S's belief that p is, and seems to us to be, insensitive (HDOM, 145–6). If our intuitions about such cases are correct, the cases are counterexamples to the theories of knowledge on which direct sensitivity accounts are based, since they show that (a) is false. But such cases also provide exceptions to the generalization (2), utilized by even indirect sensitivity accounts, for about such cases we are not inclined to judge that the subject doesn't know, despite the apparent insensitivity of the subject's belief. Of course, I've formulated (2) so that it is perfectly compatible with there being exceptions to the tendency it posits. (Indeed, I've formulated it in a way that positively anticipates exceptions.) Still, it would be better to explain by means of a generalization that has absolutely no exceptions, so counterexamples like Sosa's are damaging to indirect sensitivity accounts.

Sosa does not present his counterexamples as something new. He is citing an old problem for sensitivity accounts to set the stage for his new, alternative account. Sensitivity theorists have long been aware of counterexamples like the two Sosa presents[4] – and some other types of cases, too. How have they (we) responded?

For one thing, by suggesting modifications to their accounts. When Nozick first presented his own brand of direct sensitivity theory, he did so along with counterexamples to the simple version – prominently including cases where the subject does know that p, despite the fact that she would have believed that p even if p had been false. As is well known, Nozick suggested complications to his account involving methods of belief formation to handle the problem cases. In my presentation of an indirect sensitivity account in SSP, I discussed several kinds of exceptions to (2), and discussed various ways in which that generalization might be modified in an attempt to handle such cases (see SSP, 19–23). Still, no sensitivity theorist, to my knowledge, has even pretended that all the cases have been successfully dealt with.

But I also argued that though the SCA generalization is not ideally precise, there is good reason to think that it is on the right track, and that it can be used in good explanations. I will repeat the essence of that argument here.

First, and obviously, I pointed out that I was using (2) to explain why we seem not to know in various cases, and the generalization needn't be exceptionless to play that explanatory role. The exceptions perhaps show that the generalization can be refined and improved in certain ways, and may even point us in hopeful directions toward finding some such refinements (some of which are no doubt important and will significantly advance our understanding, and, indeed, some of which I explore), but heaven help us if we have to wait until the generalizations we use in philosophy (or elsewhere) have to be perfectly Chisholmed and exceptionless before we can put them to explanatory work!

But why think the sensitivity account is even on the right track? Why think the exceptions reveal only the need for further tinkering, rather than for a completely different account? Without repeating the case variants I discuss (see SSP, 23–7), the reason is that where the account works, it works so impressively well. First, that a subject would have believed p even if p were false does intuitively seem like a good reason to think the subject doesn't know that p. And, secondly, and more impressively, when we take cases like the familiar specifications of the situations in which our current Es are usually placed, and then start imagining the most natural ways of modifying the situation in question so that the subject *does* seem to know the relevant proposition, we will find in an imposingly impressive array of case variants that the very changes needed to make the subject seem to know also render the subject's belief sensitive. As I conclude in SSP, "Again and again, SCA posits a certain block [the insensitivity of the belief] to our judging that we know, and the changes that would clear the way for our judging that we know also remove this block. This makes it difficult not to believe that SCA is at least roughly correct" (SSP, 25).

Are we to suppose that it's just a *coincidence* that these Es seem not to be pieces of knowledge when they are in their usual settings, where they are insensitive beliefs, but that they no longer give this "no-knowledge" appearance in the modified situations in which they are sensitive – that the very changes needed to make the appearance of no-knowledge fade away also render the beliefs in question sensitive? Perhaps someone will devise a good explanation, having nothing to do with sensitivity, for why our Es seem not to be knowledge in their usual settings (in which they're insensitive beliefs), and will also allow us to see why they seem to be knowledge in the modified situations (where they are sensitive). Perhaps. But I'm not holding my breath.

3   Sosa's Safety Account

Sosa, though, is not a hit-and-run counterexampler. He has an alternative account, based on his notion of safety, for why (E4) can seem not to be knowledge, and his account seems to be generalizable to cover our other Es as well. Using '$\rightarrow$' for the subjunctive conditional, Sosa explains his notion of safety, and its relation to sensitivity, as follows:

> A belief is sensitive iff had it been false, S would not have held it, whereas a belief is *safe* iff S would not have held it without its being true. For short: S's belief B(p) is sensitive iff $\sim p \rightarrow \sim B(p)$, whereas S's belief is safe iff $B(p) \rightarrow p$. These are not equivalent, since subjunctive conditionals do not contrapose. (HDOM, 146)

Sosa claims that safety is (while sensitivity is not) a requirement for knowledge (HDOM, 147). One's belief that one is not a BIV is safe, according to Sosa, and so one does know that one is not a BIV.[5] The appearance that (E4) is not known is an *illusion* (HDOM, 147). What accounts for this illusion? Here we're asking for an explanation of the same phenomenon that SCA is designed to explain – why (E4) can seem not to be knowledge. In short, Sosa's explanation is that the belief that one is not a BIV is an insensitive belief, and, though sensitivity isn't required for knowledge, it is easily confused with safety, which *is* a requirement for knowledge. In Sosa's own words:

> Safety and sensitivity, being mutual contrapositives, are easily confused, so it is easy to
> confuse the correct requirement of safety . . . with a requirement of sensitivity. It is easy to
> overlook that subjunctive conditionals do not contrapose. (HDOM, 148)

Sosa's account can handle our other Es (in their familiar settings) as well: Because, in their familiar settings, beliefs in (E1)–(E3) are insensitive, Sosa's safety account will apply to them as well as it does to (E4).

Furthermore, Sosa's account can explain why it so often happens that the very changes to the examples that remove the "no-knowledge" appearance also have the result that the beliefs in question are not sensitive: once the beliefs in question are rendered sensitive, Sosa's explanation for the appearance of no-knowledge no longer applies to them.

So it can appear that Sosa has indeed produced a non-sensitivity account which can deliver at least many of the main advantages of sensitivity accounts.

4 Sosa's Account as a Sensitivity Account – and His Counterexamples

But wait! Isn't Sosa's own account a sensitivity account? And isn't it precisely in being a sensitivity account that it is able to deliver those advantages? Sosa's explanation for why (E4) can seem not to be known clearly employs the first of SCA's two claims:

1 S's belief that p is insensitive.

He combines this with the following in his explanation:

(b) Safety is a necessary condition for knowledge.
(c) Because it is the contrapositive of sensitivity, we easily confuse safety with sensitivity.

In fact, we can construe Sosa's account as an indirect sensitivity account, which uses (b)–(c) as its explanation for why (2) holds: it's because of (b)–(c) that we so often think that insensitive beliefs are not knowledge.

So far, this is just a matter of classification. It's no surprise that some broad category of explanations can be constructed which includes both Sosa's account and the accounts he is opposing. Do the shared features in virtue of which I'm grouping Sosa's account in with the others bear on the advantages/disadvantages of the accounts?

Yes, it seems. It's in virtue of partaking of the form of SCA that Sosa's account is able to achieve the advantages of the other sensitivity accounts. But, in virtue of that same form, Sosa's account seems to be rendered as vulnerable to his own counterexamples as are the accounts he attacks. At least it's hard to see why Sosa's account, as a sensitivity account, isn't as susceptible to the counterexamples he presents as are other sensitivity accounts. I've noted that Sosa's account seems to apply to (E1)–(E3) (in their usual settings), as well as to (E4), and it should be given credit for being able to explain the appearance of no-knowledge in the cases of those other insensitive beliefs. But Sosa's account would also apply equally well to his own counterexamples. Sosa's counterexamples involve insensitive beliefs that do not give the no-knowledge appearance given by our Es. Since these are insensitive beliefs, Sosa's explanation – built on (1), (b), and (c) – would apply to them as well as to our Es. Sosa's explanation, then, would lead us to expect the appearance of no-knowledge also in the case of his counterexamples, but, of course, no such appearance materializes.

So we should ask Sosa: Why don't we get that appearance of no-knowledge in the case of the counterexamples? Ideally, of course, Sosa will refine his explanation so that it will apply where and only where it should – so that it will explain the appearance of no-knowledge where and only where it occurs. (Perhaps in the case of his particular form of indirect sensitivity account, the refinement will consist in an articulation of the circumstances under which we're not likely to confuse sensitivity with safety.) In the meantime, Sosa can, like me, point out that (2) needn't be exceptionless to do the explanatory work to which it's put, and he can have the same grounds I have for thinking that indirect sensitivity accounts are on the right track. (Though I won't presume that he will endorse that argument that I rest on.)

In short, as far as I can see, Sosa is in the same boat I'm in with respect to the exceptions to (2). And I don't even see that he has any important advantage over *direct* sensitivity accounts here – provided that those accounts are sufficiently modest. Suppose a direct sensitivity theorist uses the phenomena I've cited as reasons for thinking that SCA is on the right track as support for the view that knowledge is *roughly* true, sensitive belief (with perhaps some other necessary conditions for knowledge also thrown in, to taste). Such a theorist may think there is an important property of beliefs, *sensitivity**, which is necessary for knowledge, and of which the conditionals in terms of which sensitivity is defined give a good first approximation. Such a modest direct sensitivity theorist will replace (a) with

(a′) Sensitivity *approximates* a necessary condition for knowledge,

and will take the counterexamples to (a) as illustrating some of the differences between sensitivity and *sensitivity** and as pointing to some of the directions one might take in refining one's account of *sensitivity**. Statement (a′) provides a foundation for (2), and, as far as I can see, the modest direct sensitivity theorist should be no more embarrassed by her need for approximation here than Sosa should be by the fact that he can only claim that we *often* confound safety with sensitivity, and yet he uses our (fairly general, but not exceptionless?) tendency to so confound in his account.

Imagine a new character, *Immodest Sosa*, who gives basically the same account as does our actual Sosa, but who claims that safety correctly and with ideal precision articulates the needed necessary condition for knowledge, and who claims that safety is always – with absolutely no exceptions – confounded with sensitivity, and so predicts that, without exception, all insensitive beliefs will give an appearance of no-knowledge. Our actual, more modest, and more sensible, Sosa will think that Immodest Sosa is on the right track – except for his foolish pretensions to precision. And our actual Sosa, I presume, thinks that there are good reasons for accepting his modest version of the safety account, despite the fact that it is not ideally precise. I don't see why our modest direct sensitivity theorist isn't in the same position as Sosa with respect to the counterexamples Sosa presents.

So, it does seem that, with respect to his own counterexamples, Sosa is in the same boat as me – and also as the direct sensitivity theorist, so long as the direct sensitivity theorist is sensibly modest.

I should add that I don't think this is a reason for Sosa to abandon his theory. The sensitivity boat is a fine boat to be in. As far as I can see, no non-sensitivity account even seriously competes with SCA in terms of successfully explaining the relevant phenomena. But it is to say that Sosa doesn't have the advantage here he thinks he has over the other sensitivity accounts. At least, I can't see why he should be counted as any less damaged by his own examples than I am – or even than the (appropriately modest) direct sensitivity theorist is.

5 Safety and the Problem of True/True Subjunctives

So far, I've only argued that Sosa's account doesn't have the main relative advantage he thinks it has. Are there any relative *disadvantages* to his safety account?

As we've seen, Sosa proposes safety as a necessary condition for knowledge, where S's belief that p is safe iff $B(p) \to p$. In perhaps the most straightforward way to convert those symbols into (semi-)English, what safety requires is this: that if the subject had believed that p, p would have been the case. I find such a condition for knowledge very problematic.

In particular, we are faced here with the problem of "true/true subjunctives." Consider: Tom is tall; Tom is a pharmacist; now, true or false:

> If Tom had been tall, he would have been a pharmacist?

My main reaction here is that there is *something* gravely wrong with using the above conditional: "*What* are you saying – 'If Tom *had been* tall'?! We've just been told that Tom *is* tall. Didn't you hear?" The conditional seems to presuppose that Tom isn't tall, but it has been stipulated in the example that he is. But what kind of supposition is this? Is it a *truth-condition* of the conditional that its antecedent is false? It isn't clear that what's wrong with the conditional here implies that the conditional is *false*. It also isn't clear that the conditional *isn't* false. As far as truth-value goes, nothing is clear here. All that's clear is that the conditional is somehow wrong. Generally, in treating such conditionals, namely subjunctive or counterfactual conditionals that have a true antecedent and a true consequent,[6] it is recognized that there are no strong intuitions about truth-value here to answer to. The use of the subjunctive or counterfactual form of conditional does in some sense presuppose that the antecedent is false, and so, when we encounter one with a true antecedent, we are overwhelmed by a sense of impropriety; however, it isn't clear that the wrongness involved is such as to render the conditional false.

The most common treatment of true/true subjunctives holds that they are *all* true. This view takes the wrongness we sense to be some form of conversational inappropriateness that does not imply falsehood. This standard view is generally arrived at by applying a theory of subjunctive conditionals that is taken to be well-motivated by its handling of other conditionals where there are strong intuitions and accepting that theory's results here, in the realm of true/true subjunctives, where the intuitive situation is considerably more murky. I find that standard view quite attractive, but, partly because I've never seen a convincing case for thinking that wrongness of these conditionals is merely one of conversational inappropriateness, I am also attracted to the rival view that *no* true/true subjunctives are true. This rival view can claim either that true/true subjunctives are all false or that they are all neither true nor false. (Or, I suppose, one can hold that some of them are false, while others lack truth-value, but I don't see why someone would hold to such a hybrid view.) What's essential to the rival view is that no true/true subjunctives are true.

If either the standard view or the rival account, in either of its forms, of true/true subjunctives is correct, Sosa's safety-based account of knowledge is in trouble. For, presumably, that S believes that p, and that p is true are requirements for S to know that p. Those requirements are standardly assumed, and Sosa doesn't indicate that he is denying them, so I take him to be proposing safety as a necessary condition for knowledge, to go alongside the standard conditions that p is true and that S believes that p, and perhaps some other necessary conditions, in his analysis of *S knows that p*. We can then use the standard conditions to narrow our focus to only true beliefs, which means that in all the important cases – the ones that satisfy the standard conditions by involving true beliefs – to which we can apply Sosa's condition of safety, the relevant conditional, $B(p) \rightarrow p$, will be a true/true subjunctive.

Now, suppose that the standard view of true/true subjunctives is correct: all true/true subjunctives are true. That renders Sosa's safety condition redundant: every case that satisfies the standard conditions for knowledge will automatically pass Sosa's safety test as well. Safety disastrously fails to eliminate from the realm of the known any case of true belief.

The rival view of true/true subjunctives is even more fatal for Sosa's theory. If *no* true/true subjunctives are true, then any belief that satisfies the standard requirements for knowledge will automatically *fail* Sosa's safety test. Thus, the rival treatment of true/true subjunctives, together with an account of knowledge which requires safety along with the standard conditions of truth and belief, will imply that nobody knows anything – a result Sosa is at great pains to avoid.

What Sosa needs is a third type of treatment of true/true subjunctives – one on which they're not all true, and on which they're not all false. Only then can safety be a necessary condition for knowledge that's both independent of and consistent with the standard conditions for knowledge. And that such a third type of theory might be correct certainly is not out of the question. Nozick posits, as a fourth condition for knowledge (in addition to sensitivity and the two standard conditions), a conditional, $p \rightarrow B(p)$, which is the reverse of Sosa's safety conditional, and so faces the same problem of true/true subjunctives that confronts Sosa.[7] Nozick presents an argument for thinking that some true/true subjunctives are true, while others are false.[8] I'm certainly not convinced by Nozick's case, and I'm not alone. The standard view (that true/true subjunctives are all true), I think, is still the standard view. And, for me, the third type of account that Nozick and Sosa need doesn't even take second place: in terms of how likely I think it is that the theories are correct, I'd put this third type of account behind both the "standard" and the "rival" account. And, of course, even if the third type of account is correct, that just gives Sosa's theory of knowledge a *chance* of being right. It's important for Sosa, as it is for Nozick, that some true/true subjunctives are true and others false, but he also needs the *right* ones to be true and the right ones to be false; they must divide into true and false in ways that render the safety account of knowledge sensible.

SAFETY, SENSITIVITY, AND SKEPTICAL HYPOTHESES 31

Even if, against my better judgment, the third type of account of true/true subjunctives is correct, I will be quite unable to check the safety account of knowledge against examples to determine if it is right. For such a task will consist of taking examples where S has a true belief that p, and then asking of them whether it is also true that if S had believed that p, p would have been true, and then checking those results against intuitions about whether S knows that p in the cases. But it's hopeless, at least for me, to try to carry out this process. Wherever S does believe that p, and p is true, the conditional *If S had believed that p, p would have been the case* will just strike me as weird and wrong; there's just no way that I'll be able to get stable and discriminating reactions that might match up with intuitions about whether the subject knows in the various cases: "Well, here the [true/true subjunctive] conditional seems true, but *here* it seems false." Apparently I'm not alone, given the typical attitude taken toward true/true subjunctives by students of conditionals. Thus, I find accounts of knowledge like Sosa's (and Nozick's) that put so much weight on true/true subjunctives highly problematic.

6 Other Formulations of Safety

Now, all of the above is based on phrasing the safety conditional, $B(p) \to p$, in "... had ... would have been ..." terms: If S had believed that p, p would have been the case. As I wrote, that strikes me as the most straightforward way to express $B(p) \to p$ as a subjunctive or counterfactual conditional and as the contrapositive of the sensitivity conditional. But Sosa expresses his safety condition in other ways – ways that don't induce the "weird and wrong" reaction in cases where S believes that p and p is true. Sosa writes:

> Call a belief by S that p "safe" iff: S would believe that p only if it were so that p. (Alternatively, a belief by S that p is "safe" iff: S would not believe that p without it being the case that p; or, better, iff: as a matter of fact, though perhaps not as a matter of strict necessity, not easily would S believe that p without it being the case that p.) (HDOM, 142)

So while I've been formulating safety as

(S1) If S had believed that p, p would have been the case,

Sosa suggests these formulations:

(S2) S would believe that p only if it were so that p
(S3) S would not believe that p without it being the case that p
(S4) As a matter of fact, though perhaps not as a matter of strict necessity, not easily would S believe that p without it being the case that p.

Suppose Tom correctly believes that I ate breakfast this morning. When I try to evaluate for truth the conditional,

(T1) If Tom had believed that I ate breakfast this morning, I would have eaten breakfast this morning, (or: *If Tom had believed that I ate breakfast this morning, it would have been the case that I ate breakfast this morning*), I just find it weird and wrong, and there's no hope that in some ways of further specifying the example I'll find the conditional true, while where the details of the case are specified in other ways, I'll find the conditional false. Things are quite different with:

(T2) Tom would believe that I ate breakfast this morning only if it were so that I ate breakfast this morning,

(T3) Tom would not believe that I ate breakfast this morning without it being the case that I ate breakfast this morning,

and

(T4) As a matter of fact, though perhaps not as a matter of strict necessity, not easily would Tom believe that I ate breakfast this morning without it being the case that I ate breakfast this morning.

Here there *is* hope for discriminating reactions. For each of (T2)–(T4), as opposed to (T1), there are some ways of filling in the case (keeping constant that I did in fact eat breakfast and that Tom believes that I did) such that the conditional will seem true, and other ways which will make the conditional seem false. What's more, at least when we check fairly obvious cases of knowledge and fairly obvious cases of no-knowledge, the initial results of the safety account of knowledge, where safety is understood here in terms of (T2)–(T4), as opposed to (T1), seem promising. Sentences (T2)–(T4) do seem true in the obvious cases that first come to mind when we try to imagine a case where Tom seems clearly to know that I ate breakfast. For example, suppose that Tom himself observed me eating breakfast, he was sure it was me, etc. And things indeed are different in the obvious cases of no-knowledge (despite the presence of true belief) that first come to mind. Suppose, for example, that Lying Larry told Tom 20 things this afternoon, including that I ate breakfast this morning. Tom believed everything Larry told him and has no basis for thinking I ate breakfast other than that Larry told him so. Though Larry thought everything he was telling Tom was false, in fact only 19 of the 20 things Larry told Tom were false, with my having eaten breakfast being the only truth in the bunch. Here Tom seems not to know that I ate breakfast, and (T2)–(T4) seem false.

So where safety is construed in one of the alternative (S2)–(S4) ways, then, a safety account of knowledge seems promising. However, where safety is so construed, I think its claim to being $B(p) \rightarrow p$, and to being the contrapositive of sensitivity is jeopardized. Much here depends on some very fine points about conditionals, but the sensitivity condition is:

If p had not been the case, S would not have believed that p,

and it seems that it's (S1), and not any of (S2)–(S4), that is the contrapositive of that. And as we've seen, it is essential to Sosa's account of why it seems that we don't know that skeptical hypotheses are false that safety is the contrapositive of sensitivity.

Sentences (S2) and (S3) would be better candidates for being the contrapositive of the sensitivity conditional if (S2)'s "would believe" and (S3)'s "would not believe" were changed to "would have believed" and "would not have believed", respectively – and perhaps if (S2)'s "only if it were so" were changed to "only if it had been so" and (S3)'s "without it being the case" were changed to "without it having been the case." But once those quite significant changes are made, the new versions of (S2) and (S3) would have the same problem that (S1) has in being applied to cases where p is the case and S has a true belief that p. Sentence (S4) is so different from the obvious way of contraposing the sensitivity conditional that its claim to being that contrapositive is extremely tenuous.

7 Safety and Strength of Epistemic Position

As Sosa notes (HDOM, 144), my own solution (in SSP) to the skeptical problem emerges from the interplay of two quite different ways of evaluating beliefs. First, there's the issue of whether the belief is sensitive or not. Second, there's the matter of how strong an epistemic position the subject is in with respect to the thing believed. Sosa presents his safety condition as something of a substitute for sensitivity – something that can be easily confused with sensitivity, but which does a better job in a theory or picture of knowledge. But when I compare the picture of knowledge that informs Sosa's treatment with my own, it strikes me that the really interesting comparison is between Sosa's safety condition, as least in its (S2)–(S4) formulations, and especially in the case of (S4), with my notion of strength of epistemic position.

Sosa's gloss on my notion of strength of epistemic position is good for our current purpose:

> One's epistemic position with respect to P is stronger the more remote are the least remote possibilities wherein one's belief as to whether p does not match the fact of the matter. (HDOM, 144)

Compare that with the (S4) version of Sosa's notion of safety:

(S4) As a matter of fact, though perhaps not as a matter of strict necessity, not easily would S believe that p without it being the case that p.

(S4)-safety seems to be a matter of degree, its formulation prompting the question, "*how* easily?" – or more precisely (though much less grammatically): "how not easily?" And the matter of how (S4)-safe is one's belief seems very close to the issue of how strong an epistemic position one is in with respect to p. Strength of epistemic position is also a matter of how easily S could have gone wrong with respect to p, this being measured by how remote are the least remote possibilities in which one does go wrong. Applying the same way of measuring "ease" to (S4), yields:

> One's belief that p is safer the more remote are the least remote possibilities wherein one believes that p without it being the case that p.

Sosa himself gives such a treatment of his safety in the last sentence of this passage:

> Here is the striking result: if we opt for safety as the right requirement then a Moorean stance is defensible, and we avoid skepticism. That is to say, one does satisfy the requirement that one's belief of not-H be safe: after all, not easily *would* one believe that not-H (which is not to say that not possibly *could* one believe that without it being true). In the actual world, and for quite a distance away from the actual world, up to quite remote possible worlds, our belief that we are not radically deceived matches the fact as to whether we are or are not radically deceived. (HDOM, 146–7)

So (S4)-safety and strength of epistemic position are very similar notions. The main difference is that (S4)-safety, if I'm understanding it correctly, is troubled only by worlds (especially very nearby worlds) in which one believes that p but p is not the case (ways in which S would easily believe that p without it being the case that p), while strength is disturbed both by that and by the presence of worlds (especially very nearby worlds) in which p is true but S disbelieves it. Which notion is more appropriate to an account of knowledge is a very difficult matter, which I won't go into here – though, of course, my preference is for the notion of strength. (Well, let me quickly mention one relative advantage of strength: its application to beliefs in necessary truths. We can, of course, believe but fail to know necessary truths. The problem for safety here is that there can be no nearby worlds in which we believe a necessary truth, but in which it isn't true, since, being necessary, there are no worlds in which it isn't true. Thus, there can be no worlds to disturb the safety of a belief in a necessary truth. But the *strength* of such a belief *can* be upset by the presence of nearby (in the relevant way) worlds in which one disbelieves the necessary truth in question.)

If I'm right that these two notions are quite close, then the picture of knowledge that informs Sosa's treatment of skepticism is very close to my own, for Sosa's rough account of knowledge is that of safe enough true belief, while mine is that of strong enough true belief. (Here, I ease exposition by simply referring to beliefs themselves as "strong," by which I mean that the believer is in a strong epistemic position with respect to the proposition that is the object of the belief.) This may be obscured by Sosa's grouping me together with direct sensitivity theorists. Unlike those direct theorists, I do not picture knowledge as being anything like *sensitive* true belief. Knowledge for me is (roughly) *strong* enough true belief, where this notion of strength seems to be quite close to Sosa's notion of safety, at least as Sosa sometimes formulates it. It is one of my main tasks, as an *indirect* sensitivity theorist, as it is one of Sosa's, to explain why insensitive beliefs so often give the appearance of no-knowledge, *even though sensitivity is no part of the concept of knowledge*, and even when the beliefs are quite strong. Correctly viewed, I'm no more a sensitivity theorist than is Sosa – and am no more damaged by his counterexamples than he is. We both appeal to certain beliefs' insensitivity to explain why they give an appearance of no-knowledge, but we both do so in an indirect way: Neither of us pictures knowledge as being anything like sensitive true belief, so we both must explain why insensitive beliefs so often seem not to be knowledge even when they have what we claim is the real knowledge-making property (safety, strength) to a high degree. As it turns out, while Sosa and I end up with strikingly similar pictures of knowledge, the explanations we give for why insensitive beliefs give the appearance of no-knowledge are very different.

So, Sosa and I are operating with very similar pictures of knowledge – knowledge as (at least roughly) safe/strong enough true belief. I take this picture in a contextualist direction: for me, the matter of how safe/strong a belief must be for it to constitute knowledge is a context-sensitive matter. In some conversational contexts, "S knows that p" can be true only if S is in a *very* strong epistemic position with respect to p, while in other contexts, S need only be in a moderately strong epistemic position with respect to p for the same knowledge-attributing sentence to be true of her. Sosa is no doubt quite sympathetic to taking our picture of knowledge in such a contextualist direction, since he is not opposed to epistemic contextualism *per se* – and in fact seems to accept it. But he does seem skeptical about the usefulness of contextualism in addressing traditional epistemological concerns – and, in particular, in providing a solution to the problem of philosophical skepticism.[9] Here, our disagreement is sharp. I believe that a contextualist version of the picture of knowledge under consideration can provide a powerful explanation of why insensitive beliefs can so often give an appearance of no-knowledge, even when they are quite strong, and can thereby provide a powerful solution to the particular skeptical paradox that both Sosa and I wrestle with, and I take its ability to provide this solution to be a strong reason – though certainly not the only reason – for accepting contextualism.

This is not the place to explain my account of why insensitive beliefs typically seem not to be knowledge. (See SSP, esp. 35–8.) But once one is operating with a picture of knowledge as (S4)-safe/strong enough true belief, and is inclined to take this picture in a contextualist direction, the materials required by my account seem all in place, and the account I give becomes almost irresistible – at least to me. So, given the problems with the safety account that I outlined above in sections 5–6, and given that the counterexamples Sosa uses against my account seem to give no advantage to his own indirect sensitivity account over my indirect sensitivity account, as I argued in section 4, I'm inclined to stick to my own account, and not accept Sosa's safety theory – at least in its current form. Of course, there's plenty of room for Sosa's safety theory to be developed in various different ways, and there's no telling at this point how successful those developments will be.

Sosa, I suspect, will weigh up the relative advantages and disadvantages quite differently. I will close by discussing two closely related issues that Sosa discusses and that bear on this weighing – the attractiveness of contextualist solutions to skepticism, and the question of just how "intuitively correct" it is that we don't know that skeptical hypotheses are false.

8 Contextualist Solutions to Skepticism

Sosa and I, along with many other current epistemologists, spend much time and energy addressing a particular form of skeptical argument, which I have called the "Argument from Ignorance" (AI). Where "O" is a proposition about the external world that one would *o*rdinarily think one knows (e.g., I have hands) and "H" is a suitably chosen skeptical hypothesis (e.g., I am a bodiless brain in a vat who has been electrochemically stimulated to have those sensory experiences I've had, henceforth a "BIV"), AI, in its simplest form, proceeds as follows:

1. I don't know that not-H.
2. If I don't know that not-H, then I don't know that O.
So, C. I don't know that O.[10]

AI's premises are both highly plausible – though more on this in section 9, below. The negation of its conclusion, however, is also highly plausible. AI thus presents us with a puzzle: (1), (2), and (not-C) (I *do* know that O) each seems individually plausible, but they can't all be true. The most attractive straightforward (non-contextualist) options for dealing with this puzzle are (following Sosa's succinct formulation):[11]

Skeptic: 1, 2, C
Nozick et al.: 1, ~C, ~2
Moore: 2, ~C, ~1 (HDOM, 144)

Sosa is a straightforward Moorean, taking the third option above. As a Moorean, he takes his counterintuitive (but see section 9, below) stand on the issue of (1), claiming, with Moore,[12] that we do indeed know that (not-H). As I've urged (see SSP, esp. 3, 42), to successfully follow this path the Moorean must explain why (1) seems true – why it seems that we don't know that (not-H). Sosa accepts this requirement (see HDOM, esp. 147), and seeks to meet it in the way outlined above in section 3 and critiqued in sections 4–6.

I endorse a non-straightforward, contextualist solution to the puzzle: I accept a contextualist theory of knowledge attributions;[13] I accept that at some very unusually high standards for knowledge (which we'll here call the "absolute" standards) we don't count as knowing that we have hands; I claim that we do know that we have hands according to the much lower standards for knowledge that typically govern most of our ordinary conversations; and I seek to explain the persuasiveness of the skeptic's argument, at least in part, by claiming that the presentation of the skeptic's argument has at least some tendency to put into play the very "absolute" standards at which we don't count as knowing that we have hands.

Sosa, who is happy enough with contextualist theory of knowledge attributions, in various ways wants a more stridently anti-skeptical solution to our puzzle than contextualist solutions provide. And the contextualist solution is indeed more conciliatory to skepticism than is the straightforward Moorean position – and in the end may be too concessive for Sosa's tastes. But I will here address one of Sosa's worries in a way that may make the contextualist solution a bit more palatable.

Sosa's most extreme worry is that the contextualist solution is simply irrelevant to traditional epistemological reflection on skepticism. Sosa does not *claim* that it is irrelevant, but is led to wonder what the relevance is (S&C, 3–4). He compares

(a1) People often utter truths when they say "Somebody loves me."
(a2) Does anybody love me?

with

(c1) People often utter truths when they say "I know there are hands."
(c2) Do people ever know that there are hands?

adding: "c2 is presented as a question we might pose in philosophical reflection, in a philosophy journal or conference." A distraught person led to ask (a2) is hoping to be reassured by the answer that indeed somebody does love them; (a1) miserably fails to provide the needed comfort. In philosophical reflection on skepticism, in philosophy journals, and in philosophy conferences, many have been moved to ask (c2). Why is (c1) any more relevant to (c2), asked in a philosophical setting, than (a1) is to (a2)?

Let's assume that philosophical discussions of skepticism are invariably governed by the "absolute" standards according to which nobody knows that there are hands. That's a highly debatable assumption, but it helps to make the question of relevance more pointed. Under that assumption, when (c2) is asked in philosophical discussion of skepticism, the truthful answer to it, according to contextualist solutions to skepticism, is the distressing "no." Why is (c1) any comfort here – any more than (a1) is in the distressing situation in which the answer to (a2) is the distressing "no"?

The important difference between (a1)/(a2) and (c1)/(c2) is that the relevant "context-sensitivity" in (a1)/(a2) – that "me" refers on each occasion of use to the speaker, and so refers to different people as it is spoken by different people – is clear to all, and so nobody is likely to be misled into thinking that (a1) implies that the answer to (a2) is positive. By contrast, if the contextualist treatment of skepticism is correct, it is only controversially so, and it is far from being clear to all. Under contextualist analysis, the skeptic raises the standards for knowledge, and our sensitivity to her standards-raising maneuvers inclines us at least some extent to give negative answers to questions about whether there is knowledge in various cases. At the same time, however, we are sensitive to the fact that it's usually correct to say that people do know all sorts of things – i.e., we realize that (c1). Not realizing that those usual affirmations are compatible with skeptical denials of knowledge, we get confused.

So far, that sounds quite skeptical. The correct answer to (c2), as we've been asking it in philosophical discussions of skepticism, is "no," and our tendency to think otherwise is based on a confusion – the confusion of thinking that (c1) implies that (c2) should receive a positive answer. But the confusion goes both ways. Not only does (c1) lead us into thinking that (c2) should be answered positively, but we can also easily be misled into thinking that a negative answer to (c2) implies (c1) is false. That, I think, is a large part of why a negative answer to (c2) can seem so menacing and so important. At least much of the sting of skepticism comes from the thought that we've been wrong all along in thinking and saying that we "know" various things. If it turns out that almost all our thoughts and assertions to the effect that we "know" various things – including *very* serious thoughts and assertions made in very serious settings where appropriately high standards (but not yet philosophical, absolute standards) for knowledge hold sway – are really correct, skepticism loses most of its sting, at least for me. Therein lies the comfort of the contextualist response.

Is that sufficient comfort? How much skeptical distress remains behind? That, it seems, depends on how important it is that we know according to "absolute" standards. If one thinks that is all-important, one will find almost no comfort in the contextualist solution. But for my part, once the skeptical strategy is seen to have no tendency to show that any of my claims to know – except those very rare ones made in settings governed by "absolute" standards – are in any way wrong, and once I start to get a clear look at what it *would* take to "know" according to the skeptic's absolute standards, I find the distress caused by my failure to meet those standards to be minimal at best – perhaps to be compared with the "distress" produced by the realization that I'm not omnipotent.

Sentence (c1) does not tell us how (c2), interpreted according to absolute standards, should be answered – any more than (a1) tells one how to answer (a2). If traditional epistemological reflection on skepticism concerned only how to answer (c2), interpreted absolutely, the contribution of the contextualist solution to that project would be to tell us that the skeptic's answer to *the* question of traditional inquiry about skepticism is the right one. Any tendency we might have to reject the skeptic's answer that's based on facts like (c1) is misguided, according to the contextualist's solution. The contextualist solution might also, in that case, lead us to believe that traditional inquiry into skepticism has not been concerned with a very important question. But insofar as philosophical inquiry into skepticism concerns, not just the question of how (c2), interpreted absolutely, should be answered, but also concerns the importance of that question, so interpreted; insofar as it addresses the relation between philosophical skepticism and ordinary thought about knowledge; and especially insofar as philosophical inquiry into skepticism seeks to address the truly menacing thought that (c1) might not be correct after all, the contextualist solution has a lot to offer, and is far from irrelevant.

9 Intuitive Complexity: Do We Know that We're Not Brains in Vats?

Finally, I will close by agreeing with Sosa on an important point, and briefly exploring the implications of that point.

Though I'm not a "straightforward Moorean" like Sosa, I am, like most who advocate contextualist solutions to skepticism, a "contextualist Moorean": I believe that according to ordinary, everyday standards of knowledge, we do know that we're not BIVs.[14] As a Moorean, I, like Sosa, have to explain why it can seem that we don't know that the skeptical hypothesis is false. (In short, *my* answer is that the unusually high standards at which one doesn't know that the hypothesis is false are the very standards that tend to get put into play when the skeptical hypothesis is brought up. But for more of the story, see SSP.) So, in SSP and now in earlier sections of this chapter, I claim that premise (1) of AI is plausible, and focus much effort on explaining why it is so plausible. Sosa insightfully responds:

> Consider, moreover, the need to explain how the skeptic's premise – that one does not know oneself not to be radically misled, etc. – is as plausible as it is. That requirement must be balanced by an equally relevant and stringent requirement: namely, that one explain how that premise is as *implausible* as it is. To many of us it just does not seem so uniformly plausible that one cannot be said correctly to know that one is not at this very moment being fed experiences while envatted. So the explanatory requirement is in fact rather more complex than might seem at first. And given the distribution of intuitions here, the contextualist and the Nozickean, et al., still owe us an explanation. (HDOM, 147)

Though I've found the distribution of intuitions a bit more tilted toward the skeptic-friendly verdict that we don't know we're not BIVs than Sosa's experience leads him to believe,[15] I certainly agree that the intuitive situation is complex, and, in fact, am myself among those to whom it is not "uniformly plausible" that we don't know that we're not BIVs. Since I first encountered philosophical skepticism in the form of AI, I personally have been fairly strongly inclined to think that I *do* know the various skeptical hypotheses to be false. Nevertheless, I at the same time felt the appeal of the skeptic's claim that we don't know this, and have found that most others feel this appeal more strongly than I do. Upon questioning, I find that almost everyone feels a conflict of intuitive forces pulling them in different directions on the question of whether they do or don't know this about themselves. My focus has been on explaining that strong pull here in the skeptic's favor.

But Sosa asks a very fair – and widely neglected – question: What about the opposing intuitive pull *against* the skeptic?

According to Sosa, one's belief that one is not a BIV is a safe, but not a sensitive belief. Our concept of knowledge, on Sosa's account, is (roughly) that of safe true belief, but we easily confuse safety with sensitivity. Thus, because the belief in question is safe, it will strike us, at least to some extent, as being a case of knowledge, but because it is insensitive, it will, at least to some extent, strike us as not being a case of knowledge.

How might the contextualist meet the challenge Sosa registers at the end of the above extract? Here, I'll speak only for myself. I think two aspects of my account that it has in common with Sosa's account provide a good start toward meeting this challenge. First, according to my solution, we are in a very strong epistemic position with respect to *I am not a BIV*[16] – which is quite close to Sosa's claim that this belief is "quite safe" (HDOM, 142). Second, knowledge is, on my account, (roughly) strong enough true belief. These together make our tendency to think that we do know that we're not BIVs quite unsurprising: on my account, as on Sosa's account, one's belief that one is not a BIV has a lot of that property that's needed to convert true belief into knowledge. Indeed, that one is not a BIV is one of the things we know best – though it's peculiarly difficult to truthfully say that we know it. In light of all this, it's the reverse of surprising that we have a tendency to think we do know it, and that we're quite conflicted about the issue.

Notes

1 "How to Defeat Opposition to Moore," *Philosophical Perspectives* 13 (1999): 141–53 (cited as HDOM); and "Skepticism and Contextualism," *Philosophical Issues* 10 (2000): 1–18 (cited as S&C).
2 I hold that, according to ordinary standards for knowledge, one does know each of the above. The reason it can seem otherwise is that the extraordinary high standards at which one doesn't know them are precisely the standards that tend to be put into play when those items are brought up.
3 *Philosophical Review* 104 (1995): 1–52; reprinted in K. DeRose and T. Warfield, eds., *Skepticism* (New York: Oxford University Press, 1999), and in E. Sosa and J. Kim, eds., *Epistemology: An Anthology* (Oxford: Blackwell, 2000).
4 I discuss a counterexample much like Sosa's first in my SSP, pp. 22–3. As Sosa points out, this sort of case is presented by Jonathan Vogel in "Tracking, Closure, and Inductive Knowledge," in S. Luper-Foy, ed., *The Possibility of Knowledge* (Lanham, MD: Rowman and Littlefield, 1987).

5   At least this is typically so. I assume Sosa would agree that there could be weird circumstances in which one doesn't know one is not a BIV. Of course, two such weird situations are: (1) where one actually is a BIV, and (2) where one is convinced that one is a BIV. But it wouldn't be hard to construct weird situations in which someone isn't a BIV, believes she isn't a BIV, but about which even "Mooreans" would want to say she doesn't *know* she's not a BIV. Consider, for example, a subject who firmly believed she was a BIV until just a few minutes ago, when Lying Larry told her 20 different things, all of which the subject believed purely on Larry's say-so, where one of the 20 was the truth that the subject is not a BIV, and the other 19 things were all falsehoods.

6   True/false subjunctives – subjunctive conditionals with a true antecedent and a false consequent – also have the problem of having a true antecedent, and thus also seem somehow wrong. Many people, though, do have a (fairly strong) intuition as to the truth-value of true/false subjunctives, intuiting that they are false.

7   In his "Postscript" to "Proper Functionalism and Virtue Epistemology" (in J. Kvanvig, ed., *Warrant and Contemporary Epistemology*, Lanham, MD: Rowman and Littlefield, 1996; pp. 271–80), Sosa proposes an account of knowledge that takes both $B(p) \to p$ (Sosa's safety condition) *and* $p \to B(p)$ (Nozick's fourth condition) to be requirements for knowledge.

8   See Nozick, *Philosophical Explanations* (Cambridge, MA: Harvard University Press, 1981), pp. 176, 680–1 (= *Skepticism*, pp. 162, 175–6 = *Epistemology*, pp. 81, 95–6).

9   Sosa opens "Skepticism and Contextualism" with these words:

> Contextualism has gained center stage in epistemology mainly through its way with the skeptic, from the early days of "relevant alternatives" to important recent publications. While myself accepting elements of contextualism, I will detail reservations about its use in epistemology, and in particular about its use to dispose of skepticism. (S&C, 1)

Sosa writes above that he accepts "elements" of contextualism. What of it does he accept? A bit later in S&C, we find:

> The main thesis of epistemic contextualism (EC) has considerable plausibility as a thesis in linguistics or in philosophy of language. In applying it to epistemology, however, it is possible to overreach, or so I am here arguing. (S&C, 3)

I think, then, that what Sosa accepts is what, in the second passage above, he says has "considerable plausibility": the main contextualist thesis. In that case, it was a bit misleading to describe himself as accepting "elements" of contextualism. He accepts contextualism, not just elements of it, if I'm understanding him correctly. What he doesn't accept is (at least many of) the applications of contextualism to epistemological problems – and particularly its alleged solution to skepticism.

In earlier work, Sosa had a brighter view of the prospects of applying contextualism to the problem of skepticism; see especially his paper, "Knowledge in Context, Skepticism in Doubt," *Philosophical Perspectives* 2 (1988): 139–55.

10 See SSP, 1, and HDOM, 143.

11 These are the most attractive straightforward options, because they take the intuitively correct stand on two of the three matters at issue, and taking the intuitively correct stand on all three questions – (1), (2), (~C) – suffers from the serious defect of being inconsistent. Of course, there are other possible, though less attractive, straightforward options on which one takes the intuitively correct position on only one of the three issues, and there's even the *very* unattractive option of (perhaps incoherently) violating intuitions on all three issues: (~1), (~2), (C).

12 As I note in SSP (p. 41, fn. 37), Moore himself responded in this way – by denying the skeptic's first premise – to the *dream argument* – the version of AI that utilizes the hypothesis

that one is dreaming as its H. I think it is very far from certain that Moore would have responded in a similar way to versions of AI that utilize other (especially more radical) skeptical hypotheses. Still, needing a label, we call all deniers of AI's first premise "Mooreans."

13 For an explanation of such theories, see my "Contextualism and Knowledge Attributions," *Philosophy and Phenomenological Research* 52 (1992): 913–29; and my "Contextualism: An Explanation and Defense," in J. Greco and E. Sosa, eds., *The Blackwell Guide to Epistemology* (Oxford: Blackwell, 1999), pp. 187–205.

14 For more on "straightforward" vs. "contextualist" Mooreanism, see my "How Can We Know that We're Not Brains in Vats?," esp. section 6 ("A Nonheroic Alternative: A Moorean Contextualist Account"): 133–6. Stewart Cohen, David Lewis, and Gail Stine all seem, like me, to be contextualist Mooreans. Mark Heller advocates a different contextualist solution – a contextualist Nozickean solution (this category of solution, as compared with contextualist Mooreanism, is explained in "How Can We Know that We're Not Brains in Vats?", cited just above).

15 In a footnote attached to the above quotation, Sosa reports:

> Informal polling of my classes has revealed (of course defeasibly) that those who find [the skeptic's first premise] false outnumber those who find it true, and quite a few prefer to suspend judgment. At every stage people spread out in some such pattern of three-way agreement-failure.

I recently took a poll in a class of over 70 introductory philosophy students, with very different results. My question was whether or not each student, in her or his own opinion, knew that she or he was not a BIV. The preparation was explaining the BIV hypothesis in some detail, while refraining from using terms of epistemic appraisal in my description of the hypothesis. (So, for instance, I was careful not to say anything like, "So, if you are such a BIV, you can't tell that you are," since I take "can't tell" to be a question-begging negative assessment of any belief one might have to the effect that one is not a BIV.) The question was put to the students before AI was even presented, so I had not indicated that a negative answer might jeopardize their knowledge of various Os – though, no doubt, many students were worrying about that on their own. I asked for a show of hands, first asking those who thought that they did not know they weren't BIVs to raise their hands. A clear majority – about two-thirds of the class, it seemed, though I didn't count – of the hands went up. So most of these students agreed with the skeptic on this issue. When I asked who thought they *did* know they weren't BIVs, only three hands went up. So, as Sosa reports often happens, a sizable portion of the class didn't vote. Still, these are very different results from what Sosa reports – and from what I've found in the past. As best I can tell, the main difference between how I presented the question at this class and how I usually present it is that I explained the BIV hypothesis in more detail than I usually do.

16 On my account, we're not only well enough positioned with respect to *I'm not a BIV* to meet ordinary standards for knowledge, but also to meet even *most* of the extraordinarily high standards that are sometimes in play – though not well enough positioned to meet the skeptic's absolute standards, of course. In SSP, I'm quite explicit about our being in as strong an epistemic position with respect to *I'm not a BIV* as we're in with respect to *I have hands*. Of course, this surprising comparative fact can be due either to our being in a surprisingly weak position with respect to the latter (as the skeptic would have it), or to our being in a surprisingly strong position with respect to the former. The surprise, on my account, is how well positioned we are with respect to our not being BIVs. This verdict is defended by means of an account of why it can *seem* that our knowledge that we're not BIVs is shaky at best. For more on this, and on the importance of defending *I'm not a BIV* as being something we're in a *very* strong epistemic position with respect to, see again my "How Can We Know that We're Not Brains in Vats?"

4

Foundational Justification

RICHARD FELDMAN

1 Introduction

Two theses characterize foundationalism. One is that there are beliefs or propositions whose justification does not depend on other beliefs. Beliefs or propositions that have this status are said to be basic or foundationally justified. The second foundationalist thesis is that everything that is non-foundationally justified has that status in virtue of its relation to things that are foundationally justified. A third thesis characterizes what is plausibly described as classical foundationalism. This is the idea that internal (or mental) factors determine which beliefs are justified. In particular, external factors such as contingent reliability or causal connectedness are not among the conditions for justification, unless they are implied by the internal factors.

For foundationalists to have a reasonably well-developed theory they must deal with at least three issues in a suitable way. First, there should be an account of which beliefs actually have foundational justification. Second, given that foundationally justified beliefs are not justified in virtue of their relations to other beliefs, there should be some account of what it is that does make them justified. And, third, if skepticism is to be avoided, there should be some account of how the foundationally justified beliefs actually manage to justify a significant body of beliefs about the world.

Familiar versions of classical foundationalism hold that propositions or beliefs about one's own current mental states are foundationally justified. Among the reasons offered for holding them to be foundationally justified are the claims that we are infallible with respect to such matters or that these states are "self-presenting." Foundationalists who limit what is basic to these mental states are faced with a difficult problem when they attempt to explain how beliefs about the external world are justified on their basis. In several recent publications Ernest Sosa has raised, in a characteristically insightful way, a challenge for such versions of classical foundationalism.[1] In this chapter I will examine Sosa's arguments and attempt to defend a version of classical foundationalism from his criticism.

2 A Problem for Classical Foundationalism

Initial formulation of the theory

Classical foundationalists have thought that there are certain qualities of experiences that are in some sense directly present to consciousness. For example, if a person has an experience of a large expanse of redness in her visual field against a sharply contrasting background, then she can know "directly" that she is having such an experience of redness. That she is having such an experience is a paradigmatic example of foundational justification. From this she can infer that there is something red before her. The traditional foundationalist picture has it that all knowledge is ultimately based on this sort of direct knowledge.

Sosa begins his discussion of this topic by quoting from Leibniz and Russell, both of whom explain foundational justification in terms of awareness. The quotation from Russell will suffice for present purposes:

> We shall say that we have *acquaintance* with anything of which we are directly aware, without the intermediary of any process of inference or any knowledge of truths.[2]

This quotation suggests a principle of foundational justification concerning things of which we are directly aware. To formulate any such principle clearly, it will be helpful to make some preliminary distinctions among the potential objects of direct awareness and also among the things that are potential subjects of foundational justification.

One might say that we are directly aware of certain experiences. Alternatively, one might say that we are directly aware of certain properties of experiences. One might also say that we are directly aware of facts about experiences and their properties. Thus, in the example in which the person is presented with a large expanse of redness, one might say that the person is aware of (i) the experience of redness; (ii) the experiential quality, redness; (iii) the fact that she has an experience of redness. It may be that the view can be developed in terms of any one of these options, but which choice is made will affect exactly how the view is formulated. For present purposes, the discussion can most easily proceed in terms of awareness of properties.

There is a clear difference between a person merely being justified in believing a certain proposition and the person believing that proposition justifiably. The former requires only something such as sufficiently good reasons for belief or an available reliable method that would lead to that belief. The person need not actually have formed the belief. The latter requires that the belief actually be formed, either on the basis of those reasons or as a result of that method. We can refer to the former sort of justification as *propositional justification* and to the latter as *doxastic justification*. We can use sentences of the form "S is justified in believing p" to report propositional justification and sentences of the form "S justifiably believes p" and "S's belief that p is justified" to report doxastic justification. At several points later in this chapter this distinction will be important.

An initial statement of a foundationalist principle about propositional justification suggested by Russell's remark is:

> (PJ1) If a person is aware of experiential property F (i.e., has an experience of F-ness), then the person is foundationally justified in believing that he is having an experience with quality F.

Given the terminology adopted here, this principle says that when a person has an experience of a certain sort, the person is justified in believing the corresponding proposition saying that she is having an experience of that sort. This holds whether or not the person actually believes the proposition. We can easily devise a principle about doxastic justification that corresponds to (PJ1):

> (DJ1) If a person is aware of experiential property F (i.e., has an experience of F-ness), and believes that he is having an experience with property F, then that belief is foundationally justified.

The difference between (PJ1) and (DJ1) will matter later.

Principles such as (PJ1) and (DJ1) should help foundationalists answer the questions for foundationalism that were mentioned at the beginning of this chapter. In answer to the first question, these principles say that the foundationally justified beliefs are the ones about directly experienced properties of experience. And, in response to the second question, these principles suggest that it is our awareness of these properties that explains why we are justified in believing them to be present.

An ambiguity

Sosa contends that there is a crucial ambiguity in principles such as (PJ1). He writes:

> One's consciousness contains experiences that go unnoticed; unnoticed altogether, or at least unnoticed as experiences with an intrinsic experiential character that they nevertheless do have. Just as one automatically jumps one's jumps, smiles one's smiles, and dances one's dances, however, so one experiences one's experiences. And since experiencing is a form of awareness, one is so aware even of experiences that escape one's notice and of which one is hence *un*aware. (PA, 4–5)

He goes on to distinguish two kinds of awareness. One he calls "noticing awareness" or "intellectual awareness." The other is mere "experiential awareness." The experiences that escape one's notice are experiences of which one is experientially aware but not noticingly aware. He asks:

> Which kind of awareness do [foundationalists] intend: (a) noticing, intellectual awareness, whereby one occurrently believes or judges the thing noticed to be present, as characterized a certain way; or (b) experiential awareness, whereby one is "aware" directly of an experience of a certain specific sort simply in virtue of undergoing it? ... That distinction ... is important as follows. From the fact that one is e-aware of something it does not follow that one is n-aware of it. (PA, 5)

And then immediately after this he adds that

To notice a fact about one's experience at a given time is to believe correctly that it is so, but just a guess will not suffice: it is required that the correct belief be also at a minimum justified, or reasonable, or epistemically appropriate, or some such. (PA, 5)

Given this ambiguity in the notion of awareness, there is a potential ambiguity in principles such as (PJ1). It could mean either of the following:

(PJ1e) If a person is experientially-aware of experiential property F, then the person is foundationally justified in believing that he is having an experience with property F.

(PJ1n) If a person is noticingly-aware of experiential property F, then the person is foundationally justified in believing that he is having an experience with property F.

Roughly, Sosa thinks that (PJ1e) is false and that (PJ1n) provides no explanation of the non-epistemic conditions in which a belief is foundationally justified. But some refinement of (PJ1n) will help make this point clearer.

To see the problem with (PJ1n), notice that it says in its antecedent that a person is n-aware of a property. But given what Sosa has said about n-awareness, n-awareness is best construed as a propositional attitude. Although one might be e-aware of properties (or experiences), n-awareness amounts to justified true beliefs about those properties. A better statement of the idea behind (PJ1n) is thus something like this:

(PJ2n) If a person is noticingly-aware of the fact that he is having an experience with experiential property F, then the person is foundationally justified in believing that he is having an experience with property F.

Given what Sosa has told us n-awareness is, this amounts to:

(PJ3n) If a person is having an experience with experiential property F, and the person believes that he is having an experience with property F, and he is justified in that belief, then the person is foundationally justified in believing that he is having an experience with property F.

Principle (PJ3n) obviously does not provide a suitable explanation of *why* beliefs about experienced qualities are justified. Its antecedent just says, in part, that the belief is justified. It does not provide non-epistemic sufficient conditions under which the belief is justified.[3] It is clear that noticing awareness cannot provide foundationalists with any helpful explanation of why beliefs are foundationally justified, since it builds into its antecedent the fact that they are justified.

Sosa uses the "Problem of the Speckled Hen" to illustrate why classical foundationalists cannot successfully appeal to experiencing awareness, as in (PJ1e), in explaining foundational justification. He writes:

Much in the intricate character of our experience can, again, escape our notice, and can even be mischaracterized, as when one takes oneself to be able to tell at a glance than an image has ten speckles although in actual fact is has eleven rather than ten. If the classical foundationalist wishes to have a theory and not just a promissory note, he needs to tell us *which* sorts of features of our states of consciousness are the epistemically effective ones, the ones such that it is *by corresponding to them specifically* that our basic beliefs acquire epistemically foundational status. (PA, 6)

I think that there may be a problem for (PJ1e) here, but it is not immediately obvious what it is.

What Sosa says is that we miss or mischaracterize some aspects of the "intricate character of our experience." This would apply most directly to a principle that says that all propositions about, or perhaps all beliefs about, features of experience are justified. But (PJ1e) does not say exactly that. It is more restrictive than that. It says that propositions about the properties of experience *of which we are aware* are justified. Furthermore, Sosa's example in which one mistakenly thinks one's image has 10 speckles rather than 11 seems to be more relevant to a principle about doxastic justification than to a principle about propositional justification such as (PJ1e).[4]

I believe that, if there is a counterexample to (PJ1e) here, it is this: when one has a mental image, sometimes one is e-aware of some of its properties without being justified in believing that one is having an experience with those properties. For example, when one has an image with 11 speckles, one is e-aware of the experience's 11-speckle property, but not justified in believing that it has that property. Similarly, when one sees a clearly displayed 23-sided object, one is aware of the experiential property of 23-sidedness, but not justified in believing that property to be instantiated in one's experience.[5] One can be e-aware of properties without being justified in believing them to apply. That is the significance of the case of the speckled hen: one is aware of some definite number of speckles, but not justified in believing that one's image has that number of speckles.

It is possible for classical foundationalists to resist the claim that one is e-aware of 23-sidedness or 11-specklehood in examples like these. They can say these are properties of experience of which we are unaware. However, I think that Sosa's point can be reformulated in response to this sort of reply. In the examples under consideration, a person has an experience of something with 23 sides or 11 speckles. These features of experience are right there in plain "view." Either the person is aware of those features or not. If he is, then the cases are counterexamples to (PJ1e). If the person is not aware of them, then classical foundationalists owe us some explanation of why not. They need to say more about what awareness of properties of experience amounts to. If they accomplish that, they might make plausible the claim, implied by (PJ1e), that all features of experience of which we are aware are "epistemically effective," i.e., all such features make one justified in believing that one is having an experience with those features.

The challenge for foundationalists is thus either to modify (PJ1e) in light of these examples or to explain why they are not counterexamples. The latter requires specifying in some informative way which properties of experience make belief in their presence justified. Further, if what results is to be a defense of anything like traditional foundationalism, this must be done without appeal to concepts such as reliability that are foreign to traditional foundationalism. After all, one possible solution would be to say that we are justified in believing our experiences to have the properties that we can reliably identify. Although this sort of reliability is a purely internal fact about a person – the person's beliefs about a certain internal fact are properly correlated with that fact – this is not the sort of theory traditional foundationalists would like.[6]

Clarifying the problem

In the previous section I ignored an important aspect of Sosa's view about foundational justification. He distinguishes three kinds of concepts: indexical, phenomenal, and simple geometrical and arithmetic (SGA). The problem he has raised for classical foundationalism concerns SGA concepts.

Indexical concepts about experience occur in thoughts of the form "I am experiencing thusly," where one simply makes demonstrative reference to some feature of experience. If one succeeds in having a thought at all in such a circumstance, that is, if one does make reference, then the thought is surely true. I think that Sosa is also willing to grant that any such thought is justified.

Phenomenal concepts are concepts that involve a certain sort of recognitional capacity. To have the phenomenal concept of redness, for example, requires the ability to recognize experiences of redness. (It might be better to call this the concept of phenomenal redness.) Sosa writes:

> Grasping such a phenomenal concept comes with a certain guarantee of reliability, then, since it is defined in part by sensitivity to the relevant feature of which it is a concept. It is defined in part by the ability to tell when that feature is present and when absent in our experiences. So we must be sufficiently reliable in the application of the concept in order to so much as grasp it. (PA, 10)

Sosa thus thinks that beliefs involving both indexical and phenomenal concepts come with a certain guarantee of reliability, and perhaps this suffices to explain why all such beliefs are justified. There is, of course, reason to wonder whether classical foundationalists can rest easy with this reliabilist explanation of why such beliefs are justified, but I will not pursue that point here.

Sosa is granting, I believe, that classical foundationalists can formulate a true principle about foundational justification involving beliefs containing indexical and phenomenal concepts. His contention, as we shall see later, is that this acceptable principle does not allow for enough foundational justification. But before turning to his argument for that conclusion, it will be helpful to get clear about exactly what he is conceding to foundationalists.

Recall the distinction between propositional and doxastic justification. Sosa's discussion of the reliability of beliefs involving indexical and phenomenal concepts suggests that he is prepared to concede that when one has a belief about one's experiences that involves one of those concepts, then that belief is justified. This suggests that he is prepared to grant the truth of a principle about doxastic justification along the following lines:

(DJ2) If a person is experientially-aware of property F, and believes that he is having an experience with property F, and refers to property F in this belief by means of an indexical or phenomenal concept, then this belief is foundationally justified.

It is less clear how to apply Sosa's remarks about indexical and phenomenal concepts to principles about propositional justification. Perhaps there is a phenomenal concept that corresponds to each experiential property, and we can specify referents for indexical concepts in propositions that no one is entertaining. If so, we might propose:

(PJ4) If a person is experientially-aware of property F, and P is a proposition that refers to property F by means of an indexical or phenomenal concept and says that the person is having an experience with property F, then the person is foundationally justified in believing P.

These are principles that link experiential awareness with foundational justification. They are not trivially true, nor are they uninformative. They do describe some factual conditions on which foundational justification might supervene. Sosa is willing to concede that they might be true because the concepts they involve come with a built-in assurance of reliability. However, he contends that these principles are not sufficient to explain all the foundational justification that classical foundationalists need. He thinks that there must be foundational justification involving arithmetic and geometric (SGA) concepts. He writes:

> We move beyond such concepts already with the theoretically richer concepts of arithmetic and geometry. When we form beliefs as to whether *these* concepts apply to our present experience, we can easily go wrong.... Classical foundationalists need some such beliefs with arithmetical or geometrical content, since from purely indexical or phenomenal concepts very little could be inferred, even allowing some explanatory induction from the given to the external.... [Has classical foundationalism] explained how we might be justified foundationally in applying arithmetical and geometric concepts to our experience? No, its lack of any such explanation is a serious problem for classical foundationalism. Might it be overcome in due course? I myself cannot see how. (PA, 11)

Thus, the problem Sosa raises for classical foundationalism concerns foundational justification for propositions and beliefs involving arithmetic and geometrical concepts. He thinks that there is no good way for classical foundationalists to explain why such propositions are foundationally justified, yet some of them must be foundationally justified if classical foundationalists are to account for the knowledge we have of the world around us. The example of the speckled hen illustrates the point. Suppose we expanded (PJ4) to include arithmetic and geometrical concepts:

(PJ5) If a person is experientially-aware of property F, and P is a proposition that refers to property F by means of an indexical, phenomenal, or SGA concept, and P says that the person is having an experience with property F, then the person is foundationally justified in believing P.

Sosa contends that the case of the speckled hen shows that (PJ5) is false. Perhaps the principle is true for some very simple SGA concepts, such as 3-sidedness. But it is not true for 23-sidedness or 48-speckledhood, SGA features that we cannot simply spot in our experiences. We are experientially aware of these properties, but we are not automatically justified in believing them to be present.

Similar considerations pose a problem for doxastic justification. Suppose we extended (DJ2) to SGA concepts:

(DJ3) If a person is experientially-aware of property F, and believes that he is having an experience with property F, and refers to property F in this belief by means of an indexical, phenomenal, or SGA concept, then this belief is foundationally justified.

The problem with (DJ3) is not simply that one can miss or mischaracterize features of experience. In such cases one does not both have an experience with that feature and believe oneself to have it. Hence, such cases are not counterexamples to (DJ3). But it is not too hard to get an example that does the job. If error is possible about the number of speckles, then it is also possible to get it right by guessing, by a pair of errors that fortuitously lead to the truth, or by a thoroughly unreliable method that happens in one rare instance to capture the truth. So (DJ3) is also mistaken.

Thus, Sosa's contention is that if classical foundationalists restrict foundational justification to beliefs and propositions involving indexical and phenomenal concepts, as in (PJ4) and (DJ2), they have too thin a base of foundational justification to support the rest of what we take ourselves to know. They can attempt to expand the base by bringing in SGA concepts, as in (PJ5) and (DJ3), but those principles are false.

One might think that the difference between the simple arithmetic concepts and the complex ones has to do with reliability. Sosa's own proposal is along those lines. But it is important to realize that to appeal to that sort of factor is to appeal to a factor of the sort classical foundationalists, as Sosa is thinking of them, would not allow into their theory. It is an external factor.

3 Sosa's Proposal

Safe and virtuous beliefs

Sosa formulates his account of foundational justification by focusing on a particular contrast. The contrast is between a case of a foundationally justified introspective judgment about the phenomenal character of experience and an unjustified belief about the phenomenal character of experience. Suppose that a person is presented with an object with 48 speckles. The object and its 48 speckles are in clear view. Thus, the person has an experience with the phenomenal character of 48 speckles. He is, if you like, appeared to 48-specklishly. And suppose that the person does believe, as a result of guessing, that he is having such an experience. That belief is not justified, or at any rate not foundationally justified. Justification does not just emerge from having an experience of this kind. Contrast this with the appearance of 3 speckles. The belief that one's experience has 3 speckles is foundationally justified.

Sosa says that to explain the difference we must appeal to more than the following 3 items:

(a) the phenomenal character of the experiences;
(b) the propositional content of the occurrent thought as one judges the image to contain so many speckles;
(c) the fit between the phenomenal character and the propositional content.

Sosa proposes that the difference between a justified introspective report and an unjustified introspective report is that the former is *safe* and *virtuous*. To say that a judgment is safe is to say that "in the circumstances not easily *would* one believe as one does without being right" (PA, 19). And a belief is virtuous provided it is "derived from a way of forming beliefs that is an intellectual virtue, one that in our normal situation for forming such beliefs would tend strongly enough to give us beliefs that are safe" (PA, 19).

These distinctions may seem to bring out nicely the difference between an unjustified belief that the image has 48 speckles and a justified belief that it has 3. The latter belief is quite safe. As a matter of fact, one is quite unlikely to have that belief and be wrong. In contrast, one could easily believe that the image has 48 speckles and be wrong. This might happen if there were 49 speckles or 47.

The need for virtuosity

As Sosa points out, merely having a safe belief is not sufficient for that belief to be justified (PA, 19). If there is a belief that could not be false, or could not easily be false, then that belief is safe. But a belief might be safe not because of any particular insight or merit of the believer, but because the proposition believed happens to be one that cannot be false. Sosa uses as an example the case of a necessary truth that one believes with little or no justification. If the proposition believed is in fact true, then it could not be false. Hence, one could not easily (or even possibly) believe as one does and be wrong. Such an unjustified belief passes the safety test. For this reason Sosa adds the requirement that the belief be virtuously formed, that the method for forming the belief be one that in normal situations leads to safe beliefs.

Sosa does not point out that unjustified contingent beliefs can also pass the safety test. It is possible that there are facts about our minds that restrict the sorts of phenomenal properties that can be present to us. Suppose, for example, that we just couldn't experience speckled images with a number of speckles near to, but not identical with, 48. Or suppose it is a law of nature that all speckled hens have 48 speckles. And suppose that the hens display either all their speckles or none of them. Thus, whenever you think you are having an experience of a 48-speckled hen, you are right. As things actually are, not easily could one be wrong about that. It's a little difficult to avoid complications involving some of the speckles being obscured, but I think that this complication is not relevant to the fundamental point. It is possible that there are propositions about experience that, like the true mathematical beliefs, cannot easily be wrong (regardless of your reasons for holding the belief). Whenever you believe such a proposition, you satisfy the safety condition. However, just as one can believe the true mathematical propositions unjustifiably, one can believe these contingently true propositions about experience unjustifiably. Thus, as Sosa realizes, safety is not enough.

Sosa describes the case in which one unjustifiably believes that one's image has 48 speckles as follows:

> One does not know foundationally that one's image contains 48 speckles even if one's image *does* in fact contain 48 speckles, and one's belief hence corresponds precisely to what is then given in one's consciousness. One fails to know in that case because too easily might one

have believed that one's image had 48 speckles while it had one more speckle or one less. But that is not so for the belief that one's image has 3 speckles. (PA, 19)

The point of the above paragraph is to show that there are at least possible situations in which a belief like this one is safe, but still not justified.

A problem?

The considerations just advanced put a considerable burden on the virtuousness condition. Sosa must say that the method by which the unjustified believer arrives at the 48-speckle belief is not virtuous. This means that it does not "derive from a way of forming beliefs that . . . in our normal situation for forming such beliefs would tend strongly enough to give us beliefs that are safe." But suppose that the person just looks at a 3-speckled image and thinks "3 speckles" and just looks at a 48-speckled image and thinks "48 speckles." Sosa must say that the latter belief, even when it is safe, derives from a different, and less virtuous, way of forming beliefs. Perhaps it does, though this is difficult to assess.

Much here depends on what counts as the "ways of forming beliefs" on which the theory depends. There is considerable flexibility in how ways of forming beliefs might be characterized. If they are characterized narrowly, it may be that the 3-speckle belief and the 48-speckle result from different ways. However, in the circumstance in which the 48-speckle belief is safe, the way in which it is formed must also extend to other beliefs, most of which are not safe. Otherwise, the theory would rule that the 48-speckle belief is both safe and virtuous. If the ways of forming beliefs are characterized in a broader fashion, it may turn out that both beliefs are formed in the same way. In that case, the theory improperly evaluates the two beliefs as being epistemically alike. Elsewhere, I've expressed doubts about there being a suitable way to spell this idea out with sufficient clarity to generate a theory capable of being evaluated.[7] Sosa does not attempt to deal with these issues in the works under discussion here.[8] To go into these matters here would take us somewhat far afield. I believe that it is fair to say that this is a difficult issue for Sosa's theory, though not fair to claim here that there is no acceptable response or even that Sosa has not provided one.

4 Defending Classical Foundationalism

We can formulate Sosa's problem for classical foundationalism as a challenge to explain the relevant differences in two pairs of examples. Consider the following pair first. In one case a person has an experience of an image with 3 speckles. The person knows with certainty that she is visually experiencing an image with 3 speckles. Contrast this with the case in which the person has an experience of an image with 48 speckles, and believes, with confidence, that it has 48 speckles. But this belief about 48 speckles results from guessing or the unjustified implicit assumption that all multi-speckled images have 48 speckles. One wants to say that the 3-speckle belief is foundationally justified and the 48-speckle belief is not. Reliability of the sort Sosa favors may seem to explain the difference, but what can a classical foundationalist say to explain the difference?

The second pair of cases that needs explanation is this. There could be people who, unlike us, can recognize 48 speckles. They might actually be sensitive to their presence. For them, the belief that they are having an experience of 48 speckles might be foundationally justified, just like the belief that we are experiencing something 3-speckled is foundationally justified for us. This shows that there is not something intrinsic to the proposition itself that determines whether or not it is the subject of foundational justification. Something about the believer matters as well. Again, reliability of some sort might seem to be an attractive answer.

Phenomenal concepts and SGA concepts

To have a phenomenal concept of a particular property is, according to Sosa, to be sensitive to the presence of that property. Now, consider the property of experiencing an image containing 48 speckles. It is possible for a person to be sensitive to the presence or absence of this property. That is, a person might be able to distinguish experiences involving images with 48 speckles from experiences involving images with any other number of speckles. But it does not follow that the person is able to tell how many speckles there are when in fact there are 48. One can know that there is something distinctive about a certain case, and reliably detect the presence of the distinctive feature, without knowing what that distinctive feature is. In the early stages of identifying things, we often are in just this situation. Perhaps a different example will make the point clearer.

The following example pertains to properties of external things, but it could just as easily be applied to features of experiences. When learning to identify different kinds of trees by the shapes of their leaves, one might learn to recognize the various different shapes without learning which kinds of trees have leaves with those different shapes. One can reliably group similar ones together and one could even make up a name for the different kinds of trees. The same thing could be true with respect to the property of being 48-speckled. One might respond differentially to experiences in which 48 speckles appear than to other sorts of experiences.

Given Sosa's account of concepts, any person who is sensitive to experiences of 48 speckles has what we can describe as a "phenomenal 48-speckle concept." Such a person can believe that he's having an experience of 48 speckles, though the person may not be able to put it that way. From the fact that one has the concept, it does not follow that one is sensitive to the concepts that we might have thought entered into it. The phenomenal 48-speckles concept is not constructed out of more primitive concepts. One might not in general be sensitive to the presence of 48 things in experience – one might not respond differentially to experiences of 48 stripes. One might be reliable at recognizing 48 speckles, but not so reliable at recognizing being speckled generally. It follows that one could even lack the phenomenal concept of being speckled. The phenomenal concept is not logically complex. Nothing much follows from it.

Presumably, most of us do not have the phenomenal concept of being 48-speckled, since we are not sensitive to the presence of the property of which it is a concept. We do not respond differentially to 48-speckled images than to 47- or 49-speckled images. We can, of course, believe that an image has 48 speckles. Thus, there must be two different "48-speckle concepts." One is the complex concept constructed out of the simpler concepts of "48" and "being speckled." Presumably, we all have this concept. Its possession does not require sensitivity to 48 speckles. This, I believe, is an SGA concept of the sort Sosa has called to our attention. The other "48-speckle concept" is a phenomenal concept, and this is one that normal people lack. This follows from the fact that most of us are insensitive to the presence of 48-specklehood.

The same distinction, of course, applies to seemingly simpler concepts. Consider the property of experiencing an image containing 3 speckles. We can often tell at a glance that we have this property. But there are both the complex 3-speckle concept and the phenomenal 3-speckle concept. Most of us grasp both of these concepts.

Which beliefs are foundationally justified?

These results about concept possession provide the basis for solving the problem for classical foundationalism that Sosa has posed. Classical foundationalists can plausibly deny Sosa's claim that they must go beyond phenomenal concepts in specifying what is foundationally justified. In other words, the reply is that principles about foundational justification restricted to indexical and phenomenal concepts are adequate. Sosa's claim that foundational justification must extend to propositions or beliefs involving SGA concepts is mistaken.

Sosa's claim that more must be foundationally justified gets little defense in his paper, and I can only speculate about why he might think that it is true. One might think that classical foundationalists have no way to explain how any beliefs involving non-phenomenal concepts are justified at all unless they allow that some beliefs involving non-phenomenal concepts are foundationally justified. This thought might gain support from the failure to take into account the distinction just noted between the phenomenal and the complex 48-speckle concept. The way the failure to take note of the distinction supports this thought is as follows. In a certain sense, things look exactly the same to the person who recognizes 48 speckles and the person who is not capable of recognizing these features of experience. Their experiences are phenomenally alike. Hence, on classical foundationalist lines, the same phenomenal beliefs are foundationally justified for them. But if what is foundationally justified were limited to phenomenal (and indexical) beliefs, then the same things would be foundationally justified for them. It is clear that nothing concerning 48 speckles is justified for the person who is not capable of recognizing this feature of experience. But then it would not be the case that the one who recognizes 48 speckles is justified in his belief. Since he is, it follows that there must be some non-phenomenal belief that is foundationally justified. And classical foundationalists have no good way to explain this.

The consequence of the discussion above is that this argument goes wrong in its assumption that the same phenomenal beliefs are justified for the person who can recognize 48 speckles and the person who cannot. The former has a phenomenal concept that the latter lacks. The former has a foundationally justified belief, involving this concept, that the latter lacks.

For most of us, if we believed that we had an experience of 48 speckles, this would not be a foundationally justified belief. We would come to this belief by inferences, perhaps from inferences involved in counting or background information about what the image was an image of and how many speckles things like that have. We could not tell, just by looking, that the SGA concept applied. For people with special abilities, however, it might be that this belief is nearly basic, though not quite. It is a simple inference from the associated phenomenal concept.

Consider again the two pairs of examples that posed the problem for classical foundationalists. One pair raised the question of what the relevant difference is, for normal people, between the 3-speckle image and the 48-speckle image. Sosa assumed that since we can tell at a glance that we have an image with 3 speckles, but not one with 48, the one belief must be foundationally justified but the other not. And he was referring to beliefs involving SGA concepts. However, most of us have a phenomenal 3-speckle concept, but not a phenomenal 48-speckle concept. There is, then, a relevant foundationally justified proposition when we experience an image with 3 speckles but not when we experience an image with 48 speckles.

Of course, this foundationally justified proposition does not involve the geometrical and arithmetic concepts on which Sosa focuses. But I think that beliefs involving those concepts are not foundationally justified. The normal person's belief involving the SGA 3-speckle concept is non-foundationally justified, depending on background information that associates that phenomenal concept with that SGA concept.

Similar considerations help explain the second pair of examples. A person who has a remarkable ability to tell at a glance that he is experiencing an image with 48 speckles differs from ordinary people in two ways. First, he, unlike us, has a phenomenal 48-speckle concept. This gives him foundational justification for that proposition, justification that most of us lack. Second, he has background information that links that phenomenal state to the complex 48-speckle concept. As a result, he is justified in believing that his image has 48 speckles, where this believes involves the SGA concept. But this last proposition is not foundationally justified. As noted earlier, the distinction between the two 48-speckle concepts also helps explain the case of a person who can differentiate at a glance an image with 48 speckles from other images without knowing how many speckles the image has. This person has the phenomenal 48-speckle concept, but has not associated that concept with the related SGA concept.

I conclude, then, that the principles formulated earlier are adequate to deal with these cases. One of those principles was:

> (DJ2) If a person is experientially-aware of property F, and believes that he is having an experience with property F, and refers to property F in this belief by means of an indexical or phenomenal concept, then this belief is foundationally justified.

Most of us do not have the phenomenal 48-speckle concept but we do have the phenomenal 3-speckle concept. So, via (DJ2) we can justifiably believe the relevant 3-speckle proposition but not the relevant 48-speckle proposition. And we can infer from the proposition involving the phenomenal 3-speckle concept, and background information, that our image contains 3 speckles. But the person with the extraordinary talent to recognize 48 speckles does have the phenomenal 48-speckle concept. Thus, when the other conditions are satisfied, he can have a belief involving that concept foundationally justified. And that belief and his background information justifies his belief involving the SGA concept.

Things are more complicated when we attempt to apply these considerations about concepts to principles about propositional justification. The principle restricted to indexical and phenomenal concepts was this:

(PJ4) If a person is experientially-aware of property F, and P is a proposition that refers to property F by means of an indexical or phenomenal concept and says that the person is having an experience with property F, then the person is foundationally justified in believing P.

Nothing said so far answers the objection to this. It would seem that (PJ4) implies that we are e-aware of both 3 speckles and 48 speckles in the relevant cases; even though we lack the phenomenal concept in the second case, (PJ4) implies that we are justified in believing each proposition. One possibility is to add to the antecedent of the principle a condition requiring that person have the relevant phenomenal concept. Another possibility is to argue that Sosa is too lenient in his assumptions about which properties we are e-aware of. In the next section I will discuss a variation on this second option. According to this view, there is a kind of awareness Sosa overlooks.

5 Another Kind of Experience?

Sosa distinguishes experiential awareness of properties and noticing awareness of them. The latter involves justified true beliefs about their presence. The former is mere passive awareness of properties of one's experience. It may be, however, that there are distinctions to be drawn among kinds of awareness that do not involve beliefs.

There is a difference between a property merely being present in one's experience and one's attending to (or "noticing," though not in Sosa's sense) that property. There are things that are, as it were, on the periphery of one's experience. The telephone in my office has a red light that comes on when there's a message for me. We recently got new, improved, state-of-the-art telephones. Unfortunately, sometimes callers are taken to the message center without allowing the phone to ring. As a result, sometimes I'll be sitting at my desk concentrating hard on my work. And a time will come when I'll notice, in Sosa's sense, that the light on my phone is on. And I'll also realize that I've been aware of its being on for a while. I was aware, in some sense, of the red on the edge of my visual field, though I did not notice it. So, some qualities of which we have experiential awareness enjoy only peripheral awareness. Things of which we are peripherally aware can be unnoticed. We miss other intrinsic qualities of our experiences for reasons of the sort discussed earlier: we are not able to pick up on them. Being 48-speckled is like this for most of us. Most of us are not able to pick up that property.

This leads me to think that Sosa overlooks in his discussion another kind of experience, something that involves more than mere experiential awareness but is less than, or at any rate something different from, noticing as he's described it. We can *attend to* features of experience. We can focus on them. In this sense, I had not attended to the light on my phone. Or, more precisely, I had not attended to the patch of red in my image. Then I did. And the difference was not just a difference in belief. It was not the case that I just came to believe that I was experiencing red. I could in principle have come to believe that because someone told me that something red was there. What happened was that I attended to the redness, and believed it was there as a result. Attention of this sort need not be purposeful or intentional. It typically just happens.

Sosa seems to mention this sort of thing when he speaks of "attending to" some features of experience (PA, 8). And, it may be that classical foundationalists would be better off saying that only features of experience that one attends to are epistemically effective. Merely having a property present to consciousness, mere e-awareness as Sosa interprets it, is not sufficient. This suggests replacing (PJ4) and (DJ2) by principles that build in the condition that the person attend to the feature of experience:

(DJ4) If a person is experientially-aware of property F, and attends to this property, and believes that he is having an experience with property F, and refers to property F in this belief by means of an indexical or phenomenal concept, then the person is foundationally justified in believing that he is having an experience with quality F.

(PJ6) If a person is experientially-aware of property F, and attends to this property, and P is a proposition that refers to property F by means of an indexical or phenomenal concept and says that the person is having an experience with property F, then the person is foundationally justified in believing P.

We cannot attend in the way required by these principles to phenomenal properties whose concepts we do not understand. That is, if one lacks the phenomenal concept of being 48-speckled, then one cannot attend to that feature of experience.[9] Thus, not all features that are minimally present in the sense sufficient for Sosa's e-awareness are epistemically effective. The epistemically effective features of experience are the ones that we attend to.

Adding to the picture the idea of attending to experiences helps with another point, one not previously mentioned. It seems to me to be a mistake for classical foundationalists to commit themselves to the view that there are certain features of experience such that, whenever they are present to anyone, a person who has the relevant concept is justified in believing that they are present. Principle (PJ5), even with an added condition requiring that the person have the relevant phenomenal concept, implies the following:

If at one time S has an experience with quality F and S is foundationally justified in believing he is having an experience with quality F, then whenever S has an experience with quality F, then S is foundationally justified in believing that he is having an experience with quality F.

There is no more reason for insisting on this thesis than for insisting that if there is one time that I see a robin and I'm justified in believing that I'm seeing a robin, then whenever I see a robin, I'm justified in believing that I'm seeing a robin. This is to say that merely seeing a robin is not a sufficient condition for the corresponding belief to be justified. Similarly, merely having an experience of a certain sort need not be sufficient for the corresponding belief to be justified. The example about the unnoticed patch of red in my visual field illustrates why. Other examples in which features of experience are difficult to identify because of factors that call our attention away from them or make them difficult to spot illustrate the same point. A richer notion of experience, the one I have tried to capture with the concept of attention, makes for a better classical foundationalist theory.

6 Conclusion

I conclude that foundationalists have the resources to deal with the specific problem concerning foundational justification that Sosa has raised. This is not to say that all is well with foundationalism. There remain hard questions about how to justify as much as seems to be justified on the basis of what is foundationally justified. And there are legitimate questions about whether traditional foundationalists are really entitled to accept Sosa's offering of the assumption that since phenomenal concepts come with a guarantee of reliability, the designated beliefs involving them are foundationally justified.[10] Nevertheless, I believe that if there are the various kinds of concepts that Sosa describes, then foundationalists are able to deal with the problems he raises.

Notes

1 My primary text here is "Privileged Access," forthcoming in Quintin Smith, ed., *Consciousness: New Philosophical Essays* (Oxford: Oxford University Press) (cited as PA). Page references in the text are to a prepublication typescript version of this essay. Similar material appears in "Beyond Internal Foundations to External Virtues," Sosa's contribution to Ernest Sosa and Laurence BonJour, *Epistemology: Internalism Versus Externalism* (Malden, MA: Blackwell, 2003) (cited as BIF). A version of "Privileged Access" was presented at the 1999 Eastern Division Meeting of the American Philosophical Association. I was commentator on that occasion, and this paper is derived from the comments presented there.

2 *Problems of Philosophy* (Oxford: Oxford University Press, 1997), p. 46. (First published in 1912.)

3 Principle (PJ3n) is not a tautology. The consequent says that the belief is *foundationally* justified, and this is not stated in the antecedent.

4 Sosa may fully intend this example to apply only to a principle about doxastic justification. I am just trying to see if there is a problem for (PJ1e) suggested by his remarks.

5 Sosa presents an example along these lines in "Theories of Justification: Old Doctrines Newly Defended," which appears in his collection *Knowledge in Perspective: Selected Essays in Epistemology* (Cambridge: Cambridge University Press, 1991) (cited as KP). See especially pp. 127–8.

6 It's not entirely clear to me why this is so. Perhaps it is because they'd worry that we could too easily be mistaken about which internal facts we are reliable about.

7 "Reliability and Justification," *The Monist* 68 (1985): 159–74. See also "The Generality Problem for Reliabilism," co-authored with Earl Conee, *Philosophical Studies* 89 (1998): 1–29.

8 Sosa suggests that relevant types are ones that can "be usefully generalized upon by us as the epistemic community of the" believer (KP, 284). It is difficult to see how this solves the problem, since multiple types may be "usefully generalized upon."

9 Sosa apparently thinks that we can attend to properties without having the associated phenomenal concept. See PA, section E. It is true that you can focus your attention at the 48-speckle array, or, say, an image of a 23-sided thing. But I don't understand how you could

attend to the phenomenal properties of being 48-speckled or 23-sided without having those phenomenal concepts.
10 In other words, there is doubt that (DJ4) exactly captures the correct foundationalist idea. It could be that a person satisfies the conditions in the antecedent of the principle, but believes that he is having an experience with quality F not directly on the basis of his awareness of the relevant experiential property but rather on the basis of some mistaken inference or assumption. An improved version of the principle will have to appeal to the idea of believing the proposition on the basis of the experience.

5

A Trial Separation between the Theory of Knowledge and the Theory of Justified Belief

RICHARD FOLEY

1   An Unfortunate Assumption

In his 1963 article, "Is Justified True Belief Knowledge?"[1] Edmund Gettier devised a pair of counterexamples designed to illustrate that knowledge cannot be adequately defined as justified true belief. The basic idea behind both of his counterexamples is that one can be justified in believing a falsehood P from which one deduces a truth Q, in which case one has a justified true belief in Q but does not know Q. Gettier's article inspired numerous other counterexamples, and the search was on for a fourth condition of knowledge, one that could be added to justification, truth, and belief to produce an adequate analysis of knowledge.

Some epistemologists proposed that for a true belief to be an instance of knowledge, not only does the belief have to be justified but in addition the justification must be non-defective, where a justification is non-defective if (roughly) it does not justify any falsehood. Others proposed that the justification must be indefeasible, where a justification is indefeasible if (again, roughly) it cannot be defeated by the addition of any true statement. However, a secondary and very different kind of response to Gettier's counterexamples was to wonder whether something less explicitly intellectual than justification, traditionally understood, is better suited for understanding knowledge. Epistemic justification is traditionally associated with being able to generate reasons in defense of one's beliefs, but in many instances of knowledge, one does not seem to be in a position to provide anything like a defense of one's beliefs.

D. M. Armstrong and Alvin Goldman were among the earliest proponents of a causal theory of knowledge, which requires, in place of justification, that there be an appropriate causal connection between the fact that makes a belief true and the person's having that belief.[2] Their proposals neatly handled the original cases described by Gettier but ran into other serious problems. Accounting for knowledge of mathematical truths, general facts, and truths about the future proved especially difficult. Nevertheless, their general approach captivated many epistemologists, in part because it fit well with the view of knowledge implicit in the emerging naturalized epistemology movement, which stressed that knowledge is best conceived as arising from one's complex causal interactions with one's environment. To assume that knowledge always requires one to have a justification is to intellectualize the notion to an unacceptable degree. Some kinds of knowledge, for example, highly theoretical knowledge, might involve justification, but other kinds typically do not, for example, simple perceptual knowledge. Our perceptual equipment collects and processes information from our environment and adjusts our opinions accordingly, and does so without deliberation except in unusual cases.

Thus, in the eyes of many philosophers, although the causal theory of knowledge had its defects, it also had the virtue of shifting the focus away from questions of our being able to justify our beliefs intellectually and toward questions of our being in an appropriate causal or causal-like relation with our external environment. The philosophical task, according to this way of thinking about knowledge, is to identify the precise character of the relation. A simple causal relation between the fact that makes a belief true and the belief itself won't do and, thus, some other causal-like relation needs to be found.

Various proposals have been made, but reliability accounts of knowledge have turned out to have the widest appeal, and again Alvin Goldman has been a leading proponent. Contrary to what he had proposed earlier, Goldman now argued that for a person's belief to count as knowledge, it is not necessary that the belief be caused by the fact that makes it true, although this will often be the case. However, it is necessary that the processes, faculties, and methods that produced or sustain the belief be highly reliable.[3]

Reliability theories of knowledge led in turn to new accounts of epistemic justification, specifically, externalist ones. Initially, reliabilism was part of a reaction against justification-driven accounts of knowledge, but an assumption drawn from the old epistemology tempted reliabilists to reconceive justification as well. The assumption is that by definition justification is that which has to be added to true belief to generate knowledge, with some fourth condition added to handle Gettier-style counterexamples. Goldman had already argued that knowledge is reliably produced true belief. Relying on the above assumption, he further concluded that epistemic justification must also be a matter of one's beliefs being produced and sustained by reliable cognitive processes. Because a cognitive process is reliable only if it is well suited to produce true beliefs in the external environment in which it is operating, this is an externalist account of epistemic justification. By contrast, more traditional accounts of epistemic justification, for example, foundationalism and coherentism, are internalist accounts, which emphasize the perspectives of individual believers.

Reliabilism and kindred proposals have sparked an enormous literature on the relative advantages and disadvantages of externalism and internalism in epistemology.[4] Most of this literature assumes that externalists and internalists are defending rival theories and that, hence, both cannot be right. An alternative and more interesting reading of the dispute, however, is that they are not, or at least need not be, competitors at all. Rather, they are principally concerned with different issues.

Externalists are principally interested in understanding the relationship that has to obtain between one's beliefs and one's external environment in order for those beliefs, when true, to count as knowledge, but in carrying out this project, they see themselves as also offering an explication of epistemic justification, because justification, they stipulate, is that which has to be added to true belief in order to get a serious candidate for knowledge. Internalists, on the other hand, are primarily interested in understanding what is required for one's beliefs to be justified, but in carrying out their project, they see themselves as also providing the materials for an adequate account of knowledge, because they too assume that justification is by definition that which has to be added to true belief to get knowledge, with some condition added to handle Gettier problems.

It is not surprising that both internalists and externalists commonly use the language of justification to report the conclusions of their projects, given that some of the most influential figures in the history of epistemology have argued that a single notion can be used to capture what is most important in knowledge as well as what is most important in internally defensible belief. Descartes, for example, urged his readers to believe only that which is internally beyond any possibility of criticism, by which he meant that which is altogether impossible to doubt. However, he also thought that by doing so his readers could be altogether assured of acquiring knowledge.

Descartes's search for an internally defensible procedure that would provide an external guarantee of knowledge proved not to be feasible, but the lesson is not that either the internal or external aspects of the Cartesian project has to be abandoned. The lesson, rather, is that there are different, equally legitimate projects for epistemologists to pursue but that these projects need to be distinguished. One project is that of exploring what is required to put one's own internal, intellectual house in order. Another is that of exploring what is required for one to stand in a relation of knowledge to one's environment. It is easy to conflate these two projects, given the assumption that the properties that make a belief justified are by definition such that when a true belief has these properties, it is a good candidate for knowledge. This is an unfortunate assumption, however. It prompts externalists and internalists to see themselves as providing rival accounts of epistemic justification, whereas a more charitable interpretation is that they are using the terms "justified belief" and "rational belief" to report the conclusions of two very different projects. Moreover, the assumption distorts both the theory of knowledge and the theory of justified belief. For the theory of knowledge, it creates a predicament: either embrace an overly intellectual conception of knowledge, which overlooks the fact that people cannot provide adequate intellectual defenses for much of what they know, or engage in awkward attempts to force back into the account some duly externalized notion of justified belief, because the definition of knowledge is thought to require it. The assumption's impact on the theory of justified belief is equally regrettable: it places the theory of belief in service to the theory of knowledge. If it is stipulated that the properties that make a belief justified must also be properties that turn true belief into a good candidate for knowledge, an account of justified belief can be regarded as adequate only if it contributes to a successful account of knowledge. The theory of justified belief is thus divorced from everyday assessments of the rationality and justifiedness of opinions, which tend to focus on whether individuals have been responsible in forming their opinions rather than on whether they have satisfied the prerequisites of knowledge.

The corrective is for epistemologists, at least at the beginning of their enterprise, to be wary of the assumption that knowledge can be adequately understood in terms of justified true belief plus some condition to handle Gettier problems. By the end of the epistemological enterprise, after accounts of justified belief and knowledge have been independently developed, interesting connections between the two may have emerged, but it ought not merely to be assumed from the start that there is a simple, necessary tie between them. Relaxing the tie between the two frees the theory of knowledge from overly intellectual conceptions of knowledge, thus smoothing the way for treatments that acknowledge that people are often not in a position to provide a justification for what they know, and it simultaneously creates a space for a theory of justified belief that is not cordoned off from the kinds of assessments of each other's beliefs that we actually make and need to make in our everyday lives.[5]

The assumption that the conditions that make a belief justified are by definition conditions that turn a true belief into a good candidate for knowledge is thus needlessly limiting. It discourages the idea that there are different, equally legitimate projects for epistemologists to pursue. One project is to investigate what has to be the case in order to have knowledge. An externalist approach is well suited to this project, and justification, which is most naturally construed as an internalist notion, plays only a peripheral role in such an account. A distinct project, also important, is concerned with what is involved in having justified beliefs, that is, beliefs supported or supportable by reasons, and knowledge is at best linked only indirectly and contingently with this account. There is no necessary, conceptual link between being justified in one's opinions and being in a position to have knowledge.

2 Sosa on Knowledge and Justification

Ernest Sosa has been at the center of virtually every major issue and dispute in recent epistemology. So, it is no surprise that he has deep and challenging views about the relationship between justification and knowledge. Like most contemporary epistemologists, he sees a close link between the project of giving an account of epistemic justification and that of giving an account of knowledge, but he is far more sensitive than most to the pressures that tend to split the projects apart. I will be examining Sosa's attempts to dissipate these pressures, relying especially on three centrally important essays from his book, *Knowledge in Perspective*: "Reliabilism and Intellectual Virtue," "Knowledge and Intellectual Virtue," and "Methodology and Apt Belief."[6] My conclusion is that despite his efforts and concessions, Sosa has not gone far enough in emphasizing the distinctness of the projects. But first, his views.

Sosa defends an intellectual virtue approach to both knowledge and epistemic justification. According to Sosa, the core characteristic of an intellectual virtue is that it helps maximize one's surplus of truth over error (*KP*, 225). A complete characterization of intellectual virtue might well also include its tendency to produce other desiderata in a belief system, for example, generality, coherence, and explanatory power, but the key, according to Sosa, is reliability:

> What makes a faculty intellectually virtuous? Its performance or powers, surely? If so what is required in a faculty is that it not lead us astray in our quest for truth; that it outperform feasible competitors in its truth/error delivery differential. (*KP*, 227)

Intellectual virtues are embedded in cognitive faculties, and Sosa distinguishes between transmission faculties and generative faculties. As the names suggest, the former produce beliefs from already formed beliefs, while latter produce beliefs from other kinds of inputs, for example, experiences. External perception and introspection are generative faculties, while memory is transmissive. In Sosa's view, reason is both: rationalist intuition (recognizing simple necessary truths) is generative while rationalist deduction is transmissive. The distinction between transmission and generative faculties is relevant for assessing the virtuousness of a faculty, because the appropriate differential between truth and error for a transmissive faculty is not its truth/error differential *simpliciter* but rather its truth/error differential when provided with true inputs.

Sosa stresses that in appraising the virtuousness of a faculty, it is important to distinguish mistakes that are primarily internal in origin from those that are primarily external in origin. Mistakes of the former kind are more closely associated with a lack of epistemic justifiedness than mistakes of the latter kind. Take perception, for example. The key to a perceptual faculty being epistemically virtuous is for its internal mechanisms to be sufficiently well calibrated with the external environment to produce beliefs that accurately reflect the presence or absence of some correlated range of properties in the external environment. Breakdowns in these internal mechanisms that have the effect of decreasing the faculty's ability to reflect the environment accurately result in a corresponding decrease in its ability to produce epistemically justified beliefs. Thus, Sosa remarks:

> Someone prone to frequent illusions or hallucinations of mainly internal origin cannot be credited with good visual perception in an epistemically most relevant sense. (*KP*, 230)

However, when the normally reliable internal mechanisms generate inaccurate beliefs because of some unusual feature in the external environment, the beliefs may still be justified:

> the falsehood of a perceptually justified belief may go unreflected in the subject's perception because of external abnormalities that he could not possibly have grasped. In such circumstances his perceptual false belief shows no defect or misconduct in the subject, and may be perceptually justified. (*KP*, 232)

Thus, briefly stated, Sosa's view is that both epistemically justified beliefs and knowledge are to be understood as the products of intellectual virtues, where intellectual virtues are faculties, or combinations of faculties, that maximize the differential of truth over error in environments that are normal for the individuals in question. I will return to the issue of an environment being normal for a subject, because focusing on abnormal situations is one way of illustrating why the project of understanding epistemic justification is distinct from the project of understanding knowledge, but here first is how Sosa himself summarizes his view (with my emphases added):

> What powers or abilities do then enable a subject to know or at least to acquire epistemic justification? They are presumably powers or abilities to distinguish the true from the false in a certain subject field, to attain truth and avoid error in that field. One's power or ability must presumably make one such that, *normally at least, in one's ordinary habitat, or at least in one's ordinary circumstances when making such judgements*, one would believe what is true and not believe what is false, concerning matters in that field. (*KP*, 236)

Sosa describes three kinds of cases that create difficulties for any view, such as his own, that seeks to understand epistemic justification and knowledge in terms of the reliability of the faculties that generate and transmit beliefs, and he makes adjustments in his account to try to handle these difficulties.

The first kind of case is that of someone who suffers an abnormality that somehow makes him clairvoyant, unbeknownst to himself. By hypothesis, his beliefs about even the remote future are reliably produced, but even so, Sosa asks "how plausible would it be to suppose him justified in his clairvoyant beliefs" if he lacks inductive or any other evidence of the reliability of these beliefs? (*KP*, 237).

A second kind of case, which raises the opposite problem, is the victim of a Cartesian evil demon:

> If his experience and reasoning are indistinguishable from those of the best justified among us, can we in fairness deny him the justification that we will claim for ourselves? Yet if we do grant him such justification, then unreliable processes do yield much belief that is in fact justified. (*KP*, 237)

A third kind of case involves faculties that are ordinarily highly reliable (but still fallible) but that operate improperly in a particular case, that is, operate in a way that would usually be unreliable. Nonetheless, because of abnormal circumstances, they generate a true belief.

> Would the belief then fall short of sound epistemic justification, and not be a true instance of knowledge? What might be missing? Perhaps some closer connection between the belief and its truth? Perhaps these cannot be so independent as when they come together only by lucky accident. (*KP*, 238)

In anticipation of the tension that I want to explore, Sosa remarks that these three kinds of cases pose problems not so much for a theory of epistemic justification as intellectual virtue, as for the combination of such a theory of justification with a conception of knowledge as justified true belief (*KP*, 239).

How does Sosa try to deal with the tensions that these cases create for the assumption that the project of understanding epistemic justification is a part of the project of understanding knowledge? With respect to the first kind of case, that of the clairvoyant, Sosa suggests that justification requires not only that the belief in question be caused by a faculty or process that is intellectually virtuous and, hence, reliable, but also that there be no equally reliable faculty or process in the subject's repertoire whose use by him in combination with the faculty or process that he actually does use would not have yielded that same belief (*KP*, 237).

A *prima facie* problem for this suggestion is that the more impoverished the repertoire of the clairvoyant's cognitive faculties, the more likely it is that the clairvoyant will have an epistemically justified belief and knowledge. Consider a "normal" clairvoyant, that is, a clairvoyant whose other faculties and methods resemble those of most other humans and, thus, whose "alternative methods would of course include the recall and use through reasoning of relevant evidence previously unused though stored in memory, including evidence about the reliability of one's pertinent faculties" (*KP*, 237–8). If we suppose that the use of these alternative methods would have undermined the clairvoyant's beliefs about events in the distant future, then these beliefs, according to Sosa's suggestion, need not be justified. On the other hand, if we imaginatively begin to strip away the clairvoyant's other faculties, creating an impoverished repertoire of faculties, and then consider analogous situations in which the clairvoyant has beliefs about the distant future, it looks as if at some point the situation will become such that, according to Sosa's account, the clairvoyant's beliefs would flip into being epistemically justified, because there will no longer be alternative faculties and methods at his disposal to undermine them.

Although this is perhaps a surprising result, I will not comment further on it, because it is not directly relevant to the central tension I want to explore. Besides, there is another case that Sosa uses to isolate what seems to him key in an account of epistemic justification.

> Superstitious S believes whatever he reads in the horoscope simply because on a day in August it predicted no snow. Tricky T intends to offer S a lemon of a used car and plants the following in the horoscope under S's sign: "You will be offered a business proposition by T. The time is ripe for accepting business propositions." Does S know that T will offer him a deal? T planted the message and would not have done so if he had been going to offer S a deal. So it is not just a lucky guess nor is it just a happy accident that S is right in thinking that a deal is forthcoming, given his daily use of the horoscope.... One thing seems clear: S does not know in such a case. What S lacks, I suggest, is justification. His reason for trusting the horoscope is not adequate – to put it kindly. (*KP*, 239)

How does Sosa understand the kind of epistemic justification that he finds lacking in this case?

> A being of epistemic kind K is prima facie justified in believing P if and only if his belief of P manifests what, relative to K beings, is an intellectual virtue, a faculty that enhances their differential of truth over error. (*KP*, 239)

However, Sosa immediately makes a key qualification having to do with issue of normal circumstances:

> What interests us in justification is essentially the trustworthiness and reliability of the subject with regard to the field of his judgement, in situations normal for judgements in that field. That explains also why what does matter for justification is how the subject performs with regard to factors internal to him, and why it does not matter for justification if external factors are abnormal and unfavorable so that despite impeccable performance S does not know. What we care about in justification are the epistemic endowments of the subject, his intellectual virtues. (*KP*, 240)

Within Sosa's epistemology, it is the qualification about "situations normal for judgements in that field" that allows victims of a Cartesian evil demon to have epistemically justified beliefs. The victims lack knowledge of their environment as a result of the demon's deceiving activities, but they do not necessarily lack epistemically justified beliefs despite the fact that their faculties in the demon-controlled environment are not reliable. This is possible, given Sosa's intellectual virtue approach to epistemic justification, because the circumstances are abnormal. In normal situations, these same faculties are reliable, and it is their reliability in normal situations that determines whether or not they are virtuous.

Notice, however, that although this qualification does allow subjects to have justified beliefs in a world where a demon occasionally deceives them, it does not allow them to have epistemically justified beliefs in a world where deceit is the norm. In particular, imagine a demon world in which not only is it the case that the demon deceives subjects with great regularity but it is also such that the demon would regularly deceive subjects in most close possible worlds as well. Given the plausible assumption that normal situations are those that are statistically frequent or at least frequent at close possible worlds, the perceptual faculties of the inhabitants of this kind of demon world are not virtuous, according to Sosa's definitions. Yet, for its inhabitants, such a world may be subjectively indistinguishable from this one.

I will return to this issue again in a moment and examine Sosa's attempt to address it, but I need first to note that Sosa makes an important additional qualification that is also relevant to the tension in question. He distinguishes two general varieties of knowledge, animal knowledge and reflective knowledge:

> One has animal knowledge about one's environment, one's past, and one's own experience if one's judgements and beliefs about these are direct responses to their impact – e.g., through perception or memory – with little or no benefit of reflection or understanding. One has reflective knowledge if one's judgement or belief manifests not only such direct response to the fact known but also understanding of its place in a wider whole that includes one's belief and knowledge of it and how these come about. (*KP*, 240)

According to Sosa, both animal knowledge and reflective knowledge require a belief that is true and epistemically justified, where justification is understood as having its source in intellectual virtue. Nonetheless, he regards the two kinds of knowledge as requiring a corresponding split of epistemic justification into two concepts: justification proper and a broader notion of justification that he calls "epistemic aptness." Justification proper is one way, but not the only way, in which a belief can be apt. Justification proper involves the subject having reasons in support of his belief, whereas aptness does not require this. The former, which is closely associated with reflective knowledge, is an internalist notion. It is reason-based and is accessible via reflection. However, Sosa insists that it is the broader notion of aptness, rather than the narrower notion of justification proper, that is necessary for knowledge:

> Apt then is perhaps what a belief must be to qualify as knowledge, in addition to being true (and un-Gettierized). One way a belief might be apt, moreover, is by being justified, which means it has the support of reasons (implicit if not explicit). But it is left open that there be other ways for one to believe aptly: it is left open, for example, that some simple memory beliefs be apt though lacking any support by reasoning (and in that sense lacking justification).... Gettier showed long ago that justified true belief is not sufficient for knowledge. On the basis of [an internalist, reason-based] conception of justification, it would now be clear that justified true belief is not so much as necessary for knowledge. (*KP*, 255)

Thus, Sosa concedes that epistemic justification proper is not the only way for a true belief to become a good candidate for knowledge. In particular, epistemic justification proper is not necessary for animal knowledge.

3 The Distinctness of Justification and Knowledge

Sosa rejects half of what I have been terming "the unfortunate assumption" that there is a conceptual link between knowledge and epistemic justification, but he does not reject the other half. He acknowledges that epistemic justification is not a necessary condition of knowledge, but he hangs on to the assumption that an adequate account of epistemic justification must explicate justification in terms of properties that turn true beliefs into knowledge absent Gettier problems. This latter assumption, although perhaps only half as unfortunate as the full assumption, is nonetheless still unfortunate.

To see why, consider again the problems that a deceiving demon creates for Sosa's accounts of epistemic justification and knowledge. He agrees that the demon's victim can have epistemically justified beliefs, noting that "if his experience and reasoning are indistinguishable from those of the best justified among us, can we in fairness deny him the justification that we will claim for ourselves?" (*KP*, 237). However, this intuition is in tension with the assumption that epistemic justification turns true belief into knowledge absent Gettier problems. A mischievous demon might allow his victim to have occasional, isolated true beliefs, but such beliefs, even though true, are not good candidates for knowledge. Sosa's strategy for addressing this tension is to insist that a faculty can be virtuous, and as such generate epistemically justified beliefs, and yet not be reliable in abnormal external circumstances, such as those present when a demon is deceiving the subject.

The problem with this strategy, as I briefly mentioned earlier, is that what is normal is a function of what is actual. If the world is pretty much as we conceive it to be, and we then imagine introducing a demon who occasionally deceives subjects, Sosa's strategy works well enough. On the other hand, if we imagine that the demon deceives not just a few people on a few occasions but rather all people with great regularity, the tensions within Sosa's account arise with as much force as ever. They do so because, by hypothesis, normal external circumstances are saturated with deceit, and, thus, perceptual faculties such as ours are not virtuous by Sosa's standards. Accordingly, the perceptual beliefs produced by them are not epistemically justified. However, this result is at odds with the intuition that the demon's victims can have epistemically justified beliefs.

Sosa tries to finesse this problem by suggesting that justification be relativized to an environment:

> Relative to our actual environment A, our automatic experience-belief mechanisms count as virtues that yield much truth and justification. Of course relative to the demonic environment D such mechanisms are not virtuous and yield neither truth nor justification. It follows that relative to D the demon's victims are not justified, and yet relative to A their beliefs are justified. (*KP*, 144)

In this passage, Sosa relies on the assumption that our actual environment is one in which deceiving demons are not the norm. With this assumption in hand, he asserts that although the victim's faculties are not reliable relative to the demon environment D and, hence, not virtuous in that environment, these same faculties are virtuous relative to the actual environment A and, correspondingly, the beliefs they produce are justified relative to A. According to Sosa, it is in this relativized sense that the victim of the demon can have epistemically justified beliefs even when being deceived.

Whatever bite this strategy has, however, derives from the assumption that our environment is pretty much as we conceive it to be. If for the sake of testing Sosa's account we suspend this optimistic assumption and instead assume that our actual environment is one in which a demon regularly deceives people, the same problems rise to the surface once again. Under this hypothesis, Sosa's relativization strategy no longer yields the desired result, because it is no longer true that relative to the actual environment A the victim's faculties are reliable. By hypothesis, the faculties in question are every bit as unreliable in our actual environment as they are in the victim's environment. Consequently, the beliefs of the victim are not products of faculties that are reliable relative to the actual environment and, hence, the beliefs they produce are not justified even in a relativized sense.

To be sure, it is possible to designate yet another possible environment, distinct from the environment of the victim and distinct also from our actual environment, and then assert that the victim's faculties are reliable relative to this third environment and that, accordingly, his beliefs are justified relative to this environment as well. But this is an uninteresting result, since for virtually any kind of faculty, there is some conceivable environment E such that the faculty is reliable relative to E. So, if there are no restrictions on picking out the environment, pretty much any kind of faculty, no matter how strange, will turn out to be virtuous in this relativized sense, and pretty much any belief will turn out to be justified in a corresponding relativized sense.

Perhaps Sosa can insist, however, that not just any environment is relevant. For example, perhaps the only relevant environments are those closely similar to what we take to be our actual environment. The claim, on this suggestion, would then be that the victim's faculties are virtuous relative to environments closely similar to what we take our actual environment to be and that, as a result, his beliefs are justified relative to these same environments. On this approach, a major issue is who the "we" is supposed to be. People in the community of the person making the evaluation? People in the community of the person being evaluated? Most people currently alive? Most people who have ever lived? Or yet another group?

It is hard to see how there can be a principled answer to such questions, but even if there were, there is a more fundamental problem with this approach. Namely, whatever is meant by "we," this approach represents an abandonment of Sosa's reliabilism, which is supposed to constitute the heart of his virtue approach. After all, "we" can have deeply mistaken beliefs about our environment, however the "we" is defined. Thus, a faculty can be virtuous relative to environments closely similar to what we take to be our actual environment and yet be deeply unreliable in what is in fact our environment, and deeply unreliable as well in other close possible environments. But if so, such faculties do not produce beliefs that are good candidates for knowledge in our actual environment. They produce good candidates for knowledge only in environments very unlike our actual environment.

No doubt there are other ways of trying to tinker with Sosa's account to try to avoid these tensions, but a better response is to root out the source of the tensions, which is the assumption that there is a conceptual tie between epistemic justification and knowledge. Sosa is correct to sever half of the commonly assumed conceptual connection between the two. He concedes that epistemic justification is not a necessary condition of knowledge. However, the other half of the connection also needs to be severed. It is not a necessary condition of epistemic justification that it turns true beliefs into knowledge, absent Gettier problems. One of the lessons to be learned from the demon cases and the like is that one's beliefs can be epistemically justified even when they are so thoroughly mistaken that the occasional true ones are not good candidates for knowledge. The assumption that epistemic justification, absent Gettier problems, turns true belief into knowledge inevitably distorts the project of trying to understand what is involved in having epistemically justified beliefs. The remedy is to jettison the assumption and instead to develop an account of justification without feeling a need to smuggle into the account constraints aimed at forging a necessary link between epistemic justification and knowledge.

The specific account of epistemic justification I favor is one that understands epistemic justification in terms of the subject not being susceptible to intellectual self-criticism. If one's opinions conform to one's own deepest intellectual standards, in the sense that they can withstand one's own most severe critical scrutiny insofar as one's goal is to have accurate and comprehensive beliefs, then those opinions are epistemically justified. This is a notion of epistemic justification that allows victims of an evil demon to have justified beliefs even when deception by the demon is the norm and, hence, even when their beliefs are produced by faculties that are not reliable in the actual world or in close possible worlds.[7]

My principal purpose here, however, is not to defend a particular account of epistemic justification but rather to illustrate the corrupting consequences of the assumption that there is a conceptual tie between epistemic justification and knowledge. The assumption distorts the project of trying to understand epistemic justification, and it also distorts the project of trying to understand knowledge. As a final illustration of how it does so, return to Sosa's case of Superstitious S. According to Sosa, S lacks knowledge in this case, and the reason he lacks knowledge is that his belief is not epistemically justified. More precisely, given Sosa's distinction between apt belief and justified belief, S lacks knowledge because his true belief is not epistemically justified and, moreover, it is not made apt by any other means.

Sosa is employing a strategy here that has become familiar in epistemology since Gettier. The strategy is to describe cases in which a subject intuitively lacks knowledge and then to employ the assumption that knowledge and justification are conceptually connected to draw conclusions, indeed often strong conclusions, about knowledge, epistemic justification, and the relation between them. The strategy can be understood as a kind of epistemology game. Call it "the Gettier game." The game starts with a case in which a subject has a true belief but intuitively seems not to have knowledge, and the play of the game is governed by the rule that justification is that which has to be added to true belief in order for the belief to count as knowledge, with perhaps some fourth condition added to handle Gettier problems. The goal of the game is to pinpoint, within the constraints imposed by this rule, the precise defect that explains why the subject lacks knowledge. A solution to the game can be one of three sorts. First, one can claim that although the subject's belief is true, it is not plausible to regard it as epistemically justified. Second, one can claim that although it is plausible to regard the subject's belief as epistemically justified, it lacks a special fourth condition (for example, non-defectiveness or nondefeasibility) that has to be present in order for a true justified belief to be an instance of knowledge. Third, one can claim that although at first glance it might seem plausible to regard the subject's belief as justified, the case illustrates why it is necessary to amend the traditional notion of epistemic justification; once these amendments are introduced (for example, by insisting that a belief is justified only if it is reliably generated), one is in a position to explain why the subject lacks knowledge, namely, the subject's belief is not justified in the amended sense.

My recommendation is not to play the Gettier game but rather a different and much simpler game. My game starts identically, namely, with a case in which a subject has a true belief but intuitively seems not to have knowledge, but it is governed by a different rule: look for other true beliefs that the subject lacks and that can plausibly account for why the subject lacks knowledge. I claim that this game always has a solution.

For example, why does Superstitious S's true belief that T will offer him a business proposition lack knowledge of this proposition? Sosa says that the explanation is that S lacks justification, but a simpler, more straightforward, and universally generalizable explanation is that he lacks so many surrounding true beliefs that he does not have an accurate, overall appreciation of his true situation. He lacks true beliefs about the unreliability of horoscopes, about T's having planted his horoscope on the day in question, and about many other aspects of his situation. As a result, he does not have a sufficiently accurate and comprehensive grasp of the topic at issue to have knowledge of it. He may also lack justification, as Sosa suggests, but there is no need to cite his lack of justification in explaining why he lacks knowledge. His lack of an adequate "picture" of his true situation is enough to explain his lack of knowledge.

Or consider Alvin Goldman's barn case.[8] You are driving in the country and stop in front of a barn. Unbeknownst to you, the surrounding countryside is filled with barn facsimiles. The facsimiles are so detailed that if you had stopped in front of any of them, you would have been fooled into thinking you were looking at a real barn, but by luck you have stopped in front of one of the few real barns left in the area. You have a true belief that you are looking at a barn but you lack knowledge. Why is this? Is it because you have been lucky, or because the process that caused your belief would have been unreliable in close counterfactual situations, or because your justification is not indefeasible? All these may be true of you, but the best explanation for why you lack knowledge despite having a true belief is the most obvious one, namely, that you lack other, relevant true beliefs. You are unaware of the barn facsimiles in the area and, moreover, the barn story has been told in such a way as to highlight that this is an important lacuna in your belief system.

So, according to the game I am recommending, in any case in which we from the outside think a subject lacks knowledge despite having a true belief, it should be possible to identify some significant aspect of the situation such that we from our external vantage point can see that the subject lacks true beliefs about that aspect of the situation. My claim, to repeat, is that this game always has a solution. In particular, my claim is that in the enormous literature generated since Gettier's article, with its vast number of cases describing a subject who has a true belief P but intuitively lacks knowledge, in each and every one of these cases it is possible to cite an important feature of the situation about which the subject lacks true beliefs and where this lack plausibly accounts for the intuition that the subject lacks knowledge.

One way of conceiving this claim is to think of it as dropping out of the approach recommended by indefeasibility theorists once the requirement that justification is necessary for knowledge is abandoned. Indefeasibility theorists buy into the assumption that justification is necessary for knowledge, and so, they are committed to the Gettier game. However, when confronted with cases in which the subject intuitively lacks knowledge despite having a justified true belief, they say, as I want to say, that the lack of knowledge is to be explained by the subject's lacking relevant true beliefs. But because they presuppose that justification is necessary for knowledge, they hook up the lack of true beliefs with the justification requirement. The subject lacks knowledge, according to them, because the missing true beliefs would defeat the subject's justification for the target belief. However, once the link between justification and knowledge is severed, as it should be in any event given that in many instances of knowledge subjects are not in a position to offer anything like defenses of their beliefs, a simpler and more elegant explanation is possible. The subject's lack of knowledge is to be explained by a lack of true beliefs about some significant aspect of the situation.

I believe this claim can be adequately defended, but for my purposes here, my aim is more limited. I am less interested in making the full case for the above claim than in showing that epistemology is better off without the assumption that there is a conceptual connection between epistemic justification and knowledge.

Notes

1 Edmund L. Gettier, "Is Justified True Belief Knowledge?" *Analysis* 25 (1963): 121–3.
2 Alvin Goldman, "A Causal Theory of Knowing," *The Journal of Philosophy* 64 (1967): 357–72; D. M. Armstrong, *Belief, Truth, and Knowledge* (Cambridge: Cambridge University Press, 1973).
3 Alvin Goldman, *Epistemology and Cognition* (Cambridge, MA: Harvard University Press, 1986).
4 For a summary and discussion of the relevant issues, see William Alston, *Epistemic Justification* (Ithaca, NY: Cornell University Press, 1989), especially chapters 8 and 9.
5 For more details on this latter benefit, see Richard Foley, "The Foundational Role of Epistemology in a General Theory of Rationality," in A. Fairweather and L. Zagzebski, eds., *Virtue Epistemology* (Oxford: Oxford University Press, 2001).
6 *Knowledge in Perspective* (Cambridge: Cambridge University Press, 1991): 131–45 (cited as *KP*).
7 See Richard Foley, *Intellectual Trust in Oneself and Others* (Cambridge: Cambridge University Press, 2001), especially chapter 2.
8 Alvin Goldman, "Discrimination and Perceptual Knowledge," *The Journal of Philosophy* 73 (1976): 771–91.

6

Achieving Epistemic Ascent

RICHARD FUMERTON

Sosa's epistemology has long been marked by an effort to avoid unnecessary polarization through compromise that incorporates the insights of opposing camps. He has recently urged us to view both the foundationalist/coherentist and the internalist/externalist controversies in epistemology as *false* dichotomies. Can we find neutral ground between these warring epistemological factions?

The Distinction between Animal and Reflective Knowledge and the Search for Compromise

In *Knowledge in Perspective* and more recently "Two False Dichotomies," Sosa stresses a distinction between animal and reflective knowledge, or, following Descartes, *cognitio* and *scientia*.[1] Put very crudely, one achieves animal knowledge simply by getting at the truth in an appropriate (non-accidental) way. The justification or epistemic virtue constitutive of animal knowledge lends itself to an externalist analysis. Reflective knowledge, the kind of knowledge that philosophers, for example, seek, requires more. It is here that internalist intuitions are most at home. I will argue that there is something profoundly right about Sosa's attempt to make this distinction, and in this chapter I will evaluate not only Sosa's suggestion as to how to understand the nature of the ascent from animal to reflective knowledge, but some competing views as well.

Sosa's Conception of Animal Knowledge

Sosa's account of animal knowledge is essentially a sophisticated variation on reliabilism. In "Intellectual Virtue in Perspective" Sosa tries to analyze epistemic concepts like knowledge employing as a conceptual building block the idea of an intellectual virtue. He suggests that we understand an intellectual virtue of a person S as a *relative* concept.[2] S has an intellectual virtue relative to some set of circumstances C, an environment E, an inner nature I, and a field of propositions F, when S has an inner nature I such that if S is in C and E and has nature I and if S either believes or disbelieves some proposition P from field F then S is very likely right with respect to P. Additional complications are introduced into the analysis to deal with potential counterexamples and to answer certain pragmatic questions that arise concerning the implicit choice of reference classes for C, E, I, and F in our ascriptions of knowledge. But the essence of animal knowledge is simply true belief that results from intellectual virtue as defined above.

Now I don't propose to evaluate here the details of Sosa's account of intellectual virtue and the way in which it might figure into an analysis of animal-level knowledge (*cognitio*).[3] Rather, I want to address the more general issue of whether we need *some* such externalist account of epistemic concepts, and the question of whether we also need more robust epistemic concepts satisfaction of which allows us to *ascend* from this sort of knowledge and justified belief to the kind of knowledge and justified belief that internalists suggest we seek in our more intellectual moments.

The Appeal of Externalism

The rise of naturalism and externalism in epistemology is, in part, a reaction to what strikes many as the traditional epistemologist's radical over-intellectualizing of belief formation. Most Modern philosophers argued that we *infer* the vast majority of what we believe about the world around us. Perceptual knowledge, they claimed, involves inference from truths we know more directly about the character of sense data or appearance. Knowledge of the past involves inference from knowledge of truths about the present content of "memory experience." Knowledge of other minds involves inference based on knowledge of truths describing the behavior of physical bodies. And the problem of skepticism loomed large on the horizon because these same philosophers held very high standards for what constitutes legitimate inference. One can reasonably believe one proposition P as a result of reasonably believing some other proposition E only if one has reason to believe that there is at least a probabilistic connection between the truth of E and the truth of P.

The traditional epistemologist's reasons for supposing that commonplace beliefs about the external world, the past and other minds must be inferentially justified, if justified at all, are familiar. The traditional epistemologist was a foundationalist who believed that the only way to end regresses of justification was with non-inferentially justified belief. Under the influence of Descartes, foundationalists sought to find their "first" truths in infallible belief or infallible justification for belief. But the best justification we can imagine for believing propositions about the external world, the past, and other minds, seems perfectly consistent with those beliefs being false. To avoid a fairly radical skepticism we would need to find justification for the beliefs of common sense in legitimate *inference* from more secure foundations.

The attempt to defeat skepticism playing by the rules of the traditional foundationalist has a troubled history, but before even attempting to reconstruct a plausible inferential justification for everyday beliefs, we might certainly pause, with Reid, to worry about the fact that we just don't seem to *make* inferences of the sort the traditional view requires. And if we don't even make inferences of the relevant sort, how can we plausibly identify the justification such beliefs enjoy as inferential justification?

It's important not to underestimate the depth of the phenomenological problem. The traditional empiricist might be tempted to shrug off the alleged problem by turning from conscious inference from occurrent belief to unconscious inference from dispositional belief. It is undoubtedly true that we don't typically consciously assent to propositions describing the character of fleeting, subjective appearance and infer from those truths propositions about the external world. Nor do we consciously infer truths about the past from propositions describing the occurrence of present memory experience. We often seem to just sense that a good friend is unhappy or pensive without first consciously noting some physical characteristic of expression or behavior. But none of this implies that we lack the relevant *dispositional* beliefs about sense experience, memory experience, or physical behavior, respectively. Furthermore, there is no reason to deny that dispositional beliefs can be causally efficacious in producing other beliefs, where the existence of those causal connections can constitute a plausible sort of unconscious inference.

But as I indicated above, the problem is more serious for the traditional epistemologist. As many have pointed out, it is not clear that we have even *dispositional* beliefs about the kinds of mental states that the traditional foundationalist takes to be the subject matter of contingent foundational knowledge.[4] Although I can't argue it here, it does seem to me almost a datum that there *is* such a thing as subjective experience, the occurrence of which does not imply the truth of any proposition about the physical world. But we typically don't *attend* to appearance in the way that would be required to form the *ground* of a dispositional belief. One of the first things an aspiring landscape painter needs to *learn* is the fascinating and subtle differences between the appearances objects present. Ordinary people aren't even very good at recognizing the details of how things look even when those very experiences serve as important *causal* clues for belief formation.

"Memory experience" is also notoriously difficult to find phenomenologically. It may exist at some level of consciousness and it may be causally operative in producing beliefs about the past, but there seems almost no plausibility to the claim that our beliefs about the past are caused by *beliefs*, occurrent or dispositional, about the occurrence of memory states. Beliefs about recent past events may be accompanied by various images, but it is far from clear that these images are essential to remembering. Indeed, as Ayer suggested some time ago, often there may be no more to remembering some fact than having a true belief caused in the appropriate way by the past event.[5]

We might suppose that we must have noticed something about our friend's behavior in order to reach a conclusion about the friend's mood, but the fact that we often can't describe, even to ourselves, what the behavioral clue was is surely *prima facie* evidence that we simply don't have a belief about that behavior. We are again hard-pressed to discover a *belief* (justified or not) in premises from which we can legitimately infer our conclusion.

Externalists bring to the table a refreshingly undemanding account of both noninferential and inferential justification. They seem to accommodate a possibility of justified belief that is more in harmony with the phenomenological data. As a species we may have evolved to respond to all sorts of noncognitive stimuli with appropriate beliefs and expectations. And if we have relatively stable dispositions to arrive at the truth in this way, why can't we view the stimulus/response belief-forming mechanisms as the very source of knowledge and justification? We need a concept of animal knowledge, of animal rationality, because we *are* animals among other animals. When the young gazelle encounters a hungry lion for the first time, it is indeed fortunate that it does not need to employ inductive reasoning to reach the conclusion that flight would be appropriate. If the world is as we think it is, nature has no doubt taken care of this for the gazelle, and although it *may* involve anthropomorphizing on our part, it is certainly noteworthy that we describe the gazelle as *knowing* instinctively (without needing to rely on experience) that there is danger present. While human beings are far more complex than gazelles, and may have the capacity to form intentional states that precede such things as flight behavior, it is hardly plausible to suppose that all of *our* beliefs and expectations are at the mercy of our reasoning ability. And this is as fortunate for human survival as it is for the survival of the gazelle. Hume put the point eloquently in discussing the way in which a person responds to sensations with beliefs about the external world:

> Nature has not left this to his choice, and has doubtless esteem'd it an affair of too great importance to be trusted to our uncertain reasonings and speculations.[6]

The fact that we don't take the plausibility of Hume's supposition to reflect on the possibility of making distinctions between reasonable and unreasonable belief, people who have knowledge and people who don't, strongly suggests that we do employ epistemic concepts the satisfaction of which does not require all that much of cognitive agents. We do, of course, find it useful to distinguish people who have capacities to get at the truth in certain predictable ways from people who lack those capacities, and it is the epistemic concepts we employ to mark such distinctions that externalists try to analyze in more formal ways.

Dissatisfaction with Externalism: Is That All There Is?

But if we hard-core internalists are occasionally tempted to flirt with externalist analyses of at least some epistemic concepts, we eventually always recoil at the suggestion that there is no more to knowledge and justified belief than what the externalist has to offer. Painting with a broad stroke, I would suggest that the fundamental internalist concern is that having knowledge or justification in the externalist sense doesn't seem to satisfy philosophical *curiosity*. It doesn't seem to provide any *assurance* of the sort the philosopher seeks when wondering about the truth of various propositions. Even some confirmed externalists seem to lose their nerve when moving up levels of knowledge and justification. Plantinga, for example, seems content to argue that, given his externalist analysis of knowledge and warrant, we *might* have non-inferential warrant for believing various propositions about the existence of God. The "might" is surely an epistemic operator. The implication is that we don't *know* anything inconsistent with the proposition that the Christian has the relevant knowledge. But the *contextual* implication of the use of the modal operator seems to make the concession that we also don't know that the Christian *does* have such knowledge.[7] But on most externalist analyses of epistemic concepts, having second-level knowledge that one knows or justified belief that one has a justified belief is not much more difficult than having first-level knowledge or justified belief. If justified belief is reliably produced belief and if beliefs about the past resulting from memory are justified because they are reliably produced, then, pace Alston,[8] the externalist should allow that one can produce a straightforward track-record argument for the conclusion that memory is reliable and get second-level justification for believing that first-level beliefs about the past are justified. If memory and induction are reliable ways of forming belief, one can *remember* remembering various events and *remember* those events having occurred and can then use an inductive argument to generalize that beliefs resulting from memories are usually true. Memory, induction, and perception can be employed together to form the reliable belief that perception is reliable. Memory and induction can be used to form the reliable belief that induction is reliable. If reliability is the essence of justification, then achieving knowledge and justified belief at the higher levels seems at our fingertips provided that there *are* the relevant reliable belief-forming mechanisms at the first level. Plantinga's Holy Spirit who aids in producing appropriate beliefs about God and His nature can surely just as easily produce warranted metabeliefs about the activity of the Holy Spirit in producing appropriate beliefs.

Despite all this, and despite having acknowledged that the externalist may have insight into at least some epistemic concepts, we almost can't help being seduced by an internalist desire for more intellectually *satisfying* knowledge and justified belief, at least at higher levels. The externalist argues that *if* memory is reliable then we have justified beliefs about the past. And *if* memory and induction are reliable then we probably have justified beliefs that we have justified beliefs about the past. The externalist has opened the door to the epistemic *possibility* of knowledge and justified belief at the first level, but for some reason we shy away from the claim that it is epistemically impossible that we lack such knowledge. It is not, I think, that the contextualist is right and that when doing philosophy all kinds of skeptical alternatives suddenly become relevant. It is rather, I think, that when doing philosophy and starting to think about the fundamental questions concerning knowledge and justification we get serious and insist that knowledge and justification require something more than a capacity to get at the truth in certain non-accidental ways. But what is the ascent we want to achieve in gaining knowledge or justification of the sort that will satisfy philosophical curiosity, provide intellectual assurance, and how can we achieve it?

Sosa's Conception of Epistemic Ascent to Reflective Knowledge

In a number of places, most recently in "Two False Dichotomies," Sosa suggests an answer to this question of what is necessary to achieve reflective knowledge. He begins by emphasizing the following principle of epistemic ascent:

(KA) If one really knows that P and one considers whether one does, then one must be justified in thinking that one does.

Notice that Sosa does not assert that knowledge implies knowing that one knows, or even that knowledge implies having the capacity to know that one knows. Nor is it clear whether he would accept an analogous principle of ascent for justification:

(JA) If one really believes P justifiably then if one considers whether one does then one must be justified in thinking that one believes P justifiably.

This latter issue is important if we fear regress from Sosa's ascent principle. After all, while one might think it initially plausible to suppose that someone's knowing P requires that person to believe justifiably that he knows that P if he considers the question, do we also want to insist that if the person were to consider the question of whether he justifiably believes that he knows that P he would find himself justifiably believing that he justifiably believes that he knows that P, and so on *ad infinitum*? In no time at all the higher-level beliefs will presumably get too complicated for any normal epistemic agent to keep things straight.

I want to be clear about the nature of the regress I fear from JA. I'm not suggesting that a principle of ascent need involve one in conceptual regress. Just because one thinks that my justifiably believing P would require me to justifiably believe that I am justified in believing P if I consider the question, it doesn't *follow* that that justified metabelief need be *constitutive* of my justifiably believing P. In other words, it needn't be an *analytic* truth that if I justifiably believe P then upon consideration I would justifiably believe that I have such justification. But even if the principle were not analytic, a principle of ascent concerning justification might require something of which finite epistemic agents are clearly incapable. Now it may be that Sosa would reject JA and for that reason deny that he faces any problematic regresses, but I'm not sure why JA has any less initial plausibility than KA, particularly if we can make a distinction between animal-level *justification* and reflective *justification* analogous to Sosa's distinction between animal-level knowledge and reflective knowledge.

Why exactly does Sosa think that KA is plausible? Well, he begins by asking us how we would react to the person who responds to the question "Do you know that P?" by saying, for example, "Maybe, maybe not." Don't we think that such a person has within his or her doxastic system a kind of disharmony that destroys the possibility of first-level *reflective* knowledge? That suggestion does seem initially plausible, but I wonder whether one could acknowledge its plausibility without introducing levels of knowledge (animal and reflective). Perhaps, for example, the plausibility of Sosa's claim stems from nothing more problematic than the fact that the subjective certainty condition for knowledge (at least knowledge of the sort that philosophers are interested in, or ordinary people are interested in when they make clear by various inflections that they want to know whether you *really* know that P) looks like it's failing when uncertainty is revealed at the higher level. When the criminal defense lawyer asks the witness if he is absolutely certain that he saw the defendant at the scene of the crime, she will no doubt claim a victory of sorts if the witness responds "Maybe, maybe not, but there's at least a 50/50 chance that I'm certain." That sort of meta-level uncertainty about certainty seems, at the very least, to be in strong tension with the *possibility* of being genuinely certain at the first level. But I'm not sure that the tension is anything other than an epistemic tension. If we suppose that generally people have a kind of unproblematic access to their own occurrent mental states, then if someone is hemming and hawing about whether or not he is certain that P, that's pretty strong evidence that he really isn't certain that P. But that it constitutes strong counter-evidence against first-level certainty needn't seduce us into thinking that a plausible metaphysical account of first-level certainty should reveal a necessary connection between possessing it and having the capacity to be certain that one possesses it.

Another perfectly plausible hypothesis as to how second-level facts concerning justified belief about knowledge might destroy the possibility of genuine first-level knowledge concerns reflection on the *truth condition* for knowledge. If I'm thinking about first-level knowledge in an orderly way, I might think separately about the various conditions that seem individually necessary and jointly sufficient for knowledge. And, of course, one of those conditions is the truth-condition. I know that P only if P is true. Now if I'm evaluating the possibility of my knowing that P by first examining the truth-condition, and conclude that I have no reason to believe that I know because I have no reason to believe P, then it follows rather straightforwardly on most Gettier-proofed justified true belief accounts of knowledge that I should infer that I don't know that P – I don't know that P because I don't have a justified belief that P, and in its absence, of course, I don't have justified true belief of the sort that could constitute knowledge.

But suppose I do have good reason to believe that P and that I have good reason to think that I am certain that P. On a justified true belief account of knowledge, what else could prevent me from having a justified belief that I know that P if I really do? Well, of course, I might not have good evidence for believing that I have good evidence for believing P. In "Two False Dichotomies" Sosa claims that "one's belief amounts to reflective knowledge only if one can say that one does know, not just arbitrarily, but with adequate justification." Now if I find myself lacking good evidence for thinking that I have good evidence for believing P it probably *would* be a violation of the rules governing conversational implicature to go around *claiming* that I know that P. In most contexts you are not supposed to make claims if you realize that you don't have good reason to believe what you claim. But from the fact that I shouldn't *say* that I know that P if I don't have good reason to believe that I know that P, it doesn't, of course, follow that I can't know that P without having good reason to believe that I know that P. If I don't have good reason to believe that it is raining outside now (or at least if I realize that I don't have good reason to believe that it is raining outside now), then I shouldn't *say* that it is raining outside now. But from the fact that I shouldn't say that it is raining outside now, it doesn't follow that it isn't raining outside now. Without a justified belief that I've satisfied the conditions for knowledge (whatever they are), I shouldn't claim to know P, but it doesn't follow that if I don't have a justified belief that I know that P, I can't know that P (even after I consider the question of whether or not I do have such evidence).

Summarizing, there may be interesting evidential connections between lacking justification for believing that one knows and lacking knowledge, and there may be interesting connections between lacking justification for believing one knows *vis-à-vis* the appropriateness of *claiming* to know, but have we yet been given any reason to suppose that there is an important kind of knowledge, reflective knowledge, that requires having the capacity to form justified beliefs that we have some other kind of knowledge? Notice that if my understanding of Sosa is correct, then this is the right way to put the relevant question. We are concerned with understanding the conditions under which one can ascend to one sort of knowledge, *reflective* knowledge, by being able to justifiably believe that we have another sort of knowledge, *animal* knowledge. Does reflection on the plausibility of a principle of epistemic ascent gives us a good reason to distinguish two different concepts of knowledge?

Let's suppose we provide an analysis of knowledge and that we have some individual S who satisfies the necessary and sufficient conditions for knowledge proposed by the analysis. Following Sosa, we can recognize the following three possibilities:

1. S might know that P but be justified in believing that he doesn't.
2. S might know that P but have no reason to believe that he knows though also no reason to believe that he doesn't know.
3. S might know that P and also have strong justification for believing that he knows that P.

Of the three epistemic situations S might be in, Sosa argues, (3) is surely *better* than (1) and (2). So if we have an externalist analysis of knowledge that seems to fall short of an epistemic ideal and we are trying to suggest some way in which one can improve one's epistemic position so that one possesses a different kind of knowledge, a *better* kind of knowledge – reflective knowledge, then isn't it plausible to define reflective knowledge in terms of knowledge *plus*? Reflective knowledge is knowledge plus at least the capacity to reach a justified conclusion that one has knowledge. We can reconcile an externalist analysis of knowledge with our internalist yearnings for something more satisfying by simply distinguishing two kinds of knowledge – animal knowledge understood in terms of arriving at truth reliably,[9] and reflective knowledge understood in terms of possessing internal justification for believing that one is getting at truth reliably. One can avoid having to choose between externalism and internalism. Furthermore, if Sosa is correct and we should understand the justification that turns animal knowledge into reflective knowledge in terms of coherence, then we may also be able to reconcile our foundationalist inclinations with our implicit recognition of the epistemic importance of coherence, by accepting an externalist, but still foundationalist, account of animal knowledge and combining it with a coherence theory of justification of the sort necessary to turn animal knowledge into reflective knowledge.

An Externalist Response

The externalist will probably reject Sosa's offer of compromise. The externalist typically offers an analysis of knowledge with an externalist justification condition. The knowledge defined will not, of course, require any logical connection between knowing and having justification for believing that one knows. When Sosa asks the externalist whether it wouldn't be better to know that P and also have the capacity to justifiably recognize that one has such knowledge, the externalist can certainly respond in the affirmative. From an epistemic point of view, it's probably better to know that one knows that P than just to know that P, better to justifiably believe that one knows that P than just to know that P, better to justifiably believe that one has a justified belief that P than just to have a justified belief that P, and so on. When one emphasizes the qualification "from an epistemic point of view," these may just be tautologies. If from an epistemic point of view more knowledge and justified belief is better than less knowledge and justified belief, then the above claims are all obviously true. But one can admit all this and propose precisely the same externalist analysis of the higher-level epistemic states that one provides of the lower-level epistemic states.

Sosa's Epistemic Ladder

Sosa will reject an attempt to climb an epistemic ladder of ascent from animal knowledge to reflective knowledge by layering meta-level knowledge or justified belief on first-level knowledge or justified belief *when the knowledge or justified belief at the meta level is given the same externalist analysis as first-level knowledge or justified belief.* And I think he is absolutely right in thinking that this sort of ascent doesn't ever really get us into the better epistemic position we seek. It doesn't really allow us to leave the realm of animal knowledge. In short, Sosa's compromise is to give the externalist an externalist understanding of animal knowledge but require for reflective knowledge something more satisfying. If what I said earlier in this chapter is plausible, the problem with leaving one's meta-epistemology with only the conceptual resources of epistemic concepts understood as the externalist understands them is that we realize that satisfying such concepts doesn't give us the kind of *assurance* of truth we seek as philosophers, or simply as cognitive agents who find ourselves reflectively worried about whether or not we really know what we think we know. If I start to wonder whether there really is a physical world with the characteristics I take it to have, my intellectual curiosity isn't affected one way or another by the fact that I happen to be getting at truths about that world in a non-accidental way. Nature or Plantinga's God may have arranged for me to get at the truth when prompted by appropriate stimuli, but that doesn't do me any good at all when it comes to assuring myself that I am indeed getting at the truth. And I believe it is precisely that sort of assurance that reflective knowledge (or reflective justified belief) is supposed to provide.

How does one get the additional assurance that would constitute having reflective knowledge? Sosa's answer is that one gets oneself metabeliefs about the sources of one's beliefs where the metabeliefs cohere in important ways. Put too crudely, perhaps, Sosa wants to understand reflective knowledge as animal knowledge with coherent belief that one has animal knowledge where the coherence of one's beliefs about the ways in which one comes to believe reliably constitutes the kind of justification that will satisfy the internalist's demands on knowledge.

But now one must insure that the account of *justification* that one employs in one's account of reflective knowledge does not *itself* leave one yearning for a more satisfying ascent to yet another sort of justification. The following observations are hardly original. Indeed, the most devastating internalist critique of coherence as a source of philosophically satisfying justification was given by BonJour when he himself was a coherence theorist.[10] BonJour argued that coherence without *access* to coherence wouldn't give the internalist the sort of justification the internalist wants. To his enormous credit, BonJour effectively reminded us that there are two sorts of coherence theories – internalist and externalist. One can define a belief's having justification simply in terms of its cohering well with other beliefs in one's doxastic system. Or one can insist that having justification for a belief requires that one be *aware* of the fact that one's belief coheres with the rest of what one believes. If one understands justification in terms of coherence without requiring *access* to that coherence, then it seems clear to me that we will now need to make a distinction between "animal" justification, and reflective justification, between justification that is intellectually satisfying and justification that is not. We can surely mimic Sosa's rhetorical questions concerning ascent with respect to knowledge and ascent with respect to justification defined in terms of external coherence. Wouldn't it be somehow better not only to have a belief that coheres with the rest of one's beliefs but also to be aware of the fact that one's belief system is indeed coherent? If satisfying reflective epistemic concepts is supposed to put us in a more satisfactory epistemic position, then surely reflective justification requires not only coherence but also access to coherence. But access coherence theories face insuperable problems.

How precisely are we to understand access to coherence? Minimally, it would involve access to our beliefs and access to logical and probabilistic connections. But "access" is itself a thinly disguised epistemic term. If "access to" means "knowledge of" or "justified belief about" our coherence theory of reflective knowledge or our coherence theory of justification faces vicious conceptual circularity. Sosa's *strategy* for distinguishing between animal and reflective knowledge avoids structural circularity. He can define animal knowledge without invoking the concept of justification (defined in terms of coherence) and he can then define reflective knowledge in terms of justified belief about animal knowledge. But the conceptual circularity will only be postponed if he concedes that coherence without access to coherence doesn't do the job of giving us the sort of justification that would satisfy an internalist. Without access requirements to coherence, however, it's not clear that we have given the internalist anything that would allow the internalist to view the internalism/externalism debate as a false dichotomy.

Coherence theorists who try to incorporate access into an account of justification may be able to escape conceptual circularity by introducing yet another epistemic concept into their conceptual framework. If coherence without access to coherence cannot constitute philosophically satisfying justification, then why not simply recognize that in addition to coherence one needs to introduce some notion of being aware of (having access to, having direct acquaintance with) belief states and relations of coherence? The answer, of course, is that in doing so one will simply cease being a coherence theorist. It does, of course, seem entirely plausible to suppose that we have a kind of unproblematic access to what we occurrently believe and certain logical, perhaps even probabilistic, connections between propositions we believe. It is revealing that historically coherence theorists just seemed to give themselves knowledge of what they believe (just as contemporary anti-realists just seem to give themselves unproblematic knowledge of the ways in which they represent reality). But what business do they have presupposing unproblematic access to mental states? If there is such a thing as direct acquaintance with mental states, and it can constitute a kind of knowledge or justification of propositions made true by those mental states, then one is a traditional *foundationalist* and not a coherentist (though one may, of course, acknowledge certain inferential connections between foundationally justified belief as providing a way of increasing the justification those foundationally justified beliefs enjoy).

But isn't the problem of getting reflective knowledge or justified belief obviously going to arise even for a traditional foundationalist who tries to understand non-inferential justification in terms of direct acquaintance with a fact? I can't really address that question fully here, but I do think the answer is "no." When one is directly acquainted with one's pain while one believes that one is in pain and while one is also directly aware of the correspondence between the thought that one is in pain and the pain, that just is the epistemic state that constitutes genuine reflective knowledge. That just is the epistemic state that satisfies philosophical curiosity, that constitutes philosophical assurance. When one represents the world a certain way and one has the relevant truth-maker for that representation unproblematically before consciousness, there is nothing more one could *want* by way of epistemic assurance.

Epistemic Descent: Another Approach to Distinguishing Reflective from Animal Knowledge and Rationality

If there is a moral to be drawn from the above discussion, it may be that one should *start* one's meta-epistemological investigations by trying to discover a kind of knowledge and justified belief that is a good candidate for *reflective* knowledge and justification. Reflective knowledge and justified belief must be such that when one possesses it one thereby gains the kind of assurance that satisfies one's intellectual curiosity. Earlier in this chapter, I argued that Sosa is right to mark a distinction between reflective and animal knowledge. I think it is equally important to mark a distinction between intellectually satisfying justification and belief the rationality of which falls short of providing intellectual assurance. Rather than start by trying to understand animal knowledge and justification, however, I think we might more profitably begin with an internalist account of reflective knowledge and justification and work our way down, so to speak, to less intellectually demanding externalist concepts of knowledge and justified belief.

I've argued at some length elsewhere for a very traditional distinction between foundationally justified belief and inferentially justified belief. As my earlier remarks indicate, I believe one should understand non-inferential justification in terms of direct acquaintance with facts, representations of those facts and correspondence holding between the representations and the facts. I want to focus here, however, on inferential justification. I argued earlier that the traditional epistemologist maintained demanding standards for inferential justification. Traditional epistemologists (and for that matter, most proponents of contemporary externalist variations of foundationalism) insist that to be inferentially justified in believing P on the basis of E one must be justified in believing E. But they also argued that an ideal epistemic agent possessing ideal inferential justification for believing P on the basis of E would be aware of either a logical or probabilistic connection between E and P. As we remarked earlier, however, these requirements for inferential justification are so strong that it seems doubtful that ordinary epistemic agents (or, for that matter, most epistemologists) can satisfy them.

We should emphasize, however, that one of the advantages of distinguishing animal rationality (knowledge) from reflective rationality (knowledge) is that we shouldn't be particularly surprised to discover that we lack *reflective* knowledge and justified belief. Epistemologists have been preoccupied, almost obsessed, with the goal of defeating skepticism. It just doesn't seem right to suppose that we must conclude from our philosophical frustration at responding in an intellectually satisfying way to skeptical arguments that we lack *any* sort of knowledge and justified belief. But the whole point of distinguishing animal rationality from the kind of rational belief that satisfies philosophical curiosity is that we can allow the possibility of animal-level knowledge and justified belief while maintaining suitably high standards for the kind of knowledge and justification we seek as philosophers. If Hume was right, we might just be out of luck when it comes to satisfying *reason* (intellectually demanding reason) with respect to the vast majority of what we believe. But that doesn't mean we will stop trying or that we will pretend to have satisfied reason when the answers to our philosophical questions remain elusive.

But what sort of rational belief or knowledge could we possess if we fail to satisfy the more intellectually demanding standards of reflective knowledge and justified belief? What could constitute a kind of inferential justification that falls short of genuine reflective inferential justification? Well, it could be the case that we have a complex set of justified dispositional beliefs which together with the occurrence of various psychological states (sensations and memories, for example) *cause* us to believe various propositions about our environment. I have argued elsewhere that one should view *facts* as the relata of causal connection, where a fact is understood in terms of particulars' exemplifying relational or non-relational properties at a time.[11] Indeed, I think that the most straightforward generality theories of causation *require* something like facts to be the relata of causal connection. Once we identify causes and effects in terms of the exemplification of properties, we have a straightforward way of identifying the regularities that constitute the relevant constant conjunctions – a's being F at t will cause it to be G at $t + 1$ when it is a law of nature that whenever something is F at one time it is immediately thereafter G.

There is an advantage to the internalist trying to make room for a derivative externalist conception of knowledge and rational belief in allowing that facts are the relata of causal connection. Facts are also the most plausible candidates for the truth-makers of propositions. The very sensory state that (together with background beliefs) causes me to believe that there is a table before me is also the truth-maker for a proposition describing that state. Perhaps we can understand the rationality of the belief that results from a sensory state in terms of the *evidential* connections that hold between propositions describing the sensory state, the propositions justifiably but only dispositionally believed, and the proposition that it is the object of the belief that is produced. Reflective inferential justification requires that we be aware of evidential connections between propositions *believed*. Unreflective inferential justification requires only that the relevant evidential connections obtain where the relata of the connections include not only propositions believed but propositions that are not believed but are made true by the experiential states that causally contribute to our "conclusions." The resulting account of unreflective justification will be importantly external in that we are allowing that one can have inferential justification without having cognitive access to the justifier. But it also can contain elements of internalism, at least if one insists that the causes that are the justifiers must all be internal states. The account of non-reflective inferential justification can be employed in an account of non-reflective inferential knowledge, although the account will be no more unproblematic than other justified true belief accounts of knowledge that need to find additional conditions to avoid Gettier problems.

The above suggestion for externalizing a kind of knowledge and justification that is less demanding than the sort that philosophers seek to satisfy is not new. Haack defends a version of it in explaining the foundationalist elements in her foundherentism.[12] Haack wants experience to play a crucial role in the justification of beliefs but, largely for the kind of phenomenological reasons discussed earlier, she doesn't want knowledge of the external world to rely on *beliefs* about the character of sensory states. She also wants to suggest that we can relate the causal role experience plays to an evidential role by defining its evidential role in terms of evidential connections between propositions describing the experience and the propositions about the physical world believed as a result of those experiences. It seems to me, however, that she has a far too liberal view as to which propositions describing experience one considers in evaluating its evidential role. At one point, for example, she suggests that the relevant proposition describing the propositional/evidential counterpart of the sensory state A has when seeing a rabbit is the following:

> A is in the sort of perceptual state a normal subject would be in, in normal circumstances, when looking at a rabbit three feet away and in good light. (*Evidence and Inquiry*, 80)

If one employs a proposition like this in assessing the epistemic contribution of the experience, one might as well make life really easy in the fight to avoid skepticism and let the relevant proposition be:

> A is now having an experience that *is* caused by the presence of a rabbit before A.

A's sensory experience will now provide A with infallible justification for believing that the rabbit is present!

Our account of non-reflective inferential justification obviously needs some principled way to choose from among the indefinitely many propositions describing experience the *relevant* one for the purpose of assessing the epistemic contribution of the experience. Again, this is where the metaphysics of causation might help. An experience exemplifies infinitely many properties, relational and non-relational, but only certain properties are such that their exemplification plays a causal role in producing belief. We can take the properties that are causally relevant to be those constitutive of the fact that is the truthmaker for the relevant evidential proposition. My belief that there is a table in front of me is caused by a visual experience that may have the property of being the kind of experience usually caused by tables under these sorts of conditions, but reflection on standard epistemological problems strongly suggests that it is only the non-relational intrinsic character of the experience that is causally relevant to producing the belief. I'd believe precisely the same thing about the table if I lived in a world in which demons typically produce hallucinatory experience. So on the account I'm suggesting the only experiential proposition relevant to assessing the epistemic contribution of the experience would be the proposition made true by the exemplification of the non-relational (intrinsic) properties of the experiential state.[13]

Unreflective Knowledge, Justified Belief, and Skepticism

I want to make clear that in introducing an intellectually less demanding concept of knowledge and justified belief, I am not asserting that we *have* knowledge and justified belief of this sort. It *may* be that we have animal knowledge even though we don't have reflective knowledge, but it *may* be that we lack both reflective and animal knowledge. The italicized modal operator is epistemic and we now have a perfectly natural way of interpreting it. Relative to what we (or at least most of us) *reflectively* know it is both epistemically possible that we have unreflective knowledge and epistemically possible that we lack it.

Conclusion

Sosa is fundamentally correct in suggesting that we needn't choose between internalism and externalism. Furthermore, he is fundamentally correct in suggesting that the ground for compromise is to be found in a distinction between kinds of knowledge, and, I would add, kinds of justification. I have strong reservations about the attempt to understand intellectually satisfying knowledge by layering justification understood in terms of coherence upon animal knowledge. Instead, I would try to find a kind of animal knowledge by stripping away some of the more intellectually demanding conditions on reflective inferential knowledge while leaving in place the fundamental role of evidential connections.

Notes

1 *Knowledge in Perspective: Selected Essays in Epistemology* (Cambridge and New York: Cambridge University Press, 1991) (cited as *KP*); and "Two False Dichotomies: Internalism/Externalism and Foundationalism/Coherentism," in Walter Sinnott-Armstrong, ed., *Pyrrhonian Skepticism* (Oxford: Oxford University Press, 2003).
2 The clearest statement of this view is presented in "Intellectual Virtue in Perspective," in *KP*.
3 I've discussed a number of concerns, particularly about the requirement concerning broadening, in "Sosa's Epistemology," *Philosophical Issues* 5 (1995): 15–27.
4 See, for example, John Pollock, *Contemporary Theories of Knowledge* (Totowa, NJ: Rowman and Littlefield, 1974).
5 A. J. Ayer, *The Problem of Knowledge* (Edinburgh: Penguin, 1956), chapter 4.
6 David Hume, *A Treatise of Human Nature*, ed. L. A. Selby-Bigge (London: Oxford University Press, 1880), pp. 187.
7 Alvin Plantinga, *Warranted Christian Belief* (Oxford: Oxford University Press, 2000).
8 William Alston, *The Reliability of Sense Perception* (Ithaca, NJ: Cornell University Press, 1993).
9 Of course, these are crude caricatures of analyses that would need to be worked out in some detail. Even within the framework of an externalist approach to understanding epistemic concepts, there are distinctions to be made, counterexamples to be met.
10 In *The Structure of Empirical Knowledge* (Cambridge, MA: Harvard University Press, 1985).
11 In *Metaphysical and Epistemological Problems of Perception* (Lincoln: University of Nebraska Press, 1985), pp. 111–13.
12 Susan Haack, *Evidence and Inquiry* (Oxford: Blackwell, 1993). I suggested that one could accommodate a derivative evidential role for experience in "Inferential Justification and Empiricism," *The Journal of Philosophy* 73, 17 (1976): 557–69.
13 Identifying the relevant propositional counterpart of sensory states is only one of the problems one faces in fully developing an account of the sort I'm suggesting. One also needs the links in the causal chain that leads from sensory experience to belief to mimic appropriately the links in a chain of conscious inference. Like most causal theories of other concepts, this one faces the daunting task of distinguishing relevant from "deviant" causal chains. I am grateful to my colleague Evan Fales for discussing this issue with me.

7

Sosa on Reflective Knowledge and Virtue Perspectivism

ALVIN GOLDMAN

One of the pervasive features of Ernest Sosa's epistemology is intellectual virtue. Not only does he elevate intellectual virtue to a central position in epistemological theory, but his work itself displays many of the same virtues of which it speaks. Sosa praises the comprehensiveness of coherence, for example, and his own writing is distinguished by its remarkably comprehensive coverage of the epistemological literature. He praises reliability and cognitive "aptness," and his own epistemological points so often hit the mark, at least by my lights, that his reliability in matters epistemic is difficult to exceed. However, the purpose of an author-meets-critics volume is not to extol the author's virtues. Presumably, it is to do something like uncover the author's vices. Even if the term 'vice' does not find any natural application in the present instance, I shall at any rate undertake the task of identifying some smallish places where I worry whether Sosa gets things right. Or, of equal relevance, I shall attempt to identify some features of his overall epistemological position where I fail to detect the rich internal coherence that Sosa sets as a standard for the highest level of human knowledge.

Reflective versus Animal Knowledge

Sosa distinguishes two kinds of knowledge: "animal" knowledge and "reflective" knowledge ("Intellectual Virtue in Perspective," "Reflective Knowledge in the Best Circles," "Beyond Internal Foundations to External Virtues"). Animal knowledge only requires that one track reality, whereas reflective knowledge requires, in addition, "awareness of how one knows" (RK, 427). In other words, animal knowledge is a matter of arriving at true belief by the employment of reliable faculties, whereas reflective knowledge involves, in addition, knowledge that one's faculties are reliable. Reflective knowledge, which Sosa sometimes links to Descartes's *scientia*, requires "relevant knowledge of one's reliability" (RK, 426). At this point it looks as if Sosa might be embracing a wholly externalist epistemology. If the second-order knowledge involved in reflective knowledge is also, like first-level or animal knowledge, a purely reliabilist or "externalist" type of knowledge, then although reflective knowledge is indeed something stronger than animal knowledge, it will not be accepted by internalist epistemologists as the best kind of knowledge of which humans are capable, or the kind of knowledge to which Descartes and other epistemologists aspire. Driven at least in part by this consideration, Sosa builds a strong coherence requirement into his notion of reflective knowledge – and also into his conception of virtue perspectivism. The link between reflective knowledge and coherence is formulated in the following passage: "[R]eflective knowledge, while building on animal knowledge, goes beyond it precisely in the respect of integrating one's beliefs into a more coherent framework. This it does especially through attaining an epistemic perspective within which the object-level of animal beliefs may be seen as reliably based, and thus transmuted into reflective knowledge" (TR, 196). The exact role and rationale for coherence in this theory is one of the main issues I wish to explore.

Before turning to the coherence proposal, let us pursue its motivation a bit further. To keep things simple, let's assume that "S has animal knowledge that p" is analyzed as "S has a reliably formed true belief that p." (Issues about Gettier-proofing and excluding relevant alternatives are set aside.) Then an initial proposal for "S has reflective knowledge that p" would be: "S has a reliably formed true belief that p, and S also has a reliably formed true belief that his belief that p was reliably formed." This clearly incorporates an element of reflection or "perspective-taking"; it requires a perspective "within which the object-level of animal beliefs [is] seen as reliably based." So why wouldn't the proposed analysis capture an adequate conception of reflective knowledge, though it does not specify a coherence component? The answer is, presumably, that if first-order reliabilist-style knowledge is somehow inferior to quintessentially human knowledge, then adding an element of second-order reliabilist-style knowledge (and further such orders) won't cure the problem. We shall still be left with inferior grades of knowledge. It appears, then, that the distinctive component of human knowledge isn't higher-orderness or reflectiveness *per se*. Coherence seems to be brought in to upgrade the general type or style of knowledge in a way that higher-orderness or reflectiveness itself would fail to accomplish. What is it about coherence that secures this upgrading?

Sosa himself raises insightful problems for the thesis that coherence *per se* contributes toward justifiedness. According to an approach to coherence that Sosa endorses, coherence requires an appropriate match between a person's experiential or sensory contents and her beliefs. Other things being equal, it would be incoherent to have a visual experience of a telephone on the wall and at the same time believe that there is no telephone on the wall. Now consider Sosa's discussion (BIF, 137–40) of Monica, who has a visual experience of a hen with 48 speckles (based on Chisholm's treatment of the same problem, in Chisholm, 1942). Although people have the reliable capacity to accurately detect the numerosity of 3 speckles without counting, they have no comparable power for accurate detection of the numerosity of 48 speckles without counting. To use a term of some psychologists, people can "subitize" 3 speckles but not 48. Suppose now that Monica believes, correctly, that her visual experience features 48 speckles; then according to the proposed condition for coherence, her belief is coherent. At least it is coherent relative to her experience, and we may also suppose that it is coherent (or not incoherent) with respect to her other beliefs. Finally suppose that she arrives at her 48-speckles belief neither by subitizing nor by counting; it's just a lucky guess. Then surely it isn't justified. So coherence *per se* does not seem to contribute toward justifiedness.[1]

This point can be elaborated with another example designed to show that coherence *per se* does not contribute toward justifiedness. Suppose Brian arrives at a set of coherent beliefs without detecting, or being aware of, their mutual coherence. For example, he might acquire a thousand beliefs by testimony, each one from a separate source. As it happens, the believed propositions constitute a highly coherent story, on any plausible criterion of coherence. Does the mere unnoticed *fact* of their coherence make a positive contribution toward the justifiedness of Brian's beliefs? It seems not. The several beliefs might each have some degree of justifiedness from their testimonial credentials, but they won't accrue any additional justifiedness from their purely accidental and unnoticed relationship of mutual coherence. At least so it seems to me.[2] Would it help if Brian *believed* in their coherence? It depends on the source of such a belief. If Brian's coherence belief is produced by mere guesswork, then, as in the 48-speckles example, there doesn't seem to be any added increment of justifiedness.

What is necessary for added justifiedness, then, is that the subject must arrive at a belief in his system's coherence by some sort of *reliable process* of coherence detection, presumably some sort of reasoning process. The same diagnosis holds for the 48-speckles example. Justifiedness of the 48-speckles belief would only accrue if the person used a reliable process of determining the number of speckles. In principle, it could be a "subitizing" process; but in fact people's capacity for subitizing doesn't extend to 48 items. Alternatively, a counting process would suffice. But now the moral is apparent. It isn't coherence *per se* – a certain relationship between the contents of one's beliefs and/or perceptual experiences – that contributes toward justification and hence toward "superior" knowledge. The coherence in question must be detected by a reliable process or method. But that seems to suggest that even in the domain of coherence, what really does the epistemic work is reliable processes.

This point is often missed by coherentists, or papered over by dubious moves. For example, BonJour (1985) candidly acknowledges that if a coherentist rests content with *de facto* coherence as the criterion of justifiedness, he may be stuck with a kind of externalism. BonJour writes: "It would be possible, of course, to adopt an externalist version of coherentism. Such a view would hold that the person whose belief is justified need himself have no cognitive access to the fact of coherence, that his belief is justified if it in fact coheres with his system of beliefs, whether or not such coherence is cognitively accessible to him" (1985: 101). As a proper internalist, BonJour rejects this externalist version of coherentism. His solution, however, is to introduce his notorious "doxastic presumption," a mere assumption or posit that every agent has cognitive access to facts of coherence and a stipulation to the effect that a person's metabelief about coherence does not itself need to be justified (1985: 103). If he hadn't helped himself to this dubious doxastic presumption, BonJour might have recognized that the spirit of internalism requires metabeliefs about coherence also to be justified. And what else could plausibly confer justificational status on such metabeliefs except their being the product of some causal process that is suitably reliable?

My question for Sosa is why *he* seems to think that an additional ingredient beyond reliability is needed for "superior" knowledge, and why he regards coherence as such an ingredient. After all, he himself seems to appreciate the sorts of difficulties for coherentism described in the preceding paragraphs. So why does he think that *de facto* coherence yields the desired "surplus" value, whereas reliably produced higher-level belief in first-order reliability doesn't yield such an element?

Sosa does offer some answers to this question. He compares reason in general, including coherentist reasoning, with retentive memory, classifying both as "transmission" faculties. Transmission faculties cannot guarantee the truth of their outputs, since that depends on the quality of their inputs as well.[3] However, he writes, "our transmission faculties are valuable . . . , if only because they combine with other faculties to increase vastly the total yield of true beliefs" (RK, 421). This is what he thinks coherence delivers. "How does internal coherence, of little significant epistemic value in itself, become more valuable when combined with external aptness? Coherence-seeking inferential reason, like retentive memory, is of epistemic value when combined with externally apt faculties of perception, because when so combined it, like retentive memory, gives us a more comprehensive grasp of the truth than we would have in its absence" (RK, 421).

The first point to notice is that this rationale for the extra cognitive value of coherence is truth-invoking, and hence just as externalist as reliability. Why would an internalist be happy with this, or prize it above and beyond reliability? To be sure, coherence is a relation among beliefs and experiences, which are themselves internal states. But other reliable cognitive processes equally involve internal states and operations. What puts coherence on to a distinct footing from them, so that it is capable of turning animal knowledge into some kind of superior knowledge whereas they are not so capable?

Return to the cited passage, where Sosa uses the phrase "a more comprehensive grasp of the truth" to identify the extra worth of coherence. What does he mean by this? Does he mean that a *single* truth is grasped more comprehensively? It is not clear what it could mean for a single truth to be grasped more or less comprehensively. What must be meant is that a larger *number* of truths are grasped as a result of coherence (combined with other, externally apt, faculties). This is confirmed by an earlier passage, also cited above, in which Sosa speaks of increasing "the total yield of true beliefs." The capacity to produce a larger number of true beliefs is a cognitive merit distinct from reliability. It is what I have elsewhere called "power" (Goldman 1986, chapter 6). The question is whether the power-increasing capacity of a process contributes to *justifiedness* and hence to superior knowledge. I don't believe that it does.

Consider two types of doxastic-attitude-forming processes, which are otherwise alike except that the first is more cautious than the second. This means that the first withholds judgment in circumstances where the second would generate belief. An example might be two processes that generate doxastic attitudes when given visual experiences. When visual experiences are "hazy" or "indistinct," the first process withholds object classifications whereas the second generates beliefs in certain classifications. Assuming that some of the riskier classifications of the second process are correct, that second process will generate a larger number of true beliefs than the first. But the reliability score of the first will be superior. Now which of these processes is associated with greater justifiedness? The first, clearly. Beliefs generated by this more cautious, and hence more reliable, process will (intuitively) have greater justifiedness, despite the fact that the less cautious counterpart generates a larger number of true beliefs. So I think it would be wrong to credit coherence as supplying an extra ingredient of justifiedness simply because it generates *more* true beliefs.

But perhaps Sosa didn't mean, on balance, to propose this. Maybe he just meant that coherence contributes to *reliability* (when combined with other reliable processes). But reliability-increasing potential is a property that might hold of other cognitive processes as well as coherence. It isn't clear why coherence should be singled out, on this basis, as the unique ingredient required to elevate animal knowledge to the superior status termed "reflective knowledge." Of course, it could be simply stipulated that reflective knowledge is knowledge involving coherence. The question then becomes: what is so great about this knowledge? That question has not been answered, in my view, in a completely satisfactory manner.

Virtue Perspectivism

In many writings during the 1980s and 1990s, as well as in *Knowledge in Perspective*, Sosa has developed a type of epistemology called "virtue perspectivism." Virtue perspectivism has major elements in common with process reliabilism, but Sosa identifies several ways in which it departs from reliabilism and regards these departures as advantages. I am inclined to regard them, at least many of them, as disadvantages.

In *Knowledge in Perspective*, several contrasts are drawn between virtue perspectivism (VP) and process reliabilism. One of these elements – the centrality of coherence – has already been discussed above, but now let us discuss some of the others. The first of these arises from Sosa's frequent preoccupation with Descartes. He apparently wants to preserve the traditional Cartesian cogito, and this leads him to be suspicious of the cognitive-process element in process reliabilism. From the vantage point of the cogito, the problem with cognitive processes is that they take *time*. Here is what Sosa says about what is entailed by, and what is right about, the Cartesian cogito:

> There is a truth-conducive "faculty" through which everyone grasps their own existence at the moment of grasping. Indeed, what Descartes noticed about this faculty is its infallible reliability. But the existence which is grasped at time t must then be [in] existence at that very moment t. Grasp of earlier existence, no matter how near to the present, requires not the infallible cogito faculty, but a fallible faculty of memory. If we are to grant the cogito its due measure of justification, and to explain its exceptional epistemic status, we must allow faculties which operate instantaneously in the sense that the outcome belief is about the very moment of believing, and the conditions C are conditions about what obtains at that very moment. (*KP*, 138)

We might summarize this argument as an instance of *modus ponens*:

> If Descartes's cogito argument is correct, justification does not always arise from temporal processes.
> Descartes's cogito argument is correct.
> Therefore, justification does not always arise from temporal processes.

Sosa accepts this *modus ponens*. But, as commonly remarked, one person's *modus ponens* is another's *modus tollens*. The process reliabilist will respond by rejecting the cogito, at least in the exact form presented by Descartes. The most the cogito can give us, according to this response, is the immediately prior existence of some episode of thinking (and therefore, perhaps, the existence of some thinking thing). This epistemic achievement is obtained by means of introspection, a process that may indeed occupy a bit of time. (Is it therefore a sort of memory, as Sosa suggests? Seeing takes time, but it isn't therefore a form of memory.) I am attracted to this variant of the cogito, which allows us to retain a desirable unity in the theory of justification and to preserve all that is worth preserving in the cogito. It does not retain the "exceptional epistemic status" of the cogito, but that exceptional status is open to question.

Sosa has additional reasons, however, for challenging the causal-process aspect of process reliabilism.

> Both [Nozick's and Goldman's] accounts focus too much on the particular target belief and on its causal or counterfactual relation to the truth of its content. A tracking requirement by itself evidently suffers from a sort of tunnel vision. It focuses too narrowly on the particular target belief and its causal or counterfactual relation to the truth of its content. Just widening our focus will not do, however, if we widen it only far enough to include the process or mechanism that yields the belief involved. We need an even broader view. Virtue perspectivism (VP) is an apt label for a broader view of what is required of the subject if he is to know through the target belief. The focus, note, is on the subject more generally and on his relevant faculties, rather than being so much on the particular belief and its causal or counterfactual relations to the truth of its content, or on the process or mechanism from which it derives on that occasion. (VE, 89)

The first point Sosa makes in this passage, against the "tunnel vision" of the tracking account, does not really apply to my form of process reliabilism. My most recent and complete account of knowledge (in the strong sense) appeared in *Epistemology and Cognition* (Goldman 1986, chapter 3). That account featured two elements, called "local reliability" and "global reliability." "Local reliability" does indeed focus on the particular target belief, and invokes a counterfactual relation between that belief and the truth of its content. My preferred version of local reliability was a "no relevant alternatives" version rather than a pure subjunctive, or tracking, version (Goldman 1986: 46), but that is irrelevant for the present point. The crucial point is that I also included an additional condition for knowledge, the global reliability condition, which goes beyond the counterfactual properties of the causal process as applied to the *particular target belief*. Global reliability requires the generic reliability of the causal process, i.e., its reliability across the entire domain to which the process applies. So the joint requirement of both local and global reliability cannot be accused of "tunnel vision."

These remarks are a defense of my own view, but now let us return to Sosa's. In contrast to the cognitive-process approach to reliabilism, Sosa's VP requires the subject to be reliable over a field of propositions encompassing the content of the target belief, and also requires the subject to be reliable over a range of conditions encompassing the conditions prevailing with regard to the target belief. (See "Intellectual Virtue in Perspective," chapter 16 of *KP*) What VP does not require is anything about the *causal process* responsible for the target belief. Is this an improvement over process reliabilism?

There is, it seems to me, a major problem with VP so formulated. A given belief can fall within the scope of a field of propositions and a range of conditions over which the subject is quite reliable, and yet the target belief token might not be justified because it is caused by a process that is not normally used for any (or many) of the other propositions and conditions in the field. In other words, the subject might have an intellectual virtue (*à la* Sosa) with respect to field F and conditions C, because he would normally use a certain process or mechanism for <F, C> that would usually generate a truth. But on this occasion perhaps he uses an entirely different process, one that does not confer justification (because it is not reliable). Here is a schematic example to illustrate this problem.

Normally, if I wonder whether I feel very tired, I will use introspection to tell how I am feeling, and introspection is very reliable on such questions. For the same reason, there is a wide range of similar propositions in the "I am feeling X" field, and a wide range of conditions, over which I am reliable. Thus, there is a field F of propositions to which the proposition "I am now very tired" belongs, and there is a set of conditions C to which my present condition belongs, such that I am generally reliable with respect to <F, C>. So according to VP, I should now be justified in believing this proposition. However, I might form a belief in this proposition without using introspection. I might instead use theoretical reasoning from other premises. For example, I might say to myself, "I seem to recall sleeping very fitfully last night, and usually when I sleep fitfully, I am very tired the next morning. This is the next morning. So I must be very tired right now." In this case, the theoretical reasoning doesn't look so bad; it might yield a justified belief. But if we slightly permute the case, we can easily produce an example where the theoretically inferred belief is unjustified. Yet, given the VP theory, it seems to follow that the belief should be justified, because the proposition believed belongs to an appropriate field and I am in an appropriate condition so that I qualify as having a pertinent intellectual virtue that "covers" the belief in question.

Perhaps I have not done full justice to Sosa's discussion of VP, at least his exposition of VP in earlier writings. Don't these earlier writings make reference to the "inner nature" of an intellectual virtue, an inner nature that might be relevant in handling the sort of case discussed above? Let us look carefully at Sosa's use of the "inner nature" element, to see whether it can save the VP approach from the preceding objection.

In *Knowledge in Perspective*, Sosa gives the following definition of what it is to possess an intellectual virtue:

> S has an intellectual virtue V(C, F) relative to environment E if and only if S has an inner nature I such that if (i) S is in E and has I, (ii) P is a proposition in field F, and (iii) S is in condition C with respect to P, then (iv) S is very likely to believe correctly with respect to P. (*KP*, 286)

He then proceeds to offer the following definition of what it is to *believe* out of intellectual virtue:

> S believes out of intellectual virtue V(C, F) if and only if:
>
> (a) S is in an intellectual environment E such that S has intellectual virtue V(C, F) relative to E,
> (b) P is a proposition in F,
> (c) S is in C with respect to P, and
> (d) S believes P. (*KP*, 287)

Notice that the definition of believing out of an intellectual virtue makes no reference to an inner nature that causes the belief. So long as an intellectual virtue is possessed, the believed proposition P is in the field of the virtue, the agent is in conditions or circumstances appropriate with respect to P, and the agent believes P, then the definition implies that the agent believes P *out of* the virtue. But this seems to imply that the inner nature that would *normally* be used to achieve an accurate belief in the right circumstances does not have to be used in order to qualify as believing "out of" the virtue.

Bearing these points in mind, return to my sketched counterexample. Let introspection be an inner nature (or capacity), let an appropriate range of first-person experiential propositions be the field F of a virtue, and let some specific conditions and environment (I don't know which would be relevant here) be conditions C and E respectively. Then it looks as if any normal human agent will possess an intellectual virtue with respect to the specified field F (of first-person experiential propositions). Furthermore, let us see if the sketched counterexample satisfies the definition of believing "out of" an intellectual virtue. It looks as if it does satisfy that definition, even when the agent uses bad theoretical inference rather than introspection to form a belief in "I am now very tired." The reason for this is that Sosa's definition of believing "out of" intellectual virtue makes no reference to the inner nature normally responsible for accurate belief formation in the experiential field. So it looks as if the agent who believes from bad theoretical reasoning will still earn credit for believing out of intellectual virtue. This presumably implies that his belief is justified. But the case is intuitively one in which the belief is not justified. That is a problem for the theory.

Suppose Sosa amends his definitions so as to include the requirement that the subject must believe out of the same inner nature that is responsible for possession of the intellectual virtue. Wouldn't this simple amendment avert the problem I have posed? It would only avert the problem, I submit, if "out of" is interpreted causally; in other words, only if the inner nature is construed as some sort of cognitive mechanism, and believing "out of" that inner nature is interpreted as believing as a *causal result* of the operation of that cognitive mechanism. But then Sosa's account would handle the problematic case only by being transformed into a version of causal reliabilism, which is precisely what he was trying to distance himself from!

One final mark of superiority that Sosa advances for his VP approach is the stability of intellectual virtues as contrasted with the possible fleetingness or accidentality of cognitive processes. This is how Sosa puts the point:

> [A]s far as Goldman's theory goes, there is no requirement of stable virtue or "intellectual character." One's cognitive life could be a kaleidoscope of functional operations from moment to moment.... [A] functional operation may never operate at any other time in the life of that subject.... Such fleeting "functional operations" could hardly count as stable virtues in the intellectual character of the subject, but they would seem to qualify as truth conducive cognitive processes that for process reliabilism would yield justification and knowledge – even if it is just luck that from moment to moment the same input–output mappings stay in place, because equally effective generating functional operations give way one to the next by a long and unbroken string of accidents. (VE, 84)

Does this (alleged) difference between process reliabilism and VP constitute a strong point in favor of the latter?

A first point to notice is that the requirement of stability could be easily added to the framework of process reliabilism. We could simply stipulate that a process (type) must be in the standard repertoire of an agent over a period of time, and that it must be reliable over that time period, in order to qualify as a generator of justification and knowledge. For similar reasons, one might add a requirement to the effect that a justification-conferring process must be one that has an appropriate evolutionary or learning-theoretic history.[4] This too would have the effect of blocking the threat of "kaleidoscopic" fluctuations in the repertoire of reliable processes.

Some of this was already anticipated in *Epistemology and Cognition* (Goldman 1986), where I proposed that reliable "methods" can only confer justifiedness if they are acquired in a meta-reliable fashion (1986: 52–3). This feature of reliabilism already constitutes an answer to the worry about its tolerating excessive accidentality. It is also true, however, that too stringent an insistence on stability may be misplaced. The acquisition of reliable methods, for example, can sometimes be accomplished quite quickly. Some people can learn a new mathematical algorithm in a flash, and immediately be capable of applying it accurately to a wide range of questions. Such a newly acquired method should surely endow a cognizer with a new intellectual virtue – the method, after all, can yield lots of knowledge – despite the rapidity of the acquisition. Moreover, one can imagine a newly acquired virtue being lost very quickly and accidentally, through a sudden stroke, for example. Such an unfortunate episode would not cast doubt on the knowledge that was spawned by the method while it was still in the cognitive grasp of the subject. So Sosa's insistence on stability threatens to be excessive, if carried too far. A moderate insistence on stability, however, seems well within the reach of process reliabilism.

On the whole, then, I am not persuaded that VP constitutes a superior approach as compared with process reliabilism.[5] Nonetheless, it remains a very attractive and carefully developed approach, which is perhaps my second-most preferred brand of epistemological theory.

Notes

1 Sosa's adduces the 48-speckles example in connection with classical foundationalism, but I think it easily transfers to coherentism as well.
2 And Sosa himself agrees, since he makes this point himself (in VE, 15), though without any elaborate example.
3 In this same connection (Goldman 1979), I have indicated that what one can reasonably seek from reasoning, like from retentive memory, is that it be "conditionally reliable," i.e., that it produce true beliefs as outputs when given true beliefs as inputs.
4 See Goldman (1975) for an early attempt to work evolution or innateness into the epistemological picture.
5 However, it is only my most recent version of process reliabilism, "two-stage reliabilism" (Goldman 1992, 1999), that I am now inclined to endorse. Sosa offers criticisms of this theory, but this is not the place to reply to those criticisms at length.

References

BonJour, Laurence, 1985. *The Structure of Empirical Knowledge* (Cambridge, MA: Harvard University Press).

Chisholm, Roderick, 1942. "The Problem of the Speckled Hen," *Mind* (n.s.) 51: 368–73.

Goldman, Alvin, 1975. "Innate Knowledge." In Stephen Stich, ed., *Innate Ideas* (Berkeley, CA: University of California Press).

Goldman, Alvin, 1979. "What Is Justified Belief?" In George Pappas, ed., *Justification and Knowledge* (Dordrecht: Reidel).

Goldman, Alvin, 1986. *Epistemology and Cognition* (Cambridge, MA: Harvard University Press).

Goldman, Alvin, 1992. "Epistemic Folkways and Scientific Epistemology." In *Liaisons: Philosophy Meets the Cognitive and Social Sciences* (Cambridge, MA: MIT Press).

Goldman, Alvin, 1999. "*A Priori* Warrant and Naturalistic Epistemology." In James Tomberlin, ed., *Philosophical Perspectives*, vol. 13 (Malden, MA: Blackwell).

Sosa, Ernest, 1991. *Knowledge in Perspective: Selected Essays in Epistemology* (Cambridge: Cambridge University Press). (Cited as *KP*.)

Sosa, Ernest, "Intellectual Virtue in Perspective." In *KP*.

Sosa, Ernest, 1997. "Reflective Knowledge in the Best Circles," *The Journal of Philosophy* 94, 8: 410–30. (Cited as RK.)

Sosa, Ernest, 2000. "Thomas Reid" (co-authored with James Van Cleve). In Steven Emmanuel, ed., *The Modern Philosophers: From Descartes to Nietzsche* (Oxford: Blackwell). (Cited as TR.)

Sosa, Ernest, 2003. "Beyond Internal Foundations to External Virtues." In Laurence BonJour and Ernest Sosa, *Epistemic Justification: Internalism vs. Externalism, Foundations vs. Virtues* (Malden, MA: Blackwell). (Cited as BIF.)

Sosa, Ernest, *Virtue Epistemology*. Draft manuscript. (Cited as VE.)

8

How to Preserve Your Virtue while Losing Your Perspective

JOHN GRECO

Ernest Sosa's "virtue perspectivism" involves two central ideas. The first is that knowledge is grounded in the intellectual virtues of the knower, where an intellectual virtue is defined as a stable disposition to arrive at truth and avoid falsehood in a relevant field, when in relevant circumstances. The second is that reflective knowledge requires also a perspective on one's truth-conducive dispositions: "For the exercise of virtue to yield knowledge, one must have some awareness of one's belief and its source, and of the virtue of that source both in general and in the specific instance."[1]

In this regard Sosa maintains a distinction between "animal knowledge" and "reflective knowledge":

> One has *animal knowledge* about one's environment, one's past, and one's own experience if one's judgements and beliefs about these are direct responses to their impact – e.g., through perception or memory – with little or no benefit of reflection or understanding.

> One has *reflective knowledge* if one's judgment or belief manifests not only such direct response to the fact known but also understanding of its place in a wider whole that includes one's belief and knowledge of it and how these come about. (*KP*, 240)

There is a tension in Sosa's thought regarding the above distinction, however. In some places Sosa maintains that animal knowledge is true knowledge, while reflective knowledge is a still higher, more rare achievement. For example, in one place Sosa writes:

> This is not to deny that there is a kind of "knowledge," properly so called, that falls short in respect of broad coherence – "animal knowledge," as we might call it. It is rather only to affirm that beyond "animal knowledge" we humans, especially those of us who are philosophical or at least reflective, aspire to a higher knowledge.[2]

In the same spirit, Sosa compares his distinction between animal and reflective knowledge to Descartes's distinction between unreflective *cognitio* and reflective *scientia*, where the latter results only from Descartes's hard philosophical work.[3]

Sosa's more common position, however, is that animal knowledge falls short of properly human knowledge. Hence he calls it "mere animal" knowledge, and even suggests that the label is only "metaphorical" (*KP*, 274–5). Here is a passage illustrating this view of the distinction.

> How then can one rule out its turning out that just *any* true belief of one's own is automatically justified? To my mind the key is the requirement that the field F and the circumstances C must be accessible within one's epistemic perspective. (Note that this requires considering servomechanic and animal so-called "knowledge" a lesser grade of knowledge, or perhaps viewing the attribution of "knowledge" to such beings as metaphorical, unless we are willing to admit them as beings endowed with their own epistemic perspectives). (*KP*, 274–5)

Thus we can find in Sosa's writing two positions regarding the animal knowledge/reflective knowledge distinction:

(a) Most human knowledge is non-reflective or "animal" knowledge. But humans are capable of reflective knowledge, which is a special and relatively rare achievement.
(b) Human knowledge is reflective knowledge. Non-reflective knowledge falls short of properly human knowledge, although we may speak of animal "knowledge" in an extended sense of the term.

It seems clear that Sosa's considered position is the second. First, the passages that reflect the position in (b) are far more numerous than those that reflect the position in (a). More telling, however, are Sosa's motivations for adopting the distinction in the first place. His two most important motivations for doing so are to address two problems for generic reliabilism: the generality problem and the meta-incoherence problem. I will say more about these two problems below, but for now the important point is this: both show that something must be added to the conditions that generic reliabilism lays down for knowledge. In response to these objections, the force of which Sosa acknowledges, he adds the requirement of an epistemic perspective. But then having such a perspective must be viewed as a *general* condition on knowledge. That is, it will not help to solve the generality problem or the meta-incoherence problem to say that *sometimes* humans have such a perspective when they have knowledge properly so called. On the contrary, Sosa's strategy for solving the two problems requires him to say that human knowledge is reflective knowledge; i.e., that an epistemic perspective is always required for human knowledge.

Once Sosa's position is interpreted this way, however, an obvious question presents itself. How plausible is it that we humans actually have the required perspective on our beliefs and our faculties, whenever we have human knowledge properly so called? On the face of things, it seems not at all plausible. It seems that, in typical cases of knowledge, people do not have *any* beliefs about their beliefs, or beliefs about the sources of their beliefs, or beliefs about the reliability of those sources. Let us call this the "Psychological Plausibility Objection" to virtue perspectivism. Two strategies suggest themselves for addressing this objection, and Sosa adopts both of them. First, he stresses that one's perspective need only be very general: "For ordinary knowledge one needs only a very sketchy and general perspective on one's own beliefs and their derivation."[4] Second, he stresses that one's perspective need only be implicit: "We need to distinguish first between fully conscious and subconscious belief; also, secondly, between what is and what is not verbalizable or symbolizable by the believer ... and, finally, also between belief that is manifested through acts of episodic acceptance of a proposition somehow present to one's mind, even if not symbolically present, from belief that is manifested only in other ways." (VP, 47)

In the remainder of this chapter I will argue that these strategies cannot help Sosa to overcome the Psychological Plausibility Objection. First, to address the generality problem and the meta-incoherence problem, Sosa must require that one's epistemic perspective is highly detailed rather than "sketchy and general." Second, once we are clear about the level of detail required, it becomes highly implausible that humans have even an implicit perspective (in the required detail) on their beliefs and the sources of their beliefs. I end by suggesting that the requirement of an epistemic perspective is not needed anyway. Rather, Sosa's virtue reliabilism has resources for addressing the generality problem and the meta-incoherence problem without invoking the idea of an epistemic perspective.

1   The Generality Problem and the Meta-incoherence Problem

Consider first the generality problem for generic reliabilism (GR). According to generic reliabilism,

(GR) S knows that p only if
(1) p is true, and
(2) S's belief that p results from a sufficiently reliable process.

The problem is that any process token is an instance of several process types, and it is not clear which process type is relevant for evaluating reliability in the context of GR. Consider that for any true belief B(p), we can describe both (a) a process type that gave rise to B(p) and that is perfectly reliable, and (b) a process type that gave rise to B(p) and that is unreliable. Clearly GR needs to say more about which process types are relevant for knowledge.

As Sosa recognizes, a version of the generality problem arises for reliabilist theories that invoke the notion of an intellectual virtue or faculty. Sosa writes:

> One has a faculty only if there is a field F and there is a set of circumstances C such that one *would* distinguish the true from the false in F in C. But of course whenever one *happens* to have a true belief B, that belief will manifest *many* such competences, for many field/circumstance pairs F/C will apply. How then can one rule out its turning out that just *any* true belief of one's own is automatically justified? (*KP*, 274)

Sosa's answer invokes the idea of an epistemic perspective: "To my mind the key is the requirement that the field F and the circumstances C must be accessible within one's epistemic perspective."[5] But of course specifying F and C too finely is only one half of the generality problem – one must not specify them too generally either.

> Such restrictions must heed a twofold objective: (a) that F and C not be made so specific that one is always perfectly reliable and justified whenever one's belief is true; but also (b) that they not be made so generic that one cannot explain how a subject could have two beliefs both derived from the given faculty (e.g., from his sight, or, more generally yet, from his sensory perception), though one is justified while the other is not. (*KP*, 284)

It is this second consideration that gives rise to the Psychological Plausibility Objection. Given the role that Sosa assigns to an epistemic perspective in solving the generality problem, it cannot be that such a perspective is "sketchy and general." On the contrary, a perspective must be specific enough to pick out dispositions that are sufficiently reliable to ground knowledge.

Next consider the meta-incoherence problem. Here is how Sosa describes it.

> In the first place, there is the possibility of reliable mechanisms for noninferential acquisition of belief other than introspection, memory, and (ordinary) perception. Clairvoyance, for instance, would be one such mechanism. If magic or surgery suddenly gives one such a gift, however, one finds oneself predicting things "out of the blue," with too little discernable connection to the rest of one's beliefs. Such a prediction might turn out to be right, of course: and not just by luck, either, since by hypothesis it derives from the operation of a reliable faculty. But I could not easily think it epistemically justified simply on that account. For anyone similarly minded, this raises a doubt as to the adequacy of mere reliability to induce justification.[6]

Once again, Sosa's solution is to invoke the idea of a perspective on one's beliefs and their sources.

> The problem of clairvoyance relative to a normal human today is, I think, its failure to meet the challenge of doxastic ascent. If a normal human today were suddenly to receive the gift of clairvoyance he would be helpless to explain the source of beliefs delivered by his new gift and how that source operates. There is much that we know at least implicitly about memory and its mode and conditions of reliable operation. And it is largely this that enables discrimination in favor of memory and against suddenly endowed clairvoyance. (*KP*, 94–5)

The general idea is that an appropriate perspective on one's belief and its source affords one a kind of internal justification that the clairvoyant lacks: specifically, one is allowed to see one's belief as reliably produced, and so not just "out of the blue."

It might appear that the Psychological Plausibility Objection is less threatening here than it is regarding the generality problem, since one might easily attribute one's belief to memory or perception, and this seems enough to distinguish it from that of the suddenly endowed clairvoyant. But this appearance is deceptive, owing to an ambiguity in the notions of memory and perception. One thing we might mean by memory and perception is *reliable* memory and *reliable* perception. But this meaning is not relevant in the present context, since it would be empty and unhelpful to have, as part of one's perspective, that one's reliable memory is reliable. For the notion of memory to do any work in the present context, it must be defined independently of reliability, so that one might helpfully think that one's belief B has its source in memory, and that one's memory is reliable in present circumstances. But now we are back to the second half of the generality problem. That is, we are back to the problem of characterizing a relevant disposition, with relevant specificity, so as to pick out a disposition that is sufficiently reliable to generate knowledge. One needs exactly the level of specificity to solve the meta-incoherence problem as is needed to solve the generality problem.

2 The Psychological Plausibility Objection Renewed

How plausible is it that human knowledge always involves a detailed perspective, i.e., a perspective detailed enough to pick out dispositions sufficiently reliable to generate knowledge? Remember, this amounts to the claim that every time S knows p, S also believes truly (1) that S believes p, (2) that p is in some field F, (3) that S is in some set of circumstances C, and (4) that S's belief B(p) results from a highly reliable disposition D(F/C). Again, it would seem that this is not plausible at all. On the face of things, in the typical case, people seem not to have beliefs about their beliefs, nor beliefs about the sources of their beliefs. The claim that they do is more plausible, of course, if we allow the second-order beliefs to be very general. It is (perhaps) not completely implausible, for example, that whenever one has perceptual knowledge, one has an implicit belief that one's knowledge derives from perception. But as we have seen above, this kind of very general belief will not do the work that Sosa needs it to do regarding the generality problem or the meta-incoherence problem. For that we need something much more specific, and now it becomes highly implausible that one has beliefs with the right level of specificity, even implicitly.

Or at least this is what I will argue below. Before getting to that, however, it is necessary to consider a suggestion that would help Sosa to answer the present concern. In reply to a related objection, Sosa has suggested that we might treat our cognitive dispositions as if they were highly implicit beliefs. For example, given S's disposition to form a belief B(p) in response to experience E, we might attribute to S the belief that E is a reliable indication that p is true.

> [T]he habit of moving from "looks round" to "is round" is strictly correct if, in the relevant circumstances, anything that looked round would in fact be round.... [T]here is some motivation to view such habits as implicit beliefs (that can be correct and justified) in the corresponding conditionals, as suggested above. (VP, 42–3)

The present suggestion would allow that we have the required beliefs about our reliable dispositions, since it simply identifies such dispositions with beliefs affirming their reliability. However, there are good reasons not to collapse the distinction between (a) implicit beliefs and (b) habits or dispositions for forming beliefs. One reason is that often there are such dispositions where there are no such beliefs. For example, simple pattern recognition in perception involves highly complex dispositions to go from perceptual cues to beliefs about external stimuli.[7] But it is implausible to attribute *beliefs* about such perceptual cues, and about their connections to external stimuli, to perceivers. That is, it is implausible to attribute such beliefs even to the most sophisticated adult perceivers, not to mention small children and animals. But all perceivers, small children and animals included, have the relevant dispositions to form perceptual beliefs.

Moreover, there is a second reason for Sosa to insist on the distinction between implicit beliefs and dispositions for forming beliefs. For without it, his distinction between animal knowledge and reflective knowledge collapses. Recall that even animal knowledge requires a source in reliable cognitive dispositions. If we say that simply having such dispositions is sufficient for having an epistemic perspective, then there will be no difference between animal and reflective knowledge.

Let us return, then, to what seems to be Sosa's considered position: that an epistemic perspective is constituted by one's second-order beliefs regarding one's first-order beliefs and their sources. And let us remember that the second-order beliefs in question must not specify one's sources in a sketchy or general way, but rather in a way that picks out sources that are sufficiently reliable to generate knowledge. The Psychological Plausibility Objection now amounts to this: It seems implausible that such second-order beliefs exist in typical cases of human knowledge, even subconsciously, and even in ways that are not verbalizable by the knower.

It is hard to see how one could have good evidence *in favor* of such beliefs if, as Sosa suggests, they are not "manifested through acts of episodic acceptance of a proposition somehow present to one's mind," but are rather "manifested only in other ways," such as in one's patterns of inference. For in that case, it will always be simpler to attribute only a disposition to make the relevant inferences, rather than a perspective on one's inferential dispositions.

More importantly, there is good evidence *against* our having the required epistemic perspective in the typical case. Let us say that one has an epistemic perspective on cognitive disposition D(F/C) only if either (a) one has an occurrent representation of D(F/C) (either consciously or subconsciously), or (b) one has a disposition to have an occurrent representation of D(F/C) (either consciously or subconsciously), where D(F/C) picks out a disposition that is sufficiently reliable to generate knowledge. There is good evidence that the reliability of our cognitive dispositions is a function of factors that are not represented at all in the typical case, either occurrently or dispositionally.[8] And if that is so, then one will not have the required perspective on such faculties in the typical case.

First, consider our perceptual faculties, which take us from various kinds of inputs to beliefs about external stimuli. The problem here is that not all of the inputs relevant to reliability are represented by the perceiver, either occurrently or dispositionally. Occurrently, we do not typically have any beliefs at all about inputs – one forms only beliefs about the objects perceived. But what is important for present purposes is that we may lack even a *disposition* to form representations of relevant inputs as well. For many of those inputs go unnoticed by the perceiver, and therefore are not available for occurrent representation at a different time. A particularly drastic illustration of this occurs in the phenomenon of blindsight. There are now several documented cases of people who are blind in some part of their visual field, but who can nevertheless discriminate size, shape, location, and/or orientation of objects in the blind part of the field. Since damage in blindsighted subjects is to the visual cortex rather than to the eyes themselves, it is hypothesized that information from the eye still reaches the brain, although bypassing the mechanisms normally responsible for conscious visual experience.[9] Of course blindsight is relatively rare, and not very reliable in known cases. Nevertheless, it is a dramatic illustration of how factors that are not represented or even available for representation by the subject can affect the reliability of our cognitive dispositions.

What makes the example of blindsight dramatic is that, at least in some cases, it seems to operate entirely on inputs that are not conscious at all. But it is now thought that less dramatic forms of non-conscious acquisition of information are common in normal human cognition. In what sense is such information acquisition "non-conscious"? Sometimes what is meant is that important initial inputs go unnoticed, perhaps because exposure time is below the threshold needed for conscious detection. At other times new information is acquired via non-conscious cognitive processing, as when a perceptual system uses algorithms and heuristics that are too complicated to be used in conscious inferences. In either case, the cognitive dispositions involved are not available for representation by the subject, either occurrently or dispositionally, because essential elements of them are not so available.[10]

Again, such inaccessibility is thought to be a pervasive aspect of human cognition, involving both our non-inferential and inferential faculties. Lewicki, Hill, and Czyzewska write,

> this lack of access to the nature of these processes (which are essentially responsible for most of what we see, experience, and feel) is not limited to the so-called low-level processes that support only the consciously controlled cognition (e.g., pattern recognition). People have no access to processes as high-level as those involved in playing chess, feeling love, forming impressions of people, or problem solving and creative thinking.[11]

I have been arguing that the reliability of our cognitive faculties is partly a function of factors that are not available for representation by the subject, either occurrently or dispositionally. That characterization of human cognition requires only the following assumption: that our cognitive functioning is importantly sensitive to information about the world without needing to represent that information, and without needing to have it available for representation. Given the available empirical evidence, it is not implausible that this assumption is true. Notice, however, that Sosa's requirement of an epistemic perspective is undermined so long as the assumption is possibly true. This is because Sosa's requirement of an epistemic perspective is a philosophical claim about the conditions for human knowledge, and so carries necessity. The above argument can therefore proceed as follows, where VP stands for virtue perspectivism, K for the proposition that some person S has human knowledge, and EP for the proposition that S has a relevant epistemic perspective.

(1) $VP \Rightarrow Nec\ (K \rightarrow EP)$
(2) $Poss\ (K\ \&\ not\text{-}EP)$

Therefore,

(3) Not-VP

Sosa might be inclined to deny premise (2), and to hold that if cognitive psychology is right about the nature of our cognition, then there is little or no human knowledge properly so called. But such wholesale downgrading of our cognitive achievements would be neither necessary nor warranted. On the contrary, it would be more reasonable to conclude that human knowledge does not require an epistemic perspective.

3 Preserving Virtue while Losing Perspective

At the beginning of this chapter I suggested that virtue perspectivism involves two central ideas: that knowledge is grounded in the reliable dispositions of the knower, and that reflective knowledge requires a perspective on those reliable dispositions. I then argued that the requirement of an epistemic perspective is psychologically implausible, given the way that such a perspective must be characterized to effectively address the generality problem and the meta-incoherence problem. In this final section I will argue that the requirement is not needed anyway, since Sosa's virtue reliabilism has resources for solving both problems without invoking the idea of an epistemic perspective.

As Sosa notes, the meta-incoherence problem is a problem about internal justification. But there are ways of defining internal justification within a virtue theory, and without invoking the idea of a perspective. In fact, Sosa gives us an important one of these. Consider the victim of Descartes's evil demon, whose beliefs seem to be justified in all respects, internally speaking. Sosa argues that we may define a relevant sense of internal justification by noting that there are two ways that a belief can fail by way of reliability. One way is that something goes wrong "from the skin inward." For example, the subject might fail to respond appropriately to her sensory experience, or might fail to reason appropriately from her beliefs. Another way to go wrong, however, is "from the skin outward." Perhaps there is no flaw to be found downstream from experience and belief, but one's cognitive faculties are simply not fitted for one's environment. It is only in this second way that the demon victim fails: internally speaking, she is in as good working order as we are.

But then there is a straightforward sense in which even the victim's beliefs are internally justified, Sosa argues. Namely, they are beliefs that result from intellectual virtues. We need only add that whether a cognitive faculty counts as a virtue is relative to an environment. The victim's perception and reasoning faculties are not reliable in her demon environment, and hence are not virtues relative to her world. But those same faculties are reliable, and therefore do count as virtues, relative to the actual world. Accordingly, we have a sense in which the demon victim's beliefs are internally justified although not reliably formed.

It is plausible that the meta-incoherence problem raises the issue of subjective justification as well as that of internal justification, where subjective justification pertains to how things are from the believer's point of view. Even if there is typically no perspective on one's reliable dispositions, the fact that a person interprets experience one way rather than another, or draws one inference rather than another, suggests an awareness of sorts of the reliability of one's evidential grounds. Or at least this is so if the person is trying to form her beliefs accurately in the first place – if the person is in the normal mode of trying to believe what is true, as opposed to what is convenient, or comforting, or politically correct. We may use these considerations to define a relevant sense of subjective justification: A belief is subjectively justified just in case it is produced by cognitive dispositions that the believer manifests when motivated to believe what is true. In cases of knowledge such dispositions will also be virtues, since they will be objectively reliable in addition to being well motivated. But even in cases where the believer is not reliable, she may nevertheless have justified beliefs in this sense, since her believing may nevertheless manifest well-motivated dispositions.

Is the belief of the newly endowed clairvoyant internally and subjectively justified, in the above-defined senses? Only if it manifests reliable and properly motivated dispositions, including dispositions to recognize and respond to relevant counter-evidence. But what if it does? Then such a clairvoyant is a far cry from cognitive agents like us, and I find it less plausible that she lacks justification or knowledge. It would be odd, in fact, to think that only cognitive faculties like our own can generate justification and knowledge. And, of course, Sosa does not think this.

The generality problem is more difficult, and I can only point to a strategy that seems promising for solving it. Once again, my claim is that Sosa has resources for addressing the problem within his own virtue theory, and without invoking the requirement of an epistemic perspective. When discussing the generality problem, Sosa often suggests that our cognitive faculties are natural kinds: "Just how fields are to be defined is determined by the lay of interesting, illuminating generalizations about human cognition, which psychology and cognitive science are supposed in time to uncover" (*KP*, 236). Sosa also stresses the social importance of our epistemic concepts and practices. For example, he writes:

> We care about justification because it tends to indicate a state of the subject that is important and of interest to his community, a state of great interest and importance to an information-sharing social species. What sort of state? Presumably, the state of being a dependable source of information over a certain field in certain circumstances. In order for this information to be obtainable and to be of later use, however, the sort of field F and the sort of circumstances C must be projectible, and must have some minimal objective likelihood of being repeated in the careers of normal members of the epistemic community. (*KP*, 281–2)

These passages contain two central ideas: (a) that our faculties are and/or involve natural, projectible kinds, and (b) that because of this they serve certain of our purposes as information-sharing beings. He then goes on to invoke a third idea: that of an epistemic perspective.

> For it is through our cognizance of such relevant F and C that we grasp the relevant faculties whose possession by us and others makes us dependable informants and cognizers. What is more, it is precisely by grasping how one does oneself have such animal aptitude over a certain field F in certain circumstances C that one bootstraps up to a higher-level of reflective justification. (*KP*, 282)

Why not keep the first two ideas while dropping the third? In other words, we can say that a disposition D(F/C) is relevant for knowledge just in case it involves an F and a C that are both (a) natural and projectible, and (b) have some minimal objective likelihood of being repeated in the careers of normal members of the epistemic community. Of course such F and C must also be defined narrowly enough so as to make D(F/C) highly reliable. Which Fs and Cs these turn out to be will depend on the psychological and sociological facts about knowledge production and knowledge sharing. But it will not depend on the relevant Fs and Cs being represented by anyone.[12]

Notes

1 "Intellectual Virtue in Perspective," in *Knowledge in Perspective: Selected Essays in Epistemology* (Cambridge: Cambridge University Press, 1991) (cited as *KP*), p. 292.
2 "Perspectives in Virtue Epistemology: A Response to Dancy and BonJour," *Philosophical Studies* 78 (1995): 233. Reprinted in *Knowledge, Belief and Character*, ed. Guy Axtell (Lanham, MD: Rowman and Littlefield, 2000).
3 For example, see "How to Resolve the Pyrrhonian Problematic: A Lesson from Descartes," *Philosophical Studies* 85 (1997); and "Post-script to 'Proper Functionalism and Virtue Epistemology'," in Jonathan Kvanvig, ed., *Warrant in Contemporary Epistemology* (Lanham, MD: Rowman and Littlefield, 1996).
4 "Virtue Perspectivism: A Response to Foley and Fumerton," *Philosophical Issues* 5 (1994) (cited as VP): 41. See also *KP*, 278.
5 *KP*, 274. Later in the same paper Sosa suggests that the relevant F and C are those appropriately usable by the knowledge attributer rather than the knower herself. Of course, the two are the same in cases where one attributes knowledge to oneself. See pp. 282 and 290. The objections I raise below are not affected by the choice between these two options.
6 "Nature Unmirrored, Epistemology Naturalized," *Synthese* 55: 49–72. Reprinted in *KP*, 94. See also "Reliabilism and Intellectual Virtue," *KP*, 132.
7 See, for example, J. Hochberg, *Perception* (Englewood Cliffs, NJ: Prentice Hall, 1978).
8 That is, such factors are not represented by the subject. According to some current theories in cognitive psychology, many states not represented by the subject are represented in a sub-personal way, for example in sub-personal mechanisms operative in perception. Of course, it is representation at the personal level that is at issue regarding Sosa's claims about an epistemic perspective. This qualification is intended in what follows below.
9 See L. Weiskrants, *Blindsight: A Case Study and Implications* (Oxford: Clarendon Press, 1986).
10 For an informative review of relevant literature, see Paul Lewicki, Thomas Hill, and Maria Czyzewska, "Nonconscious Acquisition of Information," *American Psychologist* 47, 6 (1992): 796–801.
11 Ibid.
12 I would like to thank Hilary Kornblith for his helpful comments on an earlier draft.

9

Sosa on Circularity and Coherence

ALLEN HABIB AND KEITH LEHRER

The exceptional contributions of Ernest Sosa to epistemology make it an honor to discuss his work. Sosa, while appreciating the role of coherence in a theory of knowledge, especially reflective knowledge, has contended that coherence among beliefs, however important a role it might play in knowledge and a theory thereof, will not suffice for knowledge, even if the cohering beliefs turn out to be true. He has argued that coherence must be supplemented with his illuminating theory of virtue perspectivism. While appreciating the merits of the proposed supplement, we wish to examine the possibility that coherence among beliefs which are true might embrace those merits and suffice for a theory of justification and reflective knowledge.

The crux of our argument is that beliefs about the relationship between internal representational states, most notably beliefs, and external conditions, most notably the truth of the beliefs, will be essential to any coherence theory that might suffice as a theory of knowledge. Examples of such beliefs are ones to the effect that the cohering beliefs are reliably connected with truth. Such beliefs about the reliability of the cohering beliefs ensure a truth connection and gain the advantages of externalism when those beliefs are true. The circularity of such an argument is transparent.

Sosa has recognized the inevitability of circularity in a full or complete theory of reflective knowledge, however. Those who, contrary to Sosa, think that circular arguments are vicious, and thus irrelevant, to justification might argue as follows:

> Circular arguments fail to have any justificational weight because they fail to have any dialectical force against a skeptic. A circular argument is of no use in a dialectic with a skeptic; it cannot move a rhetorical opponent, since it appeals to the conclusion that the opponent contests. This failure in a dialectic results in a general failure of circular argument to provide justification at all. If circular arguments completely lack justificational weight, then they cannot serve as a justification. If justification is to be a matter of providing good reasons with dialectical force to support or defend a belief, then circular arguments cannot provide any justification because they cannot provide us with reasons having dialectical force

against a skeptic. If arguments are to be admitted as justifications for beliefs, they must have sufficient dialectical force to refute potential skeptic opponents.

We may reasonably abandon the skeptical dialectic as the primary method of evaluating theories of knowledge and justification, however. If we instead evaluate our theories of knowledge and justification in terms of the explanations they provide, we lose our motive for construing justificational weight as requiring dialectic force and the objection to circularity falls away. To see why, imagine that you form the belief that the cat is on the mat because you see it. You now have an argument for your belief that the cat is on the mat:

> (P1) I see a cat on the mat
> (C): There is a cat on the mat.

But now imagine that you also believe that your eyesight is epistemically reliable. If we add this belief to the argument, we get:

> (P1) I see a cat on the mat
> (P2) My eyesight is reliable
> (C): There is a cat on the mat.

The second argument is superior to the first. Of course, the defense of the second premise of that argument will ultimately become circular by appealing to our reliability. But does this detract from the second argument? Does it make the conclusion less coherent, or does it rather make it more so? Does the first argument or the second offer a better explanation of why we are justified in our belief that we see a cat on the mat? The second, clearly.

Sosa agrees that circular argument can increase explanatory effectiveness through rational coherence. In discussing how we might be justified in our beliefs about the reliability of our epistemic processes, Sosa affirms that an argument, even a circular argument, would result in more overall coherence:

> [O]nce we had an argument A for W [our overall way of forming beliefs] being reliable from premises we already accepted, we would embed our faith in W's reliability within a more comprehensively coherent whole that would include the premises of the argument A. And it must be granted that such an argument *would* bring that benefit. (PSEC, 283; original emphasis)

However, he finds coherence, even supplemented with truth, insufficient as a theory of knowledge. He says,

> (A) "Suffice it to say that the most comprehensive coherence accompanied by the truth of what one believes will not yet amount to knowledge" (PSEC, 268).

His argument is that in an evil demon world we may have justification resulting from coherence and the addition of truth of what one believes is insufficient for knowledge.

(B) "However, if by sheer luck one happened to be right in the belief that one faces a fire, one's being *both* thus justified *and* right still would fall short of one's knowing about the fire. So whatever is to be said for coherence, or even for comprehensive coherence, one thing seems clear: none of that will be enough just on its own to explain fully what a true belief needs in order to be knowledge" (PSEC, 268).

This is not to say that Sosa fails to appreciate the importance of coherence. On the contrary, in his more recent work he remarks:

(C) "Broad coherence adds to a subject's intellectual worth or merit, first, because of the integration and harmony that it imports, but, also, because it is truth conducive: that is to say, broad coherence is valuable and admirable in a subject because it increases the likelihood that the subject will have true beliefs and avoid false ones" (VE, 93).

This kind of coherence must include something beyond coherence among beliefs, however. As he clarifies the matter,

(D) "For example, it must be coherence not only among one's beliefs, but among one's beliefs *and* experiences. And, further it must be coherence that turns perspectival and includes some view of the sources of one's beliefs and reliability of these sources" (VE, 91).

He concludes,

(E) "In conclusion, I claim that: (a) our broad coherence is necessary for the kind of reflective knowledge traditionally desired; and (b) such broadly coherent knowledge is desirable because of the integration it imports and also because in our actual world it helps us approach truth and avoid error" (VE, 100).

There is much agreement, consequently, between Sosa and coherentists like Lehrer (2000) who claim that coherence supplemented with the truth of what one believes is sufficient for knowledge. However, there is an important wedge of distinction, according to Sosa, between the coherence theory restricted to coherence among beliefs supplemented with a requirement of the truth of what one believes, and the virtue perspectivism that Sosa advocates. Our purpose is to question whether that wedge of distinction is a difference that makes a theoretical difference. It would be no objection to Sosa's account if it were to be equivalent to a coherence theory, especially from the point of view of one of the present authors, but Sosa stresses the importance of the distinction, and so it is worth testing the power of the wedge to effect the distinction.

First of all, it is important to avoid a verbal dispute based on claim (A) above. Sosa appears to be claiming that if the sort of justification arising from coherence is supplemented by only the truth of a target belief, then this will not suffice for knowledge. With this we agree. However, the further remarks, especially those in the later work and (D), suggest that coherence among beliefs must be supplemented by something other than beliefs and the truth thereof. One must add, for example, experiences.

Now consider, *pace* Lehrer, a kind of coherence that is sufficiently constraining so that it requires of coherence that a target belief which is justified by a coherent background system of beliefs, or which coheres with that system, must be so strongly supported by the system that all objections to the belief can be answered. Thus, if it is an objection to the belief that it was not formed in an appropriate way or derived from a reliable source, then the system must contain the belief that the forming was appropriate or the source reliable. Similarly, if it is an objection to the belief that the circumstances in which it is formed are not propitious for the truth of the belief, then the system, to be coherent with the belief, must contain the belief that the circumstances are propitious. Finally, if it is an objection to the belief that it is not properly connected to experience, then, if the belief coheres with the system, it must contain the belief that the belief is so connected to experience. So let us call this constraint, one requiring that a target belief that coheres with a system of beliefs can be defended by the system against objections to the belief, the *defensibility constraint*.

Thinking about coherence in this manner, constrained by demand that objections be answerable, seems compatible with Sosa's intuitions about coherence. Sosa allows that the circularity of a belief system which contains beliefs about one's reliability is necessary for reflective knowledge. Both Sosa and Lehrer agree that there is a kind of knowledge, what Sosa calls animal knowledge, that does not require such beliefs about reliability which would be required to meet the defensibility constraint. However, reflective knowledge, intended as it is to provide us with an understanding of what we know, seems to require a kind of coherence that satisfies the defensibility constraint. Sosa might not agree with this, and we should like to be informed if he demurs, but he appears to propose a view consistent with it.

In defense of this interpretation, note his remarks above that the kind of coherence required "must be a coherence that turns perspectival and includes some *view* [our italics] of the sources of one's beliefs and reliability of these sources." If coherence must include a *view* of such matters, then, it seems it must include a belief to that effect. For what is a view if not a belief? And what is the motivation for requiring such a view if not to provide a defense against a possible objection? We think that the attribution of the defensibility constraint to Sosa is a reasonable one concerning reflective knowledge.

However, these simple reflections suggest to us that Sosa's virtue perspectivism is contained in the coherence theory restricted to coherence among beliefs provided only that the beliefs are true. For a system sufficiently coherent to defend a target belief against objections to it, which seems required to yield reflective knowledge, must contain the beliefs concerning reliability and connection with experience which virtue perspectivism supplies. Moreover, if those beliefs are true, their truth appears sufficient, when added to coherence satisfying the defensibility constraint, to yield knowledge. To be sufficient for defense of the target belief, the beliefs with which it coheres must affirm that the context and our perspective are truth-conducive. So, if the beliefs with which a belief coheres are fully adequate to the reflective defense, then, if they are true, they will insure what is required in terms of ways, means, and circumstances by virtue perspectivism.

We thus propose a question to Sosa. What is supplied by virtue perspectivism that is not required for the defensibility of the belief by a coherent system to yield reflective knowledge? Perhaps Sosa has a positive answer we have not discerned, and we would be glad to be instructed by him. If the answer is negative, and nothing additional is supplied, then why does a highly coherent system, one with a high enough grade of coherence to provide for the defensibility of the target belief, fail to suffice for knowledge when the beliefs in the system are true? Notice, to return to the new evil demon problem, that coherence with a system plus the truth of the target belief alone cannot be expected to suffice. Far too many of the beliefs belonging to the system could be false, and thus the system might fail to yield knowledge despite the truth of the target belief. That is to be expected. If we think of the beliefs belonging the system as supplying premises to support or defend the target belief, then, of course, the support or defense will only suffice if the premises are true. Our suggestion is that the truth of cohering premises, if adequate for the defense of the target belief, suffices for knowledge.

We can anticipate one reply concerning the supplementary role of experience. It is that it is the experience itself rather than a belief concerning it that plays the crucial role in knowledge. Now, construed in one manner the answer to this objection is simple. For a belief about the existence of an experience (or about the relation of a belief to an experience) to be true, more is required than the belief. The truth of the belief that I am experiencing a fire requires the experience of the fire and not just a believing attitude. So, the truth requirement imports the reality of the thing believed to exist, the experience, and that is something beyond the believing attitude.

Another way of construing the objection that it is the experience itself rather than belief that is crucial, and a stronger one, is to say that no belief at all is required for the experience to be crucial. I might have some experience which plays a role in justification and knowledge without ever having any corresponding belief that it exists. Here there is a possible ambiguity. Many things of which we have no conception may play a causal role in our beliefs and so, indirectly, in our knowledge. But the existence of such things is not our justification for the belief, though it may play a crucial role in aetiology of the belief. Of course, sometimes aetiology constitutes part of the justification for a belief, in perception, for example, but then the truth of beliefs concerning the aetiology, that an object causes my experience, for example, and their coherence with the target belief suffices for reflective knowledge.

It should be allowed, moreover, that the word "belief" covers many different states from the weakest impression of something being the case to the most careful and certain conviction. It is important not to let ambiguities in the doxastic vocabulary generate verbal dispute and philosophical confusion. So, let us use the term in the broadest manner and think of those representations of sense which we quickly reject, e.g., of the water on the highway ahead on a sunny day, as weak short-lived beliefs, as well as the most reflective judgments. I think we may then say that experience is either represented, in which case it is at least a kind of short-lived belief that may play a role in justification, or it is unrepresented altogether, in which case it is no belief at all and plays no role in justification. No justification without representation.

Thus, to rephrase our question for Sosa: Suppose that coherence among beliefs is broad enough to provide justification for a target belief in a demon world. In the demon world, the justification is defeated by the falsity of the cohering beliefs providing the defense of the target belief. Now consider the target belief defended by a coherent system of beliefs providing a justification that is undefeated by error in the actual world. Why would such coherence combined in this way with truth not suffice for knowledge, as the coherentist avers? Note that coherence theorists have not been reluctant to add the requirement of truth to that of the internal attitudes, though they have differed concerning its nature. If truth be something external, then something external is part of the coherence theory of knowledge. The crucial question is whether our system of beliefs, when sufficiently coherent with each other to defend a target belief, suffices for knowledge when those beliefs required for the defense are true. Moreover, do not such beliefs constitute our perspective? And is it not those beliefs, which include the belief that they will lead us to truth and not error, whose virtue from our perspective yields knowledge? In short, then, why isn't the virtuous perspective required for knowledge a view that is part of the system of belief that coheres with other beliefs to yield knowledge when undefeated by error? Why isn't virtue perspectivism contained within coherence constrained by defensibility and supplemented by truth?

We conclude by expressing our appreciation for the remarkable clarification that Sosa has provided of the conditions of knowledge by advocating his position of virtue perspectivism. No one has done more to clarify issues pertaining to the relationship between knowledge and skepticism than Sosa. He has clarified beyond all others the way in which evidence that fails to be adequate for knowledge in a demon world may nevertheless be adequate for knowledge in the actual world. Moreover, his clarification of the role of reliability and what it can and cannot accomplish is a remarkable contribution. He has sorted through the details in a way that leaves us in his debt. In asking for further clarification of the relationship between the coherence theory of knowledge and his virtue perspectivism, we hope to obtain one final step in the process of clarification he has effected.

References

Lehrer, Keith, 2000. *The Theory of Knowledge*, 2nd edn. (Boulder, CO: Westview Press).
Sosa, Ernest, 1994. "Philosophical Skepticism and Epistemic Circularity." In *Proceedings of the Aristotelian Society*, supp. vol. 68, pp. 263–90. (Cited as PSEC.)
Sosa, Ernest, n.d. "Virtue Epistemology," unpublished manuscript. (Cited as VE.)

10

Skepticism: Ascent and Assent?

PETER KLEIN

Ernest Sosa has developed a comprehensive theory of propositional knowledge, which he labels "virtue perspectivism."[1] It integrates many of the salutary aspects of foundationalism and coherentism, internalism and externalism, evidentialism and reliabilism. In this chapter I want to focus on his treatment of philosophical skepticism and offer some friendly criticisms. I say "friendly" for two reasons. He is a friend of mine and I share many of his basic commitments in epistemology.

In order to understand Sosa's response to philosophical skepticism it is crucial to see that Sosa adopts a Cartesian distinction between two forms of knowledge – *cognitio* and *scientia*. *Cognitio* is true, justified belief that is appropriately caused or subjunctively related to the object of the belief. Tempting though it would be, I will not comment on Sosa's account of *cognitio* beyond what is required to discuss his response to skepticism.[2] *Scientia* is a reflective form of knowledge that results from "ascending" to a position from which we can assess whether we satisfy the conditions required by *cognitio*. Bluntly and somewhat contentiously put, this form of knowledge is reserved for epistemologists (professional or amateur).[3]

Here is a crucial passage from Descartes's replies to the objections to the *Meditations* cited, by Sosa, in which Descartes draws the distinction between the two grades of knowledge:

> That an atheist can clearly know that the three angles of a triangle are equal to two right angles, I do not deny: I merely say that this knowledge (*cognitio*) of his is not true science (*scientia*), because no knowledge which can be rendered doubtful should, it seems, be called science. Since he is supposed to be an atheist, he cannot be certain that he is not deceived even in those things that seem most evident to him, as has been sufficiently shown; and although this doubt may never occur to him, nevertheless it can occur to him, if he examines the question, or it may be suggested by someone else, and he will never be safe from it, unless he first acknowledges God. (HRPP, 236)

I say that this is a crucial passage for two reasons. In addition to displaying the two types of knowledge taken over from Descartes by Sosa, it illustrates the deep structural similarities between Sosa's view, virtue perspectivism, and Descartes's overall approach. As Sosa writes:

In structure, virtue perspectivism is thus Cartesian, though in content it is not. Radical rationalism admits only (rational) intuition and deduction (along with memory) as its faculties of choice (or anyhow of top choice) and wishes to validate all knowledge in terms of these faculties; thus the Cartesian grand project. Virtue perspectivism admits also perception and introspection, along with intuition and deduction, as well as inductive and abductive reasoning. (RK, 423)

Virtue perspectivism is structurally Cartesian because it seeks to show that we have *cognitio*, not through rational theology as Descartes attempted, but through other means that will be discussed below. Thus, developing a response to philosophical skepticism is an integral part of virtue *perspectivism*.

Sosa takes philosophical skepticism to be the view that there is "no way to attain full philosophical understanding of our knowledge. A fully general theory of knowledge is impossible" (PSEC, 93). Thus, the skepticism that Sosa has in mind is a form of Academic Skepticism rather than a form of Pyrrhonian Skepticism that would refrain from assenting to either the view that we can attain a full philosophical understanding of our knowledge or that we cannot attain such an understanding. In this chapter I want to consider Sosa's reasons for *rejecting* Academic Skepticism because they strike me as less than compelling. I don't think the reasons *for* Academic Skepticism are compelling either (and have argued for that elsewhere[4]). Thus, I side with the Pyrrhonians on this issue. But I won't defend Pyrrhonism here – at least not directly. The issue here is whether Sosa has found a good response to Academic Skepticism.

As I see it, Sosa's response to Academic Skepticism has two main tenets:

(T1) There is no good purely internalist response to philosophical (i.e., Academic) skepticism, where "internalism" is understood as the view that appropriate reasons, and only such reasons, can convert a true belief into reflective knowledge.

(T2) There is a viable externalist response where "externalism" is the denial of internalism.[5]

I think neither of these tenets has been established.

Consideration of (T1)

The argument for (T1) is that in order to develop an adequate response to Academic Skepticism one would need a "legitimating account of absolutely all one's own knowledge" and such an account is impossible, from a purely internalist perspective, because such an

account admits only justification provided by inference or argument and, since it rules out circular or endlessly regressive inferences, such an account must stop with premises that it supposes or "presupposes" that one is justified in accepting, without explaining how one is justified in accepting them in turn. (PSEC, 96)

In other words, pure internalist responses fall victim to the Pyrrhonian trilemma.[6]

Thus, by a "legitimating account" Sosa means an argument that is not circular and not "endlessly regressive" and whose premises are not arbitrarily appealed to and whose conclusion is that the person giving the argument has methods of arriving at beliefs which when properly deployed are at least likely to produce knowledge. Sosa thinks this kind of argument can't be given, but he also thinks that once the reason for that is recognized, it is no longer bothersome that there is no such internalist response available.

Sosa claims that an internalist argument which concludes that our methods of arriving at beliefs are reliable will have to employ that proposition as a premise (overtly or covertly) and will then, of necessity, beg the question. He likens the situation to the one in which we desire to locate a saint who blesses all and only those who don't bless themselves. (Shades of the barber who shaves all who don't shave themselves!) As he says, in the search for such a saint, we may "turn up likely prospects each of whom eventually is seen to fall short, until someone . . . reflects that there could not possibly be such a saint, and this for evident, logical reasons" (PSEC, 109).

Thus, even though he claims that we could not produce such an argument without begging the question (having eliminated justificational surds and endless regresses as appropriate ways of responding to the skeptic), once we recognize that what is being requested by the skeptic is logically impossible to produce, we can "go ahead and 'beg' the question against *such* a sceptic (though 'begging the question' and 'arguing circularly' may now be misnomers for what we do, since it is surely no fallacy, not if it constitutes correct and legitimate intellectual procedure)" (PSEC, 111).

I want to ask three questions:

Is Sosa correct that the kind of anti-skeptical argument required, though circular, is not viciously so?
Is Sosa correct that every attempt at providing a legitimating argument for the claim that we have knowledge will either beg the question or lead us to a *vicious* infinite regress or be based upon some arbitrary supposition?
Is Sosa correct that every legitimating response to academic skepticism must be in the form of an argument powerful enough to justify us in believing that we have reflective knowledge?

It will probably not be surprising that I think the answer to each question is a qualified "no." Let us take them one at a time.

(a) What makes an argument circular is not easy to pin down and I have no well worked out general account to offer here. Nevertheless, I do think we can say that the fallacy of circular reasoning occurs when the conclusion of an argument is warranted only on the basis of the transfer of warrant from the premises *and* the conclusion is used (either overtly or covertly) as one of the premises. A fallacy has occurred because in order for the argument to transmit some warrant to the conclusion, there must be some warrant already present in each of the premises but there is no such prior warrant for the proposition that doubles as the conclusion. Note: This does not rule out the possibility that there might be some form of legitimate reasoning both from and to propositions that are mutually probability enhancing *if* those propositions have some warrant from sources other than that provided by the reasoning in question. Such reasoning, though circular in some sense, might augment the initial warrant of the propositions.[7]

So, there might be some room for "self-supporting arguments" (PSEC, 111) that are not viciously circular. But I take it that (i) the kind of reasoning employed by the anti-skeptic envisioned by Sosa is designed to produce some warrant for the proposition, *our methods of arriving at beliefs are reliable when properly employed*, and further, (ii) Sosa thinks that the anti-skeptic internalist has no means of arriving at that conclusion without employing it as a premise. That is why he holds it to be logically impossible for such an anti-skeptic to avoid begging the question. But, if such an anti-skeptic has no warrant for that proposition independent of the reasoning offered *and* that proposition is employed as a premise, then the reasoning is fallacious and, *pace* Sosa, the anti-skeptic ought not to be allowed to "go ahead and beg the question" against the skeptic because this form of arguing is surely fallacious since it does not constitute "correct or legitimate intellectual procedure."

Now, to (b). I think that there are many arguments that conclude with the appropriate general claim about the reliability of belief processes that are not instances of circular reasoning.

Consider this argument:

(1) My methods of arriving at beliefs are M-type methods.
(2) M-type methods are reliable.
(3) My methods of arriving at beliefs are reliable.

Does that argument commit a fallacy of any sort? No. No premise employs the conclusion. And I can see no reason why an argument for either premise must employ the conclusion in one of its premises, etc.

Consider this argument:

(1) If some condition C holds, then my methods of arriving at beliefs using M-type methods is reliable.
(2) Condition C holds.
(3) My methods of arriving at beliefs using M-type methods are reliable.

Does that argument commit a fallacy of any sort? No. No premise employs the conclusion. And I can see no reason why an argument for either premise must employ the premise in one of its premises, etc.

So, why think that for "evident, logical reasons" every argument to the conclusion that my belief acquisition methods are reliable must be circular? I think the answer is that any sufficiently careful and self-conscious person who believes that his/her use of M-type belief acquisition methods are reliable will employ those very methods in acquiring the belief in the conclusion. But that is *not* a fallacy of circular reasoning. It is merely making one's practices consistent with one's beliefs. If I thought that my reliable belief acquisition methods were M-type methods, it would be imprudent of me, to say the least, to use some *other* method of acquiring beliefs – no matter what the beliefs were. Indeed, I would legitimately be accused of an inconsistency between my practices and my beliefs.

Now, perhaps this is what Sosa meant when he said that it might be a "misnomer" to call the argument he had in mind an instance of circular reasoning because there is no fallacy involved. If this is what he meant, we are in complete agreement here. An argument to the conclusion that my belief acquisition methods are reliable need not be circular.

But avoiding that horn of the Pyrrhonian trilemma only throws us back on the other two horns. Must internalists embrace arbitrary foundations or fall victim to a *vicious* regress of reasons? I agree with Sosa that foundationalism is not a viable theory for explaining what provides a belief with the suitable epistemic quality to pass muster as knowledge, and I have argued for that elsewhere.[8] I realize that to reject foundationalism without giving an argument here might be considered brash, to say the least. But I hope it is understandable in the context of this discussion. So, that leaves us with the regress.

I have argued elsewhere that some infinite regresses of reasons are not vicious.[9] Here, I merely wish to consider Sosa's reasons for thinking that all such regresses are vicious. That is important in the context of this discussion, since if he has not provided us with a good enough reason for thinking that all such regresses are vicious, then there remains the possibility of a purely internalist response to Academic Skepticism. Here is what he says:

> the main reason for accepting formal foundationalism [as against infinitism] . . . is the very plausible idea that epistemic justification is subject to the supervenience that characterizes normative and evaluative properties generally. . . . Epistemic justification is supervenient. The justification of a belief supervenes on such properties of it as its content and its basis (if any) in perception, memory or inference. (RP2, 142)

Now I am not certain that the normative does generally supervene on the non-normative or even that this way of understanding properties cuts nature and non-nature correctly at the joints, but let us assume that it is essential that a good account of justification must not preclude such supervenience.[10] The question before us then is this: Why think that the supervenience of the normative on the non-normative is precluded if a proposition is justified if and only if there is an infinite set of non-repeating propositions each of which serves as a reason for an earlier one in the chain?[11] Probably because it is thought that since the justificatory status of one proposition obtains *if and only if* there is another proposition with the same justificatory status, *ad infinitum*, the justificatory status of any proposition *depends upon* the justificatory status of another in a sense of "depends upon" that rules out the possibility that justification supervenes on some non-normative properties.

But that is an unwarranted inference. To see that, suppose that the following (contrary to fact) were true: A child is a genius *if and only if* its parents are geniuses. If that were true, would it follow that every account of what it is to be a genius must depend upon appealing to geniusness? No. We could say that a person being a genius *depends upon* their scoring above a certain level on some designated IQ test. That is compatible with the infinite regress of genius transmission. The same holds here. A proposition, *p*, might be justified if and only if there is another proposition, *q*, that is justified and transmits to *p* whatever non-normative features in virtue of which it is justified. In other words, whatever non-normative properties on which justification supervenes can be carried along by one justified proposition to another justified proposition. Thus, I think this argument by Sosa gives us no good reason for thinking that every infinite regress of reasons is vicious.

In "Philosophical Scepticism and Epistemic Circularity," he hints at another reason for thinking that such regresses are vicious. There he says when considering the resources available to an internalist for responding to skepticism:

> the justification of any given belief requires appeal to *other* beliefs that constitute one's reasons for holding the given belief. Of course, when one combines this with rejection of circularity, the case for scepticism is very strong, assuming that for limited humans an infinite regress of reasons or justifications is out of the question. (PSEC, 100)

This paragraph seems to suggest that the demand that there be an infinite number of distinct reasons available for our beliefs cannot be satisfied because we are "limited humans." But I think this misconstrues what an infinitist must require. The infinitist need not require that in order for us to have a good enough reason for believing a given proposition, we have traversed an infinite path of reasons – that would, indeed, be impossible for a mortal being, who, like us, can only entertain a finite number of propositions at any given time. That requirement is tantamount to insisting that we complete the process of justifying a proposition in order for us to have good enough reasons for believing it. And the infinitist would certainly eschew that requirement. Rather, the infinitist could require only that there be an infinite set of distinct reasons *available* for justifying the proposition and that we *actually have* some good reasons for the proposition that are not ultimately overridden by our currently held reasons against it. The latter is sufficient to make it more reasonable to believe than withhold. *Assenting* to it – that is, thinking that we know the proposition to be true – might require having completed the process of justifying the proposition, and that is why a Pyrrhonian infinitist would not assent to any proposition that requires a justification. Tentative, provisionally justified belief – yes; assent – no.

In partial summary: I think Sosa's reasons for holding that the regress would be vicious are inadequate for motivating the conclusion that there is no viable internalist response.[12] Such a response can hold both that a proposition is justified if and only if there are the appropriate reasons for it while also maintaining that epistemic properties supervene on non-epistemic ones. Further, our "finite minds" pose no obstacle to requiring that the set of such reasons is infinite and non-repeating.

But that being said, is it even required that, in order for the internalist to have a "legitimating response" to the Academic Skeptic, she have some sort of argument that concludes with the claim that we are capable of *cognitio*? That brings us to question (c).

(c) If "legitimating response" is being used as term-of-art and is defined in such a way that only the possession of such an argument would qualify, then the claim would be true by decree and lose its interest. I think, however, there is a deep difference here between what a Cartesian and Sosa would find to be a legitimating response to Academic Skepticism and what a Pyrrhonian and I would find to be a legitimate response. The Academic Skeptic is claiming that we do not have *cognitio*. The Cartesian-like philosopher is claiming that we do. The Pyrrhonian alternative is to withhold assent to the proposition that we have knowledge and, consequently, to its denial.

The Pyrrhonians would try to foster the habit of withholding assent to the proposition that we have reflective knowledge by one of two methods. The first would be to provide some *general* reasons for thinking that all *stated* arguments, and *a fortiori*, all stated arguments for Academic Skepticism or for its denial either beg the question or rest on arbitrary assumptions.[13] Thus, even if there were a non-circular, non-vicious infinite series of reasons for the claim that we have knowledge, we could never *state* that argument and so we ought to withhold assent to the proposition that we have reflective knowledge. The second method would be to carefully consider both the arguments *for* Academic Skepticism and those *for* its denial in an effort to show that they are equally good or equally bad. In my defense of infinitism (mentioned earlier) I do argue for the *general* claim. But, once again, this is not the place to rehearse that general defense. However, I would like to take up the second alternative. So let us begin with the specific argument *for* Academic Skepticism that Sosa seems to think is the most powerful.

Here is his account of that argument:

> A version of the [skeptic's] argument may be laid out as follows:
>
> 1 All your sensory experience and information at t is compatible with your dreaming at t.
> 2 So you need some test which "indicates" that you are not then dreaming, such that you know both (i) it is satisfied and (ii) if it is satisfied then you are not dreaming.
> 3 But how could such a test ever be available to you, if it is a condition of your knowing (perceptually) *anything* beyond your experience that you know yourself *not* to be dreaming? . . .
>
> This nowhere assumes that in order to know that *p* one must be *absolutely* and justifiably *certain* that *p*. We are not setting the standards too high and then complaining that we can't possibly measure up. Our argument is designed to show rather that, when compared with the possibility that we are just dreaming, our thought that we really see is based upon *no good reason whatever. A sufficient reason must enable us to rule out alternatives that clearly would preclude our knowing, as above* [emphasis added]. The dismissal of the skeptic as setting the bar too high is superficial because it overlooks this argument. (BIF, 142)

There is much in this diagnosis of the argument for Academic Skepticism with which I agree. For example, the argument does not appeal to a "too high standards" requirement but it does appeal to a version of the "eliminate all contraries" principle.[14] The question before us is this: Does the Academic Skeptic have the right to insist that I must eliminate all incompatible propositions to *p before* we can attain *scientia* that *p*? I think Sosa and I agree that he/she does not. (See BIF, 141) But, then, there is a legitimating internalist response to Academic Skepticism available: namely, the Academic Skeptic has not given us a good reason for thinking that we do not have *cognitio*.

That response could begin by pointing out that a consequence of the "eliminate all contraries" principle is that in order to know that *p* our reasons for *p* must entail *p*. And that strikes me as a burden that no internalist need accept.

To see that this is a consequence of adopting that prerequisite, note that both ($\sim p$ & q) as well as ($\sim p$ and $\sim q$) are contraries of *p*. Thus, our evidence for *p* would have to include both $\sim(\sim p$ & $q)$ and $\sim(\sim p$ & $\sim q)$. But that set of propositions entails *p*. So, the requirement that we eliminate all contraries of *p* before we have any form of knowledge (*scientia* or *cognitio*) amounts to requiring that our evidence entail p.[15] That is a requirement we need not accept especially if we are coherentists who employ both abduction and induction. Thus, it strikes me that the argument for Academic Skepticism which Sosa finds most plausible is based upon a view of the requirements for having adequate reasons or, in his terms, for employing a virtuous process of reasoning, that sets inappropriate conditions on having good reasons for our beliefs.[16]

But suppose that the requirement is weakened. Perhaps the only alternatives we have to eliminate are those which are known to be incompatible with *p*? That won't help because if we are circumspect and informed about what is incompatible with our knowing that *p*, we would have to eliminate both of the contraries of *p* mentioned above, since we know them to be incompatible with *p*.

Suppose that we weaken the requirement even further and require that the alternatives that have to be eliminated are known to be incompatible *and* are mentioned or thought of in the context?[17] Even this weaker principle seems incorrect. Recall Dretske's oft-cited Zebra-in-the-Zoo Case.[18] We are standing before some zebra-like looking animals and someone says, "How do you know that these animals are not *very* cleverly disguised Seventh-Day Adventists who dress up as zebras in order to catch you off guard so that they can begin their spiel?" Or "How do you know that these are not aliens from another galaxy who have disguised themselves as zebras in order to observe large numbers of humans as they visit the zoo?" Pretty silly. Pretty unmotivated. Now, if Seventh-Day Adventists or aliens have resorted to such disguises, or perhaps, even if you just *thought* they had, then such an alternative might need to be eliminated with epistemic "priority," as Sosa puts it (CEP). But in the absence of either of those obtaining, even this weakened requirement seems too restrictive.

Perhaps it could be claimed that although it is not normally required that we eliminate all known and raised alternatives, it is required by anyone seeking *scientia*? Doing philosophy brings with it unusual epistemic burdens. Keith Lehrer writes as follows:

> generally arguments about where the burden of proof lies are unproductive. It is more reasonable to suppose that such questions are best left to courts of law where they have suitable application. In *philosophy* [emphasis added] a different principle of agnoiology [the study of ignorance] is appropriate, to wit, that no hypothesis should be rejected as unjustified without argument against it. Consequently, if the sceptic puts forth a hypothesis inconsistent with the hypothesis of common sense, then there is no burden of proof on either side.[19]

The point here could be put in our present terminology as follows: When we are seeking *scientia*, we put on the cloak of a philosopher and, then, it becomes appropriate to require that we eliminate all known and raised alternatives. Recall Descartes's method of "pretending" that all his former opinions were false in order to arrive at what, if anything, is certain. A question, then, becomes this: Is that an appropriate requirement when we are doing philosophy? Of course, we could stipulate that it is appropriate. But then the results of employing such a requirement could be ignored by anyone not agreeing to that precondition. I think the more interesting questions are these: Why should anyone think that the mere raising of the skeptical scenario imposes any obligation upon us to eliminate it in order to have the highest form of human knowledge? Where does that obligation come from? Not our ordinary practices. From where, then?

Presumably the obligation originates from some reflections about our *philosophical* practices, and in particular, from examining the Cartesian-like goal mentioned above of settling, in so far as possible, whether we have *cognitio*. Interestingly enough, that is a goal shared by the Academic Skeptics as shown by their adherence to some version of the elimination principle. (I might note parenthetically that this is why the Pyrrhonians considered both to be dogmatists.) But if the practice of philosophy includes Pyrrhonism, namely, continuing to inquire about matters that were not self-evident ("skeptic" does come from the Greek "σκέπτομαι" meaning to inquire), then the obligation to eliminate all known and raised incompatible alternatives would likely disappear. Why should we be obliged to eliminate alternative hypotheses about the scope of our knowledge for which we have *no reason whatsoever*? Thus, I think there is a "legitimate response" to Academic Skepticism that does not require us to have an argument powerful enough to fully justify us in believing that we have *cognitio-style* knowledge. We can come to see that the argument for Academic Skepticism imposes obligations on us that need not be accepted.

Now, this is not to gainsay the possibility that a legitimate question could arise about the general reliability of our belief acquisition and sustaining methods.[20] As I have argued above, I see no reason why we can't give non-circular arguments to the conclusion that those methods are generally reliable. Those arguments would, of necessity, employ those methods. Further, those arguments would initiate a process of reasoning that is unending and further inquiry would always be in order for there would always be one more step to take. But that is a prospect that can be gladly embraced once the Cartesian-like goals are put aside.

Consideration of (T2)

It is now time to turn directly to (T2), namely Sosa's suggested response to the Academic Skeptic. As I see it, the essential step involves the Principle of Ascent (PA – mentioned in "Two False Dichotomies"). If that principle were true, it would allow us to *ascend* to a meta-level and be justified, on coherentist grounds, in believing that we do indeed have *cognitio*. That is, we can ascend and then assent. If correct, it would provide a basis for rejecting Academic Skepticism and at the same time it would lead to the rejection of Pyrrhonism since it would provide the basis for assenting to a hitherto non-evident proposition. Here is that principle:

(PA) [Ksp &CsKsp] → JsKsP

That is, if S knows that *p* and S considers whether he/she knows that *p*, then S is justified in believing the proposition that he/she knows that *p*. I say it provides a basis for rejecting Academic Skepticism because, if true, iterative reflective knowledge is made possible and *even necessary* if we consider whether we do have first-order reflective knowledge. For if one knows that *p* and considers whether one knows, and one is justified in (actually) believing that one knows, then, according to Sosa, one knows that one has knowledge (barring defeaters, of course). Thus, a limited version of the KK thesis holds.[21]

What makes Sosa think PA is true? Here is what he says in "Two False Dichotomies":

> Suppose, first, one consciously and occurrently believes that *p*, and, in that same specious present, second, one consciously and occurrently considers whether one not only believes but knows that *p*. Exactly three options open up: one might say either (a) "No, I don't know that," or (b) "Who knows whether I know it or not; maybe I do, maybe I don't," or (c) "Yes, that is something I do know." One is better off, surely, if able to give the later answers;

better off with the second answer than the first, and better off yet with the third. Answer a, and even answer b, would reveal a certain lack of integration in that stretch of consciousness; only answer c, of the three, entirely avoids disharmony within that consciousness in that specious present. If one has to give answer a, or even answer b, one thereby falls short, and one's belief that p falls short. It is not all that it could be.

The more general claim about any belief, p, in the above citation is particularized in the following passage from "Philosophical Scepticism and Epistemic Circularity":

> But now suppose that by using way W of forming beliefs ... we arrive at the conviction that W is our way of forming beliefs. Now, so long as we do not go back on that conviction, does that not restrict our coherent combinations of attitudes? Take: *(e) B:[W is my overall way of forming beliefs]*. And compare *(f) B:[W is reliable]*, *(g) D: [W is reliable]* and *(h) Wh:[W is reliable]*. It is not evident that (e) & (f) would be more satisfyingly coherent than either of (e) & (g) or (e) & (h)? (PSEC, 107)

I cite these passages at length not only because they are crucial in the argument for PA and in understanding Sosa's argument that we can know that we have *cognitio*, whenever we reflect on whether we do, but also because it underscores the deep difference between Sosa and me, mentioned above, concerning our powers to justify beliefs. His model is the Cartesian; mine is the Pyrrhonian.

The first thing to note about the argument for PA is that the conjunct, "Ksp," plays no role. The argument is that it is simply more coherent in the specious present to believe that my beliefs are knowledge than to deny or withhold that they are knowledge. The quick response to this is that it strikes me as at least bordering on what the Pyrrhonians would have thought was dogmatism. From the mere fact that I believe something, is it more coherent to believe that I also know it? I say that is the "quick" response. I would now like to consider PA a bit more carefully, but I admit that my "long" response will merely be an elaboration of this initial reaction.

To begin that more careful response, let us grant the privileged access to our occurrent belief states presupposed in these passages. The issues, though, are these: Is it more "satisfyingly coherent" to believe that I know that p whenever I believe that I believe that p? Is that the only alternative among the three possible epistemic attitudes (believe, deny, withhold) that "avoids disharmony?" I think the answer to those questions is "It depends upon what else I believe in the same specious present."

Now exactly what falls under the scope of all the beliefs of mine in the specious present is difficult to determine. Perhaps I can only have one (perhaps compound) occurrent belief at a time. But in that case, the specious present might not contain both the belief that p and the belief that I know that p unless one's account of JKp was such that it contained Bp. That strikes me as plausible but not obviously correct. The more important consideration is that if the specious present didn't include a significant portion of the beliefs relevant to p, it is difficult, if not impossible, to conceive of "coherence" as doing much work in a theory of justification. With what set of beliefs is a particular one, say p, supposed to cohere in order to be justified? It must be more than p's constituent beliefs. So, let us assume that in whatever way relevance is determined, a significant portion of my most relevant beliefs about some subject matter, p, are to be included in the scope of the beliefs to be considered when the question of what best coheres with p arises.

To see why I think that the options for achieving coherence among *my* beliefs are not as Sosa thinks are "surely" correct, let's begin by considering my belief about the reliability of methods W employed by *someone else* in arriving at their beliefs. Suppose that I'm at a carnival and, in particular, at the booth where the carnival employee "guesses" a person's weight. The rules of the "game" are simple: Someone gives the carnie 25 cents and that someone gets a panda bear IFF the carnie misses by more than 3 lbs of the person's correct weight. I hear the carnie say to someone, "You weigh 185." Assuming he/she believes what they said, am I justified in believing that the carnie knows that the person weighs 185 lbs?[22] Yes, because I think that the carnie has employed some *special* skill – a skill not had by just any person – in determining people's weights.

On the other hand, suppose that I overhear someone – let's call that person "Anyperson" – say to someone else, "You weigh 185 lbs." Let us assume that I think Anyperson's skills in determining weights is typical – that is, Anyperson is at least not more likely to be right than wrong. In that case, would I be justified in believing that Anyperson knows that the person weighs 185 lbs? It strikes me that the answer to that question is that it would be preferable on coherence grounds to at least withhold such a judgment if not to deny that it is justified. Most people are not very good at telling another's weight within 3 lbs.

Now, suppose I am Anyperson and believe that someone weighs 185 lbs. I believe of myself that I don't have any special weight-guessing skills. I'm just like anyone else. I ask myself: Do I know that the person weighs 185 lbs.? I believe the person's weight is 185 – he looks to be about Bob's weight and Bob told me a while ago that he weighed 185. It seems to me that in this case the most "satisfyingly coherent" attitude to ascend to is at least withholding assent about whether I have knowledge.

A person with Cartesian leanings might *wish* that humans, and in particular they themselves, were disposed not to believe something until they also believed (in the same specious present) that the belief is known. And a Cartesian might feel some "disharmony" here. But *must* we be Cartesians? The question here is whether if I discover a belief of mine it *must* be more "satisfyingly coherent" to believe that such a belief rises to the level of knowledge than to withhold assent to the proposition that it is knowledge. Before answering that question, wouldn't I first want to believe that I had figured out what the conditions of knowledge were and then wouldn't I want to believe that my belief satisfied them? Suppose that I thought that the conditions of knowledge required something akin to eliminating all known and raised incompatible propositions. Would I think I had done that? In particular, would I think that I had eliminated the evil genius hypothesis? I, for one, do not see how to do that.

Note, my argument here does not in any way depend upon accepting the elimination requirement. Indeed, I don't accept it. The point here is that whether it is more coherent to believe about an occurrent belief of mine that it is knowledge rather than have either of the other alternative epistemic attitudes depends upon what else I believe. In particular, it depends upon what I believe my skills are in determining the truth in matters that are not already evident and it depends upon whether I thought that I could then conform my beliefs, or the particular belief in question, to the results of that determination. If I thought that my skills were no better (or not that much better) than those of Anyperson and that my epistemic virtues were no better (or not that much better) than those of Anyperson, then *merely* discovering that I have a belief would not provide a basis for thinking that the belief is knowledge. Indeed, I see no "disharmony" at all in the mental states of persons who withhold believing that their beliefs rise to the level of knowledge. Pyrrhonism strikes me as a viable "harmonious" option. When they ascend, they don't assent.

Acknowledgments

I would like to thank Anne Ashbaugh, John Greco, Brian McLaughlin and especially Ernest Sosa for their help with this paper. Needless to say some of those people don't agree with all of the claims that I make!

Notes

1 In this chapter I will be relying primarily on the following papers by Sosa: "Philosophical Skepticism and Epistemic Circularity," *Proceedings of the Aristotelian Society* 68 (1994), 263–90 (cited as PSEC); "How to Resolve the Pyrrhonian Problematic: A Lesson from Descartes," *Philosophical Studies* 85 (1997): 229–49; "Reflective Knowledge in the Best Circles," *The Journal of Philosophy* 94 (1997): 410–30 (cited as RK); "The Raft and the Pyramid," as reprinted in Ernest Sosa and Jaegwon Kim, eds., *Epistemology* (Oxford: Blackwell, 2000) (cited as RP2); "Two False Dichotomies: Internalism/Externalism and Foundationalism/Coherentism," in Walter Sinnott-Armstrong, ed., *Pyrrhonian Skepticism* (Oxford: Oxford University Press, 2003); and "Circularity and Epistemic Priority," in R. Schantz, ed., *The Externalist Challenge: New Studies in Cognition and Intentionality* (de Gruyter, forthcoming) (cited as CEP).
2 I plan to discuss these issues in another paper.
3 I have a slight worry – that sometimes rises to the level of a nagging fear – that attributing the highest form of human knowledge to those of us who are epistemologists might be a bit jingoistic.
4 See my "Skepticism and Closure: Why the Evil Genius Argument Fails," *Philosophical Topics* 23, 1 (Spring 1995): 213–36.
5 More specifically, Sosa's form of externalism includes both the requirement that there is some appropriate hook-up between our beliefs and the world so that it is not accidental that our beliefs, however coherent, are true when justified, as well as a requirement that there be broad coherence among our beliefs. Thus "externalism" can include some internalist features but it is incompatible with pure internalism that holds that the epistemic quality of our beliefs depends completely on the reasons we have for them.
6 See Sextus Empiricus, *Outlines of Pyrrhonism*, 1, 166–9.
7 Sosa does give some examples of the kind of argument that might be circular in some sense but not vicious. See CEP: "Is there no difference between having and lacking an 'affirming' perspective on oneself, on the surrounding world, and on the relations between the two, a perspective on the basis of which one can coherently endorse one's own beliefs? Is such a coherent picture of things of no value simply because it cannot possibly be elaborated while avoiding all circularity? This should seem the opposite of obvious to a philosopher, since it discounts a main perennial objective of philosophical reflection: namely, the elaboration of such a coherent, 'affirming' view of oneself and one's place in the scheme of things. What is more, the member beliefs of such a system are enhanced precisely through being part of the

integrated view and not just loose from other beliefs in a less integrated mind. So these member beliefs attain a higher epistemic grade, a higher grade of knowledge, reflective knowledge, than they would attain otherwise, other things being equal."

8 I agree with his reasons and have offered some of my own in "Human Knowledge and the Infinite Regress of Reasons," in J. Tomberlin, ed., *Philosophical Perspectives*, vol. 13 (Malden, MA/Oxford: Blackwell, 1999), pp. 297–325; "Why Not Infinitism?" in Richard Cobb-Stevens, ed., *Epistemology: Proceedings of the Twentieth World Congress in Philosophy* (Bowling Green, OH: Philosophy Documentation Center, 2000), vol. 5, 199–208; "The Failures of Dogmatism and a New Pyrrhonism," *Acta Analytica* 15, 24 (2000): 7–24; and in "Academic and Pyrrhonian Skepticism," to appear in Steven Luper, ed., *The Skeptics: Contemporary Essays* (Ashgate Press).

9 See the papers cited in note 8, above.

10 Could it not be that some ancestor properties are essentially neither normative nor non-normative and that both "emerge" under various circumstances? I am not here endorsing this view. Rather, I merely wish to point to the importance of the assumption that all properties are either normative, non-normative, or both.

11 Strictly speaking, the existence of such a chain is not sufficient for a proposition's being justified. There must also not be reasons subjectively available (i.e., either a reason which S currently has or one that is appropriately epistemically hooked-up with S's currently held reasons) that would override a step in the chain of reasons. But that is not the admission of an externalist feature into an internalist account as Sosa views internalism and that complication can be ignored here.

12 I have discussed objections to infinitism, including the two that Sosa presents, more fully in the papers cited in note 8, above, as well as in "When Infinite Regresses are *Not* Vicious" to be given at the Pacific APA, March 2001, and published in *Philosophical and Phenomenological Research* 66 (2003): 718–29.

13 The qualification, namely "stated" arguments, leaves open the possibility that there is an infinite regress of reasons on either or both sides of the issue. Of course, if that were the case, then it would not be settled that either Academic Skepticism or its denial is the correct view to hold.

14 See *Certainty, a Refutation of Skepticism* (Minneapolis: University of Minnesota Press, 1981); and my "Skepticism and Closure: Why the Evil Genius Argument Fails."

15 See *Certainty*, esp. pp. 100–4.

16 Here I would identify my views closely with those of Michael Williams in *Unnatural Doubts* (Oxford: Basil Blackwell, 1991).

17 Some contextualists have held that merely raising the various alternatives is sufficient to make them such that they ought to be eliminated. See David Lewis in "Elusive Knowledge," *Australasian Journal of Philosophy* 74 (1996): 549–67. It is also endorsed by Keith DeRose in his "Solving the Skeptical Problem," *Philosophical Review* 104 (1995): 1–52 and his "Contextualism and Knowledge Attributions," *Philosophy and Phenomenological Research* 52 (1992): 913–29.

18 The Zebra-and-the-Zoo case is due to Fred Dretske. See his "Epistemic Operators," *The Journal of Philosophy* 67, 24 (1970): 1015–16.

19 Keith Lehrer, "Why Not Scepticism?" in Pojman, ed., *The Theory of Knowledge* (Belmont, CA: Wadsworth Publishing, 1993): 53. Lehrer no longer seems to hold this view, or at least, it is highly qualified since he now believes that we can use "I see a zebra" in our response to the skeptic who posits this objection, "You are asleep and dreaming that you see a zebra." See Lehrer, *Theory of Knowledge*, 2nd edn. (Boulder, CO: Westview Press, 2000): esp. 133–4 and chapter 9. Thus, he is claiming that we can use the very proposition that is being challenged to rebut the challenge. In that case, it does appear that we must believe that our current belief

(or "acceptance" as Lehrer would prefer) can be used to rebut a challenge to it and, hence, there is at least an implicit implication that our current beliefs are epistemically privileged over a challenge to them.

20 Perhaps we find ourselves regularly believing p and then not-p. Perhaps we share the worry that Descartes raised, namely that "nevertheless in whatever way they suppose that I have arrived at the state of being that I have reached . . . since to err and deceive oneself is a defect, it is clear that the greater will be the probability of my being so imperfect as to deceive myself ever, as is the Author to whom they assign my origin the less powerful" (Descartes's "First Meditation" in *The Philosophical Works of Descartes*, trans. Haldane and Ross (New York: Dover Publications, 1931): 147).

21 Note that PA does commit Sosa to an infinite regress of propositions of increasing complexity for which S *has* a justification. He is not committed to S's being able to believe them – since S might not be able to consider propositions with many iterated knowledge predicates.

22 By "justified" here I mean to be speaking somewhat casually. That is, I do not mean to be endorsing the view that it is settled that the carnie's belief is justified (in the sense that there is a completed justification available to him).

11

Sosa on Human and Animal Knowledge

HILARY KORNBLITH

Intuitively, it seems that both humans and non-human animals know a great many things. Just as it is part of Moorean common sense that human beings have a good deal of knowledge, it is also part of common sense that non-human animals have a good deal of knowledge. We explain the behavior of many animals[1] by attributing beliefs and desires to them and, more than this, we often speak of animals, at least colloquially, as having knowledge. Indeed, the attribution of knowledge to non-human animals seems to be more than just a matter of colloquial usage. An examination of the scientific literature on cognitive ethology shows that there too talk of animal knowledge is a commonplace.[2]

Philosophers, however, have not always been content to join with common usage on this issue. The question of whether non-human animals have genuine knowledge, and even the question of whether they have genuine beliefs, was a subject of great debate among the ancients.[3] More recently, Donald Davidson,[4] Robert Brandom[5] and John Haugeland[6] have all denied that non-human animals have beliefs, and Michael Williams[7] and Keith Lehrer,[8] accepting that they have beliefs, have nevertheless denied that they are capable of knowledge. Interestingly, Ernest Sosa seeks a middle ground here.[9] Sosa holds that non-human animals have knowledge, but he draws a distinction between two different kinds of knowledge – animal knowledge and reflective knowledge – with the standards for the latter being considerably higher than the former. If Sosa is right to draw such a distinction, then it would be appropriate to speak of *mere* animal knowledge, as opposed to the more demanding kind of knowledge which humans are capable of.

The distinction between these two sorts of knowledge plays an important role in Sosa's epistemology because Sosa's virtue perspectivism is itself a kind of middle ground between uncompromising externalism and uncompromising internalism.[10] While reliabilists insist that knowledge is, roughly, true belief which is reliably produced, and internalists insist that knowledge is, roughly, true belief which satisfies certain internally specified standards (such as foundationalist or coherentist demands), Sosa defends a view of knowledge as, roughly, true belief which is reliably produced and which also meets certain internally specified demands (of coherence). The move from reliabilism to Sosa's virtue perspectivism is connected to the view that human beings are capable of something more than mere animal knowledge.

But how well motivated is Sosa's distinction between animal knowledge and reflective knowledge? In this chapter, I argue that the distinction is not well motivated. I myself would defend a more unitary view of knowledge. I believe that human knowledge and animal knowledge are one and the same, and thus that no concession to internalism is required.

I

Sosa first draws the distinction between animal knowledge and reflective knowledge in "Knowledge and Intellectual Virtue."[11]

> One has *animal knowledge* about one's environment, one's past, and one's own experience if one's judgments and beliefs about these are direct responses to their impact – e.g., through perception or memory – with little or no benefit of reflection or understanding.
>
> One has *reflective knowledge* if one's judgment or belief manifests not only such direct response to the fact known but also understanding of its place in a wider whole that includes one's belief and knowledge of it and how these come about. (*KP*, 240)

A few comments about these definitions are called for. First, the distinction, as introduced here, makes the difference between animal knowledge and reflective knowledge a matter of degree, for animal knowledge involves "little or no benefit of reflection or understanding," while reflective knowledge involves "understanding of [the belief's] place in a wider whole that includes one's knowledge of it and how these come about." Second, reflective knowledge requires a substantial amount of second-order knowledge, precisely because it requires understanding of the belief's place in one's larger body of beliefs, as well as an understanding of the belief's origin. Without this second-order knowledge, or without very much of it, one is reduced to mere animal knowledge. Animal knowledge involves responsiveness to the environment with little or no second-order understanding. On this way of viewing things, one would think that non-human animals have a great deal of animal knowledge but probably no reflective knowledge;[12] human beings, however, are capable of reflective knowledge, but on at least many occasions, it seems, have nothing more than animal knowledge. Reflective knowledge sets a high standard, a standard to which we might aspire; and yet often, in the ordinary course of events, it is a standard which we do not reach or even attempt to reach.

These comments set out my own understanding of the distinction Sosa draws, and some of the things which follow from that distinction, or which follow from the distinction together with some commonsense truths about humans and non-human animals. But what Sosa says about the distinction is actually quite different. Sosa comments,

> Note that no human blessed with reason has merely animal knowledge of the sort attainable by beasts. For even when perceptual belief derives as directly as it ever does from sensory stimuli, it is still relevant that one has *not* perceived the signs of contrary testimony. A reason-endowed being automatically monitors his background information and his sensory input for contrary evidence and automatically opts for the most coherent hypothesis even when he responds most directly to sensory stimuli. For even when response to stimuli is

most direct, *if* one were also to hear or see the signs of credible contrary testimony that would change one's response. The beliefs of a *rational* animal hence would seem never to issue from *unaided* introspection, memory, or perception. For reason is always at least a silent partner on the watch for other relevant data, a silent partner whose very *silence* is a contributing cause of the belief outcome. (*KP*, 240)

So Sosa wishes to claim, contrary to what I suggested earlier, that human beings never have mere animal knowledge. Let us take a closer look at the relationship between Sosa's definitions and the comments he makes about them, and also at the larger philosophical issues which are raised here.

The definition of reflective knowledge, as the term suggests, explicitly requires second-order knowledge. If one is to have reflective knowledge that a certain proposition is true, one must have an "understanding of its place in a wider whole that includes one's belief and knowledge of it and how these come about." With little or no second-order knowledge of these things, one's knowledge is reduced in status to mere animal knowledge. But in the passage just quoted, Sosa allows that no actual reflection, and no actual second-order knowledge, are required for reflective knowledge. Human knowledge never descends to the level of animal knowledge because even if we do not reflect on a particular belief at all, and even if we have no understanding whatsoever of its place in our wider body of beliefs, and even if we have no thoughts about its origin, we still satisfy a certain counterfactual condition: if we were to come to have relevant counterevidence, we would be responsive to it. And it is the satisfying of this counterfactual condition which makes all of our beliefs, however unreflectively arrived at or sustained, cases of reflective knowledge. On its face, these comments seem to change the standards for reflective knowledge quite substantially.

Now I agree with Sosa that human beings are, on the whole, responsive to counterevidence even when they do not actually reflect on their beliefs; human beings thus typically satisfy the counterfactual condition. But Sosa goes further than this: he says that this makes us "rational" animals, or "reason-endowed" beings, and, again, according to Sosa, this makes us unlike mere "beasts." But if the requirement for reflective knowledge is read in this way, and so it does not require actual reflection, or even the ability to reflect, but only a certain sort of responsiveness to counterevidence, then non-human animals – animals incapable of reflection – turn out to have reflective knowledge as well; indeed, all of their knowledge turns out to be reflective knowledge. More than this, the requirement of responsiveness to counterevidence is arguably a requirement on having beliefs at all. Certainly a creature all of whose alleged beliefs were entirely unresponsive to counterevidence would not have any genuine beliefs.[13] The beliefs of non-human animals are not like this. They are strikingly responsive to counterevidence.[14] So if Sosa's definitions are taken at face value, human beings do indeed have mere animal knowledge a good deal of the time, simply because we frequently do not stop to reflect; non-human animals, on the other hand, do not ever have reflective knowledge. But if we substitute the counterfactual sensitivity requirement for reflective knowledge, human beings never have mere animal knowledge; but non-human animals do not ever have mere animal knowledge either.

There is something odd about introducing a distinction between animal knowledge and reflective knowledge as a distinction between mere responsiveness – what animals have – and responsiveness together with a broad reflective understanding of the place of one's belief in one's larger body of beliefs together with an understanding of the belief's origin – what humans are capable of – and then suggesting that the latter requires no more than a certain kind of responsiveness. If reflective knowledge is meant to be something more than just responsiveness, it must, as the definition does require if taken at face value, add something beyond responsiveness.

There are ways of reading the counterfactual requirement so that it does require something which non-human animals do not have. Sosa does say, in the quoted passage, that human beings would respond differently if they were to be presented with counter-evidence, and this suggests the counterfactual requirement which trivializes the notion of reflective knowledge. But he also says:

> A reason-endowed being automatically monitors his background information and his sensory input for contrary evidence and automatically opts for the most coherent hypothesis even when he responds most directly to sensory stimuli. (*KP*, 240)

Talk of an agent "monitoring" his background information, as opposed to merely being sensitive to changes in background information may suggest an account of reflective knowledge which does not trivialize it. One way to understand this is to see the monitoring as something which is essentially conscious; monitoring is nothing more than a kind of reflection. But on this reading, humans frequently fail to monitor their background beliefs, even if the new beliefs they form are sensitive to the content of their background views. A different way to understand the monitoring condition is to see it as a kind of counterfactual reflection condition: reflective knowledge requires that one would reflect on one's counterevidence if one had any.[15] Thus, the way in which one is sensitive to counterevidence, on this reading, is that it would be self-consciously reflected upon if it existed. This condition is arguably not met by non-human animals, but it is only sometimes met by human beings. We frequently form beliefs in a way which not only fails to involve self-conscious reflection, but would not involve self-conscious reflection even in the presence of counterevidence, even though on some of these occasions, we would be responsive, in an unreflective way, to the counterevidence. I do not see any way of reading the distinction, however, which gets human knowledge to fall on one side of it in every case and non-human animal knowledge to fall on the other side. And yet this is what Sosa claims for the distinction.

Sosa wishes to claim that reflective knowledge is, in some important sense, better than mere animal knowledge. After introducing the definition of reflective knowledge which requires a good deal of second-order understanding, he comments:

> Since a direct response supplemented by such understanding would in general have a better chance of being right, reflective knowledge is better justified than corresponding animal knowledge. (*KP*, 240)

But the relationship between reliability – the chance of being right – and the kind of second-order reflection mentioned in the definition of reflective knowledge is surely more complex than this would suggest. First-order mechanisms of belief production – those which operate without any reflection at all – vary in reliability. Some such mechanisms are very unreliable; others are extremely reliable. The same, of course, is true about reflection itself. In addition, there are some mechanisms of reflection which seem to do little more than ratify whatever beliefs are produced by one's first-order mechanisms; they play the role of cognitive yes-men.[16] So it does not seem generally true that reflective knowledge is more reliable than unreflective knowledge. Sometimes reflection acts as a corrective on less reliable first-order processes. But it can also interfere with the smooth working of more reliable first-order mechanisms. And sometimes it just leaves things as they were. Reflection should not be recommended across the board as a route to increased reliability.[17]

In a later piece, Sosa introduces the distinction between animal knowledge and reflective knowledge in a way which solves this problem by definitional fiat:

> we can more generally distinguish *animal* knowledge, which requires only that one track reality, on the one hand, and *reflective* knowledge, on the other, which in addition requires awareness of how one knows, in a way that precludes the unreliability of one's faculties.[18]

Here it is simply stipulated that, if something is to count as reflective knowledge, then one must have reflected in a way which is especially reliable. But the solution by definitional fiat has problems of its own. In particular, it is not at all clear that there are ways of reflecting which "preclude the unreliability of one's faculties," at least if talk of "ways of reflecting" is to map on to any plausible taxonomy of psychological processes. On this account, it is not clear that anyone ever possesses, or even could possess, reflective knowledge.

Even apart from requiring that reflection be so reliable as to preclude unreliability in one's cognitive faculties, Sosa is concerned to stress the merits of reflection.

> This is not to deny that there is a kind of "animal knowledge" untouched by broad coherence. It is rather only to affirm that beyond "animal knowledge" there is a better knowledge. This reflective knowledge does require broad coherence, including one's ability to place one's first-level knowledge in epistemic perspective. But why aspire to any such thing? What is so desirable, epistemically, about broad coherence? Broad coherence is desirable because it yields integrated understanding, and also because it is truth conducive, even if in a demon world broad coherence fails this test and is not truth conducive. Even so, we can still regard broad coherence as intellectually valuable and admirable so long as we do not regard our world as such a world. (RK, 422)

We have already dealt with the suggestion that adding a requirement of reflection automatically raises the reliability of the belief-producing process. But what is the other benefit which Sosa attributes to reflective knowledge, the respect in which it is said to be better than animal knowledge? Here Sosa says it is "desirable because it yields integrated understanding." This is not altogether satisfying as an explanation of the epistemic benefit of coherent belief since talk of integrated understanding seems perilously close to talk of coherence itself. To say that reflecting so as to produce more coherent belief yields integrated understanding sounds very much like saying that reflecting so as to produce more coherent belief yields more coherent belief. Why should we think that this is an epistemically good thing? And even if broadly coherent belief is a good thing epistemically, to what extent does this show that reflective knowledge is a better thing, epistemically, than mere animal knowledge?

There is no question that reflecting on one's beliefs and the processes by which they are produced can lead not only to a body of beliefs which are broadly coherent, but also to a wider understanding of things than one would have had without reflection. And when it comes to understanding, more is better. But now consider two individuals, each of whom knows that a certain proposition p is true. Individual A believes that p, p is true, and his belief that p is produced by an extremely reliable process. A has not, however, reflected on his beliefs; he has not reflected on the extent to which his belief that p coheres with his other beliefs, nor has he reflected on the manner in which his belief that p was produced. At least on this particular occasion, A is being a thoroughly unreflective, although extremely reliable, individual. B, on the other hand, is, at least on this occasion, very reflective. B believes that p; p is in fact true; and the belief that p is produced in a reliable way. But B also reflects on the way in which her belief that p fits in with her other beliefs, and, noting that it does cohere with them, she draws out a number of additional consequences from her overall body of beliefs. In addition, B reflects on the manner in which she arrived at her belief, and she comes to believe that she did, in fact, arrive at her belief reliably, and this belief too coheres with her other beliefs; this further point is something which she reflectively notes.

Now B knows many things which A does not, and reflection on her situation has produced a good deal of knowledge which she has but A lacks. More than this, A could have had this knowledge if only he too had reflected on his epistemic situation. So there is no question that, at least in this situation, reflecting has produced epistemic benefits. It has, on this occasion, improved B's epistemic situation. I certainly do not wish to deny that this kind of thing can occur.

But let us return to an evaluation of the belief that p. Both A and B believe that p. And if we follow Sosa's initial introduction of the terms, we should say that A has mere animal knowledge that p while B has reflective knowledge that p. How does having reflective knowledge that p put one in a better epistemic situation *with respect to p*? Thus far, the epistemic benefits we have noted in B's situation have to do with her knowing many other things *in addition to* p, but this, by itself, does not clearly show that her knowledge that p is in any respect superior to A's knowledge that p. And as we have seen, her reflecting, and coming to know many other things which A does not, does not in any way entail that she is more reliable with respect to p than A is. For all that has been said, A's belief that p may have been produced by a far more reliable process than B's, even when we include the effects that B's reflection has on the overall reliability of the way in which she arrived at her belief that p. So how is B's knowledge that p supposed to be superior to A's?

Consider an analogy. Suppose that I have a handful of friends whom I trust a great deal, and I frequently consult with them before reaching a conclusion about matters of importance. When an issue arises that matters to me, I think things through, and then consult with my friends. I not only ask them what I should believe about the relevant matter, I also ask them for their reasons, and what it is that they know about related issues.[19] Let us leave aside, for a moment, the issue of my friends' reliability, and whether the beliefs I come to as a result of these consultations are more or less likely to be true than beliefs arrived at independently of these friends; let us also leave aside the reasons, if any, I have for trusting them. One of the results of my consultations is that I come to have a wider range of beliefs than I would have had without consulting. On occasions on which I consult with my friends, I thus have a larger and more deeply interconnected body of beliefs than I otherwise would. I also come to have greater confidence in the beliefs I reach after consulting my friends than the ones I arrive at without consultation.

Let us call the knowledge I come to have after consulting with my friends *consultative knowledge*, and knowledge which I have which is not screened by these friends *non-consultative knowledge*. Suppose I come to believe that consultative knowledge is superior to non-consultative knowledge. Indeed, I recognize that, while other people do form their beliefs in ways which benefit from the testimony of others, very few if any others have a group of friends on whom they rely in just the way I do to inform my epistemic decisions. And suppose that I come to believe, as a result, that the knowledge which others have, since it is merely non-consultative, is inferior to mine.

Would I be justified in drawing a distinction between these two alleged kinds of knowledge, and would I be correct in thinking that consultative knowledge is superior to non-consultative knowledge? As far as the first question goes, it seems to me that so-called consultative knowledge is not a different kind of knowledge from non-consultative knowledge. Yes, in order to possess consultative knowledge, one must have gone through a certain process which the possessor of non-consultative knowledge has not followed. But if this is a ground for drawing a distinction between different kinds of knowledge, then we will have as many different kinds of knowledge as there are processes of belief acquisition and retention. Surely this multiplies kinds of knowledge far beyond necessity. On the second question, it seems that until we know something about the reliability of my friends, the question of whether going through the additional consultation improves my epistemic situation remains unanswered. If my friends are like most, and they are reliable about some areas and unreliable about others, then the epistemic value of my checking with them will be a mixed bag. But, to return to my first point, even in the unlikely event that this checking increases my reliability across the board, it hardly seems right to suggest that consultative knowledge is a different sort of knowledge than that possessed by others. We may better address the epistemic issues involved here by asking about the advantages and disadvantages of consultation with a small circle of friends than by introducing a distinction between different sorts of knowledge.

It seems to me that the distinction between reflective knowledge and animal knowledge is no better grounded than the distinction between consultative and non-consultative knowledge. There is no ground, I believe, for regarding reflective knowledge and animal knowledge as two different sorts of knowledge, nor is there adequate ground for thinking that knowledge which is produced or sustained by means of reflection is, *eo ipso*, better knowledge than knowledge which does not draw upon reflection. The epistemic utility of reflection is, to my mind, an interesting and important topic, but it is most clearly addressed directly. Insisting on a distinction between animal knowledge and reflective knowledge gets in the way of, rather than aids, such an assessment.

Animal knowledge, roughly, is just reliably produced true belief.[20] Sosa's blend of externalist and internalist requirements on knowledge comes about only because he draws a distinction between mere animal knowledge and reflective knowledge, and then insists that reflective knowledge presents us with an appropriate epistemic goal as human beings. But if the distinction between animal knowledge and reflective knowledge is no better motivated than the distinction between consultative and non-consultative knowledge, or the distinction between knowledge which makes use of any arbitrarily chosen belief-influencing process and knowledge which fails to draw on that process, then the motivation for a blend of externalist and internalist requirements on knowledge is undermined. Reflection can be drawn upon by human beings in producing knowledge, but when it is drawn upon, we should continue to see the requirements on knowledge as unchanged: the requirements on the use of reflection, like those on every other belief acquisition process, involve nothing more than reliably produced true belief.[21]

Acknowledgments

It is a pleasure to contribute to this Festschrift in honor of Ernie Sosa. I have been learning from Ernie's work since my undergraduate days and I am delighted to have the occasion, finally, to acknowledge my debt. Ernie's sober good sense, deep understanding, and unwillingness to indulge in rhetorical overstatement are a model for us all.

Notes

1 From now on, I will use the term 'animal' to refer to non-human animals.
2 I have discussed the importance of this literature for epistemology in "Knowledge in Humans and Other Animals," *Philosophical Perspectives* 13 (1999): 327–46; and, at greater length, in *Knowledge and Its Place in Nature* (Oxford: Clarendon Press, 2002).
3 For a review of this literature, see Richard Sorabji, *Animal Minds and Human Morals: The Origins of the Western Debate* (Ithaca, NY: Cornell University Press, 1993).
4 See, e.g., "Thought and Talk," reprinted in his *Inquiries into Truth and Interpretation* (Oxford: Oxford University Press, 1984). Davidson holds that non-human animals lack propositional attitudes because they are not users and interpreters of language.
5 *Making It Explicit* (Cambridge, MA: Harvard University Press, 1994), and *Articulating Reasons* (Cambridge, MA: Harvard University Press, 2000). Brandom holds that non-human animals lack propositional attitudes because they do not participate in the social practice of giving and asking for reasons.
6 *Having Thought* (Cambridge, MA: Harvard University Press, 1998). Haugeland holds that non-human animals lack propositional attitudes because they lack "existential commitment."
7 See, e.g., "Dretske on Epistemic Entitlement," *Philosophy and Phenomenological Research* 60 (2000): 607–12. Williams holds that non-human animals lack knowledge because they have not been "induct[ed] into a linguistic community, with its shared epistemic practices" (p. 609).
8 *Metamind* (Oxford: Oxford University Press, 1990). Lehrer holds (in that book) that non-human animals lack knowledge because they lack knowledge of their beliefs and the relations among them. He has since expressed a more conciliatory view, drawing a distinction between "discursive knowledge" and "the primitive knowledge young children and animals possess." "Discursive Knowledge," *Philosophy and Phenomenological Research* 60 (2000): 637–53. This latter distinction is quite similar to the distinction Sosa draws which is the subject of this chapter. Fred Dretske critically discusses Lehrer's view in "Two Conceptions of Knowledge: Rational vs. Reliable Belief," reprinted in his *Perception, Knowledge and Belief: Selected Essays* (Cambridge: Cambridge University Press, 2000), pp. 80–93.
9 More recently Sosa suggests a view which may be closer to that of Davidson, Brandom and Haugeland: "A mere thermometer reaction to one's environment cannot constitute real knowledge, regardless of whether that reaction is causally mediated by experience. It is not enough

that one respond to seeing white and round objects in good light with a 'belief' or 'proto-belief' that one faces something white and round." "Two False Dichotomies: Foundationalism/Coherentism and Internalism/Externalism," in R. Schantz, ed., *The Externalist Challenge: New Studies on Cognition and Intentionality* (de Gruyter, forthcoming; cited as TFD). This passage at least seems to hint at a view in which non-human animals, because they lack the capacity to reflect, are thereby deprived not only of knowledge, but of genuine belief as well. I will focus in the body of this chapter on the more moderate view, however, both because it is developed at greater length in Sosa's work and also because it is the more highly intuitive view, and thus, to my mind, fits far better with Sosa's overall Moorean orientation. That said, a few remarks I make later in the chapter will apply to this more radical view as well.

10 Sosa himself puts it this way. See TFD.

11 "Knowledge and Intellectual Virtue," *The Monist* 68 (1985): 226–45. Reprinted in *Knowledge in Perspective: Selected Essays in Epistemology* (Cambridge: Cambridge University Press, 1991) (cited as *KP*). Here I follow the pagination in the reprint.

12 For relevant work on this question, see, e.g., Dorothy Cheney and Robert Seyfarth, *How Monkeys See the World: Inside the Mind of Another Species* (Chicago: University of Chicago Press, 1990); and Marc Hauser, *The Evolution of Communication* (Cambridge, MA: MIT Press, 1996).

13 Compare Fodor's view on this issue: "Why Paramecia Don't Have Mental Representations," *Midwest Studies in Philosophy* 10 (1986): 3–23.

14 See, e.g., Colin Allen and Marc Bekoff, *Species of Mind: The Philosophy and Biology of Cognitive Ethology* (Cambridge, MA: MIT Press, 1997).

15 This reading of the reflective awareness condition is, perhaps, suggested by a phrase in "Intellectual Virtues in Perspective": "one's reflective awareness, implicit though it normally remains." In *KP*, 282.

16 For a review of some of the psychological literature relevant here, and a discussion of its importance for epistemological theorizing, see my "Introspection and Misdirection," *Australasian Journal of Philosophy* 67(1989): 410–22.

17 For interesting discussion of this issue and its connection to the notions of epistemic responsibility, epistemic virtue, and coherence, see Michael Bishop, "In Praise of Epistemic Irresponsibility: How Lazy and Ignorant Can You Be?" *Synthese* 122 (2000): 179–208.

18 "Reflective Knowledge in the Best Circles," *The Journal of Philosophy* 94 (1997): p. 427 (cited as RK).

19 The analogy with reflection will be even closer if we suppose that the friends I consult show a certain deference to my opinions, tending to encourage me to believe just what I would have believed even without consultation. See "Introspection and Misdirection," cited in note 16 above.

20 There are, of course, reasonable concerns about how precisely an externalist account of knowledge should be presented, but they are beyond the scope of this chapter. For the sake of simplicity of exposition then, I assume a straightforward reliability account.

21 David Christensen and John Greco provided helpful comments on a draft of this paper.

12

Skepticism Undone?

PAUL MOSER

Epistemologists have long given special attention, if typically unfriendly attention, to circularity in warrant for beliefs. Such attention might stem just from a dislike of circularity, in the way that some people dislike circular shapes in their evergreen bushes. Perhaps some epistemologists simply do not *like* the look of circles in warrant. That is a real possibility, of course, but why would these epistemologists then bother to *make a general case* against circles in warrant? If they are moved just by a personal dislike of circles, they might as well keep their dislike to themselves. In that case, their dislike would not be relevantly different from my antipathy to eating coconut. It would be unconvincing for me to make a general case against eating coconut on the ground that *I* dislike its taste. You may very well like the taste of coconut, and that would settle that, my personal dislike notwithstanding.

In opposing circles in warrant, epistemologists customarily have a reason, not just a dislike. Their reason allegedly has *general* significance, bearing on circularity generally, not just on the circularity in their own doxastic backyard. So their opposing circularity in warrant differs from my disliking the taste of coconut. What, however, underwrites their opposition, and does it underwrite convincingly? This twofold question has attracted the critical attention of Ernest Sosa in at least two recent essays: "Philosophical Scepticism and Epistemic Circularity" and "Reflective Knowledge in the Best Circles." In general, Sosa contends that a common species of epistemic circularity is not automatically vicious and that therefore some familiar skeptical and relativistic worries are misplaced. I shall argue that the latter worries are surprisingly resilient and troublesome after all, but that skepticism does not thereby triumph.

1 Epistemic Circles

William Alston has characterized a common kind of epistemic circularity as involving "a commitment to the conclusion [of a relevant argument] as a presupposition of our supposing ourselves to be *justified* in holding the premises" (see Moser 1993,15). Skeptics in the tradition of Sextus Empiricus would be uneasy with at least such circularity. They go further, however, in challenging us to secure *non-question-begging* warrant for our beliefs. In securing such warrant, we would be able to avoid simply assuming (the truth of) a position under dispute by skeptics. In particular, such warrant would free us from merely *presuming* an answer to skeptics' questions that favors our having reliable beliefs about a disputed matter.

The demand for non-question-begging warrant exceeds opposition to the kind of epistemic circularity identified by Alston. This demand calls for non-question-begging warrant even in cases where we are neither wielding nor supposing ourselves to be justified in holding the premises of an argument. We can beg questions about truth and reliability even when we do not consider ourselves to be justified in holding an argument's premises. Let's call the key challenge here *the non-question-begging challenge*. Let's also restrict our talk of skeptics to those who promote this challenge. Skeptics come in many shapes and sizes, but we shall limit our focus to those advancing the non-question-begging challenge. They are, after all, the most formidable skeptics, as I have tried to explain elsewhere (Moser 1993; Moser 2000).

Sooner or later, skeptics raise *comprehensive* questions about the reliability of our belief-forming sources. Such questions concern our belief-forming sources altogether, or *in total*. Specifically, they concern what non-question-begging warrant we have to regard *any* subset of those sources as reliable, even minimally reliable, for acquiring truth and avoiding error. Such warrant would enable one, at least regarding some source, to avoid begging questions against skeptics in virtue of merely presuming the correctness of a disputed view regarding truth or reliability. We thus gain nothing of real value in an exchange with skeptics by trying to have the reliability of one belief-forming source, such as touch, checked for reliability by another source, such as vision. *Any* such source is now under question by skeptics regarding even minimal reliability. These skeptics are not necessarily obtuse in raising their challenge. They may simply be curious about whether anything speaks convincingly in favor of the reliability of our belief-forming sources *as a group*. We seem to face intelligible questions about the reliability of those sources as a group. So it seems worthwhile to ask whether non-question-begging answers to such questions are forthcoming. Once we answer that question, we can assess the significance of the answer for the viability of skepticism.

Suppose we had an answer to the *comprehensive* question of the reliability of our belief-forming sources. Would that answer necessarily rely on input from one of the very sources under question by skeptics? Specifically, would it rely on one of the sources in a way that presumes reliability under question? If so, the answer would suffer from question-begging. One might find it obvious that we cannot test the reliability of our belief-forming sources without relying on (at least one of) them in a way that takes for granted something under dispute by skeptics. In particular, our offering support for the reliability of our belief-forming sources will evidently rely on such sources as perception, introspection, belief, memory, testimony, intuition, and common sense. It evidently will rely on such sources in a way that begs a question about reliability against skeptics. *All* such sources are now under question by skeptics, with regard to even their minimal reliability. The problem is not that we *use* such sources in forming our beliefs by way of reply to skeptics. The problem is rather that in offering support for the reliability of our sources, we evidently rely on those sources *in a question-begging manner*. We thereby would violate the non-question-begging challenge. So reliance on the sources in question evidently will not deliver the kind of evidence of reliability sought by skeptics.

What, then, might deliver the needed non-question-begging warrant? Must we seek a position independent of our own belief-forming sources to deliver a non-question-begging indication of their reliability? Is such an independent position possible? If so, how? What exact kind of independence, if any, is available here? Aside from how we answer these questions, the success of the non-question-begging challenge would entail that we lack the resources for avoiding evidential circularity. This would raise problems in some epistemically relevant areas but not in others. It would *not* preclude our having reliable beliefs, evidence-based beliefs, or even knowledge as reliably produced true belief. It would, however, undermine our answering comprehensive skeptical challenges in a manner free of the kind of arbitrariness characteristic of circular reasoning. In that case, we would not be able to silence skeptics convincingly. From the standpoint of being judicious truth-seekers, rather than mere knowers, we would be incapable of releasing the bite of skepticism.

Our problem does not arise from a demand for certainty or even for deductive inference in warrant. Skeptics can grant that the epistemic support for (at least contingent) propositions may be fallible and defeasible and fail to yield epistemic certainty, and they can allow for non-deductive inference in rational belief-transmission. A demand for non-question-begging evidence is not a demand for certainty or deductive inference. It arises rather from a concern to avoid question-begging evidential circularity. Such circularity, if exonerated, would make reasoning in debates about skepticism ineffective.

If question-begging is generally permissible, one can support *any* position one likes. In that case, one may simply beg the key questions in any dispute regarding the position one happens to like. Given the permissibility of such a rationally arbitrary strategy, argument will become ineffective in the way that viciously circular argument is ineffective. Question-begging strategies, if exonerated, would condone arbitrariness in argument and in philosophical exchange generally. Such strategies are thus rationally ineffective with regard to the questions begged. This position differs from the dubious claim that a particular instance of question-begging must be unreliable. Skeptics need not endorse the latter claim. It might be tempting to try to restrict the permissibility of question-begging to certain kinds of issues. Arbitrariness, however, is a constant threat to such a ploy.

A natural response is that, with regard to answers to comprehensive skeptical challenges, question-begging is unavoidable. Sosa comments as follows, in treating a somewhat different topic:

> So far we have been told that we must avoid epistemic circularity because it entails arriving at a generally positive view of one's faculties only by use of those very faculties. But why should that be frustrating when it is the inevitable consequence of its generality? (RK2, 282)

The non-question-begging challenge, I have suggested, does not oppose epistemic circularity on the ground that "it entails arriving at a generally positive view of one's faculties only by use of those very faculties." It rather opposes relying on those faculties *in a question-begging manner* in offering support for their reliability.

Regarding circularity as an "inevitable consequence," let's suppose (if only for the sake of argument) that it is indeed such a consequence of generality. We still should withhold an inference from

(a) the view that we *inevitably* beg questions in the face of a comprehensive skeptical challenge

to

(b) the view that some questions *rationally may* be begged.

Skeptics properly doubt that any inevitability in our begging comprehensive skeptical questions *rationally entitles* us, as judicious truth-seekers, to beg those questions.

The inevitable is not necessarily the rational. At least, we have no compelling reason to hold that inevitability entails rationality. On the contrary, epistemic rationality in truth-seeking (however the details go) seems inherently normative in a way that inevitability is not. That is, what we inevitably believe may run afoul of the standard of what is valuable by way of judicious truth-seeking. In fostering arbitrariness (of the kind noted above) in the area of epistemically rational truth-seeking, begging skeptical questions hinders our goal of judiciously, or non-arbitrarily, acquiring truth and avoiding error. It would yield a position that is epistemically arbitrary relative to intelligible skeptical questions about truth or reliability. Arbitrariness here would undermine any convincing recommendation against skepticism, even if we nonetheless have reliable belief, evidence-based belief, or knowledge. As epistemologists, we properly inquire about the availability of skeptic-resistant judicious truth-seeking. We should not limit our inquiry to the conditions for reliable belief, evidence-based belief, or knowledge.

Sosa suggests that we are unable to answer skeptics without begging the question against them, but that nothing important is thereby lost:

> in epistemology we want *knowledgeable* understanding, and not just "understanding by dumb luck".... But there is no apparent reason why we cannot have it with a theory such as T [= A belief X amounts to knowledge if and only if it satisfies conditions C], without compromising the full generality of our account. Of course in explaining how we know theory T... we have to appeal to theory T itself, given the assumptions of correctness and full generality that we are making concerning T. Given those assumptions there seems no way of correctly answering ... a sceptic except by "begging the question" and "arguing circularly" against him. But, once we understand this, what option is left to us except to go ahead and "beg" that question against ... a sceptic (though "begging the question" and "arguing circularly" may now be misnomers for what we do, since it is surely no fallacy, not if it constitutes correct and legitimate intellectual procedure). (PSEC, 324)

Sosa rightly notes that "it is not just *in virtue of being self-supporting* that our belief in T would acquire its epistemic status required for knowledge. Rather it would be in virtue of meeting conditions C" (PSEC, 324). This is not only correct but also transparently correct. Even so, the skeptic's challenge, namely the no-question-begging challenge, does not concern merely "explaining how we know theory T." The challenge concerns, as noted above, answering *without question-begging* skeptics' comprehensive questions about the reliability of our belief-forming sources. This challenge is not met by our "explaining how we know theory T," even if such explaining demands an appeal to theory T itself. So we are not out of the woods yet.

Moving a bit closer to the non-question-begging challenge, Sosa asks whether epistemically circular arguments enable us to discriminate between reliable and unreliable belief-forming practices. He proposes that "one can make such discriminations with epistemically circular arguments (ones with premises that are in fact true and justified, etc.) even if it is not the circular character of the reasoning that by itself effects the discrimination" (PSEC, 328, n.34). That is certainly true on at least one sense of "discrimination." The key issue, however, now becomes: What *kind* of discrimination is relevant to exchanges with skeptics, particularly when they raise the non-question-begging challenge? Some kinds of discrimination will be irrelevant in virtue of failing to engage *in a non-question-begging manner* skeptics' comprehensive questions about the reliability of our belief-forming sources. An appeal to irrelevant kinds of discrimination would yield our talking past skeptics rather than effectively answering or challenging them. In particular, it would weaken Sosa's desired conclusion that "we have found no good reason to accept *philosophical scepticism*" (PSEC, 324).

As epistemologists challenged by skeptics, we still have work to do after separating reliable from unreliable belief-forming practices and even after identifying and satisfying conditions *C* for knowledge. Beyond the kind(s) of discrimination needed for those important projects, we need another kind of discrimination to handle the non-question-begging challenge. We need a kind of discrimination that does not beg questions against skeptics who raise comprehensive questions about the reliability of our belief-forming sources. Otherwise, in settling for question begging, we foster the kind of arbitrariness opposed above. That is, we open the door to one's being able to support *any* arbitrary position one likes, in virtue of the permissibility of question-begging. Condoning such arbitrariness, we in effect make argument ineffective in the way that viciously circular argument is ineffective. The value of argument in philosophy is thus at stake in our concerns about question-begging in reply to skeptics.

Skeptics, we might say, seek a *comprehensive* answer to the issue of whether our belief-forming sources are reliable. Such an answer would not rest on question-begging in light of skeptical questions about reliability or truth. The issue is not whether we simply *possess* truth or reliability in our beliefs or sources of beliefs. The issue is rather whether we can answer skeptics' intelligible comprehensive questions without begging those questions. Do our reasons (whatever they include) for our beliefs ultimately lack robustness in the teeth of this challenge?

Sosa would evidently reply with some considerations about the roles of argument and aptness in knowledge and rational belief concerning reliability. He rightly notes that the validity of an argument delivers at most a restriction on one's available coherent combinations of attitudes regarding premises and conclusion (PSEC, 318–19). Such validity guarantees at most a kind of internal coherence in combinations of attitudes towards premises and conclusion. This kind of coherence does not take us very far at all toward answering skeptics without begging questions. Fortunately, we do not have to end the story of epistemic value with the coherence stemming from valid arguments or with any kind of rational coherence. Other factors are equally important.

Sosa explains as follows:

> In order to know that *P*, one's belief must not fail the test of rational, internal coherence. But it must be tested in other ways as well: it must be true for one thing. And, more than

that, it must be *apt*: it must be a belief that manifests overall intellectual virtue, and is not flawed essentially by vice.... Finally, if it is to amount to knowledge a belief must be such that, in the circumstances it *would* be held by that subject if it were true, and this in virtue of its being apt in the way that it is apt. (PSEC 320; cf. RK2, 279, 284)

The use of "test" in this quotation is metaphorical. Non-reflective knowledge, on Sosa's own account, can exist without any testing. Sosa proposes, then, that at least epistemic aptness must be added to proper reasoning to account for epistemic value (or in his language "epistemic welfare"). Accordingly, he offers this rhetorical question: "why not distinguish between the [crystal-ball] gazers and the [ordinary] perceivers in that, though both reason properly and attain thereby coherence and justification, only the perceivers' beliefs are epistemically apt and constitute knowledge?" (RK2, 283).

Reliability of a belief-forming source is evidently a logically *sufficient* condition of epistemic aptness. Sosa claims: "Perception is, of course, reliable while [crystal-ball] gazing is not. Therefore, the perceivers are right and apt both in their particular perceptual beliefs, at least generally, and in their theory of knowledge – for it all rests in large measure on their reliable perception" (RK2, 283). In addition, reliability is evidently a logically *necessary* condition of epistemic aptness. Sosa remarks: "the [crystal-ball] gazers are wrong and inapt both in their particular gaze-derived beliefs and in their theory of knowledge – for it all rests on their unreliable gazing" (RK2, 283). Reliability, then, is both necessary and sufficient for epistemic aptness, and this takes epistemic value well beyond rational coherence. For the sake of argument, let's concede Sosa his aptness approach to epistemic value and to knowledge. Our immediate concerns now lie elsewhere.

We turned to Sosa's notion of epistemic aptness after asking whether we can answer skeptics' intelligible comprehensive questions without begging those questions. How then does epistemic aptness figure in our deliberations about skeptics' non-question-begging challenge? Let's try this likely question from skeptics: what non-question-begging reason, if any, have we for thinking that our ordinary perceptual beliefs come from sources that are genuinely apt in Sosa's sense? Sosa has said, as noted, that "perception is, of course, reliable." How can this remark figure in the needed answer to the non-question-begging challenge? It simply *presumes* something under dispute by skeptics. Notoriously, they dispute whether perception, among other belief-forming sources, is in fact reliable. Skeptics do not have to say that perception, or any other belief-forming source, is actually unreliable. They may rest content with asking, in the familiar comprehensive manner, for non-question-begging warrant for its reliability. An appeal to aptness will not take us very far in reply. It will merely assume something now in question by skeptics. So skeptics will not be effectively challenged by an aptness approach to epistemic value, even if that approach illuminates the nature of knowledge and epistemic value.

2 Epistemic Burdens

The non-question-begging challenge aims to place a serious epistemic burden on us. Should we accept that burden? Or does the challenge contain a defect that removes its force? Let's consider an application of the challenge, in connection with visual perception.

The challenge assigns us the epistemic burden of identifying what non-question-begging reason, if any, we have for thinking that our ordinary visual beliefs have a reliable source. Do our available epistemic reasons (whatever they actually include) for the truth or the reliability of our visual beliefs crumble in the face of this challenge? Such reasons would evidently have a central role in any answer to the non-question-begging challenge regarding visual beliefs.

The term "reason" is dangerously slippery and often suffers from unacknowledged but confusing shifts between "reason," "inference," and "argument." In Sosa's "Philosophical Scepticism and Epistemic Circularity," epistemic internalism is initially characterized as requiring epistemic backing in "reasons or arguments" (PSEC, 304), but this shifts to talk of "inference or argument" (PSEC, 306) in a way that may misleadingly suggest that epistemic reasons are an argument's premises. Epistemic reasons are best understood, however, as (possibly defeasible) truth-indicators that may be non-propositional (e.g., sensory experiences that do not essentially involve either propositions as objects or propositional attitudes) and thus need not be premises of an argument. Sosa has made a major contribution to epistemology, in "The Raft and the Pyramid" and elsewhere, in clarifying that epistemic justifiers need not be premises of arguments. We should embrace the same view for reasons, particularly epistemic reasons (on which see my *Knowledge and Evidence* [1989]).

What about skeptics? What concept of "reason" figures in their demand that we have non-question-begging *reasons* for thinking that our visual beliefs have reliable sources? (An analogous question bears on my alternative talk of "warrant" in the no-question-begging challenge, but favoring evidentialism about warrant, I shall focus on reasons.) Charity toward skeptics requires that we allow them a plausible concept of epistemic reason. Let's allow them, then, the notion of an epistemic reason as a (possibly defeasible) truth-indicator that may be non-doxastic and even non-propositional. The non-question-begging challenge regarding vision thus becomes the demand that we have a non-question-begging truth-indicator for thinking that our ordinary visual beliefs have a reliable source. Such a non-question-begging truth-indicator could be non-propositional; so it would not have to be a belief. We definitely would not make any progress by offering skeptics the proposition that ordinary vision is reliable. The same point holds, as suggested above, for the proposition that another belief-forming source (say, touch) confirming the reliability of vision is itself reliable. Such propositions are directly under dispute now by skeptics. Non-skeptics need a different kind of truth-indicator to challenge skeptics.

Skeptics who question the reliability of belief-forming sources should not thereby question the reliability of *all* truth-indicators. They should not call for a non-question-begging truth-indicator for visual beliefs, for example, while calling into question all truth-indicators. That would be to demand with one hand what has already been taken away with the other. A better metaphor: that would be to demand that we stand somewhere while we are not allowed to stand anywhere. Such a demand would suffer from a kind of incoherence: *demand incoherence*, we might say. Skeptics *could* coherently question the reliability of all truth-indicators (available to humans), but then they could *not* coherently demand a non-question-begging truth-indicator from their interlocutors. Necessarily, if *all* truth-indicators are under question, then *none* will be non-question-begging. That much is analytically true, and importantly analytically true. The important lesson is that the non-question-begging challenge cannot coherently come with *unrestricted* questioning of truth-indicators. Skeptics, in their skeptical zeal, have not always taken this lesson to heart. So we do well to remind them of the real threat of demand incoherence in their position.

The non-question-begging challenge cannot coherently include the questioning of all truth-indicators, and typically it does not. Typically, skeptics wielding this challenge focus on truth-indicators supplied by our familiar belief-forming sources: perception, memory, reason, testimony, and the like. Their comprehensive challenge concerns the reliability of such sources. It demands a non-question-begging reason to hold that any such source actually is reliable. Do we have any place to stand, and to answer, without question-begging reliance on the familiar sources in question? This is the crucial, and the most difficult, question arising from the skeptical challenge.

We have just one durable ultimate place to stand against skeptics: with our semantic, concept-forming intentions. Such intentions give meaning to our terms, including our evidence-related terms (such as "evidence," "justification," "warrant," and "reason"). Consider the key term "epistemic reason." Skeptics and non-skeptics alike use the term, and their uses of the term often overlap in meaning, at least at a level of generality. They can share, as suggested, the general notion of an epistemic reason as a (possibly defeasible) truth-indicator. Many perennial disputes in philosophy, including epistemology, persist as a result of semantic indefiniteness in key terms, but we cannot pursue this diagnosis here. Analogous points hold for the *concepts* we form as the standards for our use of linguistic terms. Justification, warrant, evidence, reason, and knowledge can still be language-independent *kinds*. Even so, *which* epistemic kinds and *which* specific variants of those kinds figure in our aims in inquiry (aims going beyond capturing truth and avoiding error) will depend on our semantic intentions. (For the details behind this quick sketch, see my *Philosophy After Objectivity* [1993].)

Ultimately our meaning-forming intentions give semantic content to our talk of an "epistemic reason" and even of "an epistemic reason for a visual belief that P." Suppose we form the settled semantic intention to use "truth-indicator" and "epistemic reason" in such a way that a visual experience of an apparent X in a situation with no accessible defeaters is a (possibly defeasible) truth-indicator and thus an epistemic reason for a visual proposition or belief that X exists. This intention, given its meaning-conferring role for us, could then serve as a directly accessible semantic truth-maker for our ascription of an epistemic reason for a visual belief that X exists. It would then be *part of what we mean* by "epistemic reason" that *such* an ascription captures an epistemic reason for a visual belief that X exists. (People might haggle over whether a particular ascription is indeed *such* an ascription, but that would be a minor squabble.) Our semantic intentions concerning "epistemic reasons" thus serve as ultimate, even if alterable, truth-makers for ascriptions of an epistemic reason. Indeed, they thus serve as non-doxastic truth-makers for a claim that a certain kind of situation includes one's having an epistemic reason for a visual belief. (If the objects of semantic intentions are not propositions, then semantic intentions are non-propositional as well as non-doxastic. We cannot digress to that ontological topic now.)

The meanings of our evidence-related terms do *not* determine the meanings of our physical-object terms and beliefs, contrary to John Pollock (*Knowledge and Justification*, 1974). The latter are not person-oriented in the way the former are. So, contrary to

Pollock, we have no straightforward semantic refutation of skepticism about physical-object beliefs (on which see my "Meaning, Justification, and Skepticism," 1988). Likewise, the meanings of our evidence-related terms do not determine the meanings of such non-evidential alethic terms as "true" and "reliable." So we lack a clean meaning-based demonstration of the truth or reliability of ordinary physical-object beliefs. Skepticism does not surrender quite so directly, at least on the semantic front.

Skeptics might propose that our semantic intentions can be "mistaken," say in virtue of failing to capture language-independent justification. Just as we can be mistaken about truth, our semantic intentions can yield misrepresentation of such epistemic kinds as evidence and knowledge. So why should we think that a skeptical challenge regarding epistemic kinds (e.g., evidence, or epistemic reason) faces any trouble from *semantic* considerations? In this connection, epistemic kinds seem no safer from skeptical challenges than alethic kinds (e.g., truth, reliability). Why then should we assume a relevant difference here? We cannot answer skeptical challenges about truth and reliability by semantic means. So why suppose that skeptical challenges about epistemic kinds are relevantly different?

As but a little reflection shows, reality settles what is true or factual independently of what humans believe or intend regarding that reality. (Dissenters usually end up in either asylums or philosophy departments.) Reality, however, does not settle how *in particular* one must seek truth. For better or worse, it does not settle which specific variant (or specific concept) of justification, warrant, or knowledge (generally characterized) is binding on a truth-seeker. Skeptics can properly demand that one seeking to acquire truth and to avoid error accommodate any necessary conditions for truth-acquisition and error-avoidance. In addition, as seekers of reliable and warranted true belief, we can properly be required to accommodate any necessary conditions for reliable and warranted belief. So we cannot coherently embrace an "anything goes" attitude toward our truth-seeking. Not just *any* concept or procedure can properly guide us as truth-seekers. Our settled objectives in inquiry place real constraints on us, for the good of inquiry. Some semantic variability is allowed, but not just anything goes.

Even so, skeptics cannot convincingly hold non-skeptics to a specific concept or strategy of truth-acquisition that settles the dispute at hand in favor of skepticism. In particular, skeptics cannot cogently mandate an epistemic concept or strategy for us that undermines the aforementioned kind of epistemic reason (for visual beliefs) grounded in semantic intentions regarding "epistemic reason." One problem for skeptics is that such an epistemic reason is, so far as we can tell, at least as effective for judicious truth-acquisition as anything skeptics offer. In addition, skeptics have no cogent foothold to propose that such a semantically grounded epistemic reason is defective as a truth-indicator. We cannot plausibly be charged with question-begging here. Recall that it is now *part of what we mean* by "epistemic reason" that the kind of ascription in question captures an epistemic reason for a visual belief that X exists. So we may now shift the burden of argument to the skeptic, and we may call this *the skeptic's burden*. This is not just self-serving or arbitrary shifting of the burden of argument. We have, after all, produced a skeptic-resistant truth-indicator grounded in epistemically significant semantic intentions. In addition, we have challenged skeptics to steer clear of demand incoherence in their skepticism. We thus may shift the burden with a clear conscience. The skeptic's burden is now *properly* the skeptic's.

3 Conclusion

Is skepticism, then, finally undone? It is, if being neutralized is sufficient for being undone. Armed with our lessons about demand coherence and the skeptic's burden, we may now proceed with the aforementioned kind of semantically grounded truth-indicators, even in the presence of skeptical questions. We may thereby add durable backing to Ernest Sosa's conclusion that "we have found no good reason to accept *philosophical scepticism*" (PSEC, 324). We might even claim to have dispensed with skepticism, so long as such dispensing does not demand the removal of defeasibility and fallibility in warranted beliefs. In any case, it is enough good news for me and my house that skepticism is finally undone. This news is long overdue, but it's better late than never.

Acknowledgments

Ernest Sosa has made highly significant pioneering contributions to numerous areas of epistemology. Indeed, his epistemological writings have been paradigms of outstanding work in the field for decades. I am honored, therefore, to have this opportunity to interact with some of his epistemological views in a volume honoring his philosophical work.

References

Alston, William P., 1993. *The Reliability of Sense Perception* (Ithaca, NJ: Cornell University Press).
Moser, Paul K., 1988. "Meaning, Justification, and Skepticism," *Philosophical Papers* 17: 88–101.
Moser, Paul, K., 1989. *Knowledge and Evidence* (New York: Cambridge University Press).
Moser, Paul K., 1993. *Philosophy After Objectivity* (New York: Oxford University Press).
Moser, Paul K., 1999. "Skepticism, Question Begging, and Burden Shifting." In Richard Cobb-Stevens, ed., *The Proceedings of the Twentieth World Congress of Philosophy*. Volume 5: *Epistemology*, pp. 209–17 (Bowling Green, OH: Philosophy Documentation Center).
Moser, Paul K., 2000. "Realism, Objectivity, and Skepticism." In John Greco and Ernest Sosa, eds., *The Blackwell Guide to Epistemology*, pp. 70–91 (Malden, MA: Blackwell).
Pollock, John, 1974. *Knowledge and Justification* (Princeton, NJ: Princeton University Press).
Pollock, John (with Joseph Cruz), 1999. *Contemporary Theories of Knowledge*, 2nd edn. (Lanham, MD: Rowman and Littlefield).
Sosa, Ernest, 1980. "The Raft and the Pyramid: Coherence versus Foundations in the Theory of Knowledge." In Peter French et al., eds., *Midwest Studies in Philosophy*. Volume 5: *Studies in Epistemology*, pp. 3–25 (Minneapolis, MN: University of Minnesota Press). (Cited as RP.)
Sosa, Ernest, 1996."Philosophical Scepticism and Epistemic Circularity," *Proceedings of the Aristotelian Society*, supp. vol. 68: 263–90. Reprinted in Paul Moser, ed., *Empirical Knowledge*, 2nd edn., pp. 303–29 (Lanham, MD: Rowman and Littlefield). (Page references are to this reprint.). (Cited as PSEC.)
Sosa, Ernest, 2000. "Reflective Knowledge in the Best Circles," *The Journal of Philosophy* 94 (1997): 410–30. Reprinted in Ernest Sosa and Jaegwon Kim, eds., *Epistemology*, pp. 274–85 (Malden, MA: Blackwell, 2000). (Page references are to this reprint.) (Cited as RK2.)

13

Sosa and Epistemic Justification

NICHOLAS RESCHER

1 Experience and Fact

Once the idea of sensory certainty is called into question, the way is cleared to seeing sense-based knowledge in a practicalistic light. Regrettably, recent philosophers have been reluctant to see the handwriting on the wall.

In a lucid and interesting article Ernest Sosa has explored the question of "the epistemic bearing of sensory experience upon our knowledge"[1] Here the salient issue – as he sees it – is whether experiences can justify beliefs directly, that is, whether the mere fact that someone has a certain experience entitles that person to adopt certain beliefs – for example, whether "the mere fact that I have a headache suffices to justify my belief that I do?" (MG, 277). And he rightly considers this problem of the epistemic bearing of experience as one of the central topics of twentieth-century analytic philosophy.[2]

As Sosa sees it, theoretical epistemologists generally divide into two camps: coherentists who espouse the Davidsonian principle that beliefs can only be justified via other beliefs, and foundationalists who accept that beliefs can appropriately be founded directly on experiential facts, without any evidential recourse to yet further beliefs.

Sosa seeks for a middle way between these two rival positions. As he sees it, both are committed to a common premise of evidentialism:

(E) The only way in which experience is ever able to justify a belief is by providing substantiating evidence for it

But this common premise, so Sosa maintains, is eminently questionable. Instead, he holds that there is another alternative, one that is causal rather than evidential in nature, being based on the causal principle:

(C) A perfectly practicable way in which experience is able to justify a belief is by causally producing it in an appropriate way.

On this basis, Sosa reaches the conclusion that to obtain epistemic justification for a belief "it is enough that experience cause belief in some appropriate, standard way" (MG, 284).

To coherentists and foundationalists Sosa in effect says, "A plague on both your houses." To be sure, he concedes some merits to each side. To the foundationalists he grants (as against coherentists) that beliefs can be justified directly on the basis of experience. To the coherentists he grants (as against foundationalists) that there can be no *evidential* link between non-propositional experiences and propositional beliefs, seeing that evidence must always be presented propositionally. But he regards both schools as inappropriately committed to the evidentialism of (E). Rejecting this firmly, he advocates in its place a (C)-geared causalistic epistemology of belief as affording a suitable third way between the two rejected alternatives.

Attractive though this prospect sounds, it has its problems. To gain a firm grip on the issue, it helps to draw a crucial distinction between cognitive *experiences* (which are always personal and subjective) and objective *situations* (which are not). "I take myself to be seeing a cat on that mat" is one sort of thing and "There actually is a cat on that mat" is something quite different. The former is purely person-coordinated and thereby merely autobiographical while the latter objective claim is decidedly impersonal.[3] (Only in the special case of automatically self-appertaining issues such as feeling aches and pains will subjective experiences authorize claims in objective territory: to feel a headache is to have a headache.)

Two facts are crucial in this connection:

- Experience as such is always personal: it is always a matter of what occurs within the thought-realm of some individual. Thus all that is ever secured directly and totally by experience is claims in the order of subjectivity.
- Such subjective claims are always autobiographical: they can never assure objective claims about facts regarding the "external" world without some further ado.

These facts separate experience from objectivity. With objectively world-regarding facts we always transcend experience as such. The assertoric context of an objectively factual statement ("There is a cat there") is something that outruns any merely experiential fact ("I take myself to be seeing a cat there"). There is always an epistemic gap between subjective experience and objective fact.

But how can one manage to cross this epistemic gap between subjective experience and subject-transcending reality? Here Sosa's idea is that *causality* provides a natural and effective bridge across the gap. Let us examine this prospect.

2 Problems of Common Cause Epistemology

Sosa's endorsement of causal epistemology pivots on the proviso that "it is enough [for epistemic justification] that the experience *cause the belief in some appropriate or standard way*" (MG, 284). However, this formula makes it transparently clear that epistemic justification will turn not just on causality alone but its suitability and thereby on the way in which this causality operates. And this little qualification of "standard appropriateness" has to carry a big burden of weight. Of course we cannot do without it: mere causality as such does not engender epistemic justification. (I was not epistemically justified in expecting the villain's death after he was shot on stage, even when the wicked prop man had substituted a real loaded pistol – unbeknownst to one and all.) And the fly in the ointment is that things become unraveled when we proceed to take this idea of *appropriate* causation seriously.

Suppose that I espouse the objective claim "that there is a cat on that mat" because I have a seeing-a-cat-on-the-mat experience, that is, because I take myself to be looking at a cat on the mat. What is now required for that experience to "be caused in the appropriate way" – that is, being appropriately produced by a cat on that mat? Clearly the only correct/appropriate/standard mode of experience production here is one that proceeds via an actual cat on that mat. Unless one construes "experience" in a question-begging way that is not just psychologically phenomenological but objectively authentic, experiences will not suffice for justifactory authentication. That is, something like the following causal story must obtain:

> There really is a cat on the mat. And in the circumstances it is this situation – duly elaborated in its causal complexity by way of involving a light source, eyes looking in the right direction, photons emanating from the light source impacting on the retina, etc. – that stimulates my cerebral cortex in such a way as to engender this cat-on-the-mat seeing experience.

But note the difficulty here. Unless a real cat on that real mat is appropriately the causal source of my taking myself to be seeing a cat on the mat, that cat-on-the-mat belief of mine is simply not "caused in the appropriate way." (If Pavlovian conditioning leads me to experience a cat-conviction when confronted by any domestic quadruped – cats included – then my "cat on the mat belief," even when indeed caused by a cat's presence on the mat, is not caused in the right sort of way for knowledge.) Thus on any such account *the* APPROPRIATE *production of that belief not merely assures but actually* PRESUPPOSES *its truth*. Only when one assumes an account which already supposes the truth of the belief at issue can one tell that the belief is epistemically justified. On this basis, determining the epistemic justification of a belief does not just substantiate the truth of that belief but requires it. On such a construction of the matter, epistemic justification is available only when it is too late because it is no longer needed.

This condition of things creates big problems when it indeed is "the epistemic bearing of sensory experience upon knowledge" that we have in view. For given that epistemic justification is our only cognitive pathway to establishing the truth of beliefs, there is no point to a concept of justification that requires an appropriateness that is available only after this truth has already been established. If appropriateness cannot be determined independently of establishing the actual truth, then it is question-beggingly self-defeating to include it among the criteria of our truth-claims.

Sosa's endorsement of the idea that "it is enough [for the epistemic justification of claims to knowledge] that the experience cause the belief in some appropriate or standard way" (MG, 284) places him squarely into the increasingly popular tradition of causal epistemology. This approach looks to the following plausible-looking thesis generally favored by causal epistemologists:

A person X *knows* that p is the case if the (causal) processes that actualize p as a state-of-affairs (in nature) and the (causal) processes that engender X's belief that this state of affairs obtains are suitably coordinated.

Implementing this idea requires the following three elements:

1 A set $[p]$ of causal factors engendering p's actualization via a causal relationship: $[p] \Rightarrow p$.
2 A set $[X\ \text{believes}\ p]$ of causal factors engendering X's belief in p via a causal relationship: $[X\ \text{believes}\ p] \Rightarrow x\ \text{believes}\ p$.
3 A (duly specified) relationship of "harmonious coordination" between the two opposite sets of causal factors $[p]$ and $[X\ \text{believes}\ p]$.

Those three elements must all be in proper alignment with one another for a knowledge claim to qualify as appropriate.

But a rocky and winding road now lies before us. For one thing, it now becomes extremely difficult ever to attribute knowledge to others. If I know anything about history, I know that Gibbon knew that Julius Caesar was assassinated. But I certainly don't have much of a clue about the specific causal factors that produced this belief in Gibbon. (Indeed, I am not even in a position to say anything much about the causal sources of my own meta-belief.) All those now requisite causal issues are lost in a fog of unknowing.[4] I can plausibly conjecture *that* a cogent causal story can be told but I do not have much of a clue as to *what* it is and would thus be hard put to evidentiate it. Moreover – and more damagingly yet – the sorts of claims that I could ever make about this causal story are epistemically far more problematic than is my belief that Gibbon knew that Caesar was assassinated. The problem is that the causal approach to knowledge explains the obscure by what is yet more so. To establish simple knowledge claims on its basis we would need to go through a rigmarole so cumbersome in its demands for generally unavailable information as to lead sensible people to despair of the whole project. If that is what is required to substantiate claims about other people's knowledge, then skepticism on the subject offers the best option. If any plausible alternatives to common-cause epistemology are available, they surely deserve our most sympathetic consideration.

3 Modes of Justification

To see how a viable alternative approach to epistemic justification might be developed it is necessary to go back to square one and begin with a closer look at the question of just what it is to "justify" a belief.

Belief justification is a complex idea subject to a considerable variety of distinctions and elaborations. But for present purposes the crucial distinction is that between:

- *strong epistemic justification*, i.e., justification for accepting the belief as definitively true, for seeing it as meriting outright acceptance.
- *weak epistemic justification*, i.e., justification for according the belief some credit, for seeing it as a plausible prospect.

With strong justification we regard the issue of acceptability as settled, with weak justification we regard it as yet substantially open, regarding whatever commitment we have to the belief as tentative, provisional, and defeasible.

Now the critical considerations in the light of this distinction are (1) that while we must grant foundationalists that perceptual experience provides epistemic justification, nevertheless where objective factual claims are concerned this can only be justification of the weak sort; and (2) that we must grant the coherentists that strong justification is in general not immediately experiential but is something that can be had only on a larger contextual and systemic basis.

Thus consider again that cat-on-the-mat experience where "I take myself to be seeing a cat on the mat." On its basis I would arrive quite unproblematically at the following contentions:

- It seems plausible to suppose that there is a cat on the mat
- There is presumably a cat on the mat

In the circumstances to claim unqualified assurance that there indeed is a cat on the mat would be stretching matters too far. But the indicated pro-inclination towards the theses at issue is certainly warranted. Conclusiveness may be absent but plausibility is certainly there.

Yet how is one to get beyond such tentativity? To step from that visual experience to an objective factual claim on the order of

- There actually is a cat there
- There actually is a mat there
- The cat is actually emplaced on the mat

is a move that can be made – but not without further ado. Let us consider what sort of "further ado" is required here.

The position at issue is a "direct realism" of sorts. The step from a sensory experience ("I take myself to be seeing a cat") to an objective factual claim ("There is a cat over there and I am looking at it" is operationally direct but epistemically mediated. And it is mediated not by an *inference* but by a *policy*, namely the policy of trusting one's own senses. This policy itself is based neither on wishful thinking nor on arbitrary decisions: it emerges in the school of praxis from the consideration that a long course of experience has taught us that our senses generally guide us aright – that the indications of visual experience, unlike, say, those of dream experience, generally provide reliable information that can be implemented in practice.

But how would this emergence of policy validation from a body of experience work in practice? Presumption is the key that unlocks this issue.

4 The Role of Presumption

The classical theories of perception from Descartes to the sense-datum theorists of the first half of the twentieth century all involve a common difficulty. For all of them saw a real and deep problem to be rooted in the question:

Under what circumstances are our actual experiences genuinely veridical? In particular: which facts about the perceptual situation validate the move from "I (take myself to) see a cat on the mat" to "There is a cat on the mat"? How are we to monitor the appropriateness of the step from "perceptual experiences" to actual perceptions of real things-in-the-world, seeing that experience is by its very nature something personal and subjective?

The traditional theories of perception all face the roadblock of the problem: How do we get from here to there, from subjective experience to warranted claims of objective fact?

However, what all these theories ignore is the fact that in actual practice we operate within the setting of a concept-scheme that reverses the burden of proof here: that our perceptions (and conceptions) are innocent until proven guilty. The whole course of relevant experience is such that the standing presumption is on their side. Barring indications to the contrary, we can and do move immediately and unproblematically from "I take myself to be seeing a cat on the mat" to "There really is a cat on the mat and I actually see it there." But what is at issue here is not an *inference* (or a deriving) from determinable facts but a mere *presumption* (or a taking). The transition from subjectivity to objectivity is automatic, though, to be sure, it is always provisional, that is, subject to the proviso that all goes as it ought. For unless and until something goes amiss – i.e., unless there is a mishap of some sort – those "subjective percepts" are standardly allowed to count as "objective facts."

To be sure, there is no prospect of making an inventory of the necessary conditions here. Life is too complex: neither in making assertions nor in driving an automobile can one provide a comprehensive advance survey of possible accidents and list all the things that can possibly go wrong. But the key point is that the linkage between appearance and reality is neither conceptual nor causal: it is the product of a pragmatic policy in the management of information, a ground rule of presumption that governs our epistemic practice.

Presumptions by nature provide a provisional surrogate for the actual truth. As Lalande's philosophical dictionary puts it: "La présomption est proprement et d'une manière plus précise une anticipation sur ce qui n'est pas prouvé."[5] Presumptions are, as it were, in tentative and provisional possession of the cognitive terrain, holding their place only until displaced by something more evidentially substantial.[6] A presumption is a putative fact which, while in the circumstances perhaps no more than probable or plausible, is nevertheless accepted as true provisionally – allowed to stand until such time (if ever) when concrete evidential counterindications come to view. Presumption is the epistemic analogue of "innocent until proven guilty."

The rational legitimation of a presumptively justified belief lies in the consideration that some generic mode of "suitably favorable indication" speaks on its behalf while no as-yet available counterindication speaks against it. When, after a careful look, I am under the impression that there is a cat on the mat, I can (quite appropriately) base my acceptance of the contention "There is a cat on the mat" not on certain pre-established premises, but simply on my experience – on my visual impression. The salient consideration is that there just is no good reason why (in *this* case) I should not indulge my inclination to endorse a visual indication of this kind as veridical. (If there were such evidence – if, for example, I was aware of being in a wax museum – then the situation would, of course, be altered.)

With presumption we *take* to be so what we could not otherwise *derive*. This idea of such presumptive "taking" is a crucial aspect of our language-deploying discursive practice. For presumptively justified beliefs are the raw materials of cognition. They represent contentions that – in the absence of pre-established counterindications – are acceptable to us "until further notice," thus permitting us to make a start in the venture of cognitive justification without the benefit of prejustified materials. They are defeasible all right, vulnerable to being overturned, but only by something else yet more secure, some other pre-established conflicting consideration. They are entitled to remain in place until displaced by something better. Accordingly, their impetus averts the dire consequences that would ensue if any and every cogent process of rational deliberation required inputs which themselves had to be authenticated by a prior process of rational deliberation – in which case the whole process could never get under way.

5 Principles of Presumption

Of course, our presumptively justified claims range beyond the indications of sensory experience. The ordinary and standard probative practice of empirical inquiry embodies a presumption in favor of such cognitive "sources" of information as the senses and memory and the declarations of others. Additionally, there are such further prospects as:

- *epistemic utility* in terms of the sorts of things that would, if accepted, explain things that need explanation;
- *analogy* with what has proved acceptable in other contexts and the natural expectations based on prior experiences;
- *fit* through a systemic coherence with other accepted theses.

On this basis, our cognitive proceedings incorporate a host of fundamental presumptions of reliability, such as:

Believe the evidence of your own senses.

Accept at face value the declarations of other people (in the absence of any counter-indications and in the absence of any specific evidence undermining the generic trustworthiness of those others).

Trust in the reliability of the standardly employed cognitive aids and instruments (telescopes, calculating machines, reference works, logarithmic tables, etc.) in the absence of any specific indications to the contrary.

Accept the declarations of recognized experts and authorities within the area of their expertise (again, in the absence of counterindications).

All such resources provide a useful and appropriate instrumentality of presumption by furnishing us with materials for answering questions.[7] All in all, presumption favors the usual and the natural – its tendency is one of convenience and ease of operation in cognitive affairs. For presumption is a matter of cognitive economy – of following "the path of least resistance" to an acceptable conclusion. Its leading principle is: introduce complications only when you need to, always making do with the least complex resolution of an issue. There is, of course, nothing sacrosanct about the result of such a procedure. The choice of the easiest way out may fail us; that which serves adequately in the first analysis may well no longer do so in the end. But it is clearly the sensible way to begin. At this elemental level of presumption we proceed by "doing what comes naturally."

For present purposes, then, the salient point is that presumption provides the basis for letting appearance be our guide to reality – of accepting the evidence *as evidence* of actual fact, by taking its indications as decisive until such time as suitably weighty counterindications come to countervail against them. What is at issue here is part of the operational code of agents who transact their cognitive business rationally.

6   The Validation of Presumption as a General Policy

Its indispensability is a salient part of the validation of a policy of presumption. For we cannot pursue the cognitive project – the quest for information about the world – without granting certain initial presumptions: they represent Kant-reminiscent "conditions under which alone" the securing of answers to questions about the world is even *possible*. And prominent among them is the consideration that we can take our subjectively experienced "data" about the world as *evidence* – that a presumption of experiential veridicality is in order. In matters of sense perception, for example, we presume that mere appearances ("the data") provide an indication of how things actually stand (however imperfect this indication may ultimately prove to be). That we can use the products of our experience of the world to form at least somewhat reliable views of it is the indispensable presupposition of our cognitive endeavors. If we systematically refuse, always and everywhere, to accept *seeming* evidence as *real* evidence (at any rate until such time – if any – when it is discredited as such), then we can get nowhere in the domain of practical cognition of rational inquiry. When the skeptic rejects any and all presumptions, he automatically blocks any prospect of reasoning with him *within* the standard framework of discussion about the empirical facts of the world. The machinery of presumption is part and parcel of the mechanisms of cognitive rationality; because abandoning it would abort the entire project of rational inquiry at the very outset.

But indispensability apart, what is it that justifies making presumptions, seeing that they are not established truths? The answer is that this is not so much a matter of evidentially *probative* considerations as of procedurally *practical* ones. Presumptions arise in contexts where we have questions and need answers. And when sufficient evidence for a *conclusive* answer is lacking, we must, in the circumstances, settle for a more or less *plausible* one. It is a matter of *faute de mieux*, of this or nothing (or at any rate nothing better). Presumption is a thought instrumentality that so functions as to make it possible for us to do the best we can in circumstances where something must be done. And so presumption affords yet another instance where practical principles play a leading role on the stage of our cognitive and communicative practice. For presumption is, in the end, a practical device whose rationale of validation lies on the order of pragmatic considerations.

The obvious and evident advantage of presumption as an epistemic recourse is that it enables us vastly to extend the range of questions we are able to answer. It affords an instrument that enables us to extract a maximum of information from communicative situations. Presumption, in sum, is an ultimately pragmatic resource. To be sure, its evident disadvantage is that the answers that we obtain by its means are given not in the clarion tones of knowledge and assertion but in the more hesitant and uncertain tones of presumption and probability. We thus do not get the advantages of presumption without the accompanying negativity of a certain risk of error. Here, as elsewhere, we cannot have our cake and eat it too.

We proceed in cognitive contexts in much the same manner in which banks proceed in financial contexts. We extend credit to others, doing so at first to a relatively modest extent. When and as they comport themselves in a way that indicates that this credit was warranted, then we extend more. By responding to trust in a "responsible" way – proceeding to amortize the credit one already has – one can increase one's credit rating in cognitive as much as in financial contexts.

In trusting the senses, in relying on other people, *and even in being rational*, we always run a risk. Whenever in life we place our faith in something, we run a risk of being let down and disappointed. Nevertheless, it seems perfectly reasonable to bet on the general trustworthiness of the senses, the general reliability of our fellow men, and the general utility of reason. In such matters, no absolute guarantees can be had. But, one may as well venture, for, if venturing fails, the cause is lost anyhow – we have no more promising alternative to turn to. There is little choice about the matter: it is a case of "this or nothing." If we want answers to factual questions, we have no real alternative but to trust in the cognitively cooperative disposition of the natural order of things. We cannot pre-establish the appropriateness of this trust by somehow demonstrating, in advance of events, that it is actually warranted. Rather, its rationale is that without it we remove the basis on which alone creatures such as ourselves can confidently live a life of effective thought and action. In such cases, pragmatic rationality urges us to gamble on trust in reason, not because it cannot fail us, but because in so doing little is to be lost and much to be gained. A general policy of judicious trust is eminently cost-effective in yielding good results in matters of cognition.

Of course, a problem remains: Utility is all very good but what of validity? What sorts of considerations *validate* our particular presumptions as such: how is it that they become *entitled* to this epistemic status? The crux of the answer has already been foreshadowed. A twofold process is involved. Initially it is a matter of the generic need for answers to our questions: of being so circumstanced that if we are willing to presume we are able to get . . . anything. But ultimately we go beyond such this-or-nothing consideration, and the validity of a presumption emerges *ex post facto* through the utility (both cognitive and practical) of the results it yields. We advance from "this or nothing" to "this or nothing that is determinably better." Legitimation is thus available, albeit only through experiential *retrovalidation*, retrospective validation in the light of eventual experience.[8] It is a matter of learning that a certain issue is more effective in meeting the needs of the situation than its available alternatives. Initially we look to promise and potential but in the end it is applicative efficacy that counts.

The fact is that our cognitive practices have a fundamentally economic rationale. They are all cost-effective within the setting of the project of inquiry to which we stand committed (by our place in the world's scheme of things). Presumptions are the instrument through which we achieve a favorable balance of trade in the complex trade-offs between ignorance of fact and mistake of belief – between unknowing and error.

7   The Evolutionary Aspect of Sensory Epistemology

A presumption-based practicalistic theory of knowledge development clearly differs from a causal physicalistic account. And it enjoys substantial advantages.

Recent philosophy of knowledge has been pervaded by a "revolt against dualism" that insists upon continuities and overlaps where earlier theorists had seen clear divisions and sharp separations. William James stressed the continuity of thought and inveighed against division and compartmentalization. Whitehead condemned bifurcation. John Dewey inveighed against all dualisms. And their successors have been enthusiastic in continuing their tendency in matters of detail. W. V. Quine strives to consign the analytic/synthetic distinction to oblivion. Donald Davidson denigrates the conceptual/substantive distinction. And innumerable contemporary philosophers of science object to the fact/theory distinction because they regard all factual claims as "theory-laden."

But, throughout all this turning away from division and dualism, one traditional distinction has remained sacrosanct: that between cause and reason, between efficient causation and final causation. Where the medievals tended to construe *causa* broadly and to group paternal and volitional "causation" together as reflecting differences in mode but not in kind, the moderns from Descartes onwards have erected a Chinese wall between the two. Immanuel Kant stressed the distinction: "There are two and only two kinds of causality conceivable by us: causality is either according to nature [and is thus efficient causality] or according to free will and choices [and is thus final causality]."[9] And so even Davidson, in the very midst of his polemic against the conceptual/substantive distinction, argues that:

> [we must] give up the idea that meaning or knowledge is grounded in something [external to cognition proper].... No doubt meaning and knowledge depend on experience and experience ultimately on sensation. But this is the "depend" of causality, not that of evidence or justification.[10]

And so as Davidson – unlike Sosa – sees it, causation is one sort of thing and justification another, and never the twain shall meet in the cognitive realm. For while beliefs may well have causes, these do not matter in the context of justification. Causes are not reasons since "nothing can count as a *reason* for holding a belief except another belief."[11] All belief validation (justification) is discursive and proceeds by means of other beliefs. "Causes are rationally inert" is the motto here: they may provide the occasion for the provision of reasons but they themselves can never provide reasons. Or so Davidson has it.

But not Sosa. With causal epistemologists in general he wants to join the two hemispheres together. And rightly so. For having abandoned such other Kantian dichotomies as synthetic/analytic, empirical/conceptual, *a priori/a posteriori*, we would do well to abandon this cause/reason division also. The fact is that causes and reasons can and should be seen as systemically coordinated not by a Leibnizian pre-established harmony but by a Darwinian process of evolution. With intelligent beings whose *modus operandi* is suitably shaped by their evolutionary heritage, the step from a suitable experience to a belief is at once *causal* AND *rational*: we hold the belief *because* of the experience both in the order of efficient (causal) *and* in the order of final (rational) causation. With creatures such as ourselves, experiences of certain sorts are dual-purpose: owing to their – and our – evolutionary nature their occurrence both causally engenders and rationally justifies the holding of certain beliefs through a disposition that evolution has engendered exactly because it is objectively justified to some substantial extent. If this is evolutionary reliabilism, then we are well advised to make the most of it.[12] Let us examine a bit more closely what is at issue here.

8 Rational versus Natural Selection

Scientifically minded epistemologists nowadays incline to consider how the workings of the "mind" can be explained in terms of the operations of the "brain."[13] But this approach has its limits. Biological evolution is doubtless what accounts for the cognitive machinery whose functioning provides for our *possession* of intelligence, but explaining the ways in which we *use* it largely calls for a rather different sort of evolutionary approach, one that addresses the development of thought-procedures rather than that of thought-mechanisms – of "software" rather than "hardware." What is at issue here is a matter of cultural-teleological evolution through a process of *rational* rather than Darwinian *natural* selection. Very different processes are accordingly at work, the one as it were blind, the other purposive. (In particular, biological evolution reacts only to *actually realized* changes in environing conditions: cultural evolution in its advanced stages can react also to *merely potential* changes in condition through people's capacity to think hypothetically and thereby to envision "what could happen if" certain changes occurred.) Once intelligence appears on the scene to any extent, no matter how small, it sets up pressures towards the enlargement of its scope, powerfully conditioning any and all future cultural evolution through the rational selection of processes and procedures on the basis of purposive efficacy.

Rationality thus emerges as a key element in the evolutionary development of *methods* as distinguished from *faculties*. The "selective" survival of effective methods is no blind and mechanical process produced by some inexorable agency of nature; rational agents place their bets in theory *and* practice in line with methods that prove themselves successful, tending to follow the guidance of those that succeed and to abandon – or readjust – those that fail. Once we posit a method-using community that functions under the guidance of intelligence – itself a factor of biologically evolutionary advantage – only a short step separates the pragmatic issue of the applicative success of its methods (of *any* sort) from the evolutionary issue of their historical survival. As long as these intelligent rational agents have a prudent concern for their own interests, the survival of relatively successful methods as against relatively unsuccessful ones is a foregone conclusion.

Rational selection is a complex process that transpires not in a "population" but in a culture. It pivots on the tendency of a community of rational agents to adopt and perpetuate, through example and teaching, practices and modes of operation that are relatively more effective for the attainment of given ends than their available alternatives. Accordingly, the historical development of methods and modes of operation within a society of rational agents is likely to reflect a course of actual improvement. Rational agents involved in a course of trial and error experimentation with different processes and procedures are unlikely to prefer (for adoption by themselves and transmission to their successors) practices and procedures which are ineffective or inefficient.

This line of consideration does not envision a direct causal linkage between the historical survival of method users and the functional effectiveness of their methods. The relationship is one of common causation. The intelligence that proves itself normal conducive also forms functional efficacy. In consequence, survival in actual use of a method within a community of (realistic, normal) *rational* agents through this very fact affords evidence for its being successful in realizing its correlative purposes.[14]

These deliberations regarding rational selection have to this point been altogether general in their abstract bearing upon methodologies of any shape or description. They apply to methods across the board, and hold for methods of peeling apples as much as for methods of substantiating knowledge-claims. But let us now focus more restrictedly on specifically *cognitive* methods, and consider the development of the cognitive and material technology of intellectual production.

There is certainly no need to exempt cognitive methodology from the range of rational selection in the evolution of methodologies. Quite to the contrary: there is every reason to think that the cognitive methods and information-engendering procedures that we deploy in forming our view of reality evolve selectively by an historic, evolutionary process of trial and error – analogous in role though different in character from the biological mutations affecting the bodily mechanisms by which we comport ourselves in the physical world. Accordingly, cognitive methods develop subject to revision in response to the element of "success and failure" in terms of the teleology of the practice of rational inquiry. An inquiry procedure is an *instrument* for organizing our experience into a systematized view of reality. And as with any tool or method or instrument, the paramount question takes the instrumentalistic form: does it work: does it produce the desired result? Is it successful in practice? Legitimation along these lines is founded in substantial part on the fact of survival through historical vicissitudes in the context of this pivotal issue of "working out best." This sort of legitimation is at the basis of the cultural development of our cognitive resources via the varieties and selective retention of our epistemically oriented intellectual products.[15]

It is clear that there are various alternative approaches to the problem of determining "how things work in the world." The examples of such occult cognitive frameworks as those of numerology (with its benign ratios), astrology (with its astral influences), and black magic (with its mystic forces) indicate that alternative explanatory frameworks exist, and that these can have very diverse degrees of merit. Now, in the Western tradition the governing standards of human rationality are implicit in the goals of *explanation*, *prediction*, and pre-eminently *control*. (And thus the crucial factor is not, for example, sentimental "at-oneness with nature" – think of the magician vs. the mystic vs. the sage as cultural ideals.) These standards revolve about considerations of *practice* and are implicit in the use of our conceptual resources in the management of our affairs.

Given the reasonable agent's well-advised predilection for *success* in one's ventures, the fact that the cognitive methods we employ have a good record of demonstrated effectiveness in regard to explanation, prediction, and control is not surprising but only to be expected: the community of rational inquirers would have given them up long ago were they not comparatively successful. The effectiveness of our cognitive methodology is thus readily accounted for on an evolutionary perspective based on rational selection and the requirements for survival through adoption and transmission.

Yet, people are surely not all that rational – they have their moments of aberration and self-indulgence. Might not such tendencies selectively favor the survival of the ineffective over the effective – of the fallacious rather than the true – and slant the process of cognitive evolution in inappropriate directions? C. S. Peirce certainly recognized this prospect:

> Logicality in regard to practical matters . . . is the most useful quality an animal can possess, and might, therefore, result from the action of natural selection; but outside of these it is probably of more advantage to the animal to have his mind filled with pleasing and encouraging visions, independently of their truth; and thus, upon unpractical subjects, natural selection might occasion a fallacious tendency of thought.[16]

However, the methodological orientation of our approach provides a safeguard against an unwarranted penchant for such fallacious tendencies. At the level of individual beliefs "pleasing and encouraging visions" might indeed receive a survival-favoring impetus. But this unhappy prospect is effectively removed where a *systematic* method of inquiry is concerned – a method that must by its very synoptic nature lie in the sphere of the pragmatically effective.

The objection looms: "But how can you say that evolutionary survival among cognitive methods is inherently rational? Hasn't astrology survived to the present day – as its continuing presence in newspaper columns attests?" The response runs: Astrology has indeed survived. But *not* in the scientific community, that is, among people dedicated in a serious way to the understanding, explanation, and control of nature. In the Western, Faustian[17] intellectual tradition of science, the ultimate arbiter of rationality is represented by the factor of knowledge-wed-to-action, and the ultimate validation of our beliefs lies in the combination of theoretical and practical success – with "practice" construed primarily in its pragmatic sense. All these "occult" procedures may have survived in some ecological niche in Western culture. But in *science* they are long extinct.

It is accordingly not difficult to give examples of the operation of evolutionary processes in the cognitive domain. The intellectual landscape of human history is littered with the skeletal remains of the extinct dinosaurs of this sphere. Examples of such defunct methods for the acquisition and explanatory utilization of information include astrology, numerology, oracles, dream-interpretation, the reading of tea leaves or the entrails of birds, animism, the teleological physics of the pre-Socratics, and so on. No doubt, such processes continue in issue in some human communities to this very day; but clearly not among those dedicated to serious inquiry into nature's ways – i.e., scientists. There is nothing intrinsically absurd or inherently contemptible about such unorthodox cognitive programs – even the most occult of them have a long and not wholly unsuccessful history. (Think, for example, of the prominent role of numerological explanation from Pythagoreanism, through Platonism, to the medieval Arabs, down to Kepler in the Renaissance.) Distinctly different scientific methodologies and programs have been mooted: Ptolemaic "saving the phenomena" vs. the hypothetico-deductive method, or again, Baconian collectionism vs. the post-Newtonian theory of experimental science, etc. The emergence, development, and ultimate triumph of scientific methods of inquiry and explanation invite an evolutionary account – though clearly one that involves rational rather than natural selection.

The scientific approach to factual inquiry is simply one alternative among others, and it does not have an unshakable basis in the very constitution of the human intellect. Rather, the basis of our historically developed and entrenched cognitive tools lies in their (presumably) having established themselves in open competition with their rivals. It has come to be shown before the tribunal of bitter experience – through the historical vagaries of an evolutionary process of selection – that the accepted methods work out most effectively in actual practice *vis-à-vis* other tried alternatives. Such a legitimation is not absolute, but only presumptive. It does, however, manage to give justificatory weight to the historical factor of being in *de facto* possession of the field. The emergence of the principles of scientific understanding (simplicity, uniformity, and the like) is thus a matter of *cultural* rather than *biological* evolution subject to *rational* rather than *natural* selection.

To be sure, cultural evolution is shaped and canalized by constraints that themselves are the products of biological evolution. For our instincts, inclinations, and natural dispositions are all programmed into us by evolution. The transition from a biologically advantageous economy of effective physical effort to a cognitively advantageous economy of effective intellectual efforts is a short and easy step.

An individual's heritage comes from two main sources: a biological heritage derived from the parents and a cultural heritage derived from the society. However, in the development of our knowledge, this second factor becomes critical. To establish and perpetuate itself in any community of *rational* agents, a practice or method of procedure must prove itself in the course of experience. Not only must it be to some extent effective in realizing the pertinent aims and ends, but it must prove itself to be more efficient than comparably available alternatives. With societies composed of rational agents, the pressure of means–ends efficacy is ever at work in forging a process of cultural (rather than natural) selection for replacing less by more cost-effective ways of achieving the group's committed ends – its cognitive ends emphatically included. Our cognitive faculties are doubtless the product of biological evolution, but the processes and procedures by which we put them to work are the results of a *cultural* evolution which proceeds through rationally guided trial and error in circumstances of a pragmatic preference for retaining those processes and procedures that prove theorists efficient and effective. Rational people have a strong bias for what works. And progress is swift because once rationality gains an inch, it wants a mile.

We know that various highly "convenient" principles of knowledge-production are simply false:

> What seems to be, is.
> What people say is true.
> The simplest patterns that fit the data are actually correct.

We realize full well that such generalizations do not hold – however nice it would be if they did. Nevertheless throughout the conduct of inquiry we accept them as principles of *presumption*. We follow the higher-level meta-rule: "In the absence of concrete indications to the contrary, proceed as though such principles were true – that is, accept what seems to be (what people say, etc.) as true." The justification of this step as a measure of practical procedure is not the factual consideration that, "In proceeding in this way, you will come at correct information – you will not fall into error." Rather it is the methodological justification: "In proceeding in this way you will efficiently foster the interests of the cognitive enterprise: the benefits will – on the whole – outweigh the costs."

9 Against "Pure" Intellectualism

The habituates of presumption accordingly provide us with a non-discursive route to knowledge. After all, it is – or should be – clear that beliefs can be justified not just by other beliefs but also by experiences. My belief that the cat is on the mat need not rest on the yet different belief that I am under the impression of seeing it there; it can rest directly and immediately on my visual experience. My reason for holding that belief of mine is not yet another belief but an experience – which both occasions and at the same time, considered from another point of view, validates and justifies that belief.[18] But in point of validation the linkage of belief to experience is not direct but systemic.

Contemporary theorists often see the cognitive domain as confined to the realm of verbalized belief. There is no *hors de texte*, says Derrida. The only reason for a belief is yet another belief, says Davidson. But this sort of postmodern cognitivistic "wisdom" is folly. The world of thought is not self-contained; it is integral to the wider world of nature, part of a realm in which events happen and experiences occur. A perfectly good reason for believing that the cat is on the mat is just that we experience (i.e., observe) it to be there. The acceptability of beliefs frequently roots not in other beliefs but in experience – and experience must here be understood in rather general and broadly inclusive terms.

For while the productive order of causes and the explanatory order of reasons are fundamentally distinct, they melt together into a seamless whole with rational agents whose thoughts and acts reflect the impetus of reasons. In the case of rational beings, these two factors of causality and justification can come together in a conjoint fusion because here informatively meaningful perceptions and physical stimuli run together in coordinated unison. Since intelligent agents operate in the realm of both the causality of nature and the causality of reason it transpires that for them experiences such as a "cat-on-the-mat vision" have a double aspect, able at once to engender and (in view of imprinted practical policies) to justify suitable beliefs. Accordingly, such intelligent agents have dual-function experiences that at once cause their beliefs and provide them with reasons for holding them. (But note the crucial difference between this position and Sosa's principle (C) discussed at the start of the chapter. Sosa in effect holds that the cat-on-the-mat belief is justified *because* the seeing the cat on the mat experience is caused by the cat on the mat. However, the present account holds (1) that the cat-on-the-mat belief is occasioned by having a seeing-the-cat-on-the-mat experience, and (2) that having this experience concurrently justifies the belief on the basis of epistemic policy considerations.) For the justifactory link of experience to belief validation is not directly causal. We can – of course – construct a causal account linking experience to belief. But what plays a *justifactory* role in the rational validation of belief is not the *existence* of such a causal account – it is, rather, the *belief* (itself the product of an ample body of experience) that such an account can be constituted.

Yet what sort of rationale is there for taking this line? The answer lies in the Darwinian revolution. For in its wake we can contemplate the evolutionary development of intelligent beings – the emergence of intelligent creatures for which the realization of reasons can be causally effective and, conversely, suitably operative causes can assume the form of reasons. We should, in fact, proceed to see intelligence itself as a capacity that renders it possible for certain modes of experience-causation concurrently to provide reasons for beliefs.

It is exactly here – in explaining the *modus operandi* of evolutionarily emergent rational beings – that causes and reasons must *not* be separated. The "experience of having a cat perception of a certain sort" – exactly because it is a cognitively significant experience – at once and concurrently constitutes the *cause* of someone's disposition to assent to "The cat is on the mat" and affords them with a *reason* for making this claim. In the cognitive experience of intelligent beings the regions of causes and of reasons are not disjoint but rather coordinated: one and the same experience can at once provide for the ground and for the reason of a belief.

The fact is that intelligent agency brings something new upon nature's scene. Certain sorts of eventuations are now *amphibious* because they are able to function at once and concurrently *both* in the realm of natural causes *and* in the realm of reasons. My perceptual experience of "seeing the cat on the mat" is at once the cause of my belief and affords my reason for holding that belief. Q: "What causally produced his belief that the cat is on the mat?" A: "He saw it there." Q: "Why – with what reason – does he claim that the cat is on the mat?" A: "He saw it there." His seeing experience is a matter of dual action. With intelligent agents, such as ourselves, *experiences* can do double duty as eventuations in nature and as reasons for belief. For we have an evolution-imprinted "rational disposition" to effect the transition from a subjective experience ("I take myself to be seeing a cat on the mat") to the endorsement of a duly coordinated objective claim ("There is a cat on the mat").

In a way, the difference between causes and reasons in the realm of cognition lies in the angle of vision, in whether those productive experiences are viewed from an agent's first-person or an observer's third-person vantage point. What we have here is one uniform sort of process experienced in two different modes: internally to the experiencing subject as psychic; externally to the third-party observer as physical. And since a single underlying process is at issue, psychophysical coordination is assured. The perspective in question provides for an automatic response to Mark Twain's question: "When the body gets drunk, does the mind stay sober?" – and also to the reverse question: "When the mind decides to get up and leave, does the body remain behind?" What we have here is not a supra-naturally pre-established harmony but an evolution-programmed coordination: two different ways of processing one uniform basic sort of material. The question of causal effect vs. rational response is not one of primacy but rather one of coordination. (That of an analogy: the same occurrence – sugar ingestion – engenders one result in relation to the tongue (taste) and another in relation to the nose (odor). The upshot is a cognitive theory close to the ontological *neutral monism* of Bertrand Russell or the *radical empiricism* of William James.

To be sure, we must distinguish the mental (conceptual, rational) order of the physical (causal) order. But where human knowledge is concerned evolutionary processes can and do coordinate these two orders into a parallel alignment. An intelligent being is by natural design one for which certain transactions in the causal order appear (from the internal experiential standpoint) as processes in the mental order capable of rationally engendering (i.e., in the *modus operandi* natural to the mental order) the acceptance of verbalized responses of the type we characterize as beliefs. In sum, the experiential route to belief validation and the causal sorts of belief production come into coordinative fusion for such a creature in virtue of its evolution-designed *modus operandi*. Only on this basis can we validate seeing our experience-provided "reasons" as authentic *reasons*. (After all, if beliefs alone could ever justify beliefs it is hard to see how the process of belief-justification could ever get under way.)

But are there not deceptive experiences – experiences that both engender and "justify" erroneous beliefs? Of course there are! It is just that on the basis of evolutionary considerations they have to be statistically subordinate exceptions to the rule. It is the systemic course of experience itself that educates us about the rationality of various routes to belief.

10 Conclusion

A whole generation of epistemologists has turned against the idea of "the experientially given" by supplementing the perfectly sound idea that *Nothing is given in experience by way of categorical truth regarding matters of objective fact* with the very mistaken conception that *In epistemic contexts GIVEN must be construed as GIVEN AS TRUE*. When these theses are combined, it indeed follows that there are no experiential givens. But of course the situation is drastically transformed when one acknowledges that beyond the given *as true*, there is also the given *as plausible*, or *as probable*, or *as presumption-deserving*. Once this step is taken, Sosa's question of "the epistemic bearing or sensory experience upon our knowledge" acquires a very different aspect. For consider the salient question: Does the fact that I take myself to be seeing a cat on a mat – that I have a "seeing a cat on a mat" experience – "entitle" or "suffice to justify" me in adopting the belief that there actually is a cat on the mat there? This question, once raised, leads back to the underlying issues: What is at issue with belief *entitlement* in such a context? Does it require guaranteed correctness beyond the reach of any prospect of error – however far-fetched and remote? It is clear that the answer is: surely not! Entitlement and justification here is no more than the sort of rational assurance that it makes sense to ask for in the context at issue: a matter of reasonable evidentiation rather than categorical proof. The fundamental question, after all, is not "Does subjective experience *unfailingly* guarantee its objective proportions?" but rather "Does it *appropriately evidentiate* it?"

The shift from a proof-oriented "given as true" to a presumption-oriented "given as plausible" also has the advantage that in epistemology we are not driven outside the epistemic realm of reasons-for into that of ontologically problematic causes-of. A sensible epistemology can without difficulty remain within the epistemic realm of reasons by drawing a due distinction between reasons-for-unblinking-acceptance-as-true and reasons-for-endorsement-as-plausible.

Accordingly, the principal theses of these deliberations regarding Sosa's question of "the epistemic bearing of sensory experience upon our knowledge" can be set out at follows:

1. There indeed are experiential givens. But these "givens" are actually "takens." They are not products of inference (hence "givens") but of an epistemic endorsement policy or practice (hence "takens").
2. Most critically, those experiential givens are not "givens as categorically and infallibly true" but rather merely as plausible. What is at issue is not something *categorically certified* but merely something *presumptive*.
3. The move from plausibility to warranted acceptance ("justified belief") is automatic in those cases where *nihil obstat* – that is, whenever there are no case-specific counterindications.
4. Although this way of proceeding does not deliver categorical guarantees or infallible certitude, such things are just not required for the rational validation (or "epistemic justification") of belief.
5. On this basis, subjective experience can – and does – validate our claims to objective factual knowledge. But the step at issue in moving across the subjectivity/objectivity divide is indeed a step – a mode of praxis. And the *modus operandi* at issue in this practice or policy is at once validated by experience and established through a complex process in which rational and natural selection come into concurrent operation.[19]

From the angle of this perspective it appears that Sosa's discussion of the "Mythology of the Given" leaves one very crucial validating factor out of sight – the process of evolution in its relation to our cognitive hardware and software. What his account offers us is, in a way, Hamlet without the ghost.[20]

Notes

1. "Mythology of the Given," *History of Philosophy Quarterly* 14 (1997): 275–96 (cited as MG), p. 275.
2. To be sure, there is an oddity in Sosa's focusing on the example of a headache, seeing that aches, pains, and feelings of dizziness and the like are "bodily sensations" rather than "sensory experiences" in the ordinary sense. The pivotal question is that of what Bertrand Russell called "our knowledge of the external world," that is, whether my sensory experiences that I have when I take myself to be seeing a cat on a mat constitute adequate warrant for my belief that there indeed is a cat emplaced on a mat over there.
3. As standardly used, the claim "I see a cat" is amphibious and moves in both regions, seeing that it *conjoins* the subjective "I take myself to be seeing a cat" with the objective "There is a cat there that I actually see."
4. In theory we can certainly have $K(\exists f)$ (f is a causal factor of an epistemically appropriate sort) without having $(\exists f) K$ (f is a causal factor of an epistemically appropriate sort). It is

just that in matters of concrete fact there is no epistemically effective way to get at the former without getting there via the latter.

5   A. Lalande, *Vocabulaire de la philosophie*, 9th edn. (Paris: Presses Universitaires de France, 1962), s.v. "présomption."

6   The modern philosophical literature on presumption is not extensive. When I wrote *Dialectics* (Albany: State University of New York Press, 1977), there was little apart from Roland Hall's "Presuming," *Philosophical Quarterly* 11 (1961): 10–22. More recently there is Edna Ullmann-Margeht, "On Presumption," *The Journal of Philosophy* 80 (1983): 143–63. A most useful recent overview is Douglas N. Walton, *Argumentation: Schemes for Presumptive Reasoning* (Mahwah, NJ: Lawrence Erlbaum Associates, 1996), which does, however, overlook our presently central theme of probability. I am also grateful to Sigmund Bonk for sending me his unpublished study "Vom Vorurteil zum Vorausurteil."

7   This is why adherence to custom is a cardinal principle of cognitive as well as practical rationality. Cf. William James, "The Sentiment of Rationality," in *The Will to Believe and Other Essays in Popular Philosophy* (New York: Longmans Green, 1897).

8   See the author's *Methodological Pragmatism* (Oxford: Basil Blackwell, 1976) for a fuller development of this line of thought.

9   Immanuel Kant, *Critique of Pure Reason*, A532 = B560.

10 Donald Davidson, "A Coherence Theory of Truth and Knowledge" in La Pone, ed., *Truth and Interpretation: Perspectives on the Philosophy of Donald Davidson* (Oxford: Basil Blackwell, 1986), pp. 313–14.

11 Ibid., p. 310.

12 To rely on evolution in this way is not to turn epistemology into an empirical science of contingent fact. For the point here is not that "what is a good reason" is contingent, but that "what a good reason is" may be contingent and depend on the empirically determinable conditions. (That "something bad for you should be avoided" is conceptual and non-contingent, but that "smoking is bad for you and should therefore be avoided" is contingent.)

13 See, for example, P. M. Churchland, *Matter and Consciousness* (Cambridge, MA: MIT Press, 1984) and P. S. Churchland, *Neurophysiology: Towards a Unified Science for the Mind–Brain* (Cambridge, MA: MIT Press, 1986).

14 No recent writer has stressed more emphatically than F. A. Hayek the deep inherent rationality of historical processes in contrast to the shallower calculations of a calculating intelligence that restricts its view to the agenda of the recent day. See especially his book, *The Political Order of a Free People* (Chicago: University of Chicago Press, 1979), volume 3 of "Law, Liberty, and Civilization."

15 The French school of sociology of knowledge envisioned a competition among a natural/rational selection of culturally diverse modes of procedure in accounting for the evolution of logical and scientific thought. Compare Louis Rougier, *Traité de la Connaisance* (Paris: Gauthier-Villars, 1955), esp. pp. 426–8.

16 C. S. Peirce, *Collected Papers*, vol. 5 (Cambridge, MA: Harvard University Press, 1934), sect. 5.366.

17 "*Im Anfang war die Tat*" as Goethe's *Faust* puts it.

18 The position maintained here is closely akin to John McDowell's argumentation against Hilary Putnam (as discussed in Putnam's *Pragmatism: An Open Question* [Oxford: Blackwell, 1995], pp. 67–78). McDowell holds that "Once we think of [obviously mental achievement such as] hearing and seeing as *accessing information from the environment* – something with full right to be regarded as a rational accomplishment – there is no reason to accept the dictum that a perception can only *cause* (and not *justify*) a verbalized thought." But my position was arrived at independently of McDowell. Already in my 1971 Oxford lectures I argued at length against "an essentially linear model of understanding" and insisted on this coordinate synthesis

of the causal and the rational order in the cognitive sphere, insisting that "these two orders must be grasped together in their systematic unity." (On the character and interrelationship of the mental and physical orders of concepts see the author's *Conceptual Idealism* (Oxford: Basil Blackwell, 1973), especially pp. 184 ff; the quote is from p. 191) Based on lectures given in Oxford in 1971, these deliberations antedate Davidson's John Locke lectures (let alone McDowell's response to Davidson in *Mind and World* [Cambridge, MA: Harvard University Press, 1994].)

19 The epistemological program this essay sketches out combines ideas set out in considerable detail in several of the author's publications: *The Coherence Theory of Truth* (Oxford: Oxford University Press, 1973), *Plausible Reasoning* (Assen: Van Gorcum, 1976), *Scepticism* (Oxford: Basil Blackwell, 1980), *Human Knowledge in Idealistic Perspective* (Princeton, NJ: Princeton University Press, 1991), *A Useful Inheritance* (Pittsburgh: University of Pittsburgh Press, 1994). The discussion has benefited from constructive comments by Alexander Pruss.

20 I am grateful to John Greco for some constructive criticism.

14

Perceptual Knowledge and Epistemological Satisfaction

BARRY STROUD

Ernest Sosa has written so well about so many different topics that there is no hope even of expounding, let alone examining, the full range of his contributions in a single essay. Even within the theory of knowledge he has directed his careful scrutiny to such issues as the definition of knowledge, contextualism, foundationalism, coherence theories, epistemic virtues, and different pictures of knowledge behind apparently intractable epistemological controversies. Recently he has been attending to a general question about the very possibility of a philosophical theory of knowledge. He finds a form of subjectivism or relativism or skepticism rampant both in the general culture and within the apparently stricter precincts of philosophy that would bring the whole enterprise to ruin. It is based on recognition of an inevitable circularity, perhaps in all intellectual endeavor, but certainly in the search for a philosophical theory of human knowledge.

Sosa wants to defend the traditional epistemological enterprise against such charges. A successful philosophical theory as he understands it would show that, and how, we know the sorts of things we think we know, and so would provide a general explanation of human knowledge. It would be established by careful study of what human beings are like and how they use the abilities they are endowed with to come to know the things they know. He insists that there is no difficulty in principle with human beings coming in this way to know such things about human knowledge. "We can legitimately and with rational justification arrive at a belief that a certain set of faculties or doxastic practices are those that we employ *and* are reliable," he says.[1]

I want to take up Sosa's defense of the traditional epistemological enterprise. I think there remains a question about its philosophical prospects that he does not consider or put to rest. In fact, I believe the kind of theory he favors is vulnerable to the difficulty I see. But I do not think it is a question of circularity. As a general objection to the possibility of understanding knowledge, I think the charge of circularity is without force.

Sosa's optimism about the epistemological project is expressed in what he appears to regard as a rhetorical question. If we have "legitimately and with rational justification" arrived at an explanation of human knowledge, he asks, "Why could we not conceivably attain thereby a general understanding of how we know whatever we do know?" (PSEC, 285). I think this raises a real question which can be given a good answer. Even if we "legitimately and with rational justification" arrived at a theory of knowledge of the kind Sosa has in mind, I think there *is* a way in which we would not thereby attain a satisfactory general understanding of how we know what we know. I will try to explain why not. This is something I have tried to bring out before, apparently with little success.[2] It is worth trying again; I think something important about the philosophical understanding of human knowledge is at stake.

Sosa starts with a question of the kind he thinks a successful theory of knowledge should answer: "Is the existence of external things just an article of faith?" (RK, 410). He takes the question from G. E. Moore, who understands external things as things to be met with in space. Tables, trees, socks, mountains, even soap bubbles, are things of a kind to be met with in space. And they occupy their positions in space, and so exist, if they do, whether anyone ever encounters them or perceives them or thinks about them or not. The question is to be understood so that if any such things exist, then there are external things. That, of course, would not settle the epistemological question. There could be such things even if no one knows that there are. Nor would everyone's believing that there are external things settle the question of knowledge; belief can be a matter of faith. But if anyone knows or has good reason to believe that tables, trees, socks, or mountains exist, then that person knows or has good reason to believe that external things exist; he is not just taking it as an article of faith. That would be a positive answer to the question about human knowledge of external things.

If many people knew that there are external things, but no one knew that anyone had that knowledge, then no one would know the answer to the epistemological question. There would *be* a positive answer — the existence of external things would be something known and not just an article of faith — but no one would know it. If many people after epistemological investigation came to believe that human beings know that there are external things, that would not be enough for a satisfactory outcome of their epistemological investigations, just as everyone's believing that there are external things was not enough to settle the question of their knowledge. Even if the investigators' belief were in fact true, that still would not be enough. The truth of the answer they accept would not give them the understanding they seek unless they could recognize that they know or have good reason to believe that answer. Rightly finding themselves with knowledge or good reason to believe that the answer they accept is true would give them a satisfactory understanding of human knowledge.

One way in which the existence of external things would be something that we know, and not just an article of faith for us, is if we could often *see* that there is a table in the room, a tree in the garden, socks on our feet, and so on. That would be knowledge by perception of the existence of external things. I think we can and do see such things to be true, and so thereby know that there are external things. That is one answer to a question about our knowledge of external things; what might be called the most straightforward answer.

If perception is indeed a way of coming to know something about external things, then I can also know by perception that that answer to that epistemological question is correct. I can often see that someone right in front of me sees that there is a table in the room and thereby comes to know that there is a table in the room. I see what he does and I see that he knows. So I can see, and thereby know, that that is how people come to know that there are external things. The truth of that straightforward epistemological explanation is something I can know to be true by perceiving that it is true, just as I can know that there are external things by perceiving that there are.

I think there is no suspicious circularity in this way of coming to know that there are external things. Circularity can enter the picture only where there is a chain of inference or a course of reasoning by which a conclusion is reached. But the straightforward answer says nothing of a chain of inference or reasoning. It says that one *sees* that there is a table in the room, not that one infers that there is a table in the room from something else. And to see that p is to know that p. It is not that one infers that one knows that p from the fact that one sees that p. Whoever sees that p thereby knows that p. Whoever sees that there is a table in the room knows that there are external things.

Just as there is no circularity in coming to know in that way that there are external things, so there is no suspicious circularity in coming to know in that same way that this answer to the epistemological question is true. This straightforward answer does not say that one reaches the "conclusion" that people know by perception that there are external things, and so perception is reliable, by inferring it from something else one sees or knows. It says simply that I can see and thereby know that people see and know in that way that there are external things. There is no inference or chain of reasoning, and so no room for circularity. It is true that I use my eyes in finding out how people find out about the things around them, and I find that they use their eyes, but there is nothing circular or illegitimate about that. There is no illegitimacy or paradox in using our eyes to find out how the human eye works, or using the larynx to lecture on the workings of the larynx. It is no different in this case, given that we can see that there are external things.

So the straightforward explanation involves no circularity, and it is something I can know to be true by seeing that it is true. If that is the answer Sosa would give to the question about our knowledge of external things from which he begins, there is no disagreement between us, either about circularity or about our knowledge of external things. We can "legitimately and with rational justification" arrive at a belief that knowledge of external things is acquired by perception, and we can "attain thereby a general understanding" of how we know many of the things we know.

Many philosophers will grant that perhaps there is nothing wrong with that answer as far as it goes, but will feel that there is a deeper and more challenging question about perceptual knowledge to which it is not a satisfactory answer. One source of this feeling is the demand that it should somehow be *established* that human beings ever do see that there is a table in the room, a tree in the garden, or any other fact involving the existence of an external thing. The straightforward answer, it is thought, simply assumes or takes it for granted that that is so. On that assumption, the answer is perhaps unobjectionable. But for a serious and satisfying theory of human knowledge, it is felt to be something that must be *shown* to be true, not simply assumed.

I think this familiar reaction, as stated, is based on a misunderstanding of the straightforward answer. That answer does not simply assume or take it for granted that people can see that there is a table in the room or that other external things exist. It says that is something that almost anyone can *see* to be true right before his eyes; it is not something that is or must be assumed. So it *can* be established that people can see that there are external things. The expressed dissatisfaction with the answer appears to rely on a lingering suspicion of circularity. But we saw that there is no room for circularity when that answer is rightly understood.

The straightforward answer would be found dissatisfying by some philosophers because they believe that no one ever does see that p, where what takes the place of 'p' implies the existence of an external thing like a table or a tree or a sock. They think certain general reflections about sense-perception should be enough to convince anyone of that fact. So they think the straightforward answer is not, strictly speaking, true. For such philosophers, this presents a deep and challenging epistemological question: how do we get knowledge by perception of the existence of such external things, given that we never, strictly speaking, see or otherwise perceive that they exist?

This is perhaps what has come to be called the philosophical problem of our knowledge of the external world. But with this understanding of the restricted deliverances of unaided perception, the word 'external' takes on new significance. It no longer just denotes things to be met with in space, like tables and trees. It now applies to everything that is not, strictly speaking, perceived to be so; and what is perceived turns out to be much less than might originally have been thought. The problem then is how we can come to know or have reason to believe anything about what is "external" to, or beyond, the limited domain of what we strictly speaking perceive.

It is to this kind of question that Sosa appears to think the theory of knowledge he has in mind can give a satisfactory answer. The question he addresses is one to which he thinks it is at least possible to give an answer that fails through circularity or regress. That is what he says is true of all "internalist" theories of knowledge. In attempting to show how we have perceptual knowledge of something beyond what is perceived, either they rely at some point on knowledge of something beyond what is perceived, and so are "epistemically circular," or they appeal only to what is perceived and so to a regress of perceptions which establish nothing beyond themselves (EC, 267–8, 286). Sosa accordingly favors a form of "externalism" that he thinks is invulnerable to that charge. But he appears to regard his "externalism" as providing a satisfactory non-circular answer to the same question that "internalism" fails to answer.

Sosa thinks the reason "internalist" theories fail is that they try to explain knowledge of facts which we do not, strictly speaking, perceive as knowledge arrived at by inference or reasoning from something we do perceive or are aware of in experience. Accepting the restrictions on unaided perception which create the epistemological challenge, the most we can strictly perceive or be aware of is what Sosa calls "the character of our experience" (RK, 412), or perhaps its "qualitative character" (RK, 413), not facts which hold independently of our experiencing them. "Experience as if there is a fire before us does not entail that there is a fire there, experience as if here is a hand does not entail that here is a hand, and so on" (RK, 413), he says. And that is the most that experience alone provides us with. But he regards it as "doubtful" that "any allowable form of inference ... will take us from the character of our experience to the sort of knowledge of our surroundings we ordinarily claim" (RK, 412).

On this too I agree completely with Sosa, demurring only at his understated 'doubtful.' I think it is not just doubtful that such inferences could support our beliefs about the independent world, but impossible. I think Sosa would not disagree. That is precisely his case against "internalism." Some philosophers would draw from this dead end the skeptical conclusion that therefore perceptual knowledge of an independent world is impossible. Sosa concludes only that perceptual knowledge of facts which go beyond what is perceived cannot be understood as inferential knowledge. The appeal of his "externalism" is that it offers "a way to explain how we can know that p without reasoning from prior knowledge" (RK, 418).

We do not have to enter into the precise details of what Sosa thinks is the most promising formulation of this "externalist" theory in order to assess it as an answer to his epistemological question. "The key idea exploited is this: you can know something non-inferentially so long as it is no accident or coincidence that you are right" (RK, 418). Applied to perception, this means that one will have perceptual knowledge of certain facts if there is a non-accidental or reliable connection between one's perceptual experiences and the facts that one believes in as a result of them. The reliability of perception for Sosa is a matter of there being "experience/belief connections" of that kind. "Good perception is in part constituted by certain transitions from experiences to corresponding beliefs – as is the transition from the visual experience characteristic of a tomato seen in good light to belief in the tomato" (RK, 421). In order for those who enjoy that characteristic visual experience to know that there is a tomato there, and so for perception to be a reliable source of knowledge of the independent world, perceivers do not need to *know* that the "transition" is reliable; it is enough for it to *be* reliable (RK, 426).

This conception of knowledge is what Sosa sees as the key to his answer to the question how we get perceptual knowledge of the existence of things like tomatoes, given that we never, strictly speaking, perceive them; their existence is never entailed by our having the perceptual experiences we have.

That presents no obstacle to knowledge if there are reliable connections between the perceptual experiences we enjoy and the independent world we believe in. This view says that human beings then know by perception that there are tomatoes and other external things. That human beings get such knowledge in that way is also something that we can come to know by observing human beings. If there are reliable connections between the perceptual experiences we enjoy while engaging in such epistemological investigations and the world of people and other external things that we are studying, and we come to believe under those circumstances that human beings have perceptual knowledge of external things, then we know (on this conception of knowledge) that Sosa's answer to his epistemological question is true. We have "legitimately and with rational justification" arrived at "a belief that a certain set of faculties or doxastic practices are those that we enjoy *and* are reliable."

Having fulfilled in this way what the "externalist" view says are sufficient conditions for knowing how human beings get perceptual knowledge of external things, have we thereby attained a satisfactory general understanding of how we know what we know about the independent world? I think there is still a way in which we have not. Sosa's account leaves us in what I think is still an unsatisfactory position for understanding whatever knowledge we have. But it is not unsatisfactory because it suffers from some kind of circularity. There is no circularity involved in fulfilling the conditions Sosa says are sufficient for perceptual knowledge. Nor do I protest that those conditions are not sufficient for knowledge. That is a complex question which turns on the precise formulation of the "externalist" definition of knowledge. But the difficulty I think we are left in would remain even if we grant that people know just the things Sosa's theory implies that they know.

Someone who accepts Sosa's theory knows (on that conception of knowledge) that the human beings he observes know by perception that there are external things. He knows that because he knows that there are reliable connections between the perceptual experiences those people receive and the external things they believe in. It is not simply that he believes that there are such connections. The theorist would concede that his believing alone would not be enough for him to know how people come to know the things they do by perception. He thinks he has a satisfactory explanation of their knowledge because he thinks that explanation is something he knows to be true. And if it is true – if there are reliable connections between people's perceptual experiences and the facts they come to believe in as a result of them – the theory implies that the theorist who accepts that explanation does know that those people know in that way that there are external things.

But that theorist, in light of his own theory, must acknowledge that he does not, strictly speaking, ever *see* or otherwise *perceive* that those human beings and other external things that he is interested in are there. Nor does he ever *perceive* the reliability of the connections that he believes hold between them. The most he is perceptually aware of or presented with in experience are the qualities or character of his perceptual experiences. Of course, he believes in those human beings and other external things, and in the reliable connections between them, even if he never sees that they are there. He comes to believe in them as a result of undergoing certain perceptual experiences. And his theory says that he thereby comes to know of them by perception *if* there are reliable connections between those perceptual experiences he has and the facts he comes to believe in as a result of them. Of course, he believes that theory of knowledge, and he believes that there are such reliable connections, so he will confidently assert that he knows what he thinks he knows about the world, and in particular that he knows that human beings get knowledge of the world by perception in the way he thinks they do.

Any theorist of this kind who reflects on his position will concede, as before, that his merely believing is not alone enough for him to know how people know what they do. He would not thereby achieve a satisfactory explanation of human perceptual knowledge. And I think he must also concede that even knowing that people know things in that way would not be enough, if knowing is simply a matter of fulfilling the conditions Sosa's theory says are sufficient for knowledge. All the theorist can appeal to in accounting for his own knowledge as more than confident belief are the perceptual experiences he knows he has had, the beliefs he holds, which he believes to be the result of those experiences, and the theory of knowledge that he also believes. That theory says that *if* one further condition holds, then he does know what he thinks he knows. And he believes that that further condition holds. But still he remains in no better position for understanding himself as knowing what he thinks he knows than someone who reflects on his knowledge with equal confidence and in an equally satisfactory way and yet knows nothing at all.

Sosa in his concern for circularity imagines beings who do not resort to ordinary sense perception but consult a crystal ball to find out about the world. He wonders whether they could show without circularity that that practice is reliable, and if not, whether ordinary sense perception is any better off in that respect. If the idea is to establish the reliability of sense perception as a source of knowledge of the world by appeal *only* to what is here taken to be, strictly speaking, perceived, then the answer seems to me "no," just as the reliability of crystal-ball gazing as a way of knowing cannot be established by appeal *only* to what is seen in crystal balls. But again, I do not think circularity is the issue in the plight of Sosa's "externalist" epistemological theorist. What matters is the poverty of the resources available to him for understanding his own knowledge. Crystal-ball gazers help make the point.

A committed crystal-ball gazer could reflect on what he takes to be his crystal-ball gazing knowledge of the world and claim to understand it in a way parallel to Sosa's imagined "externalist" theorist. He believes many things about the independent world, but he has never seen or otherwise perceived anything except what he finds on gazing into his crystal ball. But he believes a theory of knowledge to the effect that if there are reliable connections between his seeing what he does in the ball and facts in the wider world that he believes in, then he knows what is so in the wider world. Often, when he gazes into the ball, he sees certain things and then finds himself believing that many other crystal-ball gazers know things about the world around them by gazing into their own crystal balls. He believes that because he believes that there are reliable connections between those people's seeing what they do and the world they come to believe in as a result of it. So, given the theory he also believes in, he takes himself to know that crystal-ball gazers know things about the world in that way.

In reflecting on his knowledge and explaining to himself and others how he knows what he knows, he will concede that his merely believing what he does about his knowledge is not alone enough for him to have a satisfactory explanation of it. He thinks he has a satisfactory explanation because he thinks he knows what he claims to know about crystal-ball gazing knowledge. He recognizes that he has certain experiences, and certain beliefs which he believes to be the result of them, and he believes a theory which says that *if* those experiences and beliefs are connected in a certain way with facts in the wider world, then he has crystal-ball gazing knowledge of that world.

The difference between the positions of the two theorists lies only in the believed-in connections between the relevant experiences and the wider world. The theory says in each case that if such connections hold, that theorist knows. Each theorist, confidently sticking to his own story, believes that they hold in his case and not the other. Each might even try to settle the matter by consulting his own experience and his own theory, and find himself content with the discovered result. In that respect, the two positions are equally satisfactory, or unsatisfactory.

It is perhaps tempting to say that what distinguishes them is only something that lies beyond the knowledge of either theorist; it is a matter only of what is actually so. But on Sosa's "externalist" conception of knowledge, that is not right. If reliable connections hold in one case, then according to the theory that theorist knows; the difference is not beyond his knowledge. But the question is not whether one of those theorists knows. The question is whether holding such a theory leaves anyone in a position to gain a satisfactory understanding of knowledge of the world, even if he fulfills the conditions Sosa's theory says are sufficient for knowledge. Could someone in such a position come to recognize himself as knowing, and not merely confidently believing, perhaps even truly, that sense perception is a way of getting knowledge of the world and crystal ball gazing is not?

I think that, on the understanding of perception that appears to be involved in Sosa's question about perceptual knowledge, the answer is "no." On that view, what we are aware of in perception is restricted to features of our perceptual experiences. The external facts we know as a result of those experiences are nothing we ever perceive to be so. What we get in sense perception therefore bears the same relation to the world we think we know by that means as what is seen in crystal-ball gazing bears to the world the gazers think it gives them knowledge of.

What we believe about the world goes well beyond the restricted domain of experience, and, if the connections are right, it is something we know. But to know of the reliability of the connections which must hold in order for us to know, we can do no more than attend to what then comes within the restricted domain of our experience and, if we believe it, and if the connections are right, thereby come to know that those connections are reliable. So we can understand the position we are in only as follows: *if* there are reliable connections between our perceptual experiences and what we think we know, then we know by perception that there are external things. And we believe that there are such connections. But anyone who thinks that all it takes to have a satisfactory understanding of perceptual knowledge is to conclude by *modus ponens* that we know by perception that there are external things would have to concede that the crystal-ball gazers have a satisfactory understanding of crystal-ball gazing knowledge. They could draw the corresponding conclusion equally confidently from what they believe about themselves.

No comparable doubts affect the straightforward answer to the epistemological question we considered earlier. It says that we know that people know that there are external things by perceiving that there are external things. That is something we can see, and thereby know, to be true of human beings and other external things. So we have no trouble seeing and so knowing that there are no reliable connections between what people see in crystal balls and what goes on in the world beyond them. If the gazers could raise their eyes from their crystal balls and see what is so in the world around them, they could see that too. It might seem that Sosa's "externalist" theorist is in a superior position in this respect, because if he could see what is so beyond his limited perceptual experience he would see that what he believes to be so *is* reliably connected with his getting the experiences he gets. But no such vindication is available to him. It would be possible only if he could see or otherwise perceive what is so in the world around him, not only the character of his perceptual experiences. And anyone who can do that thereby knows what is so in the world; he has no need for an "externalist" theory of knowledge to explain how his experiences enable him to know what he knows.

The conclusion I would draw from all this is that in order to achieve a satisfactory understanding of our knowledge of the world we must set aside or overcome the idea that the deliverances of perception even at its best are limited to the character of one's perceptual experiences alone. Sosa appears to regard that idea as unthreatening as long as knowledge of the wider world is not thought of as a result of *reasoning* from that prior knowledge. But even without invoking reasoning his "externalist" account still leaves us with something that is epistemically prior to any knowledge of an independent world. If there are no reliable connections between the perceptual experiences we receive and the world we believe in as a result of them, we know nothing of the wider world even though we know what experiences we are having. Perceptual knowledge of external things is seen as a combination of some prior knowledge which is not knowledge of external things plus something else. That is what I think leaves us in the plight I have described.

Perhaps I am wrong to attribute to Sosa without qualification the view that we perceive at best only the character of our perceptual experiences. That seemed necessary to make sense of him as trying to answer the kind of question his "externalist" theory is meant to answer. He insists that knowledge requires "that one be adequately related, causally or counterfactually, to the objects of one's knowledge" (RK, 430). He thinks that would be so if there were reliable connections between one's perceptual experiences and the wider world, so he appears content with a severely restricted view of the objects of perception. But one is also "adequately related . . . to the objects of one's knowledge" if one sees, and in that way knows, that there is a table in the room, or a tree in the garden. One could not see that such a thing is so unless it were so; there being a table, or a tree, there is a condition of anyone's seeing that there is a table, or a tree, there. This is a form of "externalism" too, but not in the sense of Sosa's epistemological theory. Of course the table, or tree, alone is not sufficient. As Sosa points out, "we must be both in good internal order and in appropriate relation to the external world" (RK, 430) in order to have knowledge of it. But seeing that there is a table, or a tree, is a highly "appropriate" relation in which to stand to the world in order to know that there is a table, or a tree. It is sufficient for knowing such facts.

It would be no simple matter to say what "good internal order" a person must be in in order to see that there is a table in the room, even when a table is right before him in good light. It is a question of what it takes for him to be capable of having the thought, and so being able to recognize, that there is a table in the room. Exploration of those conditions would contribute to an explanation of how perceptual knowledge of external things is possible. But it would not explain it as a combination of some knowledge that is prior to any knowledge of external things plus something else. It would leave us in a position to say: "The existence of external things is not just an article of faith; it is something we can see and thereby know to be true." If Sosa would give that answer to his question, then again there is no disagreement between us. But that is just the straightforward answer; something everybody knows. It does not look like an answer to a deep and challenging question that we need an "externalist" or any other kind of philosophical theory of knowledge to answer.

Notes

1 Ernest Sosa, "Philosophical Scepticism and Epistemic Circularity," *Proceedings of the Aristotelian Society* supp. vol. 68 (1994) (cited as PSEC), p. 285.
2 See my "Understanding Human Knowledge in General," in M. Clay and K. Lehrer, eds., *Knowledge and Skepticism* (Boulder, CO: Westview Press, 1989). Sosa found the alleged shortcoming illusory in PSEC. I replied in my "Scepticism, 'Externalism', and the Goal of Epistemology," *Proceedings of the Aristotelian Society* supp. vol. 64 (1994) that he had not correctly identified the difficulty I have in mind. In his "Reflective Knowledge in the Best Circles," *The Journal of Philosophy* 94 (1997): 410–30 (cited as RK), he appears to understand it as a charge of circularity. Both papers by me are now reprinted in my *Understanding Human Knowledge: Philosophical Essays* (Oxford: Oxford University Press, 2000).

15

Mythology of the Given: Sosa, Sellars, and the Task of Epistemology

MICHAEL WILLIAMS

I

In "Mythology of the Given," Ernest Sosa investigates the contribution of experience to our knowledge of the world.[1] He proceeds by way of a critical examination of Wilfred Sellars's famous repudiation of the "myth of the given": the idea that knowledge of the world requires experiential *foundations*. Sosa uses his discussion of Sellars as a way of motivating and developing his own ideas about the relation of knowledge to experience.

Sosa introduces his discussion by placing Sellars's position in the history of analytic philosophy: particularly the debate concerning the apparently forced choice between a foundational and a coherence theory of knowledge and justification. He is particularly interested in whether what are now known as "externalist" or "reliabilist" accounts of knowledge can be seen as breathing new life into the foundationalist option. However, Sosa sees even this recent development as continuing a discussion that goes back to antiquity. This is the discussion prompted by the Pyrrhonian problematic: the skeptical argument that any attempt to justify a belief leads inevitably to a vicious infinite regress, an arbitrary assumption, or circular reasoning. Assuming that the regress is genuinely vicious, but that justification is still possible, we seem forced to find a way of putting a better face on one of the remaining options. Foundationalists say that the regress is halted by beliefs that are basic: non-inferential but also non-arbitrary. Coherentists say that the mutual support beliefs give each other in a developed system must be distinguished from simple circularity.

Within the terms that he sets himself for exploring these issues, Sosa develops both a sharp critique of Sellars and an extremely suggestive strategy for escaping the Pyrrhonian problematic. Nevertheless, I shall argue that Sellars can be defended against Sosa's criticisms. Sosa's arguments, I shall claim, fail to engage Sellars's deepest misgivings about epistemological foundationalism, misgivings that apply with equal force to Sosa's own position. But this is not the end of the matter. The division between Sellars and Sosa is not simply over issues *in* epistemology but raises questions *about* epistemology and its place in philosophy at large.

II

Sosa holds (plausibly) that analytic philosophy owes a great deal to the legacy of logical positivism. With respect to sensory experience, the positivists saw two questions as vitally important. Sosa writes:

> Central European analytic philosophy in the first half of [the twentieth] century focused on the relation between science and experience.... The issue of how experience relates to thought and language had two components: First, how does it relate to meaning? Second, how does it relate to knowledge? (MG, 275)

On the first issue – the relations of experience to thought and language – the positivists were in broad agreement: the empiricist criterion of meaningfulness brought the positivists together as a group and set them against all other philosophers. But on the second issue – the relation of experience to scientific knowledge, which is Sosa's topic – they were sharply divided. The division was typified by the debate between Neurath and Schlick. Neurath thought that, since the ship of knowledge is always inevitably rebuilt while at sea, knowledge depends in the end solely on the coherence of one's belief system. Schlick replied that this kind of coherentism was a license to believe (with justification) anything whatever. All you had to do was avoid internal contradictions, with the result that nothing distinguishes consistent fairy stories from textbooks of chemistry. Schlick held that the only way to avoid this "astounding error" was to recognize that knowledge depended on experiential foundations that were both indubitable and incorrigible.

This debate continues today, if not in exactly the same form. As Sosa explains, the "quixotic" pursuit of absolute certainty, a "throwback to Cartesian epistemology" (MG, 276), soon gave way to a more moderate foundationalism, embodied in what Sosa calls "Hempel's insight":

(H) Beliefs held on the basis of direct experiential evidence are not arbitrary. Yet to state the evidence for such a belief is just to voice the belief. Hence, in the context of cognitive justification, these beliefs function as primitive or basic.

So, for example, if I say that I have a headache, and you ask me how I know, all I can do by way of citing evidence is to repeat myself: to assure you that I really do have a headache. But no one would say that my belief that I have a headache (when I really do have a headache) is "arbitrary." This, then, is the hallmark of a basic belief: it is justifiably held, even though it cannot be regarded as based on further evidence.

Hempel's insight became central to other moderate foundational epistemologies, Chisholm's for example.[2] However, Sellars objects not only to the quest for absolute certainty but also to the moderate foundationalism of Hempel and Chisholm. And the way he objects suggests that he belongs to the party of Neurath. How, Sellars asks, can its merely being a fact that P justify a person's believing that P? Sellars suggests that Hempel's thesis points towards inferences of the form:

(α) It is a fact that a is F;
So, it is reasonable (for me) to believe that a is F.

Sellars then objects that such an inference will be effective only if its premise itself has the right kind of authority: if it is something that it is reasonable to believe. Accordingly, (α) gives way to

> (β) It is reasonable to believe it to be a fact that a is F;
> So, it is reasonable to believe that a is F.

As Sellars says, this is "obviously unilluminating."[3]

Sosa thinks that the problem Sellars points to here is by no means unique to his particular critique of foundationalism. Sellars's crucial move is to treat Hempel's account of foundational justification as involving a kind of inference. In making this move, Sellars indicates an affiliation with later critics of foundationalism, such as Rorty and Davidson. Rorty, who sees himself as taking his cue from Sellars, attacks foundationalism on the grounds that it confuses causation with justification. Sosa cites Davidson, approvingly citing Rorty:

> As Rorty has put it, "nothing counts as justification except by reference to what we already accept, and there is no way to get outside our beliefs and our language so as to find some test other than coherence."[4]

Davidson's thought is that to justify is to give a reason. But nothing can count for or against a belief unless it can be consistent or inconsistent with that belief. Reasons are thus propositional in nature, and the only reasons I can give are propositions that I accept: i.e., my beliefs. Insofar as experiences are contrasted with beliefs, experiences may indeed cause us to hold certain beliefs. But to cause a belief is not to provide a reason for holding it. To cause a belief is not to justify it.

Sosa is not impressed by Sellars's objection. Hempel's insight (H) is that certain beliefs – foundational beliefs – have authority in virtue of being true. Beliefs of this kind can be reasonably (or non-arbitrarily) held without the believer's employing *any* form of reasoning. In converting Hempel's condition for the reasonableness of a basic belief into the premise of an inference – a premise which itself needs authority – Sellars simply begs the question against (H).

Still, while rejecting Sellars's argument, Sosa has his own reservation about Hempel's position. There is a compelling argument, Sosa thinks, for recognizing foundationally justified beliefs. If we do not recognize such beliefs, we must suppose that justification can accrue to a belief by way of circular or regressive reasoning. But the transfer of justification by inference "presupposes that justification is already there in the premises, and that is . . . what neither the pure circle nor the pure regress is able to explain" (MG, 278). However, eliminating the circle and the regress entitles us to conclude only that there must be non-inferentially justified beliefs. It licenses no conclusion about their content. Thus Hempel's identification of foundational beliefs with beliefs about immediate experience requires further argument.

The upshot is that we seem to be left with a choice between two unsatisfactory options. On one side, philosophers like Neurath, Sellars, Rorty, and Davidson hold that, at most, experience bears causally on our beliefs about the world: even our simplest perceptual beliefs. Since causation is not justification, these philosophers are forced to seek justification in relations between beliefs and other beliefs, i.e., in coherence. On the other side, Schlick, Hempel, and Chisholm claim that coherence is not enough. Our beliefs need external constraint, and it is hard to see what, other than sensory experience, could provide it. Accordingly, they postulate basic beliefs about experience. In so doing, however, they invite Sellars's objection. Worse still, in looking to beliefs about sensory experience to provide the foundations for knowledge, they "notoriously [fail] to find foundations contentful enough to found our rich knowledge of an external world" (MG, 279).

Let us return to Sosa's dismissal of Sellars's objection to "Hempel's insight." Hempel holds that belief that-P is foundational if it is made reasonable by the fact that-P. Sellars treats this relation of "making reasonable" as involving a kind of inference and, in so doing, according to Sosa, simply begs the question against Hempel. However, we might wonder whether Sosa is being hard on Sellars here. How exactly does a fact make a belief reasonable? If Hempel is not pointing to the kind of inference Sellars offers, just what is he suggesting? We should see Sellars as challenging Hempel to provide an explanation. Or more pointedly, as suggesting that Hempel has either no explanation or a bad one.

Of course, the key issue here is the epistemic character of experience. Neither Hempel nor anyone else supposes that beliefs at large are made reasonable by truth alone. Only special kinds of beliefs – paradigmatically experiential beliefs – have this peculiar feature. So for Sellars, the fact that Hempel and Chisholm single out experiential beliefs for special treatment shows that they are trapped in a particular form of the myth of the given. They think that experiential beliefs are foundational because they think that experiential states are somehow "self-presenting": we know about them simply by being in them. Only the idea that experiential states are self-presenting in this way would lead us to think that basic knowledge had to be sought at the level of experiential beliefs, rather than at the level of (fallible) beliefs about objects in our surroundings. But to put it no more strongly, it is questionable whether an appeal to what Sellars calls "self-authenticating, non-verbal episodes" is any kind of an explanation of how basic, non-inferential knowledge is possible. Certainly, Sellars takes it that we would not invoke such episodes if we could think of a better account of non-inferential perceptual knowledge. It is hard to disagree.

This aspect of Sellars's objection to foundationalism is of course perfectly well understood by Sosa. But in Sosa's eyes, the argument rebounds on Sellars himself, for it points towards a crucial assumption shared by traditional foundationalists and their coherentist critics:

(A) Experience can bear epistemically on the justification of belief only by presenting itself to the believer in such a way that the believer directly and non-inferentially believes it to be present, and can then use this belief as a premise from which to reach a conclusion about the world beyond experience. (MG, 279)

Assumption (A) drives Hempel and Chisholm to postulate self-presenting states. Skepticism about such self-authenticating non-verbal episodes leads Sellars to reject experiential foundations altogether, leaving him aligned with the coherentists. The way forward, then, is to reject (A). The crucial point is that the link between experience and perceptual belief is *causal* rather than inferential. Thus:

> Experience can bear epistemically on the justification of a perceptual belief by appropriately causing that belief. Thus while viewing a snowball in sunlight I may have visual experience as if I saw something white and round, which may prompt the corresponding perceptual belief. In that case it will be an important part of what makes my belief epistemically justified – and indeed of what makes it a perceptual belief – that it is caused by such experience. (MG, 279)

On this view, experience plays a critical role in our acquisition of basic non-inferential beliefs. However, those beliefs need not be *beliefs about experience*. Rather, they can be experientially grounded beliefs about familiar objects in our surroundings.

III

Does the fact that a perceptual belief is causally mediated by an appropriate experience make that belief foundationally justified? As Sosa says, Sellars would meet this question with an emphatic "no." As Sosa points out,

> When Sellars inveighs against the Myth of the Given, he targets not only the radical version of the myth involving direct apprehension of given experience. He objects also to the more moderate version that postulates foundational knowledge through perception. Indeed the key passage that encapsulates his opposition to a foundational epistemology targets not a foundation of introspective direct apprehension but a foundation of perception. (MG, 279)

Sosa's moderate foundationalism, which traces the foundational status of a belief to a particular kind of aetiology, is a version of externalist reliabilism. But Sellars repudiates reliabilism. As Sosa says, this was a neat trick since when Sellars wrote reliabilism had not yet been explicitly formulated.

So what is wrong with reliabilism? Before getting to this, let me enter a caveat about Sosa's contrast between radical and moderate forms of the myth of the given. One of the stranger features of Sellars's discussion of the myth is that, although he introduces many forms that the myth has taken, he never pauses to characterize the myth in general terms. However, it is not difficult to isolate what is perhaps the myth's central motif. This is the idea that, as Robert Brandom puts it, "some kinds of non-epistemic facts about knowers could entail epistemic facts about them" (EPM, 121). Sellars regards this idea as wholly mistaken, for what we must realize is that

> in characterizing an episode or state as that of knowing, we are not giving an empirical description of that episode or state; we are placing it in the logical space of reasons, of justifying and being able to justify what one says. (EPM, 76)

Sellars's thought is that "epistemic" facts are essentially normative: they concern what a person *may* or *ought* to accept in her particular circumstances. And normative facts cannot be entailed by purely "naturalistic" considerations. From this standpoint, the view that beliefs are justified by their causal history is no less radical than the view that they are justified by the preconceptual presence to the mind of sensations. Both views are forms of the same basic error, an error akin to the "naturalistic fallacy" in ethics. In any event, not only is it not surprising that Sellars would reject reliabilism, we could predict the direction his objection would take.

Sellars discusses perceptual knowledge in terms of a person's making authoritative observational *reports*, e.g., by uttering "This is green" in the presence of a green object. In consequence, Sellars's argument is expressed in terms that reflect ideas about mind and language. But Sosa, who would rather avoid extra-epistemological entanglements, thinks that the epistemological core of Sellars's argument can be abstracted from Sellars's ancillary commitments. Accordingly, he restates Sellars's argument in more straightforwardly epistemological vocabulary. So here is Sellars's argument, in Sosa's version:

> We have seen that to constitute knowledge, an observational belief must not only *have* a certain epistemic status; this epistemic status must *in some sense* be recognized by the person whose belief it is. And this is a steep hurdle indeed. For if the positive epistemic status of the belief that this is green lies in the fact that the existence of green items appropriately related to the observer can be inferred from the occurrence of such observational beliefs, it follows that only a person who is able to draw this inference, and therefore has not only the concept *green*, but also the concept of an observational belief that this is green – indeed the concept of certain conditions of perception, those which would correctly be called "standard conditions" – could be in a position to believe observationally that this is green in recognition of its epistemic status. (MG, 280)

Here Sellars rejects reliabilism on the grounds that a belief is not justified unless its positive epistemic status – Sellars says "authority" – is recognized by the believer. In the case of basic perceptual beliefs, the requirement that authority be recognized implies that it is not sufficient that a person *be* a reliable detector of certain features of his environment, in standard conditions. Rather, he must *know that* he is reliable in this respect. To suppose otherwise is to suppose that non-epistemic facts could entail epistemic facts, thus to fall prey to the myth of the given.

We saw that Sosa charges Sellars with begging the question against Hempel's supposed insight (H). We might have expected the same response here. After all, externalism just is the view that a certain kind of non-epistemic fact (about the reliability of a person's recognitional capacities) can entail an epistemic fact (about the positive epistemic status of the person's beliefs). For an externalist, no further epistemic fact (about the person's awareness of his reliability) is required to make the entailment go through. Sellars's "refutation" of externalism is no more than a dogmatic expression of internalist prejudices. However, Sosa takes a different line. I shall return to this interesting feature of his dialectic in due course.

The problem Sosa sees is that the difficulty Sellars points to does not seem to be specific to foundationalism. To be sure, the demand that epistemic status be recognized dooms crude reliabilism. But if accepted in full generality, it seems to present no less steep a hurdle for other approaches, including the coherentism that Sellars appears to embrace. How could one acquire knowledge of one's reliability as an observer without relying on a lot of prior observational knowledge, which itself presupposes a body of reliability-knowledge, which presupposes further observational knowledge, and so on. Sellars's criterion for a non-foundational view of perceptual knowledge seems to invite the traditional charge of vicious regress.

Sellars is aware of this problem. Here is his solution, again as rephrased by Sosa:

> All the view I am defending is that no belief by S *now* that this is green is to count as observational knowledge unless it is also correct to say of S that he *now* knows the *appropriate fact of the form X is a reliable symptom of Y*, namely that the observational belief that this is green is a reliable indicator of the presence of green objects in standard conditions of perception. And while the correctness of this statement about Jones requires that Jones could *now* cite prior particular facts as evidence for the idea that such belief is a reliable indicator, it requires only that it is correct to say that Jones *now* knows, thus remembers, that these particular facts *did* obtain. It does not require that it be correct to say that at the time these facts did obtain he then know them to obtain. And the regress disappears. (MG, 280–1)

Sellars's thought, in this rather difficult passage, is that the ability to acquire and express perceptual knowledge is a complex, multi-faceted capacity that must be mastered whole. Thus a mature person's ability to acquire and express observational beliefs is built on a long history of training, in the course of which he acquires (with the help of already competent believers) both observational concepts and the requisite information about his reliability in deploying them. At a fairly early stage of training, he may be able to respond on cue to a green object with "That's green." But he will not be able to defend or assess his response because (e.g.) he won't understand questions like "Are you sure you recognize F-things when you see them?" Later on, he will be able to deal with such questions by citing his reliability-history. This is because, in a fully competent adult, spontaneous memory-reports (themselves buttressed by relevant reliability-information) also express knowledge, though at an early stage of training they do not. However, since training is a gradual business, no bright line separates knowers from mere proto-knowers.

Sosa finds this response to the threat of regress problematic, but once again not in the way we might have expected. Sellars interprets the regress problem genetically: if observational knowledge presupposes prior reliability-knowledge, which itself depends on observations, which presupposes prior reliability-knowledge, and so on, how can we ever get started? But the real problem is not genetic at all. By Sellars's own standards – which enjoin us not to confuse epistemic with causal questions – the real problem has to do with the structure of epistemic justification *in the mature adult's belief-system*. And here Sellars seems to embrace circularity: particular items of observational knowledge are justificationally dependent on reliability-knowledge, which is justificationally dependent on items of observational knowledge of the very same kind (or even the very same items). So we might have expected Sosa to say that Sellars's response is no response at all: that Sellars's genetic story is irrelevant to his epistemic problem. But he doesn't. This too is worth further discussion.

The objection Sosa actually makes is to the plausibility of Sellars's picture. First, how plausible is it to suppose that one remembers one's past history of reliable observing? Think of things that you know perceptually right now: "Is it realistic to suppose that, in believing perceptually that before you there lies . . . a sheet [of paper], you are relying on recollected incidents in which you successfully perceived thus?" (MG, 281). Second, since memory no less than perception seems to presuppose reliability-knowledge, if there is a regress-problem regarding perception, there seems to be just as much of a problem regarding memory. If the response is that earlier proto-memories can become data supportive of generalizations about the reliability of memory, an analogue of the first objection immediately arises. Do we really have memories of exercises of memory, which constitute a data bank we can draw on to defend the reliability of remembering? Surely not.

For a way beyond the regress or circle, Sosa suggests that we go back to Descartes. As Sosa reads him, Descartes is much concerned with the Pyrrhonian problematic. Sosa notes that with Aristotle appealing to rational intuition as a way to found scientific knowledge, and the Stoics appealing to natural, animal perception as a way to found ordinary empirical knowledge, givenist foundationalism and something like reliabilism had already emerged in the ancient world as accounts of the possibility of knowledge. But anticipating Sellars and contemporary critics of reliabilism, the Pyrrhonians charge that Stoic externalism dignifies mere "groping in the dark" with the title of "knowledge." Like Sellars, they hold that only enlightened belief, "acquired and sustained in awareness of one's epistemic doings" (MG, 282), is knowledge properly so called. However, they also argue that any attempt to move beyond foundations leads us into circles or regresses. As we have seen, this appears to be Sellars's fate.

Descartes offers us an escape from this skeptical dialectic. According to Sosa, Descartes has been "long miscast as the archetypal foundationalist and givenist" (MG, 281). In fact, Descartes conducts his epistemological project in a much more subtle way. Central to Descartes's epistemology is a distinction between two kinds of knowledge. The first kind, *cognitio*, involves particular truths grasped with immediate, intuitive certainty but without any meta-theoretical understanding why our basic faculties are to be relied on. The second and higher kind of knowledge, *scientia*, adds to *cognitio* precisely this element of epistemic self-understanding. Sosa explains:

> First [Descartes] meditates along, with the kind of epistemic justification and even "certainty" that might be found in an atheist mathematician's reasonings, one deprived of a world view in which the universe may be seen as epistemically propitious. Descartes's reasoning at that stage *can* be evaluated, of course, just as can an atheist mathematician's reasoning.... Absent an appropriate world view, however, no such reasoning can rise above the level of *cognitio*. If we persist in such reasoning, nevertheless, enough pieces may come together into a view of ourselves and our place in the universe that is sufficiently comprehensive and coherent to raise us ... into the realm of a higher, reflective, enlightened knowledge, or *scientia*. There is in none of that any circle. (MG, 282)

Thus Descartes allows for an inference-independent kind of knowledge, *cognitio*. The need to allow for such a kind of knowledge is the truth in foundationalism. At the same time, he agrees that this is not the best possible epistemic state to be in. The coherentists are therefore right to demand more. There is a higher state of knowledge, reflective knowledge involving a comprehensive and coherent world view in which we understand our own epistemic capabilities. If we can trace a path from *cognitio* to *scientia*, a project whose success is not guaranteed in advance, we gain enlightened knowledge without being trapped in vicious circles or regresses.

Of course, Sosa is more interested in the form of Descartes's strategy than in its particular content. Descartes's key insight is simply this:

that while we do need to underwrite, at the later stage, the reliability of our faculties, what enables us to do so is the appropriate use of those very faculties in yielding a perspective from which reality may be seen as epistemically propitious. (MG, 283)

Where Descartes's perspective is theological, Sosa's is naturalistic. For Descartes's appeal to clear and distinct perception, backed by a Divine guarantee, Sosa suggests we substitute an externalist-reliabilist approach to our basic cognitive faculties: perception, memory, reasoning (deductive and inductive), etc. Provided that these faculties are not hopelessly unreliable, we will be able to acquire beliefs with some kind of positive epistemic status. With hard work and good luck, we may be able to use these beliefs (no doubt revising as we go) to piece together a picture of ourselves and our world that underwrites the continued use of those faculties, but now with reflective assurance.

We noticed earlier that Sosa's argument takes a couple of unexpected turns. Although Sellars's anti-externalist argument turns on the demand for knowledge of our own reliability, he does not accuse Sellars of simply begging the question. Nor, relatedly, does he suggest that Sellars's own conception of knowledge, in which perceptual knowledge necessarily co-exists with reliability-knowledge, is unacceptably circular. Now we see why. Sosa accepts the legitimacy of Sellars's demand for reliability-knowledge. His objection is that Sellars overgeneralizes this otherwise legitimate demand, failing to see that it is definitive only of a higher kind of knowledge, reflective knowledge. In consequence, Sellars remains trapped in the Pyrrhonian problematic. Rejecting the foundationalist option, in both its traditional and its externalist forms, Sellars finds himself forced into a version of pure coherentism.

Sosa argues that his own broadly Cartesian response to the Pyrrhonian problematic allows us to move beyond the mythology of the given, but in a way that avoids the problems that bedevil Sellars. We no longer have to think of experience as providing premises for (problematic) inferences to beliefs about the world around us. Experience can endow basic, non-inferential perceptual beliefs with positive epistemic status by causing them in the appropriate way. At the same time, we can agree with Sellars and other critics of crude reliabilism that a mere thermometer reaction to one's environment is not real knowledge. Real knowledge demands enlightenment, some awareness of the status of one's belief. Real knowledge is reflective knowledge. The crucial insight is that reflective knowledge can grow out of animal knowledge. Armed with this insight we can halt the regress and break the circle.

IV

Sosa offers a powerful response to the Pyrrhonian problematic. But how different is his position from that of Sellars? And has he really escaped the mythology of the given?

Sosa does not say in so many words that Sellars is a coherentist. But he does say that the controversy between Sellars and Chisholm continued the controversy between Neurath and Schlick, the topic of which just *was* the choice between foundationalism and the coherence theory. Sosa's way of situating Sellars in the recent history of analytic philosophy thus presents him as choosing sides in this traditional debate, and this gives a distorted impression of what Sellars is trying to do.

First of all, it is not Sellars's intention simply to throw his weight behind the party of Neurath. Sellars writes:

> One seems forced to choose the picture of an elephant which rests on a tortoise (What supports the tortoise?) and the picture of a great Hegelian serpent of knowledge with its tail in its mouth (Where does it begin?). Neither will do. (EPM, 78–9)

Sellars's account of perceptual knowledge is designed to show that we are *not* forced to choose between foundationalism (the elephant on the tortoise) and the coherence theory (the great serpent). Like Sosa, Sellars sees himself as offering an escape from the Pyrrhonian dialectic.

Second, Sellars is by no means unqualifiedly hostile to foundationalism, or even to empiricism. As he explains:

> If I reject the framework of traditional empiricism, it is not because I want to say that empirical knowledge has *no* foundation. For to put it this way is to suggest that it is really "empirical knowledge so-called," and to put it in a box with rumours and hoaxes. There is clearly some point to the picture of human knowledge as resting on a level of propositions – observation-reports – which do not rest on other propositions in the same way as other propositions rest on them. (EPM, 78)

Traditional empiricism responds to, but mishandles, the legitimate demand that empirical beliefs be responsive to the world. Since we are linked to the world (epistemically) through observation, this means that observational knowledge must play a special role in the growth of empirical knowledge. Our task is thus to respect what traditional empiricism tries to do while avoiding its mistakes.

Finally, what Sosa presents as Sellars's critique of perceptual foundations – and as an *avant la lettre* repudiation of externalist reliabilism – occurs in the context of Sellars's elaboration of *his own alternative* to "traditional empiricism." Again like Sosa, Sellars thinks that our observational link to the world is to be understood in terms of causation rather than confrontation. Sellars is, in fact, *a kind of reliabilist*, though he departs from pure reliabilism in insisting that reliable reporting dispositions will not generate knowledge unless embedded in a complex reporting practice that includes reliability-knowledge as an essential component.

So what is the difference between Sosa and Sellars? Sosa and Sellars both repudiate experiential foundations for knowledge, where those foundations are thought to provide evidence for inferences to beliefs about the world. They both hold that our link to the world is to be understood in causal terms, and that such an understanding allows us to seek the foundations of knowledge in non-inferential perceptual knowledge of ordinary objects. They both repudiate pure externalism, on the grounds that fully fledged human knowledge – reflective knowledge, in Sosa's terms – involves knowledge of our cognitive capacities. Finally, they agree that reflective knowledge grows out of a more primitive state: animal knowledge, according to Sosa; mere proto-knowledge, according to Sellars. Are they separated by more than a terminological difference?

There is at least one way, I think, in which Sosa might claim that his approach has the advantage over that of Sellars. Let us return to Sellars's response to the charge that, by making reliability-knowledge a precondition of perceptual knowledge, he opens up a vicious regress. Sellars meets this charge by invoking the distinction between knowing and proto-knowing. According to Sellars, observation-reporting is a complex, multi-faceted practice that must be mastered as a whole. At early stages of our training, we may be able to react to the presence of green objects by reliably producing tokens of "That's green." But being unable to defend our reliability in such matters, we will not yet have entered the epistemic game and so will not count as knowers. In considering this suggestion, I remarked that there seems to be a more powerful complaint than the one registered by Sosa: namely, that Sellars offers a genetic story in response to what is really an epistemic problem, in contravention of his own insistence on keeping causal-psychological and epistemological questions distinct. The real question is not how we learn the game of observation-reporting, but how we are to understand the internal structure of the game itself. And here Sellars seems to embrace circularity, accepting the *epistemic interdependence* of perceptual and reliability-knowledge. These reflections suggest that, like it or not, Sellars really is a kind of coherence theorist, just as Sosa suspects. Indeed, they suggest that Sellars is a *pure* coherentist, which Sosa assuredly is not.

As Sosa says, the problem with the pure coherence theory is that it does not explain how justification ever enters the system. Sellars is unable to solve this problem precisely because he disallows all talk of justification at any level below that of fully fledged reflective knowledge. For Sellars, the facts about our training-history are justificationally relevant only to the extent that they are themselves represented in our belief system, just as the reliability of our reporting dispositions is epistemically relevant only to the extent that we are aware of it. Sellars allows *merely* external facts no justificational significance whatsoever. Sosa, by contrast, recognizes a kind of knowledge – primitive, but still knowledge – for which some kind of externalist-reliabilist epistemology gives the proper account. Sosa is thus able to claim that some measure of positive epistemic status accrues to our beliefs prior to and independent of their acquiring the reinforcement that comes from coherence: i.e., from our piecing them together to form a world view that represents our situation as "epistemically propitious." But while this argument appears to give Sosa the upper hand, it still seems to require only the slightest inflection of Sellars's position to turn it into Sosa's. So the question is, why doesn't Sellars go down Sosa's road?

The answer is that he can't, but we will not see why if we continue to conduct our inquiries within the methodological guidelines laid down by Sosa. Sosa thinks that epistemological issues can and should be detached from issues in the philosophy of mind and philosophy of language, which is exactly what Sellars thinks cannot be done. Sellars's great polemic against foundationalism bears the title "Empiricism and the Philosophy of Mind," not "Empiricism and the Theory of Knowledge." This is something we need to take seriously. Sosa wants to know how justification enters the system; Sellars wants to know how content enters. Sosa takes belief for granted in order to explain justification, hence knowledge. But for Sellars, belief – hence meaning – is the problem. Issues about meaning form a connecting thread through the complex dialectic of Sellars's critique of empiricist foundationalism. Set them aside and it is impossible to understand why Sellars's argument proceeds as it does.

While conceding that there is "some point" to it, Sellars identifies two ways in which the empiricist picture of justification is misleading. The first is that, while it registers the epistemic primacy of observation, it blinds us to the ways in which the capacity for observational knowledge is not altogether freestanding but is necessarily embedded in further kinds of conceptual competence. The second has to do with what Sellars sees as the picture's "static" character. I shall discuss these defects in turn.

> The first problem with the metaphor of foundation is that it . . . keeps us from seeing that if there is a logical dimension in which other empirical propositions rest on observation reports, there is another logical dimension in which the latter rest on the former. (EPM, 78)

To see what Sellars has in mind here, we must go back to his account of traditional empiricist foundationalism. According to this important form of the myth of the given,

> there is, indeed must be, a structure of particular matter of fact such that (a) each fact can not only be noninferentially known to be the case, but presupposes no other knowledge either of particular matter of fact, or of general truths; and (b) such that the noninferential knowledge belonging to this structure constitutes the ultimate court of appeal for all factual claims – particular and general – about the world. (EPM, 68–9)

Sellars notes that some philosophers will find this characterization of foundationalism redundant, on the grounds that "knowledge which logically presupposes knowledge of other facts must be inferential." But according to Sellars, this claim "is itself an episode in the Myth" (EPM, 68). The crucial point is this: empiricist foundationalism takes seriously the idea of a freestanding body of observational knowledge: knowledge that is not just *epistemically distinguished* in its role as ultimate court of appeal for all non-observational claims but *semantically independent* of all non-basic commitments. In other words, the foundationalist takes seriously the possibility of a person's having *only* basic observational knowledge. Clearly, Sosa fits this description, as is evident from his talk of our "piecing together" a system of reflective knowledge from beliefs that are instances of mere animal knowledge. So if Sosa thinks that Sellars is really just another coherentist, thus someone who has failed to escape the Pyrrhonian dialectic, Sellars can return the compliment. From Sellars's standpoint, Sosa is just another foundationalist.

As we know, Sellars thinks that empiricists like Hempel and Chisholm favor experiential foundations for knowledge because they think of experiential states as somehow "self-presenting," an idea that embodies "givenness in its most straightforward form" (EPM, 73). However, Sellars's exploration of this idea is more subtle than my earlier brief discussion may have suggested. According to Sellars, in order to respect the demands for epistemic ultimacy and semantic autonomy, traditional empiricism builds in a distinctive view of the content of basic beliefs. First, basic beliefs or judgments are assumed to involve a demonstrative element: the content of such a judgment is always something like "*This* is (or appears) red *now*." In making a basic judgment, I focus my attention on a particular aspect of my current experience, noting its character. This brings me to the second point, which is that the descriptive element always involves a concept that is (indeed, must be) acquired through ostensive definition: i.e., by exposure to examples. I learn what "red" means by directly correlating the word with items that present themselves to me as red (and of course redness here is phenomenal redness). Terms whose meanings are fixed in this way cannot mindfully be misapplied in simple demonstrative judgments, where what is pointed to is a meaning-fixing paradigm. Thus although basic experiential judgments are synthetic – there needn't be anything that looks red in front of me now – they are *like* analytic judgments, in that someone who has mastered the rules governing the concepts they involve, and who is paying proper attention, cannot be mistaken. Here we find not just verification by confrontation but meaning-constitution by pure ostension. We have before us the "Augustinian" model of meaning famously criticized by Wittgenstein in the opening section of his *Philosophical Investigations*.

As I said, the passage that Sosa treats as Sellars's critique of perceptual (as opposed to experiential) foundations occurs in the course of Sellars's attempt to outline an alternative to the traditional empiricist's Augustinian account of basic judgments. According to Sellars, the ability to make non-inferential observation-reports rests on a capacity for acquiring reliable reporting dispositions. This capacity rests in turn on a primitive capacity for discriminative response. But there is no element of givenness here, since the causal relation in virtue of which we come reliably to produce tokens of "That's red" in the presence of red things, while a logically necessary precondition of the expression of basic non-inferential knowledge, is not in and of itself a "cognitive" fact at all. This is the absolutely critical point. The mere inculcation of reliable discriminative reactions – whether these reactions are external or internal, vocalized or not – is insufficient for the mastery of observational concepts. Thus merely to be subject to such reactions does not constitute acquiring beliefs with a low (though still positive) epistemic status. Lacking semantic content, such reactions do not express beliefs at all.

It is at this juncture that Sellars insists on adding the recognition of the *authority* of non-inferential reports to their mere reliability, making reliability-knowledge a precondition of observational knowledge. The reason for his making this move is that the alternative to the Augustinian conception of meaning is some kind of functionalism. Observation-reports differ from mere conditioned responses in being treated as evidence for further, non-observational claims. It follows that no one can have only observational beliefs. Again, Sellars's point here is not primarily about justification but about meaning. Sellars is arguing for a limited form of semantic holism. It is in virtue of this holism that there is a logical dimension in which even non-inferential reports presuppose collateral knowledge.

Of course, Sellars needs a view about the justification, as well as the semantic character, of non-inferential reports. In particular, he needs a view that allows him to distinguish semantic embedding from inferential dependence. His suggestion is that a particular report may be justified "as being an instance of a general mode of behaviour which, in a given linguistic community, it is reasonable to sanction and support" (EPM, 74). It is a feature of our (on the whole well-functioning) reporting practice that linguistically competent adults are generally reliable observers of familiar features of the passing scene, observers whose reports are thus not only non-inferentially *produced* and *accepted* but non-inferentially *acceptable*. However, the authority of observation is defeasible, not absolute. Sometimes we misperceive: the light is bad, we are too far away, things happen quickly. So while we do not always need a justification for relying on our spontaneous observations, sometimes we do. While not necessarily based on reasons, observation-reports are *essentially epistemically evaluable*. This is built into their being reasons rather than mere responses. But there is no possibility of assessing particular observational beliefs except against the background of a rich body of reliability-knowledge.

If Sellars's suggestion is so much as coherent, the twin commitments of traditional foundationalism with respect to observational belief – epistemic primacy and semantic autonomy – can be prised apart. The linguistically competent adult is capable of acquiring spontaneous, default-credible observational beliefs/reporting dispositions. This gives observation the epistemic primacy that empiricism insists it must have. But such beliefs or reports are essentially embedded in a larger reason-giving practice. First, they serve as evidence for claims that are not or cannot be observed to be true. Second, their authority being defeasible, the larger system of beliefs in which they are necessarily embedded includes extensive reliability-beliefs as essential components. The semantic autonomy of basic beliefs is thus an illusion. Only the myth of the given would lead one to think otherwise.

I now turn to a brief consideration of Sellars's second reservation about the metaphor of foundation. Sellars writes:

> *Above all*, the picture is misleading because of its static character. One seems forced to choose between the picture of an elephant which rests on a tortoise (What supports the tortoise?) and the picture of the great Hegelian serpent of knowledge with its tail in its mouth (Where does it begin?). Neither will do. For empirical knowledge, like its sophisticated extension, science, is rational, not because it has a *foundation* but because it is a self-correcting enterprise which can put *any* claim in jeopardy, though not *all* at once. (EPM, 78–9)

A notable feature of Sellars's discussion of epistemological questions in "Empiricism and the Philosophy of Mind" is that skepticism is never made an explicit theme. Now we see why. Philosophical skepticism is characterized by its extreme generality. The skeptic wants to know how anything whatsoever that we believe is justified. His suggestion is that, for all we know, *all* our beliefs might belong in a box with "rumours and hoaxes." Given Sellars's conception of meaning, this is not a worry to take seriously. Without an extensive system of beliefs, keyed in certain ways to direct observation, one would not be in the believing game at all. Having a lot of justified beliefs is therefore a precondition of having any beliefs whatsoever. What we need to understand is not how our entire system of beliefs counts as justified, but how changes in the system can be seen as rational. The focus of our attention should shift from the statics of anti-skeptical legitimation to the dynamics of rational changes in view.

All this should explain my claim that Sosa's arguments fail to engage Sellars's deepest reservations about foundationalism. By enforcing a sharp separation between epistemological questions and issues in the philosophy of mind and language, Sosa precludes his registering the extent to which Sellars sees empiricist views about mind and meaning as constituting the indispensable underpinnings of empiricist views about knowledge. Thus Sosa repudiates empiricist foundationalism on much narrower grounds than does Sellars. Sosa's objection is that experiential foundations provide an insufficient basis for our rich knowledge of the world. For Sellars, no beliefs, experiential or otherwise, could be basic in the strong sense of "basic" that traditional empiricism is committed to. The profound methodological divergence between Sosa and Sellars leads them, in turn, to take very different attitudes to the Pyrrhonian problematic. Sosa offers a genuine constructive solution. Sellars repudiates the problem.[5]

There is more at stake here than a clash of arbitrary methodological preferences. Sellars holds, rightly, that his is the only way to proceed, because foundationalism itself *inevitably involves commitments that go beyond epistemology narrowly conceived.* Sosa says, in defense of his practice of transmuting Sellars's arguments into more straightforwardly epistemological terms:

> I avoid issues about the nature of thought and its relation to language and society..., leaving aside whether to understand [belief, justification and knowledge] in terms of moves in a language game governed by social rules. I am not denying that our main epistemic concepts are to be understood thus in terms of language and society. I am simply not joining Sellars in affirming it. Thus my preference for the transmuted argument does not prejudge these issues. (MG, 279–80)

However, no such neutrality is possible. Sosa is himself committed to a view of meaning that allows animal beliefs to swing free of all reflective knowledge; and the question whether there is room for such a view is the nub of Sellars's critique of foundationalist epistemology. It is not hard to see where Sellars would take issue with Sosa's strategy for escaping the Pyrrhonian problematic. His point of attack would surely be Sosa's talk of our "piecing together" a system of reflective knowledge from elements of animal knowledge. If this piecing together involves inferring and hypothesis-testing, on the basis of defeasible evidence – and how else could it be understood? – then, Sellars would say, animal knowledge is already implicitly understood as subject to epistemic assessment, thus as no longer merely animal.

We are led in the end to radically opposed conceptions of epistemology and its place in philosophy. Descartes, like the Skeptics and Stoics before him, puts epistemology first. The most fundamental question we can ask, as philosophers, is "What can we know and how can we know it?" Sellars holds that one could think this way only if one were prepared to take meaning for granted. For Sellars, Sosa's professed neutrality with respect to this issue must mark him out as an adherent of the Skeptic-Stoic-Cartesian tradition. Sellars has another view of the task of epistemology. Reflection on knowledge and justification is "but part of the task of explicating the concept of a rational animal or ... of a language-using organism whose language is *about* the world in which it is used."[6]

Notes

1   "Mythology of the Given," *History of Philosophy Quarterly* 14, 3 (July 1997): 275–86 (cited as MG).
2   See Roderick Chisholm, *The Foundations of Knowing* (Minneapolis: University of Minnesota Press, 1982).
3   This argument is taken from Sellars's paper "Epistemic Principles," in H. N. Castaneda, ed., *Action, Knowledge and Reality* (Indianapolis: Bobbs Merrill, 1975); reprinted in Ernest Sosa and Jaegwon Kim, eds., *Epistemology: An Anthology* (Oxford: Blackwell, 2000), pp. 125–33. References are to this reprinting. Sellars presents this paper as further developing some central ideas of his "Empiricism and the Philosophy of Mind," in Wilfred Sellars, *Science, Perception and Reality* (London: Routledge, 1963). (Hereafter cited as EPM.)
4   Sosa (MG, 277), citing Donald Davidson, "A Coherence Theory of Truth and Knowledge." The most convenient source for this important essay in now Davidson, *Subjective, Intersubjective, Objective* (Oxford: Oxford University Press, 2001). The quotation is at p. 141 in this reprinting.

5 In my view, Sellars's remarks on narrowly epistemological issues are too brief, and it is open to question whether he was completely clear about how to avoid the traditional choice between foundations and the coherence theory. I discuss this issue in detail in "Knowledge, Reasons and Causes: Sellars and Scepticism," in James Conant and Andrea Kern, *Scepticism and Interpretation* (Amsterdam: Elsevier, 2002).

6 Sellars, "Epistemic Principles," p. 132; emphasis in original.

16

Epistemic Value Monism

LINDA ZAGZEBSKI

1 The Value Problem

Where does the state of knowledge get its value? Virtually everyone agrees that it comes partly from the value of the truth that is thereby acquired, but most philosophers also agree that knowledge is more valuable than mere true belief. If so, what is the source of the extra value that knowledge has? Curiously, several well-known contemporary epistemic theories have trouble answering this question. In particular, I have argued that reliabilism is unable to explain where knowledge gets its value. I call this the value problem.[1] Sosa addresses the value problem in a recent paper, moving his theory in a more Aristotelian direction.[2] In this chapter I will review the moves Sosa makes to solve the problem and will suggest a simpler approach that I believe does justice to all his desiderata.

Here is a statement of the value problem as I have previously presented it against reliabilism:

(i) A reliable process or faculty is good only because of the good of its product.

A reliable espresso-maker is good because espresso is good. A reliable water-dripping faucet is not good because dripping water is not good. Reliability *per se* has no value or disvalue. Its value or disvalue derives solely from the value or disvalue of that which it reliably produces.

(ii) Given that the value of the reliability of a source derives from the value of the product, the value of the product cannot derive additional value from the reliability of the source.

A reliable espresso-maker is good because espresso is good, but the espresso made now doesn't get any better just because it was produced by a reliable espresso machine. The garden I am planting now is no better just because it was planted by a reliable gardener. The pleasure produced now is no better just because it was produced by a reliable source of pleasure. And so on. The moral is that value can be transferred in one direction only, not back and forth.

> (iii) Hence, a reliable truth-producing faculty or process is good because truth is good. But if I acquire a true belief from such a source, that does not make my belief better than it would be otherwise. A state of true belief resulting from a reliable process or faculty has no more value than mere true belief.
> (iv) But knowledge is more valuable than mere true belief.
> (v) Therefore, knowledge cannot be true belief resulting from a reliable process or faculty.

Notice that this argument can be generalized to apply to any theory in which the additional value that a true belief has when it is an instance of knowledge derives from something that in turn derives from the good of truth. The problem therefore arises from the conjunction of the following three claims:

1 Knowledge is true belief with property x.
2 Knowledge is more valuable than mere true belief.
3 Any epistemic value other than the truth of a belief derives from the good of truth. (Thesis of epistemic value monism.)

Although Sosa's theory is not a pure form of reliabilism, he is attracted to epistemic value monism.[3] But any theory that accepts (1)–(3) is prey to the value problem, not just reliabilism. That is because it follows from (1) and (3) that any value x has derives from the value of truth, but if so, it is hard to see how x can add value to a true belief that is x. There is, therefore, a problem in maintaining (2). Sosa is aware of that and has proposed a solution that gives up (3) while continuing to give truth "pride of place" in epistemic value theory.

2 Sosa's Solution

Sosa says that true beliefs attributable to the agent are better than true beliefs that arise in other ways. True beliefs are attributable to the agent when they arise from the agent's own intellectual deeds. Such deeds have what he calls praxical value, a kind of instrumental value. It is the value of bringing about something of value in a way that is attributable to an agent. Since praxical value is a form of instrumental value, it derives from the value of what it produces, in this case, true belief. The praxical value of an intellectual deed in virtue of which we attribute the attainment of truth to the agent is therefore consistent with the thesis of epistemic value monism.

Praxical value does not solve the value problem. The praxical value of an excellent deed that brings about true belief does not enhance the value of the true belief. The excellent performance of an espresso-maker does not enhance the value of the espresso produced. The good espresso in this cup is no better in virtue of the fact that it is attributable to the excellent performance of this espresso-maker. But espresso-makers are not agents and what we value as agents differs from what we value in machines. Sosa concludes that the epistemic value of an intellectual deed that gives the agent the truth is not limited to extrinsic value deriving from the value of true belief. We value arriving at the truth in a way that is attributed to an agent differently than good espresso attributed to a good espresso-maker.

What, then, is the source of the value of the deed in addition to its instrumental value? Where does the value come from if not from truth? Sosa says the value is intrinsic:

> But in addition to the extrinsic praxical value, we seem plausibly committed to the *intrinsic* value of such intellectual deeds. So the grasping of the truth central to truth-connected reliabilist epistemology is not just the truth that may be visited upon our beliefs by happenstance or external agency. We desire rather truth gained through our own performance, and this seems a reflectively defensible desire for a good preferable not just extrinsically but intrinsically. What we prefer is the deed of true believing, where not only the believing but also its truth is attributable to the agent as his or her own doing. (PT, 19)

So intellectual deeds of successfully getting the truth in a way that makes the attainment of truth attributable to the agent have intrinsic value.

But Sosa actually has identified another source of the value of such intellectual deeds. Notice that in the above passage he says that we *prefer* that our successes be due to our own performance rather than by happenstance or some other cause. Three paragraphs earlier he says that we *rationally* prefer a world in which our true beliefs derive from our own cognitive performances (PT, 18). What makes the preference rational? That a value is intrinsic is only one possible ground for the rationality of preferring it. Sosa has another, although I do not think he notices that they are distinct. He speaks approvingly of Aristotle's view that performances creditable to an agent as his own are components of *eudaimonia*, a good life (PT, 19). So a different reason why it is rational to prefer successes due to our intellectual performances over successes due to some other cause is that the former contributes to a good life. If so, Sosa need not insist that the value of true believing that arises from one's own intellectual performances is intrinsic. He can say instead that it is good extrinsically because of its relation to the good of *eudaimonia*.

Either way, (3) has to go. If knowledge is true belief with property x, and if x is the property of arising from an intellectual source that makes the attainment of truth attributable to the agent, and if the value of x is either intrinsic or valuable as a component of *eudaimonia*, (3) is false. Epistemic value monism must be rejected. Nonetheless, I will argue in section IV below that if Sosa takes the second option, he can maintain a modified form of epistemic value monism. Nonetheless, epistemic value is not monistic. It is not the case that all epistemic goods other than truth derive from the value of truth. This makes our search for the source of epistemic value more complicated.

3 Epistemically Valuable False Beliefs

At this point Sosa has reached the position that knowledge is true belief with property x, and x is the property of arising from an intellectual source in the agent that makes the truth attributable to the agent. But there is a problem with this position. We usually think that there can be false x beliefs. The x part of a false x belief is still good. Sosa anticipates this problem. There is a reason why the truth is attributable to the agent when it arises from the agent's own intellectual performances, and that is that the performances themselves are excellent. Performances of that kind can be evaluated independently of the environment in which they occur, an environment which determines whether or not the resulting belief is true. So the performance can be evaluated as excellent apart from its actual truth-acquiring consequence. This makes it possible for an intellectually virtuous performance to have value even on those occasions in which it yields a false belief. We think that the agent's performance is admirable because it is one that in a benign world would lead to truth, at least characteristically.

On Sosa's account, the admirability of the intellectual performance is derived from the value of truth even when the resulting belief is false since its admirability derives from the truth that would be acquired when it is "properly installed" in the right environment. In fact, Sosa says that even if an agent's intellectual equipment never is properly installed due to the action of an evil demon, we would still want to be a person whose intellectual performances are good – such that they would lead to the truth in a benign universe (PT, 21).

Notice that since the value of a performance derives from the value of truth, it alone cannot solve the value problem. A true belief deriving from an excellent intellectual performance does not get any extra value from the performance if what makes the performance excellent is just that it is a reliable source of true belief in a benign universe. The value of a performance is needed to explain false x beliefs, but to solve the value problem Sosa needs something else, such as the value he identified earlier in the paper as either intrinsic or contributive to a life of *eudaimonia*.

Sosa concludes that there are four kinds of epistemic value:

(a) The value of the truth of a belief.
(b) The praxical, extrinsic value of true believing where the agent brings about the belief. This value derives from the value of truth.
(c) The eudaimonist, intrinsic value of true believing when getting the truth is attributable to the agent as his own deed.
(d) The extrinsic value of one's intellectual performance, whether or not the performance leads to the truth, when that performance is such that it would produce the truth if properly installed in a suitable environment (PT, 21–2).

In my view this picture is more complicated than is necessary. The four values are related in ways that beg for a more unified account of the source of epistemic value. Sosa is right that we prefer successes due to our own agency, and even when we are not successful, we prefer to act in ways that in a benign universe *would* be successful. That says more than that we prefer successes and we prefer acts of agency. I think that Sosa's account naturally leads us to the view that we prefer the *organic unity* of true beliefs arising from good intellectual performances. Such a view would permit him to incorporate all four of the values he identifies in a single account of epistemic value.

4 Organic Unities

So far we have seen that Sosa has to reject epistemic value monism in the form of (3) in order to solve the value problem. Not all epistemic value derives from the value of truth.

Nonetheless, there are variations of epistemic value monism that can be saved, if that is what Sosa wants. Take, for instance:

(4) There is no intrinsic epistemic good other than truth.

Claim (4) does not say that all epistemic value other than truth derives from the value of truth. Claim (4) is compatible with the existence of extrinsic epistemic good that derives from something other than the good of truth, e.g., some non-epistemic good such as *eudaimonia*. Or an epistemic good could be a component of such a non-epistemic good; it can contribute to the value of the whole. Both of these alternatives show that Sosa is not forced to claim that (c), the third epistemic value he identifies above, is intrinsic. Let us take a closer look at the way the value of the parts can contribute to the value of a whole.

Notice first that if contributory value is permitted, it does not follow from (1) and (2) that x has value itself since it is possible that x is valuable only in that it contributes to the value of the whole. So it does not follow from the fact that knowledge is true belief with property x and that knowledge is more valuable than true belief, that the value of knowledge in addition to true belief just is the value of x. That is because the value of a whole may exceed the value of the sum of its parts. This is the theory of organic unities, advocated by G. E. Moore and Franz Brentano.[4]

According to Brentano, the value of a whole may be either greater or less than the value of the sum of its parts. When the value of a whole exceeds the value of the sum of its parts, it may be impossible to assign the additional value of the whole to the contribution made by any given part. An obvious way this can happen is when the additional value arises from a relation among the parts. Brentano maintains, for example, that increasing good is better than decreasing good. Brentano writes: "Let us think of a process which goes from good to bad or one which goes in the opposite direction. The latter shows itself as the one to be preferred. This holds even if the sum of the goods in the one process is equal to that in the other. And our preference in this case is one that we experience as being correct."[5] What Brentano seems to have in mind here is that we prefer a life in which pleasure continuously increases over one in which pleasure continuously decreases even when the sum total of pleasure in the two alternative lives is equal. The order of the goods affects the value of the whole process, but order itself is neither intrinsically nor extrinsically good. The total intrinsic and extrinsic value of the parts is identical in both processes.[6]

It seems to me that another internal connection between the parts of a whole that can affect the value of the whole is the presence or lack of a causal connection among the parts. The whole consisting of pleasure caused by benevolently motivated acts is better than the value of benevolently motivated acts plus the value of pleasure. A world containing benevolently produced pleasures is a better world than one containing the same quantity of pleasure and the same quantity of benevolently motivated acts, but without a causal connection between the acts and the pleasure. The parallel point applies to a cruel world, a world in which pain is inflicted intentionally. Arguably, a world of pains produced by cruelly motivated acts is worse than a world with the same quantity of pain and the same quantity of cruelly motivated acts, but without a causal connection between them. If this is right, benevolently produced pleasures and cruelly produced pains are organic unities.

The relations among the parts can therefore increase or decrease the value of the whole. Brentano also maintains that parts can contribute to the good of a whole when they are not good themselves. It is even possible that something intrinsically bad can contribute to a larger good. For example, Brentano believes that pleasure is intrinsically good and sorrow is intrinsically bad, yet he also says that wickedness accompanied by sorrow is less bad than wickedness accompanied by pleasure.[7] (Presumably, he means sorrow over the wickedness.) So something bad can contribute to the good of a whole, as can something good. We have already seen that something evaluatively neutral can contribute to the value of a whole as well. The examples of temporal order and causal connection are probably in that category.

Suppose now that knowledge is an organic unity. Knowledge is an organic unity of x and true belief, where the value of knowledge is more than the sum of the value of x and the value of true belief. This means that either x or truth or some relation between them contributes to the value of the whole in addition to any intrinsic or extrinsic value possessed by x and by truth. I think that Sosa would agree with me that an internal causal connection within the state of knowledge can explain the difference in value. The organic unity of virtuously produced true belief is better than true belief *simpliciter* for the same reason that benevolently produced pleasure is better than pleasure *simpliciter*. Furthermore, the organic unity of virtuously produced true belief is better than true belief plus virtuously motivated performance for the same reason that benevolently produced pleasure is better than pleasure plus benevolently motivated action where there is no causal connection between them.

Compare two worlds, W1 and W2, that have the same number of true and false beliefs and the same number of intellectually virtuous acts. But suppose that in W1 there is no causal relation between the acts and the beliefs, whereas in W2 the true beliefs are virtuously produced. Sosa says we prefer the second, although he commits himself to the paradoxical position that W1 and W2 are equal in value (PT, 8).[8] I agree that we prefer W2, but there is no need to maintain that W1 and W2 are equal in total value. Even if there is no difference in intrinsic value in the two worlds, the second is a better world as long as virtuously produced true belief is an organic unity.

So my suggestion for Sosa is as follows:

(a) The truth of a belief is valuable, perhaps intrinsically so.
(b′) Virtuous intellectual performances are extrinsically valuable (derived from the value of truth). This is a value performances can have whether or not they lead to the truth on a given occasion.
(c′) The organic unity of a true belief produced by a virtuous intellectual performance is better than the value of truth plus the value of the performance. That is why knowledge is better than mere true belief.

The answer to the deeper question "Why is the organic unity of knowledge better than the sum of its parts?" should probably be that such an organic unity contributes to a life of *eudaimonia*. The organic unity of virtuously produced true believing is a component of a yet larger organic unity of a good life.[9]

On this proposal Sosa would not be forced to say that the value of getting the truth in a way that is attributable to my own deed is an intrinsic good distinct from the good of truth. That means he could maintain the form of value monism given in (4), although he must still reject (3), and on the proposal I made in the preceding paragraph, he also has to give up the idea that epistemic value is an autonomous kind of value. Knowledge is valuable because it is a component of *eudaimonia*, a life that is ethically valuable. But as far as I can see, he has already given up the autonomy of epistemic value anyway. Still, since Sosa apparently wishes to defend some form of epistemic value monism, I think he can get it in the form of (4).

If Sosa accepts my suggestion that the value of knowledge should be understood as an organic unity, that would also resolve his apparent ambivalence about the intrinsic value of truth. He points out that some truths are trivial (PT, 2, 5). In fact, he seems to think that the value of true believing is conditional on certain interests (PT, 4). Alternatively, he sometimes speaks as if true believing is good in so far as it contributes to a life of *eudaimonia* (PT, 19). That suggests that he would prefer to say that the truth of a belief has only contributory value, not intrinsic value, although he seems tempted to call it intrinsic in one place (PT, 19). If it is not intrinsic, neither component value in knowledge would be intrinsic, nor need either be extrinsic. Both might have only contributory value. I think this is a perfectly coherent position, and if it is what Sosa has in mind, the dependence of epistemic value on some non-epistemic value to which it contributes would be obvious. But Sosa need not go so far as to deny the intrinsic value of true believing. The value of the truth of a belief can be intrinsic even if it is trivial and its more interesting value is contributory. As far as I can see, the theory of organic unities is the best way to understand this.

In short, Sosa must give up epistemic value monism in the form of (3) in order to solve the value problem. Nevertheless, he is not forced to maintain that there is another intrinsic epistemic value such as the value of true believing when getting the truth is attributed to one's intellectual deeds. If knowledge is true belief with property x, the value of knowledge can exceed the value of truth plus the value of x. The value of truth may be intrinsic or merely contributory to the organic whole. The value of x also may be intrinsic, extrinsic (because it is derived from the value of truth), or merely contributory to the whole. In any case, the value of the whole exceeds the value of the sum of the parts. The solution to the value problem is that knowledge is an organic unity.

5 Gettier

It is a good idea to think of knowledge as an organic unity for a completely different reason. That is Gettier problems. I have argued previously that Gettier-style counterexamples can be given for any theory according to which knowledge is true belief plus x, where the truth is not entailed by x.[10] As long as it is possible for there to be a false x belief, a counterexample can be generated following this recipe: Find a false x belief. Then amend the situation to make the belief true for reasons that have nothing to do with x. The belief will then be true and will be x, but will not be knowledge. This means that x cannot be a component of knowledge independent of truth. On the other hand, as we have seen above, it does seem intuitively right that there can be beliefs that are just as epistemically admirable as ordinary cases of knowledge except that they are false. Is there a way to satisfy both intuitions in a single account of knowledge?

Yes, there is. I have proposed that in instances of knowledge the truth is reached *because of* the other epistemically valuable components of the state of knowledge. What I call an act of intellectual virtue is an act that reaches the truth because of the intellectually virtuous motives and behavior of the agent.[11] And, as we have seen, Sosa's new account of the value of knowledge has a similar feature. He insists that we value getting the truth in a way that is attributed to our own intellectual deeds. We ought to conclude, then, that it is misleading to formally define knowledge as true belief plus x, where x designates the epistemically valuable ingredients in knowledge other than truth. Rather, x is the property of getting the truth because of those ingredients. It is possible to have the ingredients without getting the truth, but getting the truth and having the ingredients is not sufficient for knowledge. Knowledge is getting the truth because of the ingredients. Knowledge is true belief acquired in a valuable way, a way that is to the agent's credit.[12]

Let me now summarize my recommendations for Sosa:

(1) The assumption that knowledge is true belief with property x does not have the consequence that the value of knowledge is the same as the value of truth plus the value of x. Knowledge may be an organic unity.
(2) Epistemic value monism based on the value of truth is false.
(3) Even if the truth of a belief is intrinsically valuable, it is still possible that there is no other intrinsic epistemic value.
(4) The value problem, as well as Gettier problems, lead in the direction of understanding the evaluative components of knowledge as causally connected, particularly in a way that makes the successful attainment of truth the result of the agent's own doing, and hence, something for which she can be commended. I think, then, that Sosa and I are in agreement that knowledge is a state of believing in which the agent reaches truth in valuable way w. We can, of course, debate about the substance of way w, but I suggest that any viable account of knowledge will have this form.

Notes

1 I raised this problem briefly in *Virtues of the Mind* (Cambridge: Cambridge University Press, 1996), 301–2. The more detailed argument reviewed here appears in "From Reliabilism to Virtue Epistemology," *Proceedings of the World Congress of Philosophy 1998: Epistemology* (Bowling Green, OH: Philosophy Documentation Center, 2000), reprinted in an expanded version in *Knowledge, Belief, and Character*, ed. Guy Axtell (Lanham, MD: Rowman and Littlefield, 2000).
2 "The Place of Truth in Epistemology," forthcoming in Michael DePaul and Linda Zagzebski, eds., *Intellectual Virtue: Perspectives from Ethics and Epistemology* (Oxford: Oxford University Press, 2003) (cited as PT). Page numbers refer to the typescript.
3 Sosa knows that there may be epistemic values such as understanding which may not be directly related to the value of truth, but he is leaving these aside. See PT, note 5.
4 A good discussion of Brentano's version of the theory appears in R. M. Chisholm, *Brentano and Intrinsic Value* (Cambridge: Cambridge University Press, 1986), chapter 7. Moore had the idea earlier and called Brentano's attention to the need for organic unities in his review of the

first edition of Brentano's *The Origin of Our Knowledge of Right and Wrong*. See Chisholm, p. 69, note 1.
5   See Chisholm, *Brentano and Intrinsic Value*, p. 71.
6   I distinguish intrinsic and extrinsic good differently than does either Moore or Brentano, but that should not matter for the point of this chapter.
7   Chisholm, *Brentano and Intrinsic Value*, p. 72.
8   Sosa says that worlds are evaluated by total intrinsic value even though particular events are evaluated by taking into account instrumental value.
9   Alternatively, he could say the organic unity of knowledge is instrumentally good, leading to a life of *eudaimonia*, but I find that less plausible.
10 "The Inescapability of Gettier Problems," *Philosophical Quarterly* (January 1994); also in *Virtues of the Mind*, Part III, sec. 3 (Cambridge: Cambridge University Press, 1996).
11 *Virtues of the Mind*.
12 Wayne Riggs and John Greco have similar positions. See Riggs, "Reliability and the Value of Knowledge," forthcoming, *Philosophy and Phenomenological Research*; and Greco, "Knowledge as Credit for True Belief," in DePaul and Zagzebski, *Intellectual Virtue*.

Part II

Critical Essays: Metaphysics

17

Sosa on Realism

WILLIAM P. ALSTON

I

To the best of my knowledge, all of Sosa's contributions to the topic of realism come from the last decade. But that is far from being a mark against it. Ripe reflection is usually more conducive to good philosophy than early enthusiasm.

What I take to be the most important and interesting of Sosa's writings on this topic have to do with the question of how realistic it is reasonable to be concerning what individuals exist. His main discussions of this are in "Putnam's Pragmatic Realism" (PPR) and "Existential Relativity" (ER). The general framework of the discussion is the same in both essays, though the issue on which I will be focusing is much more extensively treated in ER, and the conclusion there is somewhat more definite. I will deal mostly with ER, with some passing glances at PPR.

PPR is organized as a critical discussion of Putnam's arguments for his "internal realism." Setting aside the notorious "model theoretic argument," Sosa concentrates on three: (a) the argument that since causation has a "perspectival character," so does reference and hence so does the reality to which reference is made; (b) the argument that depends on tying metaphysical realism to materialism or scientific realism; (c) the argument that what exists is relative to "conceptual schemes" or "theories." Sosa is severely critical of (a) and (b), rightly so in my judgment, but much less so of (c). He finds in it "a valuable insight" (PPR, 619). It is his development of, and discussion of, this argument on which I will concentrate here.

II

First we need to spell out the position the argument is designed to support. The intended conclusion is that what exists, what "objects" there are, is relative to a "conceptual scheme," to a certain way of conceptualizing the world, a certain way of, *inter alia*, dividing it up into kinds of things, "countenancing" certain kinds of things, and thereby determining what individual objects there are. Moreover there is a plurality of such schemes, actual and possible, that have an equal claim to acceptability. Hence there is no unique, "absolutist" answer to the question of what objects exist, or what kinds of object exist. This is the anti-realist thrust to this *conceptual relativity*. It is directly counter to one of the three cardinal theses of *metaphysical realism* that is enumerated in Putnam (1981: 49), namely, "the world consists of some fixed totality of mind-independent objects." According to Putnam's conceptual relativity, any list of what objects exist is valid only relative to a certain way of conceptualizing the world among innumerable alternatives, and hence no such list can pick out a totality of *mind-independent* objects.

Putnam's favorite example of conceptual relativity concerns the issue over mereological sums. Does any arbitrary collection of objects count as an object? Is there a composite object made up of my computer, Chartres Cathedral, a speck of dust on my desk, and a pile of snow on my front lawn? Putnam claims that there is no rational basis for making a choice between a positive and negative answer. We can only say that relative to one conceptual scheme there is such an object, and relative to an equally acceptable scheme there is not. Sosa obviously feels, as do I, that the mereology issue is not the best way of recommending this approach. There are too many ways of handling the problem without succumbing to conceptual relativity. (The following is taken from my reactions to Putnam's conceptual relativity in chapter 6 of Alston 1996.) We might grasp the nettle and claim that there are sufficient reasons for, e.g., the anti-mereological position. Or we might say that it's just a matter of how we are going to regiment language or logic for a certain purpose, and that it has no metaphysical implications for what reality is like. Or we might say that it is more reasonable (than conceptual relativity) to think that there is an objective answer to the question, even though at present we can't conclusively determine which that is. So Sosa and I both think that conceptual relativity would appear in a stronger light if we were to consider an issue that is, or at least clearly appears to be, of undeniable metaphysical importance.

The example that Sosa picks for this purpose involves snowballs and some of their close relatives:

> Artifacts and natural objects are normally composed of stuff or of parts in certain ways. Those that endure are normally composed of stuff or of parts at each instant of their enduring ... Thus a snowball exists at a time t and location l only if there is a round quantity of snow at l and t sufficiently separate from other snow, and so forth; and it endures through an interval I only if, for every division of I into a sequence of sub intervals $I_1, I_2 \ldots$, there is a corresponding sequence of quantities of snow $Q_1, Q_2 \ldots$, related in certain restricted ways. I mean thus to recall our criteria of existence and perdurance for snowballs.
>
> So much for snowballs. The like is true of chains and constituent links, boxes and constituent sides, and a great variety of artifacts or natural entities such as hills or trees; and the same goes for persons and their constituent bodies....
>
> Compare now ... the concept of a "snowdiscall," which we may define as an entity constituted by a piece of snow as matter and as form any shape between being round and being disc-shaped. At any given time, therefore, any piece of snow that constitutes a snowball constitutes a snowdiscall, but a piece of snow might at a time constitute a snowdiscall without then constituting a snowball.... Whenever a piece of snow constitutes a snowball, therefore, it constitutes infinitely many entities all sharing its place with it.

> Under a broadly Aristotelian conception, therefore, the barest flutter of the smallest leaf creates and destroys infinitely many things, and ordinary reality suffers a sort of "explosion." (ER, 132–3)

Since there is a continuum of shapes between roundness and disc-shaped, we could draw a line anywhere along that continuum and define another kind as a piece of snow the shape of which falls somewhere between roundness and that line. So just this example provides the resources for distinguishing an indefinite number of kinds. And since analogous proliferations are all over the map, we are faced with an (presumably very high order of) infinity of kinds of things, each exemplified, not to mention all the unexemplified kinds we could envisage.

This explosion is one of the options to which, according to Sosa, the above considerations lead us. A second is conceptual relativism:

> Constituted, supervenient entities do not just objectively supervene on their requisite, constitutive matters and forms, outside all conceptual schemes.... Just as we do not countenance the existence of snowdiscalls, just so another culture might be unwilling to countenance snowballs. We do not countenance snowdiscalls; our conceptual scheme denies the snowdiscall form ... the status required for it to be a proper constitutive form of a separate sort of entity – at least not with snow as underlying stuff. (ER, 133)

So whether a certain matter–form pairing generates a distinctive kind of individual is relative to a conceptual scheme, to whether that scheme "recognizes" or "countenances" that pairing as suitable for that function:

> The third option is a disappearance or elimination theory that refuses to countenance supervenient, constituted objects. But then most if not all of reality will be lost. (ER, 134)

At the end of PPR Sosa simply leaves these three options, none of them unqualifiedly attractive, as ones between which we must choose, but without himself making a choice. But in ER he carries the investigation further. He first provides convincing answers to some obvious objections to conceptual relativism. To complaints that it absurdly represents us and our conceptual doings as responsible for the existence of whatever exists (usurping a divine prerogative), thereby implying that before we existed with our conceptual activity nothing existed, he distinguishes between "*in virtue of* a conceptual scheme" and "*as a result of* a conceptual scheme," construing the position in terms of the former. In answer to the objection that so long as we "countenance the matter and form in question" (which Sosa never questions), we are stuck with the "absolute" existence of individuals constituted of that matter and form, whether we "recognize" them or not, Sosa distinguishes between recognizing that, e.g., many pieces of snow exemplify the snowdiscall shape, which he is prepared to do, and, on the other hand, recognizing that this matter–form combination generates (absolutely, not relative to some conceptual scheme) a type of individual with distinctive existence and persistence conditions, which is another matter altogether. His discussion indicates that it is the persistence conditions that are the real clinker here. If a snowball is sufficiently squashed, it will no longer be a snowball, but it will still be a snowdiscall. So it seems that the same hunk of snow is two different individuals with different persistence conditions. And if that is so, no limit can be put on the number of different individuals it is. This is a bitter pill to swallow unless one is prepared, with Geach and others, to take identity to be relative to property, an idea Sosa does not discuss in this connection.

Another objection is that if we admit that things exist prior to the development of any conceptual scheme, we are committed to absolutism after all. If they do so exist, "reality itself manages somehow to cut the cookies unaided by humans" (ER, 137). In reply Sosa introduces an analogy with familiar indexical statements:

> If I say, "The Empire State Building is 180 miles away," my utterance is true, but the sentence I utter is true only relative to my present position.... However it is not so that the Empire State Building is 180 miles from here *in virtue of* my present position.... Whether I am here or not does not determine the distance of the Empire State Building relative to this place here.
>
> Existential relativity can be viewed as a doctrine rather like the relativity involved in the evaluation of the truth of indexical sentences or thoughts. In effect, "existence claims" can be viewed as implicitly indexical. (ER, 137)

That is, there are snowdiscalls relative to a certain conceptual scheme, but it is not in virtue of (as well as not as a result of) the conceptual scheme that there are snowdiscalls. It might seem that to give his analogy the required force, Sosa presupposes the possibility of making these indexically relative statements in a non-indexically relative way, that he is required to assume this if he wants to hold that what makes the statement true is not itself relative. But later he denies this:

> Actually stating the fact in virtue of which my thought "Boston is nearby" is true may be a problem if one tries to do so non perspectivally; I actually think it cannot be done, not by humans anyway. But that need not prevent us from supposing that a fact *is* stated and could be stated by any one of a large number of coordinated propositions, which would be used by different, appropriately positioned subjects; a fact, moreover, that is not mind-dependent, in the sense that its being a fact is independent of its being thought of by anyone, in any of the various perspectival ways in which it might be thought of. What is that fact, one might well ask, what could it be? Why not "the fact that Boston is nearby"? The point is that I have no way to state it except perspectivally.... As far as I can see, it simply does not follow that the fact itself must therefore be mind-dependent. (ER, 140–1)

If, like myself, one objects to treating sentences, or utterances, as basic bearers of truth-values, one might be unimpressed by the invocation of this indexical analogy, on the grounds that it depends on that way of identifying truth-value bearers. But I do not believe that the force of Sosa's analogy depends on the commitment to sentences as basic truth-value bearers. Note that in the above quotations Sosa freely oscillates between speaking of sentences (utterances) and thoughts or propositions. What saves him here, from my perspective on truth, is his position that *what one says* using indexical terms cannot be said (i.e., precisely the same cannot be said) in any other way. That is as much as to say that the indexicality affects the proposition one utters (the thought expressed) and not just the particular linguistic devices one employs. Hence the analogy survives the transition from sentences to propositions as basic truth-value bearers.

I could continue the discussion of these defenses of conceptual relativity, but on the whole I find them sound, and in any event I prefer to move on to a consideration of Sosa's final verdict on his three alternatives in ER.

III

It turns out that by the last section of ER the list of choices has been transformed. Eliminativism remains as before, but absolutism has undergone fission. The general position is described as follows:

> *Absolutism*: Eliminativism is false. Moreover, there are no restrictions on the appropriate matter–form pairs that can constitute objects. *Any* matter–form pair whatever ... determines a corresponding derived entity ... so long as the matter takes that form. This is the "explosion" of reality.

The two forms of this are distinguished by adding alternative views on the interpretation of existential claims:

> *Unrestricted absolutism*: any existential claim is to be assessed for truth and falsity relative to all objects and properties without restriction.

> *Conceptual relativism*: existential claims are true or false only relative to the context of speech or thought, which restricts the sorts of objects relevant to the assessment. Such restrictions are governed by various pragmatic or theoretical considerations.

So both forms of absolutism take the existence of objects to be non-relative and also agree in rejecting eliminativism. They differ over the interpretation of existential propositions, whether the existential operator takes as values all objects, or only those deemed relevant by a certain "context." The second form of absolutism is the position Sosa (tentatively) endorses.

What is puzzling about this array of alternatives is that the original, "hard-nosed" conceptual relativism on which nothing exists except *as relative to* some conceptual scheme has simply disappeared without so much as a by-your-leave. Sosa does not make explicit his reasons for this. Here is my shot at a reconstruction. If I have misrepresented his intent, he will, no doubt, let me know.

There are Sosa's criticisms in PPR of Putnam's arguments for his position. We might just assume that Sosa thinks that he decisively disposed of Putnam there and doesn't need to repeat it at the end of ER. But for two reasons the matter is more complicated than that. (a) At the end of PPR Sosa remains in suspense between three alternatives, one of which is Putnam's "hard nosed" conceptual relativity. (b) More pertinent to our present concern, certain features of the discussion in PPR can be taken as pointing to the conclusion that whatever solid reasons there are for conceptual relativism, they support Sosa's revised version, not Putnam's more extreme version. In particular, much of his criticism amounts to accepting a relativity or "perspectival character" of reference, causation, talk, and thought, but balks at deriving from that a relativity of reality itself. This amounts to holding that these considerations support only Sosa's version, in which the relativity is restricted to the content of what we think and say. The idea that this is the direction in which Putnam's arguments point is already suggested by the fact that Putnam's canonical formulation of his existential relativism is: "*what objects does the world consist of?*" is a question that it only makes sense to ask *within* a theory or description. This is in terms of our discourse, not of what exists.

This line of reaction to Putnam's position hooks up with certain aspects of the answers to objections to conceptual relativism in ER, answers briefly sketched above. Recall his answer to the objection that unless we fall into thinking that our conceptual activity creates whatever exists we must recognize that indefinitely many things exist independently of the character of our conceptual schemes. Sosa's response was to point out that with indexical statements, though the character of *what we say* is relative to a position, that does not prevent the *fact* that makes what we say true from being what it is independently of the speaker's position. This is as much as to say that the only way to avoid a crushing objection to conceptual relativism is to restrict it to the content of existential *statements* and not try to extend it to what makes such claims true when they are. Moreover, he explicitly uses indexical statements as a model for contextually relative existence statements. "In effect, 'existence claims' can be viewed as implicitly indexical, and that is what my existential relativist is suggesting" (ER, 137).

Finally, in leading up to his revised list of alternatives at the end of ER Sosa presents examples like "That figure is shapeless" (said of a very irregular figure), though, of course, it has *some* shape, but one that does not belong to some contextually determined list of "significant" shapes (ER, 142). The implicit suggestion is that this is the kind of context relativity that is found in whatever relativity of existence we have significant reason to accept.

Putting all this together, my reconstruction of Sosa's argument that the only kind of conceptual relativism worth considering is one that is limited to our thought and discourse, runs as follows.

(1) The considerations that support Putnam's conceptual relativity only go so far as to support a relativity of thought and discourse (RT), not Putnam's more extreme form (RE), in which there is also a conceptual scheme relativity of what exists.
(2) Moreover, RE, to the extent that it goes beyond RT, is subject to devastating objections.
(3) Therefore RT is the only form of conceptual relativism worth considering.

Sosa also seems to support his revised conceptual relativism in the following way. He reports an "inability to find any well-motivated objective restriction on the matter–form pairs that constitute derived entities. Our relativism applies to the truth or falsity of existential and other ontologically committed claims. It is here that a restriction is imposed by the conceptual scheme of the claimant speaker or thinker" (ER, 143). But just how is that inability supposed to contribute to the rejection of a hard line conceptual relativism that applies to facts as well as to propositional content? It is not as if that position supposes there to be such a "well-motivated *objective* restriction." On the contrary, it disavows any such restriction, as well as any other context-independent objective facts about what there is. Of course, Putnam does think that there are restrictions on what matter-form pairs constitute derived entities, i.e., restrictions within one or another conceptual scheme. That is what his existential relativism amounts to. But he would heartily agree with Sosa that there are no well-motivated *objective* (context-independent) restrictions. The absence of such objective restrictions supports the "explosion" of reality, so long as the hard-line conceptual relativism can be ignored. But it does nothing to contribute to eliminating it. The only position it is opposed to is a form of absolutism that recognizes only some matter–form pairs as constituting existing individuals, in a context-free way. And that alternative is conspicuously absent from Sosa's list and, indeed, from his discussion. It does not appear in court at all. It has been condemned without a hearing. (Such a hearing will be provided shortly in this chapter.)

The only remaining element in Sosa's case for his final position in ER is his objection to eliminativism. After a brief flirtation with that position, he points out that it would dispense with (the strict reality of) not only familiar complex objects, but even their most minute constituents so long as the latter are constituted of distinct parts. That would leave us with only absolutely simple "atoms." But how do we know there are any such? Science, he says, postulates no such level. It is, at best, a philosophical dogma.

I have been conducting this discussion as if in ER, unlike PPR, Sosa makes a definite commitment to one of his list of alternatives. But that is not quite accurate. He ends the essay by saying:

> My preference can only be tentative.... I do point to a way in which one might be able to accommodate some of the intuitions that drive the desire for restriction, through a kind of metalinguistic or metaconceptual ascent [as well as recognizing the objective truth of the "explosion"]. And it is through this ascent that our relativism emerges. It remains to be seen, however, whether the accommodation thus made possible will be accommodating enough. (ER, 143)

Nevertheless, for so cautious a thinker as Sosa, this is close enough to a definite commitment to be treated as such for purposes of discussion.

IV

What are we to make of all this? First I shall raise an internal problem with Sosa's position. Then I will present an alternative reaction to his alternatives.

Sosa winds up with an "objective metaphysics" that is "absolutist and latitudinarian." Since, as we have seen, he finds no "well-motivated objective restriction on the matter–form pairs that constitute derived entities" (ER, 143), he recognizes them all as objectively (non-context-relatively) existent. But at the same time "the objects on the derived level relevant to the truth evaluation of an existential claim are those in some restricted set, the context somehow determining the restriction" (ER, 142). Thus any existential claim one makes is made in some context that determines some restricted set of entities that constitutes the values of the existential quantifier. But then what about the claim Sosa makes in setting forth his "latitudinarian" objective metaphysics: "There is an existing individual for every realized form–matter pair." How can the truth conditions of this statement involve objects from some "restricted set?" If it did, the statement could not possibly be true. It would be self-defeating.

In order to make the claim square with his total position, including the other claim that existential statements are made relative to contextual restrictions on existents, Sosa would have to modify that latter claim to make this relativity optional rather than necessary. Though one *can* make existential statements subject to restrictions of this sort, one need not. Nothing is forcing one to do so. The thesis would have to be weakened to an affirmation of the *possibility* that one *can* make any existential statement subject to such restrictions, while leaving open the alternative possibility of making such statements without any restrictions as to what kinds of existents count for its assessment. To use one of Sosa's examples, one could ask "What's in the box" while keeping the presupposed list of possible contents unrestricted, rather than presupposing an exclusion of "air" from the possible answers, as Sosa suggests, rightly, that we ordinarily do. But the fact that this is our ordinary practice is a fact about our interests, needs, concerns, and limitations, rather than a necessary feature of any discourse employing an existential quantifier. Ordinary existential discourse works with such restrictions because otherwise we would never get through assessing existential claims or answering existential questions. If I were to set out to tell you what's in the box, with no restrictions as to what counts for this purpose as *something*, I would never finish the job. But if this is what the context relativity claim amounts to, it fails to be a deep fact about the necessary structure of existential discourse as such.

Here are a couple of other ways of seeing how unexciting the *context relativity of the content of existential statements* would become on this understanding. (1) It is totally uncontroversial that this kind of relativity to context infects most ordinary discourse. One need only remind us with a couple of well-chosen examples, as Sosa does on p. 142 of ER, that this is the way we ordinarily proceed. We don't need profound philosophical investigations to uncover or defend that! (2) Moreover, it would lose its analogy with indexical statements, as Sosa portrays them, where we are unable to say the same thing in non-indexical terms. And Sosa hangs a lot of his argument on this analogy.

Thus the position seems to have run into a dilemma. Either the *conceptual relativity of content* component makes it impossible to state the *objective metaphysics* component, or the former becomes innocuous and truistic. I can't see my way around this difficulty. Perhaps Sosa can help me here.

V

Now for a suggested alternative to Sosa's middle way. I have no objection to his relativism of existential claims, in the innocuous form in which he presents it. As I said, that seems maximally uncontroversial. But as for the "explosion of reality" thesis, it seems to me that Sosa unduly neglects certain possibilities for a well-motivated objective restriction on which matter–form pairs constitute derived entities. Or, at least if no such restrictions are imposed, there are still reasons for denying that all such entities have the same ontological status, the same claim to be "really there" independent of our choices, in the same way. Let me explain.

My basic point is a very familiar one. It seems that some forms determine kinds that are, as it were, thrust upon us by the fact that the members of such kinds share numerous properties that are of importance for our attempts to understand the world. They prove fruitful for taxonomy, for prediction, and for the construction of powerful explanatory theories that often provide drastic unification of what heretofore seemed to be diverse phenomena. Salient examples include the forms that differentiate species of organisms, chemical elements, chemical compounds, crystalline and other physical structures, fundamental physical particles, basic types of forces, and so on. This is so oft-told a tale that it is unnecessary for me to belabor the point. The idea that the form definitive of snowdiscalls has an ontological claim to "be there" equal to that of hydrogen, a head cold virus, water, the strong nuclear force, or protons, runs into the crushing objection that snowdiscalls share no theoretically or practically interesting properties that indicate they are pulling some independent weight in the economy of the universe. Thus snowdiscalls and the infinitely numerous other artificially marked-out kinds can be distinguished by a "well-motivated objective criterion" from natural kinds and their members as much less worthy of being recognized as existing independently of our interests and choices.

The issue here between Sosa and myself evokes echoes of Locke's critique of the scholastic doctrine of "substantial forms" that marked out kinds by nature, independently of the peculiarities of human language and thought. To this position Locke opposed his doctrine of "nominal essences" that are constituted by the criteria we use to pick out the extension of a general term. For Locke, any individual substance belongs to many such "nominal kinds," possesses indefinitely many nominal essences, as many as there are general terms that are true of it. Thus I belong to the kinds, *human*, *male*, *animal*, *mammal*, *professor*, *American*, etc., etc. Locke thinks, to use Sosa's term, that there is no "well-motivated, objective criterion" for picking out one of these nominal essences as determining the objective natural kind to which I belong, which makes me what I am. Sosa, with his "latitudinarian, absolutist objective metaphysics," seems to embrace something like a Lockean account of nominal essences, except that he is willing to recognize a distinct individual for each essence; whereas I am suggesting that something more like the scholastic doctrine of real essences that are constituted by "substantial forms" is forced on us by nature. To be sure, the real essences I envisage differ from those of the medieval scholastics, just because we know a great deal more than they did about what properties are crucial for understanding, predicting, and explaining natural phenomena.

My opening shot only involved claiming that there are certain properties (kinds, essences, forms) the instances of which have a special claim to context-neutral existence by virtue of their role in strongly influencing the course of natural processes. That claim stopped short of denying to other forms and the putative individuals for which they count as essences any conceptual scheme-independent status at all. But this is a natural further step to take once we appreciate the enormous difference between a key essence like that of hydrogen and an inert one like snowdiscallity. Why not say that "snowdiscalls" have no autonomous foothold in objective reality, but, at most, exist only relative to some context in which there is some interest in individuals with those kinds of identity and persistence conditions? What would be the objection to that? Once we appreciate the magnitude of the explosion thus generated, and the insignificance of practically all its products, one is hard pressed to find a sufficient reason for "countenancing" all those distinct individuals. It seems perverse to be as latitudinarian as Sosa was suggesting (albeit tentatively).

So my suggestion is that in the logical space of form–matter pairs, there is a line to be drawn between those that constitute individuals there is sufficient reason to count as existing "on their own," whatever we *choose* to recognize, and those for which there is no such sufficient reason. Just where we draw the line is a subject for further consideration. I have been urging that natural kinds fall in the former group, but there are other candidates as well. What should we do with artifacts? They can't claim the theoretical importance of organic species, living cells, chemical elements, or fundamental forces. And yet it does seem that desks and chairs are "out there" confronting us in a way that snowdiscalls are not. And I think that there is a significant basis for this intuition. They do have intrinsic, non-arbitrary principles of identity and persistence, though these come not from nature but from art. I will bring this out by reference to a point Sosa makes near the end of ER. He says that a hammer could also be used as a doorstop. The remark was designed to provide another illustration of the ontological explosion. Is there both a hammer and a doorstop confronting us? The example leads me to reflect that the hammer has a kind of foothold on reality that the doorstop lacks. And that is due to the intentions of the maker(s). The object was manufactured in order to do such things as drive in nails. Like anything else, including organisms, it can be used for various other purposes. But the intention of the maker, the purpose for which it was constructed, takes a certain precedence. That provides the primary identity and persistence conditions by contrast with which the conditions stemming from other possible uses have only a secondary status, if that. If we may think of the essences of natural kinds as intended by a divine maker, we have a close analogy between the products of nature and art. There is still the difference that the standard way of discovering the natural kind to which natural substances belong does not go through an investigation of the intentions of the maker, whereas the opposite is true of artifacts. And yet in both cases there are objective facts of the matter that provide a basis for placing an item in one kind rather than others to which it nominally belongs, and giving that kind a special ontological status.

The reference to Locke and the scholastics made a few paragraphs back suggests another way of posing the issue I am discussing. Instead of asking what counts as natural kinds or "artificial natural kinds," we can proceed in terms of essential and accidental properties. In asking what form–matter pairs constitute genuine individuals, with built-in identity and persistence conditions, we are asking what properties count as essential properties of individuals. For the necessary condition of persisting identity just is the continued possession of the properties that are essential to the individual. Or to turn this around, a property counts as an essential property of x *iff* x cannot be the individual it is without possessing that property. This is a familiar theme nowadays with the revival of essentialism sparked by such thinkers as Kripke. And Sosa himself gives clear indications that he thinks of the "explosion of reality" issue in just this way. Recall his answer to the second objection to conceptual relativism. There he said:

> of course there are snowdiscalls if all one means by this is that there are pieces of snow with a shape somewhere between disc-shaped and round.... When I introduced the term "snowdiscall" this is not what I had in mind. In my sense, a "snowdiscall" is not just any piece of snow with a shape between round and disc-shaped. Nor is a snowball just a round

piece of snow, a snowround. For a round piece of snow can survive squashing, unlike the snowball that it constitutes, which is destroyed, not just changed, when it is squashed. The question is, what is special about the form of being round combined with an individual piece of snow, what is special about the ordered pair, let's say, that makes it a suitable matter–form pair for the constitution of a constituted individual, a particular snowball? Would any other shape, between roundness and flatness, also serve as such a form, along with that individual piece of snow? Could they together yield a matter–form pair that might also serve, in its own way, for the formation, the constitution of its own individual: not a snowball, presumably, but its own different kind of individual? It is to *this* question that the absolutist would answer in the affirmative, while the existential relativist might well answer in the negative. (ER, 136)

This is as much as to say that the question is as to whether *any* form is suited to be an essential property of the individuals of a certain kind, when it informs some matter. That is what it would take to yield what Sosa here calls a "constituted individual," one that has its own distinctive identity and persistence conditions. A piece of snow, like anything else, could have any one of various *accidental* properties without the loss of any of them amounting to the destruction of any individual. It is only when the property is such that its loss would be the going out of existence of an individual that it serves to "constitute" an individual to which it is *essential*. It is the indefinite proliferation of "constituted individuals" that amounts to the "ontological explosion" that the Putnamian conceptual relativist, along with the eliminativist, rejects, and that Sosa (tentatively) accepts. In other words, the explosion consists of treating *every* exemplified form as an essential property of individuals of a correlated kind.

My reluctance to join Sosa in accepting the ontological explosion stems not only from my earlier point that some kinds of putative individuals have a claim to that status, regardless of our conceptual choices or preferences, whereas innumerable others do not. There is also the point that this infinite proliferation of constituted individuals is even more forbidding than the "snowdiscall" example would suggest. Not only does the same quantity of snow house indefinitely many distinct individuals of different kinds. The same applies to us. On Sosa's view there are many distinct individual substances sharing my space-time chunk with me, as many as I have accidental properties, not to mention the infinite snowdiscall-type variations that can be derived from each. All my accidental properties – details of my life history, my height and weight, my likes and dislikes, my professional involvements, etc. – that I could lose without ceasing to be me, are also essential properties of different individuals occupying the same spatiotemporal regions as myself. So when I lose or gain an accidental property, some member of this cluster (or, remembering the snowdiscall and its cousins, an infinite series of such) is destroyed and another one comes into existence. This is very uncomfortable, to say the least. It would seem to run counter to our deepest sense of what or who we are. I am not sure how serious a problem this is, but it calls for further reflection.

Getting back to the discrimination of what does and doesn't exist independently of conceptual scheme choices, thus far I have suggested members of natural kinds and artifacts as candidates for the former. But Sosa's example of the snowball reminds me that there are artifact-like things to be found among ways of dividing up stuff. It is much more plausible to take snowballs as existing in a context-free way than to accord that status to snowdiscalls or any of the other indefinitely numerous putative individuals that we could dream up in the same way. Why is that? Presumably it is because there are standard procedures for shaping snow into balls for a well-defined purpose – to throw them at people. Though it is much simpler to design and construct a snowball than a gun, it is not too much of a stretch to think of them as endowed with an essence by their creators in basically the same way, and hence as having the same kind of title to context-independent existence. The same cannot be said of snowdiscalls, etc. This opens up the field to an enormous variety of stuff shaped for a purpose – sugar cubes, medallions of veal, gold rings, etc. And there are even "pieces of stuff" analogues to natural kinds – snowflakes and drops of water, for instance.

At this point the reader may be wondering what is left to be consigned to the category of individuals that exist only relative to a conceptual scheme. I won't try to give a complete inventory of those inhabitants. That would extend this chapter beyond reasonable bounds. But here are a few plausible candidates. First, the arbitrarily demarcated hunks of stuff typified by Sosa's "snowdiscalls." Other candidates would be *sugar that is in a bowl, canister, or bag* and *some water that is still when and only when impeded from flowing by an artificial obstacle*. But I wouldn't restrict the category to form–matter pairs where the form has this made-up character. Even putative individuals with more "natural" essences such as *snow on my front lawn in March* and *sugar currently in the bowl on our breakfast room table* lack the "thrust on us by nature" character that is required for conceptual-choice-independent existence. Second, there are Putnam's favorite mereological examples. I can't see that "individuals" like *the sum of my fingernails, a certain leaf on a tree in my front yard, and the Alhambra* are forced on us, willy-nilly, by nature. If and only if we are interested in doing something (perhaps in logic) that requires reference to such entities will we have a sufficient reason for recognizing them as individuals. Otherwise they can be safely ignored. If I were to continue this enumeration, I would soon run into much more controversial candidates. And even with the types just mentioned I am hardly immune to contrary arguments. But I hope that these are plausible enough to give an idea of the sorts of putative objects I contrast with those that have the status of individuals that exist, with their distinctive conditions of identity and persistence, whatever our interests or choices.

One final point about Sosa's problem as to whether all, some, or no form–matter pairs engender "constituted" individuals that are independent of our conceptual or theoretical choices. If I follow him correctly, the problem only arises for forms that are exemplified somehow or other, forms that actually inform something. This means that it does not include questions as to what exists in any way at all. Thus questions as to whether there are such things as gods, angels, propositions, non-actual possible worlds, meanings, immaterial souls, etc., etc., fall outside Sosa's discussion altogether. It is only after we have decided that angelic or divine essences, or what it takes to be a proposition or a meaning, really are exemplified that the question of whether the resultant putative individuals exist independently of conceptual choices can arise.

VI

The exploration of those kinds of individuals that are "thrust upon us" by nature (or art), whatever our interests and choices, could and should be carried on far beyond the bounds of this essay. Here I aspire only to explore a few examples that hold out hope for avoiding an unrestrained ontological explosion. Thus far my discussion has been conducted along the lines Sosa laid down. I have been focusing on when a form–matter pair does, or does not, constitute an individual, independently of our interests and choices. But the distinction between essential and accidental properties of individuals opens up a different field for research into independent existence, namely whether, or when, or to what extent an individual has its accidental properties independently of our conceptual scheme choices. Is an individual's possession of some or all of its accidental properties a matter of the way (that bit of) the world is in itself? Or is it the case, always or sometimes, that this possession obtains only relative to one or another of the alternative possible conceptual schemes?

The first point to be made about this is that in a very large proportion of the cases there is little if any reason to deny that the properties in question are possessed by the individuals in question in a conceptual-scheme-free way. More specifically, there is little if any reason that is specific to the property in question, as contrasted with highly general reasons for the thesis that there are no facts whatever that obtain apart from some dispensable conceptual scheme. Restricting ourselves here to the more specific reasons, we would be hard pressed to find any sensible reason for doubting that it is true absolutely (not conceptual-scheme-relatively) that a tree has a certain height, a desk has a certain weight, an organism has a certain anatomical and physiological structure, a light bulb a certain wattage, and so on. And this point holds with respect to the putative individuals that I have suggested to be relative to context as well as those possessing a more absolute status. A snowdiscall, if such there be, sports a shape, weight, and volume as absolutely as a snowball.

Nevertheless, when we probe deeper we discover that not all cases are as cut and dried as this. We run into controversial issues over many ethical and evaluative features of individuals, human and otherwise. To stick with the human, each of us is regularly evaluated as more or less virtuous or vicious, worthwhile or worthless. Our actions are deemed justified or the reverse, as, in a somewhat different sense, are our beliefs. We are sometimes said to be doing our duty, carrying out our obligations, and sometimes the reverse. Widening the field, individuals of many other kinds as well as humans are considered to be more or less beautiful or the reverse, are regarded as admirable or disgusting, well- or ill-formed. It is one of the most controversial of philosophical issues whether some or all of these characterizations can lay claim to encoding an objective, conceptual-scheme-independent truth about its subject. And to give one more turn of the screw, how about being a saint or a sinner, being a prophet or a charismatic leader, in one or more of the distinctively religious senses of those terms?

Controversial issues of the sort just aired are, in a way, much more serious and more connected with real life than Sosa's problems as to what form–matter pairs constitute independently existing individuals. Sosa is on the right track in representing those latter issues as hanging on highly abstract ontological considerations that have little or no connection with problems that engage all human beings. Imagine trying to persuade a diverse group of students in an introductory philosophy course to get exercised over the mereology problem, much less getting the patrons of the bar on the corner interested. But it is a quite different story with issues concerning the absoluteness or objectivity of moral, aesthetic, religious, and other evaluative characterizations. These are of intense interest to many people who are innocent of technical philosophy, and people often feel strongly about one or another answer to the questions they raise. Think of the violently opposed attitudes on the question of whether one who performs an abortion is thereby doing something horribly wrong, or even transgressing a commandment of God.

Obviously, I cannot go into these issues in this chapter. I have only sought to give a sense of stretches of the landscape that extend beyond that portion cultivated by Sosa in his writings I have been discussing. A further examination of these and other matters will, I am sure, reveal many more complexities that must be accommodated in a comprehensive survey of the ways in which what is true of things in the world is so absolutely, or relative to some one of a number of alternative conceptual schemes.

References

Alston, William P., 1996. *A Realist Conception of Truth* (Ithaca, NY: Cornell University Press).
Putnam, Hilary, 1981. *Reason, Truth, and History* (Cambridge: Cambridge University Press).
Sosa, Ernest, 1993. "Putnam's Pragmatic Realism," *The Journal of Philosophy* 90, 12: 605–26. (Cited as PPR.)
Sosa, Ernest, 1999. "Existential Relativity," *Midwest Studies in Philosophy* 22: 132–44. (Cited as ER.)

18

Reference and Subjectivity

BILL BREWER

In "Fregean Reference Defended" (FR), Sosa presents a sophisticated descriptive theory of reference, which he calls "Fregean," and which he argues avoids standard counterexamples to more basic variants of this approach. What is characteristic of a *Fregean* theory, in his sense, is the idea that what makes a person's thought about some object, *a*, a thought about *that particular thing*, is the fact that *a* uniquely satisfies an appropriate individuator which is suitably operative in her thinking.[1] On his version, (hereafter labeled FT), any individuating concept, or definite description, is an *appropriate individuator*, whether it picks out its referent entirely independently of context, and is therefore *absolute* (e.g. <the smallest positive even number>), or it picks out its referent only with the aid of a context of use, and is therefore *perspectival* (e.g. <the football team I support>); and such an individuator, α, may be *suitably operative* in a person's thinking in one of two ways. First, she may be thinking, *de dicto*, a proposition predicating some property ϕ with respect to α. Second, she may be thinking, *de dicto*, a proposition predicating ϕ with respect to another individuator, β, which is a member of a *referential conception* for her at that time, whose *epistemic basis* contains α as one of its great preponderance of individually co-referential members. The second possibility is designed to avoid standard counter-examples, in which, insofar as a person is thinking, *de dicto*, a proposition predicating ϕ with respect to some individuator, β, she is nevertheless intuitively thinking about something other than the unique satisfier of β, either because there is no such thing, just a near miss, or because, although there is, she is really thinking about something else, which may generally be believed to be the β (e.g., Donnellan 1966; Kripke 1980). For Sosa argues that, in such cases, the intuitive object of thought uniquely satisfies an appropriately related α. Thus, Sosa secures the right results by appeal only to the relation of unique satisfaction between *a* and *some* individuator, rather than offering an alternative relation between *a* and β itself, combining a degree of satisfaction with additional causal components.[2] So he remains faithful to the official Fregean rubric.

What is so desirable about this rubric, though? Suppose α is <the *A*>. The truth-conditions of the subject's thought therefore have the following form.

$$\exists x \forall y [[Ay \leftrightarrow x=y] \& \phi x]$$

Individuator α is suitably operative in the subject's thinking in one of the two ways given above. Hence *A* is *subjectively accessible to her*: it is entirely determined, in one of these two ways, by how things are *for the subject*, by what is available within her subjective perspective. Assume that ϕ is likewise subjectively accessible. FT therefore has the consequence that the truth-conditions of a person's thought about some object, *a*, are entirely determined by how things are subjectively for her. That is, it meets the condition which I call *the subjective determination of truth-conditions* (SDTC).

I believe that this plays a key role in Sosa's motivation for FT, for two reasons. First, the "competing doctrine," with which he explicitly contrasts FT, fails to meet SDTC. Second, SDTC has strong intuitive support of its own. I take these in turn.

Sosa characterizes the "competing doctrine" as follows.

(N) A genuine relation of reference must be constituted by some special relation binding the thinker with the object of reference, probably some causal psychological relation like perception or memory.

The key contrast with FT is that (N) introduces additional causal determinants of the truth-conditions of a person's thoughts, *over and above anything which is determined by her subjective condition*. Against this, Sosa insists that any such causal conditions upon reference enter only "in a derivative, or 'by the way' fashion," as necessary conditions upon an object's unique satisfaction of subjectively accessible individuators, like <the man I see drinking a clear liquid>, or <the person I saw drinking just now>. His opposition to (N) therefore indicates an endorsement of SDTC.

Furthermore, SDTC has powerful independent appeal, along the following lines. It is a necessary condition upon a person's having a thought about an object, *a*, that she grasps its content. That is, she must have some conception of what it would be for it to be true. Any such conception, *of hers*, though, of what it would be for that thought to be true, draws only upon how things are subjectively *for her*. Suppose that SDTC is not met: truth-conditions are determined in part by causal factors external to the thinker's subjective perspective. Then, although a person, S, is actually thinking the thought, T_1, with truth-conditions TC_1, things might have been just as they are for her subjectively, had she instead been thinking the distinct thought, T_2, with truth-conditions TC_2, where the difference between her actually thinking T_1 and counterfactually thinking T_2 are accounted for entirely by the extra-subjective, causal, determinants of truth-conditions. Thus, S thinks T_1. So she must have some grasp of what it would be for its truth-conditions, TC_1, to obtain. This draws only upon how things are subjectively for her. Hence it is identical to the conception which she would have had of what it is for TC_2 to obtain had she been thinking T_2 instead. For, recall, the only difference between her actual T_1-thinking and her counterfactual T_2-thinking is external to her subjective perspective. This conception of what it is for TC_1 to obtain is supposed to constitute her grasp of the content of her thought. Yet we have just seen that it is entirely insensitive to the distinction between TC_1, and TC_2. Ascribing T_1 to her, *as opposed to* T_2, is therefore to make a distinction between thoughts which is more fine-grained than the subject's own understanding of their contents. Hence it follows from the rejection of SDTC that a person may think a thought without grasping *its content*, as distinct from that of some other. This is unacceptable. So SDTC stands. It is simply an expression of the pretheoretic requirement that which thought a person is thinking is determined by *her understanding* of its content.

This intuitive motivation for SDTC may in the end be found wanting; but it does in my view justify Sosa's strategy of exploiting the mechanism outlined above in defense of SDTC against the counterexamples offered in the literature in support of (N).[3] I am not going to take up the issue here of whether this mechanism is successful in every case. What I offer instead is a discussion of the fate of FT at the hands of a more general worry about the definitive Fregean proposal that reference to spatiotemporal particulars is to be secured by their unique satisfaction of appropriate individuators.

These individuators are either absolute or perspectival. The "aid" of a context which is required in the latter case effectively embeds into a perspectival individuator a brute stipulation of the numerical identity of some object, place or time, in relation to which the target referent is to be identified. Correlatively, absolute individuators are *purely qualitative*: they pick out their referents, either directly, by their own qualitative features, or by their relations with other things, which are in turn picked out, either directly, by their own qualitative features, or by their relations with yet other things, which are likewise, ultimately, qualitatively identified.[4]

Particular spatiotemporal objects allow for a distinction between qualitative and numerical identity.[5] For any such object, or system of related objects, that is, there is the possibility, at least in principle, of another, qualitatively identical object, or system, which is nevertheless numerically distinct; and this is so however complex or extensive the system may be. To this corresponds the possibility, for any absolute individuator, α, that it may be multiply satisfied, and therefore that it fails to refer, since its mode of reference is supposed to be *unique* satisfaction. Call this the possibility of *massive reduplication* relative to α. Suppose that FT is correct, and that a person, S, is thinking about an object, a, in virtue of having individuator α suitably operative in her thinking; and suppose further that α is absolute. It follows that S only knows that she is referring to anything at all, never mind that she is actually referring to a, if she knows that the possibility of massive reduplication relative to α is not actual. This is something she can never know, though. For any reduplicated system may be indefinitely distant from her in both space and time. FT therefore has the consequence that a person can only know that she is succeeding in thinking about something if the relevant individuator operative in her thinking is perspectival (see Strawson 1959; Brewer 1999).

I assume, I hope uncontroversially, first, that any theory of reference must acknowledge the existence of at least some cases in which the subject is in a position to know that she is successful, and, second, that it must treat such cases as more basic than those in which she is not in such a position. Thus, FT must regard reference in which a *perspectival* individuator is operative as both essential to the very possibility of reference to spatiotemporal objects, and as more basic than any case in which the operative individuator is supposed to be absolute.

Perspectival individuators secure reference to particular objects by stipulating the numerical identity of some entity relative to which the target referent is identified. Call this the *anchor* of the individuator in question. An anchor may be supposed either to be a mind-dependent experiential item, or to be an element of the mind-independent world.

The first alternative yields an account of singular reference along the lines proposed by Searle in *Intentionality* (1983, esp. ch. 2). The most basic reference to mind-independent objects proceeds by description embedding anchoring reference to some particular token experience. Thus, [That (seen) F is ϕ] is rendered, roughly, as [The F appropriately causally responsible for this F-type visual experience is ϕ]. I consider this option in detail below.

Perspectival individuators with a *mind-independent* anchor, on the other hand, automatically require a supplement to Sosa's official Fregean theory FT, by *some* commitment to (N). For brute stipulation of the numerical identity of some such anchor, relative to which the target referent is to be identified, just *is* "a genuine relation of reference constituted by some special relation binding the thinker with the object of reference."

One might admit this supplement, but insist that the appeal to (N) need only be very limited. Perhaps the *only* non-Fregean singular term required is the first person pronoun, "I." There is some evidence that this is Sosa's view. For the examples he gives of perspectival individuators are such expressions as <the person I saw drinking just now>, and <the one I seem to see drinking>. So, the suggestion is that the first person pronoun yields a unique mind-independent anchor. The remaining apparatus of singular reference operates by embedding this into perspectival individuators which therefore pick out their target referent in the world on the basis of some psychological relation, such as present or past perception, memory, or whatever, in which it stands *to the subject*.

This certainly *is* a concession by the proponent of FT as a complete account of singular reference; but it seems to me also to have serious difficulties of its own. The current proposal simply *presupposes* a satisfactory account of reference to mind-independent particulars in perception and memory. For a given subject, S, and in favorable circumstances, C, it is taken for granted that there is a determinate answer to the question which object in the world is, say, the F which S is perceiving in C. So the question immediately arises how *this* singular reference is supposed to be secured.

Either a person's subjective condition in perception uniquely determines which particular object she is perceiving, or it does not. If it does, then we have lost any real motivation, in this case at least, for the distinctively Fregean idea that reference is secured by the unique satisfaction of an appropriately operative individuator. For we have the possibility of direct demonstrative reference to the object itself, exploiting its presence within the thinker's subjective perspective. To say that this uniquely determines its numerical identity is just to say that she is subjectively acquainted with *that thing*, in such a way as to make possible her identification of it in thought *without the aid of any descriptive individuator*. This is precisely the line which I shall eventually be recommending; but it really is a radical alternative to FT, and it is certainly not Sosa's response at this point.

He would say that a person's subjective condition in perception does not uniquely determine which particular object she is perceiving. Then there seem to me to be just two options. Either the object of perception is fixed directly as that object (of the right kind) which happens to stand in the appropriate causal relation with the subject's experience, or this causal condition itself shows up in an individuator suitably operative in the subject's perceptual condition, which therefore fixes the object of perception by description, *as* the object standing in such a causal relation with this experience. The first option is really a version of (N). For it is *the fact that* the object in question stands in the causal psychological relation we call perception which is supposed to constitute the relation of perceptual reference. SDTC therefore fails at this most fundamental level.[6] Yet SDTC is Sosa's legitimate motivation for FT from the outset. On the second option, the perspectival individuator <the F I now see> is effectively shorthand for, or epistemically based upon, something like <the F appropriately causally responsible for this F-type visual experience>. So we return to the Searlean account, on which perspectival individuators secure reference to mind-independent particulars by stipulating the numerical identity of a mind-dependent anchor. I think that this is Sosa's only real option at this stage.

Call the model individuator on this view – <the F appropriately causally responsible for this F-type visual experience> – α_0. This is intended to provide the subject with his knowledge of which object he is thinking about, only given which does he genuinely understand the thought which he is supposed to be having about that particular F in the world around him. So we should ask precisely what conception α_0 provides of such a mind-independent thing. I shall argue that this is bound to be unsatisfactory.

The crucial issue concerns the relation between reference to particular Fs, and reference to F-type experiences, as these occur in α_0. I can see just two possibilities. First, the subject grasps what particular Fs *are* – the nature of such things, as individual mind-independent objects of a certain kind – independently of, and prior to, any capacity for the identification and categorization of F-type experiences, which he acquires only on the basis of the former understanding. Second, his most basic capacity concerns the identification and categorization of particular F-type experiences, which is independent of, and prior to, any grasp of what mind-independent Fs might be; this latter understanding being in some way constructed out of, or derived from, the former. These correspond, respectively, to the standard ways of thinking of the relation between concepts of the primary qualities and of experiences of those qualities, on the one hand, and concepts of the secondary qualities and of experiences of those qualities, on the other. Thus, the orthodoxy has it that the most basic distinctions concerning primary qualities are those between squareness, circularity, and the rest, *as properties of mind-independent things*. Having first identified which property squareness is, we can then identify square-type experiences as those which present something as having *that property* – squareness. Conversely, on the standard view, the most basic distinctions concerning secondary qualities are between red-type and green-type *experiences*, and the rest, conceived quite independently of the question of what their worldly correlates, if any, may be. Having made such distinctions, we may then define a property – redness – which applies to mind-independent objects, as that of being disposed to produce those kinds of experiences – red-type ones – or, alternatively, as the property of having whatever underlying physical constitution happens in the actual world to ground that disposition.[7]

In the current context, where the question is which of these two directions of explanation governs the relation between reference to Fs and reference to F-type experiences, as these figure in α_0, the first option – assimilating this case to the orthodox treatment of the *primary qualities* – is untenable. For it ascribes to the subject a way of thinking of particular Fs, which informs his basic understanding of *what such things are*, which is prior to, and independent of, his being in any position to entertain α_0, which embeds reference to an F-type experience as its mind-dependent anchor. Yet the whole point of the current version of FT is to account for the most basic reference to mind-independent Fs *as mediated by* grasp of α_0.[8]

Thus, only the second option is really open, at this point in the dialectic. Reference to *F*-type experiences must be the prior, and independent, *source* of a person's understanding of what particular mind-independent *F*s are, the source, that is, of his conception, on any occasion on which he thinks about a specific such thing, of which thing it is that he is thinking about. The question to press now is how exactly this conception is supposed to be constructed out of, or derived from, his more basic capacity for reference to particular mind-dependent *F*-type experiences. Again, I can see only two possibilities; and I shall argue that neither is the source of a proper conception of *F*s as particular mind-independent things.

First, the subject regards *F*-type experiences as aspects, or elements, of mind-independent *F*s themselves. Their own nature, as the particular experiential items which they are, constitutes an exemplar, or model, on the basis of which he attains his understanding of what particular *F*s in the world might be. This is *precisely* Berkeley's view (1975a, 1975b).[9] Although there is some latitude in the details of its development, it is, as he is fully aware, bound to lead to a form of empirical idealism. For, if particular physical objects are conceived as a construct of some kind out of particular mind-dependent experiences, then they cannot themselves be genuinely mind-independent. It may be possible to accommodate a degree of incompleteness and inaccuracy in a given person's view of the world; but the world itself is explicitly *mind-dependent* in nature. So this cannot be the way in which individuators like α_0 yield a satisfactory conception of particular mind-independent *F*s as the objects of a person's empirical thoughts.

Second, the subject regards mind-independent *F*s as the *explanatory causes* of his *F*-type experiences. Worldly *F*s are theoretical postulates, invoked in explanation of the nature and order of particular *F*-type experiences. Such experiences *may* have mind-independent causes. For all the subject knows, though, they may equally well not have. In any case, this recipe provides him with no inkling whatsoever of what worldly *F*s might actually be. For, in being forced to adopt the order of explanation on which the identification and categorization of *F*-type experiences is logically prior to, and independent of, that of worldly objects of any kind, the theorist is at this point barred from making any appeal to *F*s in his characterization of *F*-type experiences. Hence nothing can be discovered about the nature of mind-independent *F*s from a person's grasp of which things these *F*-type experiences are. What on earth worldly *F*s might be is quite obscure so far as these experiences themselves are concerned. So the capacity for reference to such experiences cannot be the source of any proper conception of *F*s at all. This approach is therefore incapable of providing a person with any genuine understanding of what he is thinking about when he purportedly thinks about a particular *F* in the mind-independent world around him.[10] Put the other way around, whatever it may be that he comes to be thinking about by these means (if anything at all), it is not a constituent of the empirical world: *this* world, which is presented to him in experience. Yet the whole point of FT is to account for reference to particular *such things*.[11]

On the reverse direction of explanation, where identification and categorization of *F*s is prior to that of *F*-type experiences, such experiences do make the nature of worldly *F*s quite evident to the subject. For these experiences are by definition those which display the world to the subject as containing such and such a particular *F*. This is unavailable on the current version of FT, though. So individuators like α_0 are quite incapable of providing a person with any satisfactory conception of mind-independent *F*s at all.

Either they provide a perfectly intelligible conception of something which is bound to be mind-dependent, or they gesture in the direction of something which *may* be mind-independent, yet of which they provide no illuminating conception whatsoever, and which is therefore not a constituent of the empirical world which is presented in experience: whatever else it may be, it certainly isn't one of *these* – an F.[12] FT is therefore unable to meet the intuitive demand of SDTC for a subjective source of a person's knowledge of what he is thinking about when he supposedly thinks about a particular mind-independent F.

The proponent of FT is led down this cul-de-sac by his commitment to the *conjunction* of SDTC with the thesis that a person's subjective condition in perception (or memory) does not uniquely determine the numerical identity of the object which he is perceiving (or remembering). The latter is common ground between Sosa and his foil, (N). They differ in that (N) dispenses with SDTC. Given that we are now at an impasse, then, insofar as there is any power to my intuitive support for Sosa's endorsement of SDTC, the only conclusion to draw is that a person's subjective condition must uniquely determine the object of his perception (or memory). This is in my view the right conclusion to draw.

The leading idea is quite simple. In order to avoid the line of objection which I have been developing to FT, it is essential to draw upon a key feature of (N). In the most basic cases, a genuine relation of reference is constituted by an actual relation between a person and the worldly object in question. In order to respect the attraction of SDTC, it is therefore necessary to recognize that this very relation, between a person and the object in the mind-independent world to which he is referring, contributes essentially to the constitution of his subjective condition. Of course, it is far less simple to give a compelling account of such a relationally constituted subjective perspective upon the world; but that, in my view, is where we must look for further progress.[13]

Notes

1 I myself follow Evans (1982, 1985) and McDowell (1984, 1986) in thinking that Frege's own position is not Fregean by Sosa's lights; but here I adopt his terminology.
2 See Blackburn's (1984, ch. 9, sect. 7) discussion of the "Right Relation," for a move in this direction. Sosa cites Boër and Lycan (1986) for insistence upon the importance of extrinsic causal requirements.
3 Putnam (1975) and Burge (1979) develop parallel objections to SDTC with respect to reference to kinds.
4 I rule out without argument here appeal to *haecceistic* individual concepts, like "the thing that pegasizes" (Quine 1980). These are supposed to be neither purely qualitative, nor, unlike brute stipulation, are they object-dependent, in the sense that their significance requires the existence of a corresponding object. Yet it is *a priori* that they apply to no more than one thing.
5 I also reject *Leibnizian* views, which hold to the identity of indiscernibles for persisting material objects.
6 It might be said that SDTC *is* met with respect to perceptually-based thoughts on this view. For such thoughts have truth-conditions of this form: $\exists x \forall y [[Ay \leftrightarrow x=y] \& \phi x]$, with "Ax" subjectively accessibly interpreted as "x is an F which I now see". The difficulty is that this

description does nothing to reveal the identity of whatever it may be that it picks out; and a Fregean theory which is satisfied with meeting SDTC in this attenuated sense loses its intuitive advantage over (N), which SDTC is intended to capture. There is also a problem with the subject's conception of what Fs might be. See note 8, below.

7 This conception of the orthodoxy is due to Campbell (1993).

8 It might be objected that a person may understand what mind-independent Fs are (or would be), in general, as it were, without reference to any particular worldly exemplar. So adopting the primary quality model is not inconsistent with FT. What could be the source of such a conception of Fs, though? Presumably, they are to be conceived as the kinds of things which play a definitive causal explanatory role, but in connection with what? It cannot be as explanatory of F-type experiences, since the primary quality model makes reference to these experiences *dependent* upon this very conception of Fs in general (see also note 11 below). So Fs must be conceived as causally explanatory of various mind-independent phenomena. Yet without a more basic account of the subject's understanding of what *those* things are, there is clearly a regress; and any such account will again be in tension with the current version of FT.

9 At least in the *Dialogues* (1975a). See Foster (1985), for discussion of the metaphysical variation in Berkeley's work; and see note 11 for a sketch of how the phenomenalism of the *Principles* (1975b) fits into my argument.

10 It might be objected that thought about mind-independent Fs is possible in the absence of any proper conception of what such things are like *in themselves*. Russell (1992) suggests that this is our own position in thinking about the physical world. I ignore this *noumenal* view here, largely because I am confident that it would not be a satisfactory destination for *Sosa's* defense of Fregean reference. The view is independently objectionable, but that is an argument for another occasion.

11 It may appear possible to avoid this difficulty by identifying mind-independent Fs with *powers* to produce F-type experiences in appropriate circumstances, rather than with the mysterious grounds of these powers. But this is effectively to adopt a form of *phenomenalism*, on which, although there may be no direct *construction* of physical objects out of experiences, as in the idealism which I rejected earlier, true sentences "about" physical objects are still held to be true *simply in virtue of* the basic facts about the actual and counterfactual order of experience.

12 This is the dilemma which Berkeley (1975b, sect. 8) offers Locke (1975), in objection to the claim that our ideas *resemble* the real qualities of mind-independent things, and hence that they provide us with a sensory-based conception of the nature of such things. Physical qualities are either perceptible or they are not. If they are, then they are ideas, and therefore plainly mind-dependent. If they are not, then they fail to resemble our ideas, which are therefore incapable of providing any intelligible conception of them.

13 Thanks to John Campbell, David Charles, Imogen Dickie, Adrian Moore, Mark Sainsbury, Matt Soteriou, and Tim Williamson, for their helpful comments on earlier versions of this material.

References

Berkeley, G., 1975a. *Three Dialogues Between Hylas and Philonous*. In M. Ayers, ed., *George Berkeley: Philosophical Works* (London: Everyman).

Berkeley, G., 1975b. *A Treatise Concerning the Principles of Human Knowledge*. In M. Ayers, ed., *George Berkeley: Philosophical Works* (London: Everyman).

Blackburn, S., 1984. *Spreading the Word* (Oxford: Oxford University Press).

Boër, S., and Lycan, W., 1986. *Knowing Who* (Cambridge, MA: MIT Press).

Brewer, B., 1999. *Perception and Reason* (Oxford: Oxford University Press).
Burge, T., 1979. "Individualism and the Mental," *Midwest Studies in Philosophy* 10: 73–121.
Campbell, J., 1993. "A Simple View of Colour." In J. Haldane and C. Wright, eds., *Reality, Representation and Projection* (Oxford: Oxford University Press).
Donnellan, K., 1966. "Reference and Definite Descriptions," *Philosophical Review* 75: 281–304.
Evans, G., 1982. *The Varieties of Reference* (Oxford: Oxford University Press).
Evans, G., 1985. "Understanding Demonstratives." In his *Collected Papers* (Oxford: Oxford University Press).
Foster, J., 1985. "Berkeley on the Physical World." In J. Foster and H. Robinson, eds., *Essays on Berkeley* (Oxford: Oxford University Press).
Kripke, S., 1980. *Naming and Necessity* (Oxford: Blackwell).
Locke, J., 1975. *An Essay Concerning Human Understanding*, ed. P. H. Nidditch (Oxford: Oxford University Press).
McDowell, J., 1984. "De Re Senses." In C. Wright, ed., *Frege: Tradition and Influence* (Oxford: Blackwell).
McDowell, J., 1986. "Singular Thought and the Extent of Inner Space." In P. Pettit and J. McDowell, eds., *Subject Thought and Context* (Oxford: Oxford University Press).
Putnam, H., 1975. "The Meaning of 'Meaning'." In *Mind, Language and Reality* (Cambridge: Cambridge University Press).
Quine, W. V. O., 1980. "On What There Is." In *From a Logical Point of View* (Cambridge, MA: Harvard University Press).
Russell, B., 1992. *The Analysis of Matter* (London: Routledge).
Searle, J., 1983. *Intentionality: An Essay in the Philosophy of Mind* (Cambridge: Cambridge University Press).
Sosa, E., 1995. "Fregean Reference Defended," *Philosophical Issues* 6: 91–9 (cited as FR).
Strawson, P. F., 1959. *Individuals* (London: Methuen).

19

Sosa's Existential Relativism

ELI HIRSCH

Ernest Sosa's notion of "existential relativism" opens new ground in one of the hardest areas of metaphysics.[1] In this chapter I want to explore two questions: first, how existential relativism relates to David Lewis's ontological position, and, second, how it relates to Hilary Putnam's conceptual relativism.

1 Existential Relativism and Explosionism

Existential relativism is initially presented by Sosa as one response to our ability – or apparent ability – to conceive of different ways of breaking the world up into objects. He asks us to consider by way of illustration the possibility of operating with the concept of a "snowdiscall." Thinking in terms of our ordinary conceptual scheme, we say that when a (suitably sized) chunk of snow is made spherical some object called a snowball comes into existence. We can imagine an alternative scheme in which "any shape between round and disc-shaped" stands to the term "snowdiscall" in the way that in the ordinary scheme "round" stands to "snowball." When a chunk of snow is made disc-shaped, in the alternative scheme, but not in the ordinary one, it would be correct to say, "Something – i.e., a snowdiscall – has come into existence." Obviously we can repeat this illustration for any shape we want. It follows that, for any shape, there will be a scheme in which it is correct to say "Some object has come into existence" whenever a chunk of snow acquires that shape.

One philosophical response to these reflections is to hold that all of the objects countenanced by the various schemes really exist. When a chunk of snow becomes disc-shaped one object – a snowdiscall – comes into existence, when the chunk is made round another object – a snowball – comes into existence, and so on for every shape that the chunk can acquire. Reality suffers from a kind of "explosion" of objects, as Sosa puts it (ER, 133). I will indeed call this position "explosionism." Sosa himself calls it "absolutism," but for reasons that will be explained later I prefer a different terminology.

To get a better feel for the scope of explosionism – for how far and wide the explosion of reality will be on this view – it may be helpful to look at an illustration a bit more extreme than Sosa's. Suppose that an ordinary tree stands in a certain yard. We can consider the succession of (stages of) objects that consists of the whole tree during each day and only the trunk during each night. Imagine a conceptual scheme in which this succession corresponds to the persistence of a "shmree." Although nothing exceptional is happening to the tree, in this other scheme it will be correct to say, "A certain brown wooden object – a shmree – shrinks in size by losing all of its branches each night, and then grows in size by retrieving the branches each morning." The explosionist will say that there is in reality that shrinking and growing object in the yard.

It is clear that explosionism is the ontological position held by David Lewis and many other philosophers. According to them, any succession of (stages of) bits of matter constitutes an object. To put it another way: if we start out with our ordinary objects, any way of mentally dividing these objects spatially or temporally yields additional objects; and any way of mentally summing these objects yields still additional objects. Any object that we can cook up, so to speak, was really already there waiting for us.

Explosionism seems to fly in the face of common sense. If this is not entirely clear with respect to Sosa's rather modest example of snowdiscalls it surely seems clear with respect to the example of shmrees. Ordinary people would regard it as sheer lunacy to suggest that when an ordinary tree stands in a yard there is some brown wooden object there that keeps gaining and losing branches every morning and evening.

Existential relativism is presented by Sosa as an alternative to explosionism. According to this position "what . . . exists relative to one conceptual scheme may not do so relative to another" (ER, 133). Is there a brown wooden object in the yard that keeps gaining and losing branches? According to the existential relativist there is such an object relative to the shmree-scheme but there is no such object relative to the ordinary scheme. Since ordinary judgments are made relative to the ordinary scheme, the ordinary person is quite right in regarding it as lunacy to judge that there is an object that gains and loses branches – relative to the ordinary scheme. On the other hand, it would be lunacy to judge that there is no such object relative to the other scheme.

Existential relativism seems to me to be an exciting position. And the first question that I want to raise in this chapter is why Sosa eventually gives it up. He evidently intends his final position – a "middle ground," as he calls it (ER, 141) – to be a kind of compromise between existential relativism, as initially explained, and explosionism. He calls his final position "conceptual relativism," but it seems to me that this terminology is likely to mislead, since, as Sosa himself stresses, this position is not relativist in any serious sense – indeed, it seems to be no more relativist than Lewis's position. Here is the way that Sosa characterizes his final position:

> Absolutism [i.e., what I am calling explosionism] is true. Moreover, existential claims are true or false only relative to the context of speech or thought, which restricts the sorts of objects relevant to the assessment. Such restrictions are governed by various pragmatic or theoretical considerations. (ER, 142)

This, I think, is exactly David Lewis's position.[2] When we do philosophy, Lewis explains, our quantifier is not restricted in any way. In terms of the unrestricted quantifier explosionism is true: there exist snowdiscalls and shmrees as well as snowballs and trees. In ordinary contexts, however, we restrict the quantifier in a way that excludes such things as snowdiscalls and shmrees. This seems to be what Sosa means when he says, "Speaking loosely and popularly we may hence say that there are only snowballs there, even if strictly and philosophically one would recognize much that is not dreamt of in our ordinary talk" (ER, 143). I think Sosa means that when we speak "strictly and philosophically" we employ the unrestricted quantifier. There appears, then, to be no real difference between Sosa's final position and Lewis's position.

Why did Sosa give up on existential relativism, which, we recall, was initially introduced as an alternative to explosionism? If we remain existential relativists then we regard the conceptual scheme adopted by the explosionist as merely one possible scheme amongst many. Relative to this scheme there exist all the objects that exist relative to all the other schemes. This scheme is not, however, metaphysically privileged, as compared to the others. It gives us one kind of "relative" truth, not the "absolute" or "philosophically strict" truth, as the explosionists – and now Sosa – believe.

I am not sure that I understand the argument Sosa gives in favor of explosionism – and against existential relativism – in the final section of "Existential Relativity." One thing that he says is that his preference for explosionism is motivated by his "failure to find attractive and well-motivated restrictions on allowable matter–form pairs" (ER, 143), that is, on allowable ways of conceptually dividing and summing bits of matter to form what will be considered unitary objects. Earlier Sosa had explained that any conceptual scheme will contain a "selection function" (ER, 138) that determines how unitary objects can be conceptually constructed out of bits of matter. In explosionism the selection function is completely permissive: any construction counts as a unitary object. What seems to be driving Sosa towards explosionism is the following train of thought. If our selection function allows snowballs then it seems quite arbitrary to exclude snowdiscalls. Surely the difference of shape between these items cannot have any ontological significance. But, then, if we are allowing snowballs and snowdiscalls, why exclude shmrees? Why exclude any construction? Explosionism seems to be the best escape from metaphysical arbitrariness.

This argument for explosionism seems to me unpersuasive, and for reasons that Sosa himself elegantly explains in earlier sections of his paper. People can speak about snowballs or speak about snowdiscalls, Sosa explains, and yet be grasping the same "facts" from different conceptual perspectives (ER, 140–1). Another way to put this point, I think, is that any truth expressible in one scheme is (*a priori*) necessarily equivalent to some truth expressible in another scheme. It follows that there is no substantive disagreement between people who employ different schemes. As Sosa says: "Of course there may be reasons why it is better to select one [scheme] rather than another, pragmatic reasons at least; rather as there may be reasons why it is better to be at one location rather than another. But this would not show that the actual judgments of 'what is nearby' made by those poorly positioned are inferior to the judgments made by those better positioned. . . . Similarly, to have different positions in ontological space might reveal a lack of coincidence in [selection functions], but little else in disagreement about what there can be or what there cannot be" (ER, 139). These points, it seems to me, apply as well to the scheme chosen by the explosionists. Perhaps there are pragmatic reasons to choose that scheme, at least when we are doing philosophy. It may be the simplest and therefore in a sense the least arbitrary scheme we can adopt. (I mean that the permissive selection scheme of explosionism may be logically simple, though it evidently generates a large number and variety of objects.) But it does not follow that the judgments of "what exists" made by those positioned in other schemes are inferior in truth – inferior in describing the facts – to the judgments made from within the scheme of explosionism. There is, I think, no persuasive argument here to give up on existential relativism and hold that explosionism is the "absolute philosophical truth."

My own preference for existential relativism – or some closely related form of relativism that I will describe later – over explosionism stems from my earlier suggestion that explosionism flies in the face of common sense. I need now to explain this a bit further. According to both Lewis and Sosa, when ordinary people say, "It's not the case that there is something brown and wooden in the yard that keeps gaining and losing branches" they are right, because they are using the quantifier expression "there is something" as restricted to "standard objects," as we might say. They are therefore not in conflict with the philosophical claims made by Lewis and Sosa that there is something there that gains and loses branches, since these philosophical claims are made with an unrestricted sense of "there is something." But this reply, it seems to me, does not really meet the point. Suppose we say the following to ordinary people: "Take a look at the tree in the yard. Is there something brown and wooden there that loses its branches each night and gains them back each morning? Now make sure that you don't restrict the range of objects you consider in answering this question. Take into account objects of any sort whatever, no matter how strange they are, and no matter how unlikely you would normally be to refer to them." Of course, they still insist that there obviously is no such object. I think this shows that even when they use the expression "there is an object" in a completely unrestricted sense they regard the explosionist claims as absurd. I have sometimes heard it suggested that ordinary people, no matter how hard they try, cannot use the quantifier in a completely unrestricted sense, so that, no matter what they say, they are not really disagreeing with philosophical explosionists like Lewis and Sosa. That retort seems extremely puzzling to me. How could a semantic rule become entrenched in the English language with the effect that fluent speakers of the language, with the exception of a few philosophers, constantly use quantifier expressions in a contextually restricted fashion, without intending it, or knowing it, or even recognizing it when it is pointed out to them? I think that makes little sense.

It needs to be emphasized that explosionists like Lewis and Sosa claim to be speaking plain English – "strict" plain English with unrestricted quantifiers. I agree that the contexts of ordinary life do indeed often restrict the quantifier in various ways, but ordinary people must be able to understand how to use in plain English the quantifier in unrestricted ways, and when they do so they adamantly reject explosionism. Explosionism does, therefore, conflict with common sense. It should be emphasized, further, that the claims in conflict concern the category of highly visible macroscopic objects – if there are such things as shmrees they belong to that category. There is, I think, something especially peculiar in philosophers' disagreeing with common sense with respect to the existence of objects within that category.

The situation seems quite different with respect to existential relativism. Suppose we say to ordinary people: "Look at the tree. Do you think that, relative to some conceptual scheme that can't be expressed in English, there exists something there that gains and loses branches?" The ordinary response will surely not be to answer this question in the negative, but rather to ask what the words "there exists something relative to some conceptual scheme that can't be expressed in English" means. If we, as existential relativists, give an affirmative answer to the question, therefore, we are not saying anything clearly against common sense. That is, I think, how it should be: philosophers have every right to say things that ordinary people, unversed in philosophy, do not understand, but they should try to avoid saying things that ordinary people do understand and regard as absurd.

Let me now say why I rejected Sosa's use of the word "absolutism" to express the explosionist position. Sosa's terminology seems confusing because philosophers who believe in "the absolute philosophical truth" need not be explosionists. Eliminativism, a position that Sosa himself cites, is one example of a belief in "absolute truth" being combined with the denial of explosionism. Another example is Van Inwagen's view that the only composite things are living things.

I take it that to believe in the "absolute philosophical truth" in the sense relevant to the present discussion is to believe that, amongst the various conceptual schemes and selection functions that we seem able to make intelligible to ourselves, one is somehow uniquely privileged, uniquely right in some sense. Suppose, now, that we believe in the "absolute truth" in this sense. I suppose we are then left trying to come up with the best philosophical hypothesis, the best guess, as to what that truth is. The simplicity and hence non-arbitrariness of explosionism may seem quite significant on this supposition. Explosionism, it may be argued, is, because of its simplicity, the best bet, the one most reasonable to accept. The appeal to simplicity, therefore, may be a good argument for explosionism, *given* that one is already committed to the "absolute truth." The appeal to simplicity, however, cannot itself support this commitment. As I argued before, the existential relativist can acknowledge the special simplicity and non-arbitrariness of the explosionist's scheme but not be moved by this to regard that scheme as expressive of the "absolute truth."

Believers in the "absolute truth" may be led to explosionism, or they may be led somehow to other positions, such as Van Inwagen's. One thing that seems quite clear is that they will not be led to the ontology of common sense. Our common-sense selection function, as far as one can make it out, seems to be an amorphous and intractably complex mess, containing in all likelihood disjunctive conditions and grue-like exceptions. How could *that* possibly be the uniquely correct selection function? It follows that if we want to be able to defend our common-sense ontology we need to reject the "absolute truth." Our common-sense ontology must be seen as one scheme amongst many, far from the simplest, but still able to express in its own way the same facts expressed by the others. It begins to look, therefore, as if existential relativism – or perhaps some variation of it – may be a requirement for common-sense philosophy. The connection goes in the other direction as well: once we are committed to existential relativism there is no good motive to repudiate our common-sense ontological beliefs, complex and messy though they may be.

2 Existential Relativism and Quantifier Relativism

What I next want to talk about is the relationship between existential relativism and Putnam's "conceptual relativism." The terminology here has evidently become difficult, since Sosa is now using "conceptual relativism" as the name for a position that includes explosionism, which is certainly not a position encompassed by Putnam's relativism. I am therefore going to refer to Putnam's relativism in this chapter as "quantifier relativism." The motivation for this terminology will, I hope, become apparent.

Let me introduce quantifier relativism by quoting a couple of passages from Putnam. "The logical primitives themselves, and in particular the notions of object and existence, have a multitude of different [possible] uses rather than one absolute 'meaning.'"[3] "All situations have many different descriptions, and ... even descriptions that, taken holistically, convey the same information may differ in what they take to be 'objects.' ... [T]here isn't one single privileged sense of the word 'object' ..., but there is only an inherently extendible notion of 'object.'"[4]

Putnam is saying that different languages, different conceptual schemes, might operate with different selection functions, and hence with different concepts of what it means for there to exist an object. In his surrounding discussion Putnam makes it clear that he is not merely saying that the same unrestricted concept of existence, operating within every language, might be contextually restricted in different ways. Rather he is saying that different languages might possess different concepts of "unrestricted existence."

In the first quote from Putnam I myself inserted the word "possible." There are really two claims here: first, that the quantifier expressions in plain English (or some other actual language), when they are in no way contextually restricted, have multiple senses; second, that there is the possibility (if not the actuality) of languages in which the contextually unrestricted quantifier has a different sense from that of plain English. It is the second claim that I am here calling quantifier relativism. The first claim might follow from the vagueness of our unrestricted quantifiers, which I in fact believe in, but I am not going into that here.[5]

The difference between existential relativism and quantifier relativism is that the former makes an object-level claim about the world, whereas the latter makes a meta-level claim about different possible languages or conceptual schemes. Quantifier relativists are not saying that different objects exist relative to different conceptual schemes; rather, they are saying that different concepts of an "object" might be employed in different conceptual schemes, schemes that are all adequate for describing the world. In each scheme, however, the relevant descriptions would take the non-relativized form, "There exist such-and-such objects," not, as in existential relativism, the form, "There exist such-and-such objects, relative to scheme S."

Sometimes philosophers initially react to quantifier relativism by regarding it as trivial. "Isn't it trivial that we could use the words 'the existence of an object' in any way we please?" Of course that is trivial; we could use those words to assert, for instance, that it is raining outside. That is not Putnam's point, however. Putnam is saying that there could be a language whose (contextually unrestricted) quantifier expressions do not have the same sense as those of English, so that the people who employ that language (as their primary language, as the language "in which they think") could be said to operate with a different concept of "the existence of an object" than the ordinary one, and yet they can describe the world as accurately and truthfully as we do.

To appreciate how untrivial this claim is, one should consider how it relates to the correspondence theory of truth. One classic understanding of that theory might be put roughly as follows:

The referential correspondence theory of truth. In any possible language the truth of a statement depends on the referential relations between its (non-logical) words and objects that exist in the world.

Another way to express this theory of truth is by saying that any possible language must admit of a standard referential semantics. If we are quantifier relativists it seems we must reject this theory of truth. Suppose we (who are speaking plain English) are considering the truth within the shmree-scheme of the statement, "There exists an object in the yard that is brown and wooden and that keeps gaining and losing branches." Without going into the details, it seems clear that we cannot (in plain English) give a standard referential semantic analysis of what makes the sentence true in the shmree-language. Such an analysis would require us to say that there is a suitable object that is referred to by the terms "brown," "wooden," and "gains and loses branches." What could that object be? From the perspective of our own scheme there is no such object for these terms to refer to in a suitable truth-making way. The referential correspondence theory requires that it be possible to match up the reference of the terms and quantifier expressions of our own language to those of any other describable language; that is what is required to give in our own language a referential analysis of the semantics of another language. Quantifier relativism claims that sometimes this will not be possible. Since the shmree-language embodies a different concept of "the existence of an object" we cannot in terms of our own concept of "the existence of an object" describe the truth of sentences in that language as deriving from the referential relations between its words and objects that exist in the world.

Quantifier relativists must reject the referential correspondence theory of truth, but they still have available to them another perennial version of the correspondence theory:

The factive correspondence theory of truth. In any possible language the truth of a statement depends on the world's being the way the statement says the world is.

Another way to put this is that the truth of a statement must depend on its correspondence to the facts. We recall Sosa's explanation that the same facts (in one intuitive sense of the word "facts") can be grasped from different conceptual perspectives. Quantifier relativists can hold, therefore, that, whichever concept of "the existence of an object" we adopt, our concept of "a fact," our concept of "the way the world is," remains the same, and it is this concept that defines the nature of truth for any conceptual perspective. (I will not at present attempt to explain Putnam's own attitude – apparently negative – towards the factive correspondence theory.)

A question might now be posed as follows: If we are quantifier relativists we claim that the expression "there exists an object," as used in the shmree-scheme, does not mean *that there exists an object*, that is, it does not mean what it means in our language. Why, then, it might be asked, should we even call this expression, as it functions in the shmree-language, a "quantifier." And why, then, should we say that speakers of the other language are operating with a different concept of "the existence of an object," rather than saying that they operate with no concept of "the existence of an object."

I think that quantifier relativists should readily concede the force of this question. Indeed, we could just as well express the basic idea of quantifier relativism by saying that the expression "there exists an object" functions in the shmree-language *in some ways like* a quantifier, and it expresses in that language a concept *in some ways like* our concept of "the existence of an object." We are merely trying to indicate these similarities when we say that the expression is "their quantifier" and that it expresses a "different concept of 'the existence of an object.'" The similarities in question are partly a matter of formal logic, since we are tacitly assuming in our construction of the shmree-language that all of formal quantificational logic will remain intact in that language. It seems on an intuitive level, however, that there are "holistic" similarities that go beyond purely formal matters. When we reflect on how the word "shmree" functions in the other language we are inclined to say that the word *does something like* referring to an object. We know that (in terms of our concept of an object) there isn't any suitable object for the word to refer to, but it is in some sense *as if* there were an object being referred to, a brown and wooden object in the yard that keeps gaining and losing branches. Of course, to say that it is "as if" there is such an object, though there is no such object, is only a way of expressing our sense that the word "shmree" functions in the other language in some ways similar to how our word "tree" functions in ours. Whether it is even in principle possible to spell out the relevant holistic similarity seems doubtful.

How should we now say that quantifier relativism is related to existential relativism? Consider, first, the following possible analogy. It is correct to make the meta-level statement, "In base 5, 'The sum of 3 and 2 is 10' is a true sentence." I think most people would, however, regard it as merely a use–mention confusion to try to make the object-level statement, "Relative to base 5, the sum of 3 and 2 is 10." Is the existential relativist committing the same confusion? The quantifier relativist makes the correct meta-level statement, "In the shmree-scheme, 'There exists an object in the yard that keeps gaining and losing branches' is a true sentence." Are existential relativists committing a use–mention confusion when they make the object-level statement, "Relative to the shmree-scheme, there exists an object in the yard that keeps gaining and losing branches"?

Existential relativists have a response, however. They will say that the cases are very different. We have no trouble describing, from our ordinary base 10, how other bases function. In base 5, we say, the expression "10" refers to the number 5, the expression "20" refers to the number 10, and so on. There is, therefore, no reason here to move to an object-level description, which would indeed be merely a use–mention confusion. In the case of alternative concepts of "the existence of on object," however, we cannot readily describe how these alternative concepts function. In the shmree-scheme the word "shmree" seems to have the function of referring to a certain kind of object, but, in terms of our ordinary scheme, there is no such object. We are, therefore, pushed in this case to make the object-level claim that, relative to the shmree-scheme, there is in fact the required sort of object.

I can accept this explanation, but only in a certain spirit. My inclination is to think that there is at bottom no genuinely substantive difference between quantifier and existential relativism. The central insight of both forms of relativism is that there are many possible selection functions, many possible perspectives on "the existence of objects," which all are adequate for truthfully describing the same facts, the same "way the world is." None of these schemes is, therefore, metaphysically privileged; none of them qualifies as somehow presenting the uniquely "absolute truth," the "strict and philosophical truth." (This point holds, we recall, even for the explosionist scheme, which the relativist regards as merely one scheme amongst many – albeit, perhaps, an especially simple one – for describing the facts.) This basic relativist insight is first formulated in the meta-level terms of quantifier relativism. That formulation attempts to remain close to plain English but strains to make itself intelligible. "In the shmree-scheme," the quantifier relativist says, "it is in some sense *as if* there exists a suitable object for the word 'shmree' to refer to." This awkward and stammering formulation is then converted by the existential relativist into the object-level formulation, "Relative to the shmree-scheme, there does exist a suitable object." I am viewing existential relativism as essentially a technical formulation of something that is hard to put in plain terms. The existential relativist departs from plain English, but does so for the purpose of presenting the basic relativist insight in a more vivid and intuitive manner. As so viewed, quantifier relativists and existential relativists need have no disagreement with each other.

I want to conclude by commending existential relativism to Ernest Sosa. This was an important idea that I wish he had not abandoned so quickly. Certainly, I must regret his reversion to the "strict and philosophical truth" of explosionism. Existential relativism and its close cousin quantifier relativism deserve to be elaborated, if for no other reason than that they appear to provide the essential philosophical backdrop for a defense of the ontological judgments of common sense.

Notes

1 All of my references in what follows are to Sosa's "Existential Relativity," in *Midwest Studies in Philosophy* 22 (1999) (cited as ER). A related discussion is in the final part of Sosa's "Putnam's Pragmatic Realism," *The Journal of Philosophy* 90 (1993): 605–26 (cited as PPR).
2 David Lewis, *On the Plurality of Worlds* (New York: Basil Blackwell, 1986), especially at p. 213.
3 Hilary Putnam, "Truth and Convention: On Davidson's Refutation of Conceptual Relativism," *Dialectica* 41 (1987): 71.
4 Hilary Putnam, "The Question of Realism," in *Words and Life* (Cambridge, MA: Harvard University Press, 1994): 304–5.
5 See my "The Vagueness of Identity," in *Philosophical Topics* 26 (1999).

20

Sosa on Internal Realism and Conceptual Relativity

HILARY PUTNAM

Ernest Sosa's 1993 paper "Putnam's Pragmatic Realism"[1] is clearly one of the most important of the many papers that were published analyzing and criticizing the "internal realism" that I defended in books and papers[2] published between 1976 and 1989. Not only is the argumentation outstanding, as is the case in all of Ernest Sosa's work, but the scope of the discussion is extraordinarily comprehensive. If I did not reply to the paper at the time, the reason is that I had only relatively recently given up some of the views that Sosa criticized, and was still in the process of working out my present position. But the present volume gives me an opportunity that I very much value to explain just which of Sosa's criticisms I accept and which I believe that I can meet. I look forward very much to learning his response!

The Model-theoretic Argument

Sosa sets the stage for his discussion of my "internal realism" with a quotation from a paper of Donald Davidson's.[3] By internal realism I had in mind not just that the truth of sentences or utterances is relative to a language. That much, Davidson observed, was "familiar and trivially correct." "But," he continued, "Putnam seems to have more in mind – for example that a sentence of yours and a sentence of mine may contradict each other, and yet each be true 'for the speaker'. It is hard to think in what language this position can be coherently, much less persuasively, expressed."[4] Sosa opens his paper by asking, "What arguments might lead to such a view?" and picks four that, as he says, "stand out." "First, the 'model-theoretic' argument; second, the argument from the non-objectivity of reference and of the sort of causation involved in contemporary accounts of reference; third, the argument from the unlikelihood of scientific convergence on a finished science that provides an objective and absolute conception of reality; and, finally, the argument from the non-absoluteness of objecthood and of existence" (PPR, 606).

Before I discuss what Sosa has to say about these arguments, permit me to object strongly to Davidson's report of my view. The place where I stated the view Davidson was attacking (the view I called "conceptual relativity") was my first Carus Lecture,[5] and *nothing like* the assertion that "a sentence of yours and a sentence of mine may contradict each other, and yet each be true 'for the speaker'" occurs in that lecture. (In fact, neither the notion of *contradiction* nor the notion *true for the speaker* occurs.) What does occur is an example: the example of a world in which the number of objects will be said to be three if one disallows mereological sums as objects and seven if one allows them, and a discussion in which I claimed that it is absurd to suppose that there is some kind of metaphysical fact of the matter as to whether "mereological sums really exist." We can extend our language so that we speak of such things, and in the sense of "exist" and "object" we thereby create, it will be true that "there are such objects as mereological sums," or we can refuse to extend our language in that way; and both procedures are legitimate. – I thereby drew the conclusion that *the logical primitives themselves, and in particular the notions of object and existence, have a multitude of different uses rather than one absolute "meaning"* [emphasis in the original]. What this implies is that the sentence "There are seven objects (in the relevant world)" (spoken by a "Polish logician" who has introduced mereological sums into his language) and the sentence "There are three objects (in the relevant world)" (spoken by my fictitious "Carnap") do *not* "contradict" each other. Moreover, as I explained in the follow-up paper "Truth and Convention," it does not help to say that the difference in the use of "object" in the two languages is a "difference in meaning" either – especially if the criterion for sameness/ difference of meaning is supposed to be "translation practice." But I shall return to this issue below.

In contrast, the model-theoretic argument was *not* an argument for conceptual relativity, but rather an argument for the identification of truth with "idealized rational acceptability."[6] In his essay, Sosa decided to "set the controversy [provoked by that argument] aside, as one with little prospect of any new progress or insight beyond what is already contained in the literature about it," and "to discuss instead, and in turn, the other three *arguments* that sustain Putnam's pragmatic realism."[7] Since Sosa does not discuss the model-theoretic argument, I shall refrain from discussing it as well.[8]

The "Second Argument"

The second of the four arguments attributed to me by Sosa he describes as "the argument from the non-objectivity of reference and of the sort of causation involved in contemporary accounts of reference" (PPR, 606). He gives what he calls "a thumbnail sketch" of this argument (which he attributes to my "Why There Isn't a Ready-made World"[9]) as follows:

(1) Truth depends on, and is constituted by, reference (at least in part).
(2) Reference depends on, and is constituted by, causation (at least partly).
(3) Causation is radically perspectival.
(4) Reference is radically perspectival (from 2,3).
(5) Truth is radically perspectival (from 1,4).
(6) Reality is "internal" to one's perspective (from 5). (PPR, 607)

As I will now explain, I do not recognize this argument in my writing. Nevertheless, what Sosa says in this section of his paper (PPR, 607–8), and indeed in each of the sections that follows, is important to consider carefully.

Before I consider what Sosa says about the argument he attributes to me, I wish to say briefly what *I* thought I was doing in the papers in which he perceives this argument. The philosophers I was debating against subscribe to the kind of scientism that Bernard Williams defended in *Descartes: the Project of Pure Enquiry* and later in *Ethics and the Limits of Philosophy*. That means that they thought the description of the world as it is in itself, mind-independently (Williams calls it "the absolute conception") could be given in the language of a perfected natural science, indeed, in physicalistic terms. In strikingly similar language, in fact, both Michael Devitt and Clark Glymour asserted that reference is some kind of "causal connection." And they conceived of "causal connection" as something that holds between (mind-independent) physical events mind-independently. In short, they held that *the semantical (or, as I prefer to say, the "intentional") can be reduced to the non-semantical.*

In the context of this debate, it was natural that I should attack this reductionist claim. In "Why There Isn't a Ready-made World," however, I envisaged only two possible positions: either my own "internal realism," with its "verificationist semantics," or a materialist version of metaphysical realism (a dichotomy I blush at today). In Sosa's reconstruction of that essay, however, (3) reads "Causation is radically perspectival" and what follows from (3) (together with (2)) is "Reference is radically perspectival." But I did *not* argue in that paper that the context-and-interest relativity of "the cause" leads to a context-and-interest relativity of "refers."[10] ("Internal realism," which I did argue for, does not automatically imply a relativity of "refers.") What I did argue is that "the cause" means, roughly, "that part of the total cause that may reasonably, given the interests appropriate to the context, be *regarded as* the bringer about as opposed to a background condition," and hence that concept "the cause" involves something *intentional*.

Thus, from my point of view, Sosa's "(4)" should have read: "Reference is *intentional*"; his "(5)" should have read "Truth is *intentional*"; and his "(6)" should not have been there at all.

One philosopher who saw that that is what I was arguing, and who was deeply concerned to rebut my arguments, is Jerry Fodor, who wrote:[11]

> I have helped myself to the notion of . . . one event's being the cause of another. I have therefore to claim that whatever the right unpacking of [this concept] may be, it doesn't smuggle in intentional/semantic notions.

That was precisely what my argument was designed to show: that "the cause" *does* "smuggle in intentional/semantic notions," and hence the *only* way that materialist metaphysical realists have suggested for avoiding the model-theoretic argument doesn't work.

Given *his* reading of my argument, however, I find it natural that Sosa writes:

> Perhaps it is true that our concepts of reference and truth are ineliminably perspectival. Even so it still would not follow that reality itself could not be largely as it is independently

of us and our thought, in the sense that plenty of reality could not have existed propertied and interrelated very extensively just as it is in fact propertied and interrelated even if we had never existed to have any thoughts, and even if no other finite thinkers had existed to take our place. What is more, our perspectival references and truths may be seen to derive necessarily from absolute and unperspectival reality.

But I never claimed that "truth is perspectival," as far as I can see, although how we express it is certainly dependent on perspective. Moreover, no anti-realist (including my former self) denies that, for example, the moon exists "independently" of our perceptions and thoughts in the sense of having existed *before* there were perceptions and thoughts. Its existence was not *caused* by perceptions and thoughts.[12] To pretend that advocates of anti-realist (or "verificationist") semantics deny the *causal* independence of the moon, or the solar system, etc., from human thoughts and perceptions is to misdescribe their position.

Sosa continues his analysis and criticism of my arguments from the "non-objectivity of reference" [Sosa's terminology, not mine[13]] in a section titled "Objectivity, Absoluteness and the Many Faces of Realism" (pp. 608–14). Here again he repeats the charge of fallacy, this time in connection with the criticisms I made many years later of Bernard Williams's position:[14]

> What the metaphysical realist is committed to holding is that there is an in-itself reality independent of our minds and even of our existence, and that we can talk about such reality and its constituents by virtue of correspondence relations between our language (and/or our minds) on the one hand, and things-in-themselves and their intrinsic properties (including their relations) on the other. This does not commit the metaphysical realist to holding that reference itself (or correspondence, or causal explanation) is among the objective properties constitutive of in-itself reality.

What Sosa claimed is that I overlooked the possibility that there could be an "in-itself" reality [in Williams's sense] *even if* reference, truth, correspondence, etc., are all "perspectival" in the sense of being relative to interests (and other features of the contexts in which we think and speak). However, Williams's position is that the description of the world in terms of its *non-perspectival* properties is a *complete* description. It isn't, that is to say, that an exhaustive description of the world in terms of all the "absolute" properties would only describe a *part* of the world, and there is another part, the "perspectival part," which would still remain to be described. But that means that if, for example, "John referred to object X" describes a "perspectival fact" – say the fact that "John referred to object X from such-and-such a perspective" – then that *whole* fact, including the perspective and the object X and the relation between them – must *somehow* appear in the "absolute conception" (Bernard Williams's term for the complete description of the world in terms of non-perspectival properties). And the absolute description is envisaged as being given in terms of the fundamental magnitudes of natural science! Thus Williams *does* need to somehow reduce facts which involve intentionality to pure physical facts if he is not to become a sheer eliminationist with respect to the intentional. I think it is because Sosa himself does not feel the appeal of the idea of reducing the intentional to the non-intentional (nor the appeal of denying its existence altogether) that my physicalist opponents are so attracted to that he (charitably) misdescribes Williams's views.

One sees such a charitable misdescription when Sosa writes (PPR, 610): "There is nevertheless an argument open to Williams's view if the latter includes commitment to 'objectivism,' which is defined by Putnam . . . *as the view that what really has a place in objective reality is only what is included in the ontology and the ideology of 'finished science,' only what the absolute conception recognizes*"[15] [emphasis added]. Sosa immediately adds: "It is not at all clear that Williams himself would accept objectivism." In fact, not only is it *clear* that Williams accepts objectivism, but he wrote a whole book defending it – namely, *Descartes: the Project of Pure Enquiry*, the gravamen of which is that objectivism is the lasting element of truth in Descartes's philosophy!

[Thus Williams wrote, "The world itself has only *primary* qualities.[16] ("The world itself" is Williams's term for everything that, in Sosa's phrase, "has a place in objective reality," and its description is consistently identified with "the absolute conception.") And he went on to say explicitly that the notion of an "absolute conception" has substance (it does not "look too pale," in Williams's phrase) because we do have a conception of "what an adequate *physics* might look like."[17]]

"Finished Science"

As Sosa points out (PPR, 613), in my criticism of Bernard Williams's views I argued that "there is no evidence at all for the claim . . . that science converges to a *single* theory. We simply do not have the evidence to justify speculation as to whether or not science is 'destined' to converge to some one definite theoretical picture. . . . Mathematics and physics, as well as ethics and history and politics, show our conceptual choices; the world is not going to impose a single language upon us, no matter what we choose to talk about." (As examples of questions on which we cannot expect science to dictate a single answer I listed whether stones are identical with mereological sums of particle-time-slices and whether points are individuals or limits.) On pp. 612–14 of his essay, Sosa reconstructs this argument as follows (p. 613):

(a) There is no real possibility of a finished science.
(b) Things-in-themselves are by definition the things in the ontology of a finished science, and intrinsic properties are by definition those in the ideology of finished science.[18]
(c) Hence, there is no possibility that that there are things-in-themselves with intrinsic, objective properties.

I do have to concede that I argued badly.

What I *should* have said was that the question "do mereological sums exist" is not a *scientific* question at all, and not that science isn't going to "converge" to an answer. "Science" couldn't care less whether we quantify over mereological sums or not, or whether we take points to be individuals or (as Whitehead and Russell did) to be limits, or, to shift to a mathematical example, whether we take sets as primitive (and identify functions with sets of ordered pairs), or we take functions and numbers as primitive (and identify sets with "characteristic functions," as is customary in recursion theory), or take functions and numbers *and* sets as *all* primitive. Even if science "converges" it isn't going to converge to *one single "ontology" and "ideology."* (But that doesn't mean there aren't other senses in which it may well converge.)

I was mistaken to write as if "one definite theoretical picture" required one single ontology and one single ideology (i.e., as if theories did not have a number of alternative versions – a point that I myself stressed in other writings). I believe that this mistake accounts for Sosa's attribution of "(a)" to me. But "(b)" is a proposition (indeed, the most important one) that *Bernard Williams* argues for. I absolutely do not see why Sosa thinks that I agree with it. I have argued against "things-in-themselves" in various places, but always, I believe, in the context of some debate, and then the term was to be understood as the particular opponent (who might not be a realist at all) understood it. What I reject is not the idea of *mind-independent things* (in the sense of things causally independent of the mind), but (1) the idea that there is one single metaphysically privileged use of "thing" (or "object," or "entity"), and (2) the idea that there is a fact of the matter as to such questions as "is a table identical with the mereological sum of its time-slices?", etc. But I would not express this by saying "There are no things in themselves," because I don't think any of the metaphysical uses of the notion I have seen to date is *intelligible*.

The situation is similar with respect to "intrinsic properties." I would not define them in terms of Williams's concept of finished science (or rather, asymptotically approachable finished science). Actually, I would say that when people talk about "intrinsic properties" they generally suppose them to be essential properties in the Aristotelian sense (properties without which something would not be the thing that it is), and also suppose them to be interest-independent. And I don't think that there is a definite set of properties possessed by, say, *dogs* which are *the* "intrinsic properties" of dogs *interest-independently*. What is "essential" to being a dog from the point of view of a molecular biologist is not what is "essential" from the point of view of an evolutionary biologist, nor what is "essential" from the point of view of someone who is interested in dogs as *pets*. (I argue this in detail in "Aristotle After Wittgenstein"[19]).

So, I throw the ball back to Sosa in the following sense: I say, "Ernie, you want to read me as *defining* these metaphysical notions ('thing-in-itself,' 'intrinsic property'), in fact defining them the way Bernard Williams did, and then asserting 'there are no things-in-themselves with intrinsic properties.' But I don't think these notions are intelligible (as used by metaphysicians), nor do I think that all the different (unfortunate) ways they have been used are captured by Williams's definition. *I* don't want to either assert or deny the thesis that 'there are things-in-themselves with intrinsic properties.' So do we have any remaining disagreement about this issue?" If the answer is "yes," I suspect the remaining disagreement(s) will come up in what I shall say now about *conceptual relativity*.

Conceptual Relativity

As Sosa describes, in *The Many Faces of Realism*, I used the following example (I quote Sosa's presentation of the example (PPR, 614), which is quite accurate):

Suppose a world with just three individuals x1, x2, x3. Such a world is held by some "mereologists" to have in it a total of seven things or entities or objects, namely, x1, x2, x3, x1+x2, x1+x3, x2+x3, x1+x2+x3. Anti-mereologists by contrast prefer the more austere ontology that recognizes only the three individuals as objects that *really* exist in that world. Talk of the existence of x1+x2 and its ilk is just convenient abbreviation of a more complex discourse that refers to nothing but individuals. Thus, suppose x1 is wholly red and x2 is wholly black. And consider

1 There is an object that is partly red and partly black.
2 There is an object that is red and an object that is black.

For the anti-mereologist, statement 1 is not true, if we assume that x3 is also wholly red or wholly black; it is at best a convenient way of abbreviating the likes of 2.

Sosa goes on to quote my response (which, as he correctly points out was in agreement with Carnap's views on similar questions), namely that "the question is one of the choice of a language. On some days it may be more convenient to use [anti-mereological] language; ... one other days it may be convenient to use [mereological] language."[20]

Explaining this answer, Sosa writes:

Take the question:
How many objects with a volume of at least 6 cubic centimeters are there in this container? This question can have no absolute answer on the Carnap–Putnam view, even in a case where the container contains a vacuum except for three marbles each with a volume of 6 cubic centimeters. The anti-mereologist may say

3 There are three objects in the box.

But the mereologist will reply

4 There are at least seven objects in the box

The Carnap–Putnam line is now this: *which statement we accept – 3 or 4 – is a matter of linguistic convenience.* The language of mereology has criteria of existence and identity according to which sums of individuals are objects. The language of anti-mereology rejects such criteria, and may even claim that by its criteria only individuals are objects. (PPR, 614–15)

Sosa begins the first of his criticisms with the following words: "There is a valuable insight here, I believe, but I am puzzled by the linguistic wrapping in which it is offered."[21]

After saying "I am puzzled by the linguistic wrapping...," Sosa continues, "After all, none of 1–4 mentions any language, or any piece of language, nor does any of them say we shall or shall not or should or should not use any language or bit of language. So I do not see how our decision actually to use or not to use any or all of the sentences 1–4 can settle the question of whether what these sentences *say* is true or false."

My reply to this objection is that what settles the question whether what these sentences say is true or false is not merely our decision to use (assert?) any or all of them, but our adoption of what Sosa himself called "the criteria of existence and identity" of mereology or "the criteria of existence and identity" of anti-mereology, *together with certain empirical facts.* The way that works is as follows: if the Eiffel Tower does not exist (and that, I agree with Sosa, is not a question with respect to which there is any "conceptual relativity") or if the Statue of Liberty does not exist (ditto), then *the mereological sum of the Eiffel Tower and the Statue of Liberty* also does not exist (no matter which of the criteria we adopt). But if they do both exist, then *if we adopt the mereological criteria of existence and identity, then we have adopted conventions of language that make it trivially correct to say that the mereological sum of the Eiffel Tower and the Statue of Liberty exist.* The example itself was meant to illustrate precisely how there can be a choice between different uses of "exist," on some of which it is true to say that mereological sums exist, while on others it is false.

["But Hilary, how can you talk of *conventions* after Quine!" I can imagine my old friend Burton Dreben (and not only Burton Dreben) exclaiming. The answer here, as I explained long ago,[22] is that while I find the notion of convention indispensable, I do not explain it in terms of the Carnapian notion of "analyticity." What is and what is not a matter of convention is something on which we may change our minds, and empirical facts may turn out to be relevant. But I do not agree with Quine that the notion is simply to be discarded.]

Perhaps anticipating some such response, Sosa immediately suggests that a linguistic formulation of the doctrine of conceptual relativity would render it trivial. He writes:

> Here for a start is a possibility [i.e. a possible interpretation]:
>
> LR1. In order to say *anything* you must adopt a language. So you must "adopt a meaning" even for so basic a term as 'object'. And you might have adopted another. Thus you might adopt Carnap-language (CL) or you might adopt Polish-logician language (PL). What you say, i.e., the utterances you make, the sentences you affirm, are not true or false absolutely, but are true or false only relative to a given language. Thus, if you say "There are three objects in this box" your utterance or sentence may be true understood as a statement of CL while it is false understood as a statement in PL.
>
> But under this interpretation linguistic relativity seems trivially true. Who could deny that inscriptions of shapes and emissions of sounds are not true or false independently of their meaning, independently of all relativization to language or idiolect?

My reply to this consists of three points:

1 The speaker of, say, PL does not do anything that would ordinarily be called giving (or "adopting") a meaning to the word "object" (if this is not clear, substitute "entity"). When he says that there are such objects (or such entities) as mereological sums, he counts, at least for linguistic purposes, as simply using "object" ("entity") in the normal (Anglo-American) way. So the trivial linguistic truth that the truth-value of our utterances depends on the meanings we give to their words (or that our linguistic community has already given them) is *not* the same as the thesis of conceptual relativity that I affirmed above, unless "meaning" is already being given a special philosophical interpretation.

2 To see that it is *not* trivially true that if we adopt CL we *thereby* make "There are seven objects in the box Sosa described [the one with 3 marbles in a vacuum]" true, consider the question from the standpoint of a *metaphysical realist* who does not

believe in the existence of mereological sums. (I called him "Professor Antipode" in *The Many Faces of Realism*.) Obviously Professor Antipode will say something like this: "I don't mind your saying that when you use the word 'object' you mean to include mereological sums as objects. But that doesn't make 'mereological sums exist' true, any more than saying 'When I use the word "object" I mean to include leprechauns' makes 'Leprechauns exist' true."

3   On the other hand, according to my own unmetaphysical sort of realism, adopting the conventions of PL does make it true to say (in PL) "Mereological sums exist," and adopting the conventions of (CL) makes it true to say "Only 3 objects exist" [in the relevant world], and *a fortiori* that mereological sums do not exist. Whether I am right in this claim or not is not an instance of trivial linguistic conventionality, as Professor Antipode's argument shows.

Sosa's "Non-linguistic" Restatement

After expressing dissatisfaction in this way with "the linguistic turn taken by Carnap and now Putnam," Sosa moves to a more positive assessment, writing, "Nevertheless, it still seems to me that there is a valuable insight in Putnam's now repeated appeal to the contrast between the Carnapian conceptual scheme and that of the Polish logician. But, given our recent reflections, I would like to put the insight without appeal to language or to any linguistic relativity" (PPR, 619).

The insight, as expressed at the close of Sosa's essay, is that by extending my reasoning, we reach a set of options in contemporary ontology that present us with "a rather troubling trilemma" (PPR, 626).

To comment on these words, I need to explain Sosa's trilemma, which he presents with the aid of an example:

> I am supposing a snowball to be constituted by a certain piece of snow as constituent matter and the shape of (approximate) roundness as constituent form. That particular snowball exists at that time because of the roundness of that particular piece of snow. More, if at that time that piece of snow were to lose its roundness, then at that time that snowball would go out of existence.
>
> Compare now with our ordinary concept of a snowball, the concept of a snowdiscall, defined as an entity constituted by a piece of snow as matter and as form any shape between being round and being discshaped. At any given time, therefore, any piece of snow that constitutes a snowball constitutes a snowdiscall, but a piece of snow might constitute a snowdiscall without then constituting a snowball. For every round piece of snow is also in shape between being discshaped and round (inclusive), but a discshaped piece of snow is of course not round.
>
> Any snowball SB must hence be constituted by a piece of snow PS which also then constitutes a snowdiscall SD. Now, SB is distinct (a different entity) from PS, since PS would survive squashing and SB would not. By similar reasoning, SD is also distinct from PS. And, again by similar reasoning, SB must also be distinct from SD, since enough partial flattening of PS will destroy SB but not SD. Now, there are infinitely many shapes S1, S2, ... between roundness and flatness of a piece of snow, and for each i, having a shape between flatness and Si would give the form of a distinctive kind of entity to be compared

with snowballs and snowdiscalls. Whenever a piece of snow constitutes a snowball, therefore, it constitutes infinitely many entities all sharing its place with it.

Under a broadly Aristotelian conception, therefore, the barest flutter of the smallest leaf hence creates and destroys infinitely many things, and ordinary reality suffers a sort of "explosion." (PPR, 620)

The first of the three responses to this threat of ontological "explosion" that constitutes the "trilemma" Sosa himself calls "conceptual relativity," and he explains it as follows:

> Perhaps snowballs do exist relative to all actual conceptual schemes ever, but not relative to all conceivable conceptual schemes. Just as we are not willing to countenance the existence of snowdiscalls, just so another culture might have been unwilling to countenance snowballs. We do not countenance snowdiscalls because our conceptual scheme does not give to the snowdiscall form (being in shape between round and disc-shaped) the status required for it to be a proper constitutive form of a separate sort of entity – at least not with snow as underlying stuff.

And Sosa points out that:

> [t]hat would block the explosion of reality, but the price is conceptual relativity. Supervenient, constituted entities do not just exist or not in themselves, free of any dependence on or relativity to conceptual scheme. What thus exists relative to one conceptual scheme may not do so relative to another. In order for such a sort of entity to exist relative to a conceptual scheme, that conceptual scheme must recognize its constituent form as an appropriate way for a separate sort of entity to be constituted. (PPR, 620–1)

Sosa now considers a possible objection to this first response, which he promptly rebuts (PPR, 621): mustn't we think of *the existence of the framers and users of the conceptual scheme as also relative to that conceptual scheme?* "Are we then not caught in a vicious circle?" And he replies that "existence *relative* to a conceptual scheme is *not* equivalent to existence *in virtue* of that conceptual scheme. Relative to scheme C the framers of C exist *in virtue* of their constitutive matter and form, and in virtue of how these satisfy certain criteria for existence and perdurance of such subjects (among whom happen to be the framers themselves). There is hence no vicious circularity." And he sums up this first response (conceptual relativity) thus:

> The picture is then roughly this. Each of us acquires and develops a view of things that includes criteria of existence and perdurance for categories of objects. When we consider whether an object of a certain sort exists, the specification of the sort will include the relevant criteria of existence and perdurance. And when we correctly recognize that an object of that sort does exist, our claim is elliptical for "exists relative to *this* our conceptual scheme." (PPR, 621)

Comments: Both Ernest Sosa and Jennifer Case have noted that all the examples I gave (and, I might add, that Sosa now gives) of "conceptual relativity" involve what Sosa called "recondite entities" (he added "of controversial status," but I have explained above why I don't think that is always the case). And Case went on to make an important suggestion:[23]

Reading Davidson's discussion of conceptual schemes as contravening Putnam's agenda requires overlooking the difference between natural languages and languages like Carnap's and the Polish Logician's. For lack of a better term, let me call languages of the latter variety "optional languages". If having a conceptual scheme is to be associated with having a language, it should be associated with having an optional language. Modifying a remark of Davidson's, we may say that where conceptual schemes differ, so do *optional* languages.

It is not necessarily the case that where conceptual schemes differ so do *natural* languages. Someone who has a single natural language may have multiple optional languages and, therefore, multiple conceptual schemes.

If one looks at the matter this way, as I think we should, then one will not say that "we" (or "our culture") *do not countenance* snowdiscalls or mereological sums. Our culture allows us to do different things in different context, including introducing, if we want, an optional language in which we quantify over snowdiscalls – and "snowdiscalls" are, after all, no more unusual than say, "the mereological sum of my nose and the Eiffel Tower."

Secondly, I don't think it is happy to say that "mereological sums exist *relative to* the Polish Logicians language" (or "snowdiscalls exist *relative to* the SD scheme"). If we use PL, in some context and for some appropriate reason, then we should simply say "there is an object which is the mereological sum of my nose and the Eiffel Tower," or "The mereological sum of my nose and the Eiffel Tower exists." We do not have to relativize existence *to* PL *in* PL. What we have to do is make clear which optional language we are speaking.

"But then what you count as the same sentence in English may have different truth-conditions in different contexts!" That is the case anyway! ("Tomatoes are vegetables" has different truth-conditions in the mouth of a grocer and the mouth of a botanist, for example, and no one is disturbed by this.)

Thirdly, I do not see why Sosa thinks he has "put the insight without appeal to language or to any linguistic relativity." Talk of criteria of existence and perdurance is *metalinguistic* talk on the face of it. (Perhaps Sosa read me as advocating that we must always restate existence claims in the formal mode, as Carnap did. But this was not the aspect of Carnap's view that I endorsed. What I endorsed was his tolerant attitude to a plurality of – to use Jennifer Case's term – optional languages, with different so-called "ontologies.")

Fourthly, as already mentioned, I think that – very importantly – conceptual relativity should be our approach not only to questions of existence and perdurance, but to many questions having to do with cross-category identification ("Are points mere limits?" "Are functions sets of ordered pairs?" etc.).[21]

Living with the Explosion

A second approach to the problem illustrated by the snowdiscball example is what Sosa calls "try[ing] to live with the explosion." This is his term (PPR, 621) for just saying that *all* the objects in *all* the alternative conceptual schemes (what I would now, taking Case's suggestion, call all the alternative optional languages) are genuine elements of reality. There are, we will say if we take this line, snowballs *and* snowdiscballs *and* who knows what else besides? ("Possible worlds"?)

As Sosa points out, however, "If we allow the satisfaction by any sequence S of any form F of the appropriate polyadicity and logical form to count as a criterion of existence for a corresponding sort of object, then reality right in front of us, before us, and all around us is unimaginably richer and more bizarre than we have ever imagined. And any way we shall still face the problem of giving some explanation of why we focus so narrowly on the objects we do attend to, whose criteria of existence and perdurance we do recognize, to the exclusion of the plethora of other objects all around and even in the very same place" (PPR, 622).

Comment: "Trying to live with the explosion" is tremendously costly for additional reasons having to do with the problem of *criteria of cross-category identity* that I mentioned a moment ago. Consider the fact that I have mentioned a couple of times in this chapter, that in recursion theory and hierarchy theory (one of the branches of mathematics I wrote quite a few papers in) we regularly take numbers as individuals, and functions of numbers, functions of functions, functions of functions of functions . . . (as in type theory, but extended through the transfinite) as primitive. We do not take sets to be still additional entities, but "identify them" with characteristic functions. In another branch of mathematics (set theory), we regularly take sets as primitive, and identify functions with sets of ordered pairs. I have never met a philosopher *or* a mathematician who thinks there is a "fact of the matter" as to which is right! Yet they can't *both* be right.[25] According to "conceptual relativity," there is only the question of a choice of an "optional language" here. But if we go for the "exploding reality" approach, what do we do? Do we say there is a (possibly unknowable) "fact of the matter" as to whether sets are characteristic functions or functions are sets of ordered pairs? That, I must admit, seems crazy to me! [Davidson and Quine have at times suggested a move that would come to this: asserting that there are *sets1* and *functions1* and *sets2* and *functions2* and that *sets1* are (characteristic) *functions1* while *functions2* are *sets2* of ordered pairs (which are . . . ?). Any takers for that one?!!!!]

Nor does the problem arise only in pure mathematics. Typically, when we find a way of "interpreting" one version of a physical (or geometrical) theory in another, the different alternative "translations" are incompatible if taken at face value. For example, even if we decide that points are limits, there are just as many ways of formalizing the notion of a "limit" as there are of formalizing the notion of a "set." Yet surely the adoption of one or another way is a choice of a linguistic option, and not a metaphysical claim.

The Last Option: Eliminativism

The third of the three options that constitutes Sosa's trilemma is "eliminativism":

> A third option is a disappearance or elimination theory that refuses to countenance supervenient, constituted objects. But then most if not all ordinary reality will be lost. Perhaps we shall allow ourselves to continue to use its forms of speech ". . . but only as a convenient abbreviation." But in using those forms of speech, in speaking of snowballs,

chains, boxes, trees, hills, or even people, we shall *not* believe ourselves to be seriously representing reality and its contents. "As a convenience": to *whom* and for what *ends*? "As an abbreviation": of *what*?

Sosa recognizes that "[w]ith alternatives so grim, we are encouraged to return to our relativistic reflections." But now he raises an additional worry – and a deep one:

> Our conceptual scheme encompasses criteria of existence and perdurance for the sorts of objects that it recognizes. Shall we say now that a sort of object O exists (has existed, exists now, or will exist) relative to a scheme C at t if and only if, at t, C recognizes O by allowing the corresponding criteria? But surely there are sorts of objects that our present conceptual scheme does not recognize, such as artifacts yet uninvented and particles yet undiscovered, to take only two obvious examples.... What is it for there to be such objects? Is it just the in-itself satisfaction of constitutive forms by constitutive matters? That yields the explosion of reality.

Part (but only a part!) of the answer to this worry is that we should not think of ourselves has having *one* conceptual scheme. We have a language within which we can already introduce an indefinite number of conceptual schemes or optional languages (and as that language develops, there will be the possibility of still more). But we must not think of all the optional ontologies as if they might be simply *pooled*: that leads right back to "the explosion of reality" (with the consequences noted a moment ago). Yet, reality does force us to recognize that we need, for example, at least *one* optional language in which we can describe (for example) quantum reality. That there are a number of such optional languages (and ways of "translating" back and forth between them) is well known.[26]

To take Sosa's two very different examples separately: we already have in ordinary language the broad (and indispensable) category *artifact*. So we can *now* say that *there are kinds of artifacts that will probably be invented that we do not now have names for*. Saying that does not, of course, permit us to answer such questions as: *what is the exact cardinal number of uninvented artifacts*, even "in principle," but that is a bad question anyway if conceptual relativity is right – bad, because there will doubtless be more than one (optional) way of counting artifacts. The question does not become sensible by relativizing it to something called "our" conceptual system, because, as I am emphasizing, we use and need to use *many*.

The problem of undiscovered sorts of particles submits to a similar treatment. But what if Sosa were simply to ask: what of *presently indescribable but yet to be discovered sorts of physical entities*? With respect to this I would say that to say that there are such is to say that reality is not exhausted by what we can talk about in any precise way, and certainly not by our relatively precise optional languages of present-day science. As I said in my Dewey Lectures, we renegotiate – and are forced to renegotiate – our notion of reality as our language and our life develop.

Sosa closes this penultimate part of his discussion by repeating his three options, *eliminativism*, *absolutism* (the "explosion of reality") and *conceptual relativism*, and writes, "Right now I cannot decide which of these is least disastrous. But is there any other option?"

Conclusion

I cannot resist quoting Sosa's closing paragraph, which I very much appreciate, in full:

> Of the four Putnamian arguments for pragmatic realism – the model-theoretic argument; the argument from the perspectival character of causation, reference and truth; the argument from agnosticism regarding scientific convergence upon a finished science; and the argument for conceptual relativity – this fourth and last of them seems to me far the most powerful and persuasive. It raises a threefold issue – the choice between eliminativism, absolutism, and relativism – still wide open on the philosophical agenda, and a most exciting issue before us today.

Thank you, Ernie!

Notes

1 *The Journal of Philosophy* 90, 12 (December 1993): 605–26. (Cited as PPR.)
2 My "internal realism" was first announced in "Realism and Reason," my Presidential Address to the Eastern Division of the American Philosophical Association (Boston, MA, December 29, 1976), reprinted in my *Meaning and the Moral Sciences* (London: Routledge and Kegan Paul, 1978). The position was further elaborated and developed in *Reason, Truth and History* (Cambridge: Cambridge University Press, 1981), in the papers collected as *Realism and Reason: Philosophical Papers*, vol. 3 (Cambridge: Cambridge University Press, 1983), and in *The Many Faces of Realism* (LaSalle: Open Court, 1987), and the concluding chapter of *Representation and Reality* (Cambridge, MA: MIT Press, 1988). I first renounced the identification of truth with "idealized rational acceptability" which had been a central element of that position (although I retained – and still retain – another element that I called "conceptual relativity") in my reply to Simon Blackburn at the Gifford Conference on my philosophy at the University of St Andrews, November 1990. The proceedings, including that reply, are published as *Reading Putnam*, ed. P. Clarke and R. Hale (Oxford: Basil Blackwell, 1993), and repeated that renunciation in more detail in my reply to David Anderson in the issue of *Philosophical Topics* (20, 1, 1992) devoted to my philosophy. The position that I sketched in the reply to Anderson was later developed as my Dewey Lectures, *Sense, Nonsense and the Senses, The Journal of Philosophy* 91, 9 (September 1994): 445–517, collected as part I of *Sense, Nonsense and the Senses* (New York: Columbia University Press, 1999).
3 "The Structure and Content of Truth," *The Journal of Philosophy* 87, 6 (June 1990): 279–328.
4 What is strange about this paper of Davidson's is that I had heard Davidson present these arguments (at a conference at the Universidad Autonoma de Mexico) several years earlier and replied to them not only on the spot but also in print in "Truth and Convention: On Davidson's Refutation of Conceptual Relativism," in *Dialectica* 41 (1987): 69–77; collected in my *Realism with a Human Face* (Cambridge, MA: Harvard University Press, 1990) as "Truth and Convention." Davidson's paper ignored my rebuttal entirely.
5 These were published as *The Many Faces of Realism*. "Conceptual relativity" is explained on pp. 16–21.
6 My internal realist notion of truth coincided with the notion that Crispin Wright calls "superassertibility" in his *Truth and Objectivity* (Cambridge, MA: Harvard University Press,

1992) (although that is not how *he* interprets me!), if we prescind from possible differences over the notion of "assertibility."

7   NB: Sosa here uses "pragmatic realism" as synonymous with "internal realism"; I would today describe myself happily as a pragmatic realist, but *not* as an "internal realist."

8   My reasons for giving up "internal realism" are given in detail in "Sense, Nonsense and the Senses," collected in *The Threefold Cord: Mind, Body and World* (New York: Columbia University Press, 1999).

9   In my *Realism and Reason*, pp. 205–28.

10 It might be thought, after all, that all the interest-relativity is already allowed for in the fact that reference is relative to a context, and that there will be no possibility of *different* answers to "what does word W refer to?" once the context *in which W was used* has been specified. Actually, I do not think this is the case: I think that the answer to this question may depend on *who is asking and for what reason* and not only on the context of the user of the word W in question. But this is something I did not argue in the paper Sosa refers to.

11 *Psychosemantics* (Cambridge, MA: MIT Press, 1988), p. 126.

12 In *Realism with a Human Face* – a work Sosa cites in his essay – I write "It is a part of [our image of the world] itself that the world is not the product of our will – or our dispositions to talk in certain ways either" (p. 29). Compare Sosa's own distinction between existing *relative* to a conceptual scheme and existing *in virtue* of that conceptual scheme on p. 621.

13 I do not myself see why the fact that something is interest-relative need mean that it is *non-objective*. As Richard Boyd (surely no "anti-realist"!) once remarked, reference can be interest-relative, but that fact that a word refers to X given certain interests is perfectly objective.

14 Sosa cites my "Objectivity and the Science/Ethics Distinction," p. 174 in *Realism with a Human Face*, as the locus of the alleged fallacy. Note that this was published in 1990, and written *after* I had given up "internal realism." Its purpose was to defend the objectivity of ethics, not to argue that "reality is perspectival," however *that* might be understood.

15 Here Sosa is quoting from p. 4 of *The Many Faces of Realism*.

16 Bernard Williams, *Descartes: The Project of Pure Enquiry* (Harmondsworth: Penguin, 1978), p. 237. That Williams agrees with Descartes on this point is made clear on p. 241: "There is every reason to think that [the absolute conception] should leave out secondary qualities."

17 Ibid., p. 247.

18 Sosa also reads the following "definition" of *subjective* into my writings (PPR, 612): "f is a subjective property = Df f is postulated by a particular language or conceptual scheme." This would commit me to the view that all the properties we ever talk about are "subjective"!

19 Collected in *Words and Life*.

20 The quotation is from my "Truth and Convention: On Davidson's Refutation of Conceptual Relativism," in *Dialectica* 41 (1987): 69–77; at p. 75.

21 (PPR, 615.) However, there is one (possibly quite consequential) change I would make in the above explanation of "the Carnap–Putnam line": in the last sentence, I would change the last clause to read "and may even claim that by its criteria *there are no such objects* as the 'sums' x_1+x_2, x_1+x_3, x_2+x_3, $x_1+x_2+x_3$."

22 See "Convention, a Theme in Philosophy," in *Realism and Reason: Philosophical Papers*, vol. 3.

23 In "On the Right Idea of a Conceptual Scheme," *The Southern Journal of Philosophy* 35, 1 (1997): 1–18; at p. 11.

24 A possible fifth point: as I say in a passage that Sosa quotes, I think yet another approach to the kind of problem he raises with the snowdiscballs example is *sortal identity*. I know that both Kripke and Quine shudder, but isn't just this sort of example a good reason to reconsider the shudders?

25 Assuming the Axiom of Foundation, anyway.
26 Such "translations" – the technical term for them is "relative interpretations" – do not, however, necessarily preserve what Quine has caused philosophers to call the "ontology" of a theory, nor are they certifiable as correct by *linguists* on the basis of what Davidson refers to as "translation practice." Rather, they are accepted because they *preserve explanations* under passage from one version of a theory to another. For a detailed discussion, see my "Equivalence," and "Truth and Convention: On Davidson's Refutation of Conceptual Relativism."

21

On What There Is Now: Sosa on Two Forms of Relativity

JAMES VAN CLEVE

It is an honor to contribute to this volume devoted to the work of Ernest Sosa. I do not know from which I have learned more over the years – reading Ernie's articles or subjecting my own to his critical scrutiny – but from each it has been much. His perspicacity and equanimity are valued by all who know him, and it is hard to imagine a better philosophical interlocutor and colleague. This is for Ernie, in appreciation.

Sosa holds that there are two important types of proposition whose truth-value can vary from one context to another: tensed propositions, which can be true relative to one perspective and false relative to another, and existential propositions, which can be true relative to one conceptual scheme and false relative to another. In this chapter I discuss both varieties of relativity.

1 The Relativity of the Present

In an early paper ("The Status of Temporal Becoming: What is Happening Now?"),[1] Sosa considers the merits of four theories about the status of the present: the objective property doctrine, the thought-reflexive analysis, the tensed exemplification view, and the form of thought account. He finds problems with each of the first three views and favors the fourth overall. In later papers, he returns to the subject from a different angle – how best to understand propositional attitudes about the present? – and develops his novel theory of perspectival propositions.[2] I believe that of the four doctrines he canvasses in the earlier piece, the tensed exemplification view is the best, and I shall argue here that it is not as problematic as Sosa originally found it. I shall then address two questions: whether his later theory of perspectival propositions can be seen as a development of the tensed exemplification view, and whether Sosa's espousal of it makes him a friend of the dynamic theory of time.

According to the objective property doctrine, there are objective but transitory properties of being future, being present, and being past. These properties are successively exemplified by all things, generating what McTaggart called the A-series. In his refutation of time, McTaggart notoriously claimed that the A-series is contradictory: the various

A-characteristics are incompatible, yet every event must have them all. That is why he pronounced time unreal.

Why did McTaggart think there is a contradiction in believing that the A-characteristics are exemplified by all events? Without entering into tangled questions of McTaggart exegesis, let me simply say that I think Sosa offers the correct diagnosis.[3] McTaggart believed that tense is dispensable – that anything we say using a tensed copula could be said using a tenseless copula and an A-characteristic instead. "S {was, is, will be} P" gives way to "the event of S's being P lies (tenselessly) in the {past, present, future}." Under this assumption, contradiction or absurdity is indeed close at hand. To say that a flash of lightning is occurring is to say that a flash is tenselessly present. But a basic rule for understanding tenseless discourse is this: if a tenseless proposition is true at any time, it is true at every time. Thus McTaggart thinks we are committed to saying that if a flash is occurring now, it must always be true to say that it is present or occurring now – that the flash is eternal. And that is absurd.

An obvious way out of the absurdity would be to accept tense as an irreducible and indispensable device for reporting occurrences. Thus, the flash is now present, but will soon be past – no more absurdity. But now, Sosa notes, the A-characteristics have become superfluous. If we have tense, we do not need them. Instead of saying that the flash is present, we can simply say that it is happening (present tense); instead of saying that a flash is past, we can say that it occurred; and so on. So the objective property doctrine is "run though" by the following dilemma:

(a) The exemplification involved when a flash of lightning is present is either tenseless or tensed.
(b) If it is tenseless, the flash is eternally present.
(c) If it is tensed, the A-characteristics are superfluous.
(d) So the ostensibly transitory A-characteristics are either not really transitory or else superfluous.

I agree with this criticism, but I also believe Sosa tends to overstate what is shown by the second horn. He says that tenses *leave no room* for the A-characteristics and *drive them out* (STB, 28 and 26). To be redundant is one thing, to be driven out another. For all that has been shown so far, a believer in objective A-characteristics could simply accept them, redundantly, alongside tense.

There is another reason, however, why a serious upholder of tense may wish to reject the A-characteristics. Consider the following three tenets, any or all of which are sometimes held to constitute a "dynamic" or A-theory of time:

(A1) Tense is an indispensable feature of thought and language.
(A2) The A-characteristics (being future, present, and past) are successively possessed by all events.
(A3) The present is ontologically privileged: things present have a reality not belonging to things past or future.

Tenet (A1) is espoused by those who "take tense seriously," (A2) is the A-theory proper, and (A3) is the currently much-debated doctrine of presentism. I wish to observe that although the three tenets are often bundled together, no one should hold all three of them. This is not because (as Sosa suggests) (A1) excludes (A2). It is rather because (A3) excludes (A2). The point is simply that if presentism is correct, then there is nothing to exemplify the A-characteristics of being past and being future. If anything exemplified the property of being past, it could only be a past moment or a past event, but for the presentist, there are no such things.[4] Which is not to deny, of course, that there have been and will be things that do not exist now. What was and will be must be reported by using tense (it was the case eons ago that dinosaurs roamed the earth) rather than by ascribing A-characteristics to things (the dinosaurs now lie eons in the past).

I would say, then, that a believer in dynamic time should accept tensed exemplification, but eschew the A-characteristics. Such, apparently, is the view Sosa calls the tensed exemplification view, which simply grasps the second horn of the dilemma above. But Sosa thinks this view comes at too high a cost. He thinks that a believer in tensed exemplification must be committed to an infinity of distinct nexuses of exemplification – one for each time. There is the property or nexus of *now* exemplifying the property of having a toothache that I attribute to myself now, the nexus of *then* exemplifying the property of having a toothache that I attributed to myself a moment ago, and so on.

Why does Sosa think the property of being presently so-and-so must be splintered in this way? He reasons along the following lines (STB, 36–7, 39–40). I now attribute to the moon the property of presently being full. What property did I attribute to the moon a month ago when I likewise believed that the moon was full? Was it the property of being presently full, or presently exemplifying fullness? No, Sosa says, for "that would at best have been to make a prediction, whereas my belief then was not predictive but was rather about the phase of the moon at that time" (STB, 39). The only way to capture what I then believed about the moon, he says, is to posit a property of then being full, or then exemplifying fullness, and we will need a distinct such property for each time. The supposedly unitary property of now exemplifying fullness thus splinters into an infinity, one for each time, which Sosa calls "bizarrely exuberant."

I fail to see myself why we really need to posit any such plethora of exemplification relations. I think what I believed about myself a moment ago (in believing that I then had a toothache) is exactly what I believe now – the proposition that I presently have a toothache. The reasoning to the contrary should be compared to the following piece of reasoning:

> I now believe that I am actually 5 feet 11 inches tall. But what would I believe in another possible world *w* in which I was an inch taller and correctly believed so? Would I believe there that I am actually 6 feet tall? Not at all, for that would be to believe something about my height in this, the actual world, whereas what I believe there in *w* must concern my height in that world.

I maintain that there is a perfectly good sense in which what I believe in *w* is the proposition that I am actually 6 feet tall. We must not, in reporting what I believe, insist on tying the actuality operator to the world of the report rather than the world of the belief. Similarly, I maintain that there is a perfectly good sense in which what I believed about my own condition a moment ago is the proposition that I presently have a toothache – the very thing I believe now.

I turn now to Sosa's more recent work on propositional attitudes about the self and the present, which gives me reason to think he may agree with what I just said in the previous paragraph.

How are we to understand beliefs and other propositional attitudes about the self and about the present? Sosa distinguishes four possible views, defined by their stance with respect to the following triad of assumptions:

(A) Propositions are true or false absolutely.
(B) Propositions are the only objects of attitudes such as belief.
(C) Propositions are abstract items that exist in every possible world.

One possible view accepts all three assumptions; the other three each select a different assumption to deny.

The first possibility is to accept all three of (A)–(C). Sosa argues that if we do so, we must be haecceitists. We must hold that each individual has its own haecceity – the property of being identical with *that* individual – and that such properties can exist even if they are not exemplified. To believe that I am F, on this view, is to accept the abstract proposition that the individual exemplifying the haecceity *being me* is F, and to believe that it is now raining is to accept a similar proposition involving the haecceity of a certain moment. Sosa notes several liabilities of such a haecceitist position.

If we reject haecceities, we must deny one of the assumptions (A)–(C). If we reject assumption (C), we are led to the idea of concrete propositions, along with a companion doctrine of acquaintance. For someone x to believe that he is wise is for him to believe the concrete proposition represented by the ordered pair <x, wisdom>. This proposition incorporates x as a constituent and therefore exists only in worlds where x exists. Moreover, in order to believe such a proposition one would presumably need acquaintance with its constituents and thus with oneself.[5] Again, Sosa notes the costs.

If we deny (B), we get the theory of self-attribution, as developed by Chisholm, Lewis, and Perry.[6] When I believe that I myself am wise, I do not believe any proposition; rather, I stand in a special unanalyzable relation of self-attribution to the property of being wise.[7]

Sosa notes that all three of the views so far mentioned (haecceities, concrete propositions, and self-attribution) have analogues for beliefs about the present. He also notes that all three views have significant liabilities. He therefore explores a fourth view, which denies the so far unchallenged proposition (A).

If we deny (A), we get Sosa's own theory of perspectival propositions. What I believe when I believe myself to be wise is the proposition *I am wise*. What you believe when you believe yourself to be wise is the very same proposition. If I am really foolish, or at least fall short of being wise, then what I believe will be false even though what you believe is true. So assumption (A) is false: the proposition *I am wise* is not true or false, period, but true for you and false for me – true in the context containing you as the believer and false in the context containing me.

The analogous view about time also denies assumption (A), holding that one and the same proposition about what is happening at present may be true at one time and false at another. Thus *it is now raining* may be true at one time, yet false at another as the sun comes out.[8] Such variability is often taken to be the hallmark of tensed propositions.

That is why I say Sosa's more recent work may be an incarnation of the tensed exemplification view, now no longer saddled with the consequence that each moment requires its own brand of the present tense.[9]

In holding that sentences containing tense or temporal indexicals express propositions whose truth-values can vary with time, Sosa joins forces with C. D. Broad, A. N. Prior, and other philosophers who take tense seriously. Is he therefore to be accounted a friend of the dynamic theory of time? I shall consider two answers to this question: (1) Sosa is a friend of dynamic time, because he believes there are propositions that change in truth-value with the passage of time; (2) Sosa is a foe of dynamic time, because he believes all truth supervenes on eternal truth.

For further light on our question, it will be instructive to compare Sosa's views with the more recent views of Ted Sider.[10] Sider distinguishes two types of propositions: *eternal* propositions, expressed by sentences like "it is raining on September 26, 2002," which are true or false *simpliciter*; and *temporal* propositions, expressed by sentences like "it is now raining" (or "Ted's pain is now over"), which are true or false relative to times. Like Sosa, Sider believes that we need temporal propositions to serve as the objects of attitudes such as relief and anticipation. He suggests that temporal propositions be construed as functions from times to eternal propositions: the temporal proposition *it is now raining* is the function that assigns to each time *t* the eternal proposition *it is raining at t*. "A temporal proposition is true at a time iff the value of that function, for that time, is true *simpliciter*."[11] Temporal propositions can be true at one time and false at another – just like Sosa's perspectival propositions.

And yet Sider is an avowed foe of the A-theory and dynamic time. Sider calls himself a B-theorist, meaning by this someone who believes (i) that tensed sentences and thoughts have tenseless truth conditions, and (ii) that past and future objects are just as real as currently existing ones.[12] Assuming Sider's views are consistent, mere espousal of propositions with changeable truth-values does not imply a theory of dynamic time.[13]

I do not wish to deny any differences between Sider's temporal propositions and Sosa's perspectival propositions. Sider's temporal propositions are precisely what Russell called propositional functions – functions from individuals (in this case, times) to propositions. And propositional functions are sometimes equated (as by Quine) with properties.[14] Sosa's perspectival propositions, on the other hand, are meant to be saturated or self-standing propositions rather than properties; he explicitly contrasts his view with the property-attribution views of Chisholm, Lewis, and Perry. Despite this difference, however, the salient point of similarity remains: Sider and Sosa both posit objects of attitudes that change in truth-value over time. If Sider is not a friend of dynamic time on that account, neither is Sosa.[15]

Indeed, there is a further point of similarity between Sosa and Sider that may cause us to suspect that Sosa is a *foe* of dynamic time: both hold (in a sense) that all truth conditions are eternal.

Sosa tells us that although first-person and present-tense propositions are true or false only relative to a perspective, we may still define a notion of absolute truth for beliefs as follows:

> A belief on the part of subject S at time t is absolutely and objectively true (false) iff the proposition believed is true (false) in the perspective <S,t>. (CSP, 41)

The right-hand side of that biconditional is true eternally if true at all. Compare this with Sider's view that tensed tokens, though expressive of temporal propositions, have tenseless truth conditions:

> Consider a token, o, at some time, t, of the tensed sentence 'It is now raining'. This token may be given a tenseless truth condition: o is true iff it is raining at t. The truth condition is tenseless because 'raining at t' is a tenseless locution: if it is in fact raining at some particular time, t, then it always has been the case and it always will be the case that it is raining at t.[16]

So beliefs in Sosa's perspectival propositions and sentence tokens expressing Sider's temporal propositions both have truth conditions that obtain eternally if at all.

Moreover, there is even a sense in which the propositions themselves have eternal truth conditions. As Sider says,

> A temporal proposition is true at a time iff the value of that function, for that time, is true *simpliciter*.[17]

Thus, the proposition *it is now raining* is true at *t* iff *it is raining at t* is true *simpliciter*. And *it is raining at t* is true *simpliciter* only if it is true eternally. So there is a sense in which all truth supervenes on eternal truth. Sosa has affirmed as much in conversation, as well as suggesting more generally that all relative truth supervenes on absolute truth. So is Sosa not a foe of dynamic time?

If every truth were entailed by some eternal truth, dynamic time would indeed be lost. But the sense in which all truth supervenes on eternal truth for Sider and Sosa is not that, but this: for every proposition, if it is true at *t*, its being true *at t* is entailed by some eternal truth. That is something a believer in dynamic time can admit.[18] Compare: a contingent proposition *p* is true at a world *w* iff the necessary proposition *p holds in w* is true *simpliciter*. In that sense, all truth supervenes on necessary truth. But while admitting that much, one could still hold that there are contingent truths that are true *simpliciter* and not simply at worlds. Similarly, while admitting that all truth supervenes on eternal truth in the sense now under discussion, one could still hold that there are perspectival propositions that are true *simpliciter* and not simply at times.

As far as I can see, then, Sosa's views on perspectival propositions are neutral on some of the issues that separate partisans of static and dynamic time. I would be glad to hear anything more he has to say either by way of declaring himself or assessing the state of the debate.

2 The Relativity of Existence

Propositions of the form *I am now F* are not the only propositions whose truth-value Sosa holds to be relative to a context. The same is true also of propositions of the form *Os exist*, which in his view are true or false only relative to a conceptual scheme. We can better understand this second form of relativity if we first review Sosa's notion of a *supervenient entity*.[19]

A supervenient entity is an entity that depends for its existence on certain more fundamental entities, but exists nonetheless in its own right, as something over and above the more fundamental entities. Every supervenient entity is a compound of matter and essential form. For example, a snowball (Sosa's favored paradigm) is a supervenient entity whose matter is a certain quantity of snow and whose form is roundness conjoined with separation from other snow. A snowball is not to be identified with the matter composing it, since before the snow was shaped into a ball, the snow existed, but the snowball did not.

Sosa identifies four kinds of principles that govern supervenient entities. Principles of *existence* tell us that a supervenient entity of a certain sort exists at a time iff its constituent matters exemplify its constituent form at that time. Thus a snowball exists at t iff a quantity of snow is round and separated from other snow at t. Principles of *identity* and *persistence* tell us the conditions under which a supervenient entity X existing at one time is identical with a supervenient entity Y existing at the same or another time. Finally, principles of *derivation* tell us how the properties of a supervenient entity X derive necessarily from certain properties of the matter of X or certain relations among those matters.

Which matters and which forms are such that when those matters exemplify those forms, a new supervenient entity is generated? An extreme answer is *absolutism*: when *any* matter instantiates *any* form, a new entity thereby exists, regardless of what anyone thinks about it. Thus consider the supervenient entity Sosa calls a *snowdiscall*, having as its matter a chunk of snow and as its form any shape between being round and being disc-shaped. If you take a snowball and flatten it, you destroy the snowball (having deprived it of its essential form), but you leave a snowdiscall in its place. Moreover, the snowdiscall you leave was there all along, sharing matter with the original snowball. Our conceptual scheme may not recognize snowdiscalls, but if the absolutist is right, that is just a parochial failure to acknowledge entities that are really there.

Absolutism gives rise to a problem Sosa calls "the explosion of reality." Consider the following series of shapes: being round, being round or flattened up to degree 1, being round or flattened up to degree 2, and so on, until we reach the property of being round or flattened up to some degree including being squashed into a disc. There are infinitely many such shapes.[20] If absolutism is correct, each of these shapes is the essential form of an entity of some type, and an ordinary snowball therefore coincides with infinitely many other entities – snowdiscalls of all possible degrees. Some may resist this result because they boggle at the sheer number of entities involved; others may resist it because they find intolerable the idea that distinct entities may share exactly the same place and matter.

What, then, are the alternatives? The alternative at the opposite extreme from absolutism is *eliminativism*, which refuses to countenance any supervenient entities at all. The only entities that really exist are the basic entities – entities that do not owe their existence to any deeper entities. Such was the program of Russell's logical atomism. Anything that depends for its existence on more fundamental entities is a logical construction or linguistic fiction, talk of which is in principle dispensable in favor of talk of how the basic entities are disposed. To say that a snowball has come into existence is just to say that some snow has been formed into a ball; it is not to announce the birth of a new being.

Sosa raises two difficulties for eliminativism. First, what if there are no basic entities? Is it not possible that every entity depends for its existence on still deeper entities? If that were the case, eliminativism would give way to total nihilism, according to which nothing whatever exists. Second, is not the claim that talk of ordinary entities like snowballs is an abbreviation simply bluff? For *of what* is it an abbreviation? How could we ever spell it out?

In view of the difficulties besetting the extremes of absolutism and eliminativism, Sosa proposes his own *via media*, which he calls *conceptual relativism*. Supervenient entities *do* exist (contrary to the eliminativist), but they do not exist *in themselves* (contrary to the absolutist). They exist only relative to conceptual schemes. As Sosa explains further:

> What thus exists relative to one conceptual scheme may not do so relative to another. In order for such a sort of entity to exist relative to a conceptual scheme, that conceptual scheme must recognize its constituent form as an appropriate way for a separate sort of entity to be constituted.[21]

'Conceptual relativism' may be a misleading term for Sosa's view, for there is no Kuhnian implication that the concept of a snowball in schemes countenancing snowballs is a different concept from that of a snowball in schemes that do not countenance them. Indeed, this implication must be denied if the same existential propositions are to be true in some schemes and false in others. Perhaps a better name for Sosa's view would be *ontic* relativism – what exists is relative to schemes.[22]

By way of probing Sosa's conceptual relativism, I shall now ask a series of questions about it. These questions may or may not amount to objections, but answers to them will further our understanding of the view.

(1) How is conceptual relativism supposed to save us from the extravagances of absolutism? How does it block the "explosion of reality?" I gather the answer is along the following lines. Questions of existence are relative to conceptual schemes, not just in the sense that answers to them vary from scheme to scheme, but also in the sense that there can be no answer to them apart from any scheme. In short, answers to existence questions are not only variable, but elliptical.[23] Sosa makes this explicit as follows: "When we correctly recognize that an object of [a certain] sort does exist, our claim is elliptical for "... exists relative to *this* our conceptual scheme."[24] It presumably goes along with this that no one scheme is privileged, in a way that would let us define absolute existence as existence relative to the privileged scheme. The explosion is blocked, then, because we are not forced to say (and are indeed forbidden to say) that all the entities in the exploded universe exist absolutely speaking. Various of them exist relative to one or another scheme, but no scheme is uniquely correct.[25]

(2) But is not absolutism itself one possible scheme? Absolutism was abjured because it leads to an incredible explosion. But then presumably any scheme that embraces absolutism should also be abjured. Doesn't that go against the spirit of conceptual relativism, if conceptual relativism holds that all schemes are on a par? To put this question another way, how does conceptual relativism avoid the explosion if it bestows its blessing equally on all schemes, including schemes that set off the explosion?

(3) One of Sosa's arguments against eliminativism was the "abbreviation *of what?*" challenge. Why can't the eliminativist respond to this challenge by saying that talk of the entities he discountenances is an abbreviation of whatever conditions figure in the principles of existence employed in schemes that *do* countenance them? If the believer in Ks can say in virtue of what Ks exist – if he can specify what matter must exemplify what form in order for them to exist – then the disbeliever can say what talk of Ks is short for.

(4) It is a premise in Sosa's other argument against eliminativism that there might not be any basic entities – that entities might be constituted out of other entities all the way down. How is this premise to be formulated if conceptual relativism is correct? The question arises because whether an entity is basic is presumably (for conceptual relativism) itself a relative matter. For an absolutist, the possibility that nothing is basic would be formulated thus: it is possible that $(x)(\exists y)xRy$, where "xRy" symbolizes "x exists because constituent matter y exemplifies some constitutive form." For a conceptual relativist, on the other hand, the premise must evidently be weakened to something like this: there are possible schemes (or scheme-world pairs) according to which $(x)(\exists y)xRy$. Is such a parochial-sounding premise adequate for purposes of the argument against eliminativism, or would we need to affirm instead the scheme-transcendent possibility of constitution all the way down?

(5) How *does* a scheme countenance entities all the way down? One possibility is that for every x countenanced by S, there is a y such that xRy and S countenances y (by endorsing relevant principles of existence). This would imply an infinite series of entities separately countenanced – not something easily accomplished. Another possibility is that the scheme simply endorses the quantified statement $(x)(\exists y)(xRy)$. This is easily enough done, but raises the question whether scheme-relative existence now comes too cheaply – i.e., whether there is too little that a scheme or its framers must "do" in order for entities to exist relative to it.

(6) Are *any* matters and *any* forms eligible as thing-makers in a conceptual scheme? Or are there certain constraints, such as that the matter of a permissible entity must lie within the spatial boundaries of the entity? To illustrate my concern, let me propose a scheme right now according to which a phantom object of kind K (e.g., a phantom desk) exists in a region R just in case a normal object of kind K (e.g., a desk) occupies the congruent region R' exactly ten yards in a specified direction d from R. Here the constituent matter of the phantom desk is the desk at R', and the constituent form is occupying a region ten yards in d from R.[26] If anyone actually operated with such a scheme, I would be tempted to say that his assorted phantoms are only *façons de parler*: when he says there is a phantom desk at a certain spot, that is really just a coded way of saying that there is a desk ten yards away. But that way lies eliminativism. The believer in supervenient entities as genuine existents and all conceptual schemes as on a par will have to acknowledge that phantom desks have the same robustness (within the scheme of the phantomizer) as substantial desks (within his own). Is Sosa's relativism that egalitarian? Or would he perhaps impose certain constraints on eligible forms and matters – e.g., that the matter of any compound must be contained within the spatial boundaries of the compound?[27]

(7) Consider the following principle of sense-datum theory: for any subject S and object x, x looks F to S if and only if x presents S with a sense datum that is F. A. J. Ayer once regarded talk of sense data merely as a second language, in which instances of the

right-hand side of the biconditional just stated are coded ways of expressing the corresponding instances of the left. But most classical proponents of sense data regarded the biconditional as a genuine existence principle, positing sense data as entities that explain (in a constitutive way) facts about how things appear to people. What would Sosa say? Would he regard the biconditional as an existence principle, according to which sense data are supervenient entities whose matter consists of an object x and a subject S and whose form is the relation of appearing-F-to? That would give us another case in which the matter of a supervenient entity does not consist of its own parts. Or would he say that the biconditional is an existence principle, but not one that specifies the form and matter of the sense datum? In either case, we could ask the following question: does he regard the truth of the biconditional as entirely relative to schemes? Whether to countenance sense data in the analysis of perceptual situations is an issue that philosophers debated for several decades and still occasionally revisit today. Would Sosa say that there is no fact of the matter about who is right in such debates – that sense data exist relative to some schemes, not according to others, and there is no more to be said?

(8) What is involved in saying that entities of kind K exist relative to a scheme S? Sosa gives us one necessary condition: the framers of S give a certain form-cum-matter pair the requisite status by incorporating within their scheme a principle to the effect that a K exists iff matter m exemplifies form F. Is that necessary condition also sufficient? Or must we add that m *does* exemplify F? In the latter case, must ms exemplifying F be a condition that obtains absolutely or only relative to S? One element or presupposition of that condition – that m itself exists – will presumably hold only relative to S. But how about the rest of it, the part that says m (if it exists) does exemplify F? Is that also relative to S? If so, are we led into a more general Protagorean relativism, according to which not only the existence of things but also their having the character they do is relative to schemes? If not, why not?

I will close this section by sketching an alternative to all three of the views canvassed by Sosa, which for want of a better name I call conjunctivism or the mereologist's view.[28] Positively, the view holds that given any entities $x, y, z \ldots$, there also exist all mereological sums of these entities.[29] The view thus countenances such entities as the scattered composite object consisting of the Eiffel Tower and my big toe. Negatively, the view holds that no entities exist sheerly in virtue of the exemplification of new forms by entities already in existence. Thus we do not obtain a new entity merely by shaping snow into a ball or clay into a statue; snowballs and statues are accorded the status of logical constructions rather than entities in their own right. The resulting view has affinities with each of Sosa's two extremes. It is like absolutism insofar as it countenances myriads of entities (namely, all the mereological sums) that exist whether they are recognized in anyone's conceptual scheme or not, and it is like eliminativism insofar as it denies that the mere rearrangement of old entities ever yields new entities. But it is enough *unlike* each view to avoid the difficulties Sosa finds in them.

The problem for absolutism was the explosion. Conjunctivism does involve an expansive proliferation of entities (for any n given initially, at least $2^n - 1$ altogether), but it is more like a controlled nuclear reaction than an atomic blast. Moreover, it does not involve what seems to me the more serious objection to absolutism, namely, that it implies the existence of infinitely many distinct entities sharing the same space and consisting of exactly the same matter as any given entity. This is because the mereologist holds that if entities *x* and *y* have all the same parts (at some level of decomposition), they are really one and the same. You cannot have two entities, such as a snowball and a snowdiscall, that are composed of exactly the same H$_2$O molecules. For a given region of space, there will be at most one entity that exactly fills it, and for a given tract of matter, there will be just one entity that is composed of exactly the matter in that tract.

The main problem for eliminativism was the threat of nihilism or, at any rate, the implication that if there are no simple entities, nothing whatever exists. Grant for the sake of argument that there are no simple or ultimate parts of matter – that there are parts within parts forever. If all composite entities are merely nominal existents, it would then follow that everything is a merely nominal existent, which is absurd. But the mereologist does not hold that *all* composites have merely nominal existence; he only holds that composites of matter *and essential form* have nominal existence. Mereological sums are composite entities that are not constituted by any essential form – as far as their existence is concerned, nothing matters but matter. Or, if you prefer, you could say that mereological sums are entities whose essential form is nothing more than co-existence of the relevant parts. In any case, as sheer aggregates of matter, they exist just so long as their parts exist, no matter how finely chopped or widely scattered. So even if there are parts within parts all the way down, the threat of nihilism is averted.[30]

3 Conclusion

I have brought present-tense propositions and existential propositions together in this chapter because Sosa holds that propositions of both types have truth-values that vary with context: propositions of the form *X is now F* can be true in one perspective and false in another, and propositions of the form *Os exist* can be true in one conceptual scheme and false in another. Moreover, Sosa makes it explicit that the two forms of relativity are of a piece:

> Conceptual relativism can be viewed as a doctrine rather like the relativism involved in the evaluation of the truth of indexical sentences or thoughts. In effect, "existence claims" can be viewed as implicitly indexical, and that is what my conceptual relativist in ontology is suggesting.[31]

In closing, I would like to ask two further questions. (1) What are the relevant similarities and differences between the relativism Sosa espouses in ontology (according to which *Os exist* can be true in one scheme, false in another) and the contextualism he opposes in epistemology (according to which *S knows that p* can be true in one context of attribution and false in another)? This is a question I would like to explore further on another occasion or, better yet, have Ernie answer for us. (2) It is a crucial component of Sosa's relativism in ontology that existential claims are evaluable *only* relative to a scheme: not only are they true in some schemes and false in others, but they are never true or false *simpliciter*. Might it be that present-tense propositions are different in that besides being true in some perspectives and false in others, they are also true or false *simpliciter*? That is the issue that separates those who believe in an absolute present and those who believe that all truth is truth *sub specie aeternitatis*.[32]

Notes

1. "The Status of Temporal Becoming: What is Happening Now?" *The Journal of Philosophy* 76 (1979): 26–42 (cited as STB).
2. My main source is Sosa's "Consciousness of the Self and of the Present," in *Agent, Language, and the Structure of the World*, ed. James E. Tomberlin (Indianapolis: Hackett, 1983), pp. 131–45 (cited as CSP); but see also "Propositions and Indexical Attitudes," in *On Believing*, ed. Herman Parret (Berlin: de Gruyter, 1983), pp. 316–32 (cited as PIA).
3. As I present it here, it is similar to the diagnosis offered by C. D. Broad in *An Examination of McTaggart's Philosophy* (New York: Octagon Books, 1976; reprint of 1938 edn), vol. 2, part I, pp. 264–323, esp. pp. 314–15.
4. Here a Meinongian could say that past or future items exemplify A-characteristics even though they are not "there" to do so. Thus it is strictly only (A3) in conjunction with non-Meinongian views about quantification that excludes (A2). For more on this, see James Van Cleve, "If Meinong is Wrong, Is McTaggart Right?" *Philosophical Topics* 24 (1996): 231–54.
5. This is apparently what the thought-reflexive account of Russell and Smart becomes when modified as Sosa suggests to avoid the objection that a certain flash might have occurred now even if there had been no thoughts (see STB, 32–4).
6. R. M. Chisholm, "The Indirect Reflexive," in *Intention and Intentionality: Essays in Honor of G. E. M. Anscombe*, ed. Cora Diamond and Jenny Diamond (Brighton: Harvester Press, 1979); David Lewis, "Attitudes *De Dicto* and *De Se*," *The Philosophical Review* 88 (1979); John Perry, "The Problem of the Essential Indexical," *Nous* 13 (1979).
7. This view has some affinities with the form-of-thought view canvassed in "The Status of Temporal Becoming."
8. I have learned from Jim Stone that the Stoics held a similar view, maintaining that the proposition *it is day* is true when it is day and false when it is night. See *The Hellenistic Philosophers*, ed. A. A. Long and D. N. Sedley (Cambridge: Cambridge University Press, 1987), vol. 1, sec. 34.
9. I am not sure that Sosa has left this worry behind, however – see the discussion that begins on p. 329 of "Propositions and Indexical Attitudes."
10. Theodore Sider, *Four-Dimensionalism* (Oxford: Clarendon Press, 2001); see especially pp. 11–21. I thank Dean Zimmerman for suggesting the comparison.
11. Sider, *Four-Dimensionalism*, p. 215.
12. In Sider's terminology, (i) is the reducibility of tense and (ii) is eternalism, the opposite of presentism. His "reducibility of tense" is the contemporary variety that gives tenseless truth conditions for tensed thoughts without claiming that tensed thoughts may be *analyzed* in terms of tenseless ones.
13. Dean Zimmerman has argued for a similar conclusion in "What Does it Take to be an A-Theorist?" a paper presented at the Spring 2002 meeting of the Philosophy of Time Society.
14. The comparison to Russell's propositional functions should dispel the impression that Sider gets his temporal propositions by *adding* something to eternal propositions. It is true that as Sider constructs them, temporal propositions have eternal propositions as constituents, namely, as second members of time–proposition pairs. But the effect is rather to create propositions with "holes" in them, like propositional functions.
15. Another reason for not regarding Sosa as a friend of dynamic time has been voiced by Robin LePoidevin and Murray MacBeath in their introduction to *The Philosophy of Time* (Oxford: Oxford University Press, 1993). According to them, a real believer in "fleeting facts" should not accept personal and spatial perspectival facts (as they take Sosa to do), since so doing obscures what is distinctive about time. I have some sympathy with this – I am sometimes inclined to think that time is the one dimension in which propositions can vary in truth-value without being incomplete. Yet it seems indisputable that there *are* personal and spatial

perspectival propositions: if we don't admit the Sosa variety, we could construct the Sider variety as functions from persons or places to absolute propositions. So while recognizing that perspectival propositions do not suffice for dynamic time, a believer in dynamic time should not fear that non-temporal perspectival propositions *do away* with dynamic time.

16 *Four-Dimensionalism*, p. 13.
17 *Four-Dimensionalism*, p. 215. This goes along with the fact that a token occurring at t is true iff the temporal proposition expressed by it is true at t.
18 Unless presentism forbids it. Perhaps presentists should deny that *it is raining at t* is an eternal truth on the grounds that that proposition asserts a relation to a time, relations hold only if their relata exist, and times other than the present time do not exist.
19 My main source in the next several paragraphs is Sosa's "Subjects Among Other Things," in *Philosophical Perspectives*, vol. 1, ed. James Tomberlin (Atascadero, CA: Ridgeview Publishing, 1987), pp. 155–87.
20 Unless the atomic nature of matter puts a limit to the possible degrees of flattening, but then there are other dimensions of variation we could invoke to make the present point.
21 "Putnam's Pragmatic Realism," *The Journal of Philosophy* 90 (1993): 605–26, at p. 621. The key section of this article for present purposes, "Nonabsolute Existence and Conceptual Relativity," is reprinted along with an addendum in *Metaphysics: The Big Questions*, ed. Peter van Inwagen and Dean Zimmerman (Oxford: Blackwell, 1998), pp. 399–410.
22 This is not the same as Quine's *ontological* relativism, which is the view that what a theory *says* exists is relative and indeterminate – indeterminate because relative to interpretations, none of which is objectively correct. Sosa's relativism presupposes the falsity of Quine's as well as Kuhn's.
23 These two dimensions of relativity are not always distinguished. It is important to distinguish them, however, and to note that the first does not imply the second. Newton allowed that a sailor may be at rest with respect to his ship and moving with respect to the ocean, yet still insisted that the sailor is either moving or at rest absolutely speaking (depending on what the ocean is doing). This illustrates the possibility of variability without ellipticality. Yet many philosophers infer automatically from variability to ellipticality. For instance, Anthony Quinton holds that because what is certain relative to one body of evidence may not be certain relative to another, there is no such thing as absolute certainty (Anthony Quinton, *The Nature of Things* (London: Routledge and Kegan Paul, 1973), p. 156). And David Lewis holds that because which world is actual varies from world to world, there is no such thing as absolute actuality (David Lewis, *On the Plurality of Worlds* (Oxford: Basil Blackwell, 1986), p. 93).
24 "Putnam's Pragmatic Realism," p. 621, or "Nonabsolute Existence and Conceptual Relativity," p. 404.
25 Or could it be Sosa's view instead that the speaker's own scheme is privileged, and that the speaker is spared the excesses of absolutism just so long as he is not an absolutist himself?
26 How do we judge the identity through time of a phantom desk? For example, when we move a desk, do we destroy a phantom in one place and create one in another, or do we cause the original phantom to move? And what color do we assign to a phantom – the color of its remote host matter, the color of any object occupying its space, or what? These questions would have to be settled by the scheme's principles of persistence and derivation.
27 Actually, it may be that the phantomizer could easily satisfy this constraint by construing the matter of the phantom as the air (or whatnot) occupying R (rather than the desk at R') and the form as being such that a desk lies ten yards in d from R.
28 I have set out the view summarized here at greater length in the following two articles: "Mereological Essentialism, Mereological Conjunctivism, and Identity Through Time," *Midwest Studies in Philosophy*, vol. 11, ed. Peter A. French, Theodore E. Uehling, Jr., and Howard K. Wettstein (Minneapolis: University of Minnesota Press, 1986), pp. 141–56; and "Inner States

and Outer Relations: Kant and the Case for Monadism," *Doing Philosophy Historically*, ed. Peter H. Hare (Buffalo: Prometheus Books, 1988), pp. 231–47. The label 'conjunctivism' is normally applied just to the positive component of the view sketched in the text, not the negative component.

29 This principle is comparable to Zermelo's *Aussonderungsaxiom*, which does not say (as Cantor's unrestricted comprehension principle did) that there is a set for any property F, but that for any set, there is a subset of it consisting of exactly those members of it that are F. Zermelo's principle tells what new sets there are relative to any set already posited. Similarly, the mereologist's principle tells us what new entities there are relative to any entities already posited.

30 What exists in this case would be what David Lewis has called "atomless gunk." I am not enamored of the label, however, for it suggests a reality altogether too homogeneous and viscous.

31 "Addendum to 'Nonabsolute Existence and Conceptual Relativity': Objections and Replies," p. 409 in van Inwagen and Zimmerman, *Metaphysics: The Big Questions*. The assimilation of existence claims to indexical claims is part of Sosa's strategy for divorcing conceptual relativism from any sort of idealism or dependency of what there is on schemes and their framers.

32 I thank Dean Zimmerman for helpful discussion of the issues in this chapter.

22

Sosa on Abilities, Concepts, and Externalism

TIMOTHY WILLIAMSON

A kind of intellectual project characteristic of Ernest Sosa is to resolve an apparently flat-out dispute by showing that it is not after all a zero-sum game. His irenic goal is to do justice to both sides and give each of them most of what it wants. In his subtle paper 'Abilities, Concepts, and Externalism' (ACE) he applies this strategy to the dispute between internalism and externalism in the philosophy of mind. It is a pleasure to engage in discussion with a philosopher of Sosa's fair-mindedness and analytical skills.

I

The dispute is familiar. For the internalist, one's mental features are fully determined by one's intrinsic state: if a thinker x in a possible situation s is in the same total intrinsic state as a thinker x^* in a possible situation s^*, then for any mental feature M, x has M in s if and only if x^* has M in s^*. Externalists such as Hilary Putnam, Tyler Burge and Donald Davidson have challenged that supervenience claim with celebrated thought experiments. In Putnam's story, the role that H_2O plays on Earth is played by the chemically quite different but observationally quite indistinguishable liquid XYZ on Twin-Earth. In 1750, Otto on Earth and his counterpart Twin-Otto on Twin-Earth are innocent of chemical theory. They are supposed to be in the same total intrinsic state. Consider the mental feature M of believing that one is near water. Otto has M; he believes that he is near water. His belief is true. If Twin-Otto has M too, then he believes that he is near water, and his belief is true if and only if he *is* near water, for in general one's belief that P is true if and only if P. Twin-Otto is not near water, for XYZ is not water. Thus Twin-Otto has M only if he thereby has a false belief. But there is no more reason to attribute false belief to Twin-Otto than to Otto; they are equally neutral about the underlying nature of the liquid in their environment with the relevant appearance. Therefore, Twin-Otto does not have M; he does not believe that he is near water. He has a different belief that he might express with the sounds 'I am near water'. Believing that one is near water is an externalist mental feature. Presumably, Twin-Otto fails to believe that he is near water because, unlike Otto, he lacks the concept *water*. Then grasping the concept *water* is another externalist mental feature.

This externalist account does not satisfy Sosa. He resists the claim that Twin-Otto lacks the concept *water*, on the grounds that it might be an indexical concept (ACE, 321–2, 326–8). The very concept that on Earth refers to H_2O might on Twin-Earth refer to XYZ. It is far from obvious that such an indexicalist account of natural kind concepts coheres with an adequate general theory of concept individuation. However, it is not the aim of this chapter to refute the indexicalist account, although its motivation will in effect be questioned. We should in any case note that it does not make all propositional attitude ascriptions internalist. Even if Twin-Otto has the concept *water*, he still fails to believe that he is near water. The supposed indexicality of the concept *water* would not undermine the argument for that conclusion. The point here is that if, in attributing a propositional attitude to S*, the attributor S uses an indexical C in the complement clause, then the reference of C depends on the context of S, not on that of S*. For example, if you believe that I am hungry, your belief is true if and only if I am hungry; you do not express that belief by saying 'I am hungry'. Similarly, if Twin-Oscar believes that he is near water, his belief is true if and only if he is near water; on Twin-Earth he does not express that belief by saying 'I am near water' or 'He is near water'. Thus believing that one is near water is still an externalist mental state.

Sosa has a second line of argument, one that does not rely on the indexicalist account of natural kind concepts. In effect, he challenges externalism by attempting to ground externalist mental states in an underlying level for which internalism holds. Such a resolution of the dispute is likely to prove more acceptable to those of internalist sympathies than to those whose sympathies go the other way. In what follows, I will argue that Sosa does not succeed in revealing an underlying internalist level.

II

Sosa's strategy depends on the widespread assumption, shared by many externalists, that concept possession is a matter of abilities or dispositions. He does not say much about which abilities or dispositions are the relevant ones, or how they are related to concept possession; indeed, it is no easy task to do so. Presumably, one has a concept if and only if one has the ability to employ it in thought, but that equivalence is not very informative. We might learn more from a link between possession of a concept C and an ability or disposition to ϕ, where having C is not already an immediate consequence of ϕing. Sosa indicates the kind of thing he has in mind:

> Having a disposition to discriminate white objects, for example, is partially constitutive of possession of the concept of white (*as* the concept of white), which in turn is required for having the thought that snow is white. (ACE, 314)

We may doubt whether much ability to discriminate white is really required to have the concept *white*; certainly not much ability to discriminate liars is required to have the concept *liar*. However, Sosa's main line of argument does not rely on the premise that the abilities or dispositions at issue are discriminatory ones. Rather surprisingly, it starts

ABILITIES, CONCEPTS, AND EXTERNALISM

just from the idea that concept possession is constituted by abilities or dispositions of some kind or other. The work is to be done by an analysis of abilities or dispositions in general.

At least for the sake of argument, we may grant the premise that concept possession is constituted by abilities or dispositions, and see what Sosa does with it. In this volume it can hardly be inappropriate to quote him at some length. He explains the idea with his usual lucidity:

if φ is an ability possessed by x then there will be *some* C and B such that the following is true:

Nec.: (x has φ iff *if x were in C, it would emit behaviour B*)

Thus consider the dispositional property that a round marble has of being a 'roller', defined as:

Nec.: (x has (the disposition of) being a roller iff, if x were released at the top of an incline, it would roll)

And let's abbreviate the form of conditional involved as

$$Cx \to Bx$$

Such a conditional is normally true only relative to certain presupposed circumstances. Thus consider the conditional about rolling – i.e. if x were released at the top of an incline, it would roll – abbreviated as:

$$REx \to ROx$$

When this is true of a basketball on the surface of the Earth, its truth is relative to the rigid sphericity of that basketball and the downward pull of gravity. If the basketball were flat or if it were in a spaceship, the conditional would not be true of it.

Let's define now the 'grounds' of a true conditional of the form $Cx \to Bx$ as conditions $G_1, \ldots, G_n$, holding of x, such that:

$$Cx \;\&\; G_1x \;\&\ldots\&\; G_nx \to Bx$$

is true in *all* circumstances, but

$$G_1x \;\&\ldots\&\; G_nx \to Bx$$

is *not* true in all circumstances; nor is any other such conditional that weakens the antecedent (without importing independent subject-matter): e.g.

$$Cx \;\&\; G_2x \;\&\ldots\&\; G_nx \to Bx$$

The grounds of such a conditional will often include both grounds *intrinsic* to the object involved (e.g. the rigid sphericity of the basketball) and grounds *extrinsic* to the object (e.g. the presence of gravitational pull exerted by a nearby massive body). Let's now combine all extrinsic grounds into G_Ex and all intrinsic grounds into G_Ix. Then the grounds of $Cx \to Bx$ will be G_Ex and G_Ix, so that:

$$Cx \;\&\; G_Ex \;\&\; G_Ix \to Bx$$

is true absolutely and in *all* circumstances. Consider now the true conditional

$$(*)Cx \;\&\; G_Ex \to Bx$$

(where, in the case of the basketball, we leave out of the antecedent all reference to the intrinsic state of the basketball: e.g., whether it is inflated or flat, etc.). This conditional (*) does in some sense *involve* matters extrinsic to the item of which it is true (e.g. the basketball) for it involves a relationship to an *incline, rolling, a massive external body*, etc. – all matters extrinsic to the item in question (the basketball). And yet conditional (*) is *concurrently determined* to hold of an item x simply in virtue of $G_I x$, which is something purely intrinsic to x (e.g. the basketball's being rigidly spherical). It is determined to hold of x by $G_I x$ in a sense entailing that

> In any factually or counterfactually possible world, if an item x had G_I, the following would be true of x: $Cx \& G_E x \to Bx$. (ACE, 315–16).

This passage raises many questions.

III

One salient issue concerns Sosa's conditional analysis of abilities. Quite generally, conditional analyses tend to fail to provide necessary and sufficient conditions (Shope 1978). The truth-value of the conditional often depends on extraneous factors. Such problems apply to conditional analyses of dispositions (see Martin 1994; Lewis 1997; Bird 1998), in particular of those dispositions relevant to the grasp of concepts (Martin and Heil 1998). Sosa applies his conditional analysis to both dispositions and abilities (ACE, 315). As we should expect, it is vulnerable to counterexamples.

The point can be illustrated by reference to Sosa's analysis of 'x has (the disposition of) being a roller' as 'if x were released at the top of an incline, it would roll'. A round marble does not lose its disposition or ability to roll merely because a malicious person follows it around with a hammer, ready to shatter it the moment it is released at the top of an incline, before it can start rolling. Equally, a plastic cube does not acquire a disposition or ability to roll merely because someone follows it around ready to squash it into a sphere the moment it is released at the top of an incline. The kinds of dispositions or abilities that seem most relevant to the grasp of concepts are also vulnerable to such problems. To take a jejune example, suppose that I am disposed to utter 'Cat!' in the presence of cats. I do not lose that disposition merely because, without my knowing it, the man with the hammer is following me around, ready to hit me on the head the moment I come into the presence of a cat, before I can utter 'Cat!' Naturally, one can always look for more complex conditional analyses, but that has the look of a degenerating research programme.

Could Sosa explain concept possession directly in terms of the conditionals, without claiming that they analyse dispositions or abilities? That line does not seem very promising, for where the conditionals diverge from the abilities and dispositions, the latter are usually more relevant to concept possession. For example, the mere readiness of my shadow to hit me with his hammer before I can speak does not prevent me from grasping the concept *cat* or understanding the word 'cat'. Of course, the relation between concept possession and dispositions or abilities is itself far from clear, as we have already noted. Without resolving this problem, let us pass on to some others.

IV

Sosa's final step in the quoted passage is to infer that intrinsic features of the item in question concurrently determine its satisfaction of the conditional (*). Thus he moves from the necessity of the conditional $(Cx \& G_E x \& G_I x) \to Bx$ to the necessity of $G_I x \supset ((Cx \& G_E x) \to Bx)$, where $\supset$ is the truth-functional conditional. This inference is of the following general form (where $\Box$ symbolizes necessity):

(!) From $\Box((p \& q) \to r)$ conclude $\Box(q \supset (p \to r))$

Here p is $Cx \& G_E x$, q is $G_I x$ and r is Bx. But (!) is an invalid rule, and would still be invalid even if $\Box$ were dropped from the conclusion. We can see that easily by considering the special case in which r is q itself. For q follows by truth-tables from $p \& q$, so $(p \& q) \to q$ is necessarily true on any reasonable theory of the counterfactual conditional $\to$. Consequently, we can infer by (!) that $q \supset (p \to q)$ holds in all circumstances, which is to say that any counterfactual conditional with a true consequent is true. That is obviously wrong; John is alive now but it is false that if he had died last year he would have been alive now.

The point seems to apply to the case at hand. Even if Cx and the intrinsic and extrinsic grounds are jointly sufficient for Bx, it does not follow that the intrinsic grounds alone are sufficient for the counterfactual conditional (*). Although Sosa's definitions are supposed to guarantee the compatibility of the intrinsic grounds with the antecedent of (*), for all that Sosa has said the intrinsic grounds might obtain in circumstances in which the following counterfactual also obtains: if the condition Cx and the extrinsic grounds had obtained, then the intrinsic grounds would not have obtained. For, in the circumstances, realizing Cx might involve an intrinsic difference in x. If so, the joint sufficiency for Bx of Cx and the intrinsic and extrinsic grounds is irrelevant to whether the intrinsic grounds are sufficient for (*). Perhaps Sosa thinks that special features of his case permit this difficulty to be resolved. One hopes that he will address the issue. As it stands, his argument does not establish that intrinsic features of the item in question concurrently determine (*) or a corresponding ability.

V

Imagine that Sosa has filled the gap in the final step of his argument. His approach still faces another and deeper problem. Why suppose that there always are intrinsic and extrinsic grounds such as he postulates? One might for a moment think that there must be, because one can pack as much detail as one likes into those grounds. But that is to overlook the logical structure of the argument. For a counterfactual conditional, the interesting cases of its truth are those in which its antecedent is false. Sosa requires the grounds of the conditional $(G_1 x, \ldots, G_n x$, subsequently refactorized into intrinsic and extrinsic) both to obtain in the original case in which the conditional $Cx \to Bx$ is true and to conjoin with Cx to form a sufficient condition for Bx. If the antecedent is false in the original case and the sufficient condition for Bx is not vacuously sufficient merely by being impossible, then the grounds must obtain in at least two cases in which the conditional is true: one in which x has the ability in question unrealized (so Cx is false) and one in which x realizes the ability (so Cx and Bx are true). The grounds must have some kind of generality to obtain in such different cases. Packing too much detail into the grounds will not serve Sosa's purpose.

So far, the point appears to require no more than moderation in defining the grounds. An example will help. I will take the ability to recognize cats, and pretend that one has this ability if and only if one is such that if one were confronted by a cat (Cx), one would say 'Cat!' (Bx). Obviously, satisfying this condition is not really either necessary or sufficient for being able to recognize cats, but that does not matter for present purposes, since they concern what Sosa says about the conditional itself, irrespective of its relation to abilities. The simplicity of the example does no harm to his argument.

Consider two cases. In case α, Anna has the ability to recognize cats ($Cx \to Bx$) but is not currently realizing it; no cat confronts her ($\sim Cx$) and she does not say 'Cat!' ($\sim Bx$). The intrinsic and extrinsic grounds for Anna's ability that obtain in α are $G_I x$ and $G_E x$ respectively. In case β, $G_I x$ and $G_E x$ still obtain but Anna realizes her ability; a cat confronts her (Cx) and she says 'Cat!' (Bx). Of course, the conditional may have different grounds in many other cases, but on Sosa's approach there should be at least one case β as described corresponding to the given case α. Now, consider a third case γ that is just like α in respects intrinsic to Anna but just like β in respects extrinsic to her.[1] Thus in γ a cat does confront Anna (Cx), because γ is extrinsically like β, but she does not say 'Cat!' ($\sim Bx$), because γ is intrinsically like α. Somehow, Anna fails to register the cat. The conditional $Cx \to Bx$ has a true antecedent and false consequent and is therefore false in γ (otherwise it would fail to satisfy *modus ponens*). According to the conditional analysis, in γ Anna lacks the ability to recognize cats. Moreover, the intrinsic grounds $G_I x$ obtain in γ, for they obtain in α, which is intrinsically like γ. The extrinsic grounds $G_E x$ likewise obtain in γ, for they obtain in β, which is extrinsically like γ. Thus the conditional (Cx & $G_E x$ & $G_I x$) $\to Bx$ is false in γ, because it has a true antecedent and a false consequent. But Sosa's argument depends on the claim that this conditional 'is true absolutely and in *all* circumstances'. At least in this straightforward example, there cannot be intrinsic and extrinsic grounds of the kind that Sosa postulates. The intrinsic and the extrinsic are too closely connected to permit such a factorization.

One might wonder whether there can really be such a case γ, intrinsically just like α and extrinsically just like β. For example, how exactly do the intrinsic part of α and the extrinsic part of β join at Anna's retinas? Now if this were a serious difficulty, it would be one for Sosa's approach. For his separation of the grounds for the conditional into intrinsic and extrinsic components requires just the kind of modal independence of the two dimensions that makes γ possible. A view on which the intrinsic state of an item necessitated external features of its environment sounds like a strong form of externalism, perhaps one that would undermine the very distinction between the intrinsic and the extrinsic. It is at least quite different from the view that Sosa suggests. In any case, we may recall that the supposed intrinsic and extrinsic grounds have a certain generality; thus γ need not match α in absolutely every intrinsic respect to reproduce the intrinsic grounds, nor need it match β in absolutely every extrinsic respect to reproduce the extrinsic grounds. Analogously, we can treat shape and colour as independent dimensions, and combine the shape of one object with the colour of another, even though in fact they are not perfectly independent, because both shape and colour depend on atomic structure (see also Williamson 2000: 73–5).

How far can the Anna example be generalized? The refutation of the conditional in γ depended on the purely extrinsic nature of its antecedent (that a cat is in front of her, whether she registers it or not). Sosa can hardly object to this, since the antecedent Cx of the original conditional in his own example (that x is released at the top of an incline) is equally extrinsic. What of antecedents that are not purely extrinsic? If Cx were 'Anna sees a cat', it would be false in γ, because she would no more internally register the cat than she does in α. Thus Sosa's conditional $(Cx \: \& \: G_E x \: \& \: G_I x) \to Bx$ would have a false antecedent in such a case, and the refutation above would not apply.[2] Obviously, it does not follow that the counterfactual conditional would be true in γ, still less that it would be a necessary truth. It may be harder to find counterexamples simply because the condition Cx has a more complex structure, mixing the extrinsic with the intrinsic. The factorization of the grounds into intrinsic and extrinsic has been shown to fail in an example in which the condition Cx is purely extrinsic. There is no special plausibility to the claim that the factorization would be more likely to succeed in examples with mixed antecedents. The natural hypothesis is that Sosa's factorization fails in a wide variety of cases.

It is not surprising that the factorization claim is vulnerable to a triad of cases with the structure of α, β, and γ. Much of the significance of thought and language involves various kinds of coordination between the internal and the external. The grounds for such coordination typically permit its achievement in more than one way. They ground both a case α, in which the intrinsic condition I is coordinated with the extrinsic condition E, and a case β, in which a different intrinsic condition I* is coordinated with a different extrinsic condition E*. Therefore, in a case γ intrinsically like α and extrinsically like β, the intrinsic condition I holds together with the extrinsic condition E*; but I need not be coordinated in the appropriate sense with E*. Yet any intrinsic grounds that hold in α and any extrinsic grounds that hold in β also hold in γ. Consequently, if the sufficient grounds for coordination that hold in α and β could be factorized into the conjunction of intrinsic grounds with extrinsic grounds, then they would also hold in γ, which they do not when coordination fails in γ. Factorization into intrinsic and extrinsic components can be shown to fail with respect to mental content, perception, belief and knowledge, and non-mental conditions too (Williamson 2000: 66–72, 75–80, 88–9).

VI

Sosa's position is moderate. He does not claim that all the abilities or dispositions that constitute understanding are determined by intrinsic features of the thinker, just that some of them are: but we have seen reason to doubt the analysis on which he bases even that moderate claim. He proposes, however, that the relevant abilities are the same for someone on Earth and someone on Twin-Earth, because 'it would seem that their pertinent abilities would be indistinguishable' (ACE, 319). But he has not supplied adequate reason to accept that claim. Consider, for example, the ability to bring water in response to the request 'Please bring me water' (for simplicity, we may individuate the request phonetically). It seems entirely natural to say that people on Earth have that ability while people on Twin-Earth do not. It is certainly legitimate to assume that Otto brought water in response to each of the hundreds of utterances of 'Please bring me water' made to him, while Twin-Otto brought water in response to none of the equally numerous utterances of 'Please bring me water' made to him. Of course, if Otto and Twin-Otto were switched without realizing it, then Twin-Otto and not Otto would bring water in response to the request. But so what? If x has the ability to ϕ and y lacks that ability, it does not follow that it is impossible to put them in other circumstances in which x unluckily fails to ϕ and y luckily ϕs. For example, although you have the ability to find a book in a certain library and I lack that ability, a malicious librarian might then interfere so that you unluckily fail to find the book while I luckily succeed. To assume that switching between Earth and Twin-Earth makes no difference to abilities and their realization is to prejudge the very point at issue. Without that assumption, Sosa has provided no reason to think that the pertinent abilities are the same. No doubt Oscar and Twin-Oscar share some abilities; what we lack is a reason to assign those abilities any special significance for the mental.

Although Sosa allows some abilities to be individuated in an externalist way, he insists on the basis of his analysis that:

> for every such environment-dependent ability possessed by a subject there is a corresponding environment-*in*dependent ability or 'ability', which must also characterize that subject. And this latter ability would no doubt supervene on (be concurrently determined by) the intrinsic character of the subject and nothing else. (ACE, 320)

Much of the interest of this claim depends on what sense of 'corresponding' is in play. In the sense defined in 'Abilities, Concepts, and Externalism', there is often no such corresponding environment-independent ability. The externalist mind does not factor into an internalist mind and a surrounding environment.[3]

Notes

1 By 'extrinsic' Sosa means more than 'not intrinsic'. For the conjunction of something intrinsic with something irrelevant to it and non-intrinsic is itself non-intrinsic; since $G_E x$ combines '*all* extrinsic grounds', it would entail $G_I x$ if 'extrinsic' meant 'not intrinsic', which is not what Sosa intends. Rather, by 'extrinsic' he means something like '*purely* non-intrinsic'. Such a sense is assumed in what follows.
2 It is not obvious that the new conditional ('If Anna saw a cat she would say "Cat!"') does better than the old one ('If Anna were confronted by a cat she would say "Cat!"') as an analysis of the ability to recognize cats. Anna might be unable to recognize cats *because* she is unable to see them.
3 Thanks to Alexander Bird for the benefit of his expertise on abilities and dispositions.

References

Bird, Alexander, 1998. 'Dispositions and Antidotes', *Philosophical Quarterly* 48: 227–34.
Lewis, David, 1997. 'Finkish Dispositions', *Philosophical Quarterly* 47: 143–58.

Martin, C. B., 1994. 'Dispositions and Conditionals', *Philosophical Quarterly* 44: 1–8.
Martin, C. B., and Heil, J., 1998. 'Rules and Powers'. In J. Tomberlin, ed., *Philosophical Perspectives 12: Language, Mind and Ontology* (Oxford: Blackwell).
Shope, Robert, 1978. 'The Conditional Fallacy in Modern Philosophy', *Journal of Philosophy* 75: 397–413.
Sosa, Ernest, 1993. 'Abilities, Concepts, and Externalism'. In J. Heil and A. Mele, eds., *Mental Causation* (Oxford: Clarendon Press). (Cited as ACE.)
Williamson, Timothy, 2000. *Knowledge and Its Limits* (Oxford: Oxford University Press).

Part III

Replies

23

Replies

ERNEST SOSA

Introduction

First I must thank the editors and critics for making this volume possible.[1] Even when I try to rebut objections, I have learned in every instance, about both substance and formulation, and am deeply grateful. It is bittersweet to read such close and excellent discussion of one's views: sweet the many responses that deepen insight, bitter the occasional misinterpretations, especially when one shoulders some blame.[2]

My responses fall under several topics of current interest in epistemology, under most of which I respond to more than one critic. It was tempting to respond in point by point detail, but this would have lengthened my replies unduly. So I have tried rather for responses that will flow with integrity within a reasonable compass. No critique seemed less than worthy of serious consideration; nevertheless, following established precedent, I have not picked every nit. I have responded only on issues of epistemology of current interest to me, and even then have not done so in every case. Sometimes I had nothing useful to add. Sometimes my response is best postponed to forthcoming work, where I intend to address my critics' concerns.

I am equally appreciative of the papers outside epistemology – such as those in metaphysics, or philosophy of mind – and hope to be forgiven for postponing these replies. To do otherwise, given my present focus, would postpone publication of the volume even beyond the present already long delay.

My response will be restricted, then, to topics in epistemology mostly near the center of contemporary discussion, as follows: contextualism; epistemic justification: internalism versus externalism; human knowledge, animal and reflective; safety, bootstrapping, circularity; coherence; philosophical skepticism; praxis and epistemology; and epistemic value. Finally, I have tried to make these sections self-contained, by making each independent of any other, and by explaining targeted objections before responding to them.

1 Contextualism

Reply to Keith DeRose

Keith DeRose aims to explain our intuitive judgments as to when it is true to say that a subject "knows" that such and such. In pursuit of this he offers the "subjunctive conditionals account" (SCA), according to which

(SCA) We tend to consider false a claim that "S knows that p" when we take S's belief that p to be insensitive.

(S's belief that p is *sensitive* iff were it false that p, S would *not* believe that p; a belief is *insensitive* iff not sensitive.)

DeRose accepts this account while rejecting the Dretske/Nozick thesis that when we consider false a claim that "S knows that p," this is because we take knowledge to require sensitivity. DeRose's own explanation is more indirect than that. According to his account, the context of attribution determines the relevant standards, the ones that fix the attribution's truth-value.

Such contextualism is thought to bear on the following skeptical paradox, where <o> is an ordinary perceptual claim – that one sees a hand, say, or a fire – and <h> describes an <o>-precluding skeptical scenario, such as one in which one is a BIV, or a demon's victim (and thus sees no hand or fire).

(1) I don't know that not-h.
(2) If I don't know that not-h, then I don't know that o.
So, (C) I don't know that o.

This allows three possible stances:

Skeptic: 1, 2; therefore, C.
Nozick et al. 1, Not-C; therefore not-2.
Moore: 2, Not-C; therefore not-1.

According to DeRose, the plausibility of the skeptic's argument derives from the fact that his very statement of the argument installs the high standards relative to which his premises then count as true.

My own response to the paradox is the Moorean, buttressed through a requirement of safety rather than sensitivity. S's belief that p is *safe* iff it would not be true that S believes p without it being true that p, whereas it is *sensitive* iff it would not be true that not-p without it being true that S does not believe p. (More idiomatically: a belief is *safe* iff it would be true if held, and *sensitive* iff it would not be held if false.)[3] These being contrapositives, they are easily confused, or at least thought equivalent; but contraposition is invalid for such conditionals.

What follows is a defense of the Moorean stance against the contextualism favored by DeRose. I will reply to objections against my stance and will argue for its superiority to such contextualism.

DeRose argues in several ways against the Moorean response to the skeptical paradox. First, he argues, it must be supplemented with an adequate explanation of why its rejected premise, namely (1), is so intuitively plausible. He defends his favored SCA explanation of this intuitive pull, and notes that I am really agreeing when I explain that we feel drawn to the skeptic's (1) because any belief with the content <h> is bound to be insensitive. My explanation does appeal to the belief that knowledge requires sensitivity, even if what knowledge actually requires is something different, but easily confused with sensitivity, namely safety.

DeRose argues that adopting this explanation makes me in effect a "sensitivity theorist," so that I can hardly object to his sensitivity explanation for our intuitive judgments that underlie such claims. But in fact it is not my aim to explain ordinary intuitions about sentences of the form 'S knows that p'. Thus, many might (correctly, at least in their dialects) assess as true sentences like these:

- Given our dire situation, I just knew our days were ending; imagine my surprise when miraculously we were rescued.
- That door somehow knows when someone is approaching.

However interesting it might be to figure out what is eliciting the intuitions that such sentences are true, that is of limited interest in epistemology, since epistemological questions are first-order questions: What is involved in knowing something? In believing it with rational justification? What are the conditions, necessary or sufficient, for knowledge and for (rational, epistemic) justification? What is the extent of our knowledge, and of our justification?

True enough, far from objecting to sensitivity in explaining the skeptic's plausibility, I myself appeal to it. What is plausible need not be true, however, and some may find sensitivity so plausible because they confuse it with the correct requirement, that of safety (as a first approximation). Of course, compatibly with all this, people may find the skeptic's premises plausible for other reasons. Thus there may be reasons that involve explanatory underdetermination, or vicious circularity, or indiscriminability by sensory experience. These may all be related at one point or another to sensitivity, but they are still distinct, and may have their own separable roles in explaining the intuitive pull of the skeptic's premises. Of course, as the underlying reasoning becomes more complex, it becomes less appropriate to call the pull exerted by that premise merely "intuitive." But this is a matter of degree. Even the fact of insensitivity will function as a *reason* for those who derive from it their sense that the skeptic's main premise is correct.

That all being so, what needs explaining is not mainly why we *say* things of the form "S knows that p" or "S does not know that p" in various contexts, or why we find these sayings intuitively plausible. Nor do we even require, in the context of our skeptical paradox, an explanation for why we find it so plausible to utter in certain contexts sentences like "we do not know ourselves to be free of radical illusion." For even if we stay in the object language, the skeptic is able to exert about as powerful a pull, since we *also* find considerable plausibility in the claim of the skeptic that we do not know ourselves to be free of radical illusion *even by ordinary standards*. True, in ordinary contexts it would be silly to demand proof that we are not radically deceived in the ways pressed by skeptics. Even if we do *not* demand such an argument, nevertheless, when the skeptic's question *is* faced, we find ourselves challenged and puzzled. And that seems adequate to explain the doubt that many feel about our ability to know such a thing even by ordinary standards.

A story can perhaps be told as to why we find the skeptic's premise as plausible as we do, even taken as a premise about empirical knowledge by ordinary standards. For such knowledge may plausibly be supposed to require ability to discriminate the true from the false on an ultimately sensory basis, however we suppose ourselves to manage it. But that appears not to be possible, no matter what we try, if the ultimate basis for discrimination, including the total experiential basis and our use of the tools of reason, are exactly the same in the two scenarios, that of ordinary reality and that of radical illusion. Surely that explains how powerfully attractive is the skeptic's premise, whether we take it as a claim about knowledge by absolute or by ordinary standards. So, the advantage of this non-contextualist explanation is that it explains what the contextualist tries to explain, and more besides.[4]

One way to try to explain the attraction of sensitivity-based skepticism, again, is to see it as based on a confusion of the misguided requirement of sensitivity with the right requirement, that of safety. An advantage of this sort of explanation may now be seen: namely, that it helps explain not only why we utter such sentences as "We do not know ourselves to be free of radical illusion." Our contraposition-confusion explanation helps explain not only that but also why we believe that we do not know ourselves free of such illusion, whether by ordinary or by absolute standards.

Even once sensitivity and safety are distinguished, and even once we recognize that these are inequivalent contrapositives, it is still surprising just *how* different they are, and how much more defensible safety is than sensitivity as a requirement for knowledge. While joining in the general rejection of sensitivity, therefore, I still find plausible some form of a safety requirement for knowledge. Note how each of sensitivity and safety secures a kind of non-accidental connection between our basis for believing and the truth of our belief. So the underlying source of the intuitive plausibility of the sensitivity requirement may still be heeded even if in the end we reject sensitivity in favor of safety. In line with this, I defend a safety-based Moorean response to the skeptical paradox.

That much is a response to DeRose's most general objection to my Moorean approach. In addition, he raises the following more specific objections.

1 My safety conditionals don't do the work that I assign to them, and in any case safety and sensitivity are not contrapositives.
2 His "strength" condition (to be explained below) is very similar to my safety condition, and where importantly different is superior.
3 By going contextualist in a way that I resist, he is able to explain the intuitive pull of the skeptic's main premise, that we cannot know ourselves to be clear of the fearsome scenarios (BIV, evil demon, etc.), whereas I lack any such explanation.

There are many other interesting points, well worth discussing, in this substantial discussion, but I will confine myself to these main points, and even here must resist the temptation to respond in close detail.

In response to objection 1: My rough-and-ready conception of a (*strong*) *conditional* is this: *sentence that expressively conditions something x on something y, either as a necessary or as a sufficient condition.*[5] If a sentence expresses <*p*> as sufficient for <*q*>, then its *contrapositive* is the same except only for negating each of '*p*' and '*q*' and inverting their positions. (Here I have avoided the corner quotes that strict formality would require.) This should suffice to indicate why I insist that, in my sense, both the sensitivity and safety conditionals are indeed conditionals, and why each conditional contraposes the other. Here are some formulations:

> *Sensitivity*   <Not-*p*> would be so only if <Not-B(*p*)> were so.
>
> *Safety*   <B(*p*)> would be so only if <*p*> were so.

At several points, DeRose proposes a particular subjunctive conditional as "the most straightforward way to convert" into (semi-)English the symbols 'B(*p*) → *p*'. He later acknowledges that I construe safety in ways that avoid his preferred conditional, namely: 'If the subject had believed that *p*, then it would have been so that *p*.'[6] About the sort of conditional used in my own construal of safety, such as: "The subject would believe (would have believed) that *p* only if it were (had been) true that *p*," he has this to say: that "its claim to being B(*p*) → *p*, and to being the contrapositive of sensitivity is jeopardized." He evidently has two reasons for this stance. First, as already noted, he claims the symbols 'B(*p*) → *p*' to be *most straightforwardly* converted into English in his preferred way. But this claim is unpersuasive. Symbols, after all, are available for stipulative definition in whatever way a theorist might prefer. My own preference is in line with the formulation of *Safety* above, and I see no reason to think that this is "less straightforward" than his preferred formulation: 'If <B(*p*)> had not been so, then <*p*> would not have been so'.

DeRose argues, against my formulation, that it is not the contrapositive of his sensitivity conditional (in his preferred formulation), which would undercut my explanation in terms of contraposition-confusion. But his formulation seems optional. Another option is to formulate the relevant conditional in my expressly preferred ways, such as: <*Not-p*> *would be so only if* <*Not-B(p)*> *were so*. (Or, especially for references to the past: <*Not-p*> *would have been so only if* <*Not-B(p)*> *had been so*.) And there are also more idiomatic variants, such as: <*p*> *would be false only if* <*B(p)*> *were false*. In any case, the important point is this: *the sorts of formulations that I prefer seem equally effective in explaining the sensitivity-based intuitions that favor skepticism*. And the sorts of formulations I prefer *are* contrapositives (in my explained sense) of corresponding formulations that capture my notion of safety.

So, it remains the case that there is a kind of sensitivity that explains the intuitions favorable to the skeptic, one easily confused with its contrapositive, although the two are inequivalent. This being so, none of DeRose's points affects my claims that safety and sensitivity (as I construe them!) are contrapositives, that the requirement of sensitivity would underwrite skepticism, but that it is *incorrect* as a general requirement, although it is easily confused with, but inequivalent to, the correct requirement, that of safety.

What is more, and this is the important point on this issue: it is not essential to my approach that safety and sensitivity be contrapositives; what is essential is that they be easily confused, and this can be so even if they are not strictly contrapositives.[7]

I turn next to objection 2. This objection highlights several ways in which we differ. First, I am mainly interested in first-order questions about the conditions for knowledge, for when someone knows something. Only secondarily am I also interested in the linguistic, second-order questions as to the conditions for correct (true) utterance of sentences of the form 'S knows that p.' An important part of my critique of contextualism is that it either avoids the first-order questions or answers them incorrectly. DeRose now offers an answer to the first-order question as to when one knows that p, as follows. To know that p is to believe that p with enough "strength," where the strength of one's belief is stronger the more remote are any worlds wherein one first fails to match the fact of the matter as to whether p. That is to say, the strength of one's belief is directly proportional to the remoteness of the least remote worlds wherein it fails to be the case both that $(p\&B(p))$ and that $(\sim p\&\sim B(p))$. If too easily one's belief might have failed to match the fact of that matter, then one does *not* know.

DeRose's strength requirement is unacceptable as a necessary condition for knowledge, or so I will now argue. If I see a large pelican alight on my garden lawn in plain view, I will know that there is a bird in my garden. And this is not affected by the fact that a small robin sits in the garden in its nest out of view. In such circumstances, there might very easily have been a bird in the garden without my believing it. If the pelican had not arrived just then while the robin was still in its nest out of view, all of which might easily have happened, then there would have been a bird in my garden without my believing it. So, while DeRose's condition is perhaps a condition for a kind of *competence* on the question whether p, it fails as a condition for *knowledge* that p. The safety condition, however, unlike the strength condition, still seems safely a live possibility.

I turn finally to objection 3, which first requires some context-setting. DeRose's account still makes an indirect appeal to sensitivity in explaining why we find the skeptic's stance so plausible, why we find it as plausible as we do that one does *not* know oneself to be free of radical illusion (brain in a vat, evil demon, realistic dream, or whatnot). However, if we insist on sensitivity as necessary for knowledge (as do Dretske and Nozick), then we must deny closure, and espouse the "abominable conjunction" that "while you don't know you're not a bodiless (and handless!) BIV, still, you know you have hands" (DeRose 1995, in DeRose and Warfield 1999, p. 201; see chapter 3, note 3). It would be preferable to avoid such abominable conjunctions consequent on the failure of closure, while still somehow using sensitivity to explain how plausible the skeptic can seem. And this is DeRose's objective in proposing his "Rule of Sensitivity" (RS), namely:

> (RS) When it is asserted that some subject S knows (or does not know) some proposition P, the standards for knowledge (the standards on how good an epistemic position one must be in to count as knowing) tend to be raised, if need be, to such a level as to require S's belief in that particular P to be sensitive for it to count as knowledge (p. 206).

DeRose's contextualism focuses on how the assertion that you know that p ups the strength required in your belief, and in associated beliefs, if they are respectively to be knowledge. Your belief on the matter in question, and on related matters, must now correspond to the facts of that matter not only in the actual world but in all worlds up to the nearest worlds where it is false that p (at least up to such worlds); and this happens because that knowledge-assertion highlights the question of the sensitivity of your belief that p. But the standards are *not* supposed to be raised similarly by the mere supposition, or even by the thought or the assertion, that your belief is insensitive. There is a reason why it is crucial to the position that the standards be raised only by attributions or denials of knowledge that one is illusion-free. The mere mention of that radical possibility must not be allowed to raise the standards. For only thus can we secure the desired combination of results: namely, to (a) give the skeptic his premise, while (b) still alleging that *in ordinary contexts people know perfectly well that they sit, despite the fact that they are in no better position to know that they sit than to know that they are illusion-free, and despite the fact that were they to believe themselves illusion-free their belief would be insensitive.* In a philosophical context we make that whole italicized claim in adopting the contextualism under scrutiny. For what makes this contextualism distinctively attractive is that it can make such a claim while still prepared to grant the skeptic his skeptical premise, once he asserts it (which changes the context). It is this that makes it a compromise position able to make reasonable sense of all sides of the controversy.

Unfortunately, it seems arbitrary to so distinguish the conversational or other relevant effects of asserting that one knows oneself illusion-free from the effects of presenting that same possibility of illusion in other, non-assertive ways. But, again, if one allows any presentation of the illusion possibility to raise the standards, then one would not be able to make the claim, as we reflect philosophically on the issues of skepticism, that in an ordinary context you can know about fires and hands, even though you're then no better positioned to know about any of that than you are to know yourself illusion-free, and even though believing yourself illusion-free would be insensitive. Unless we protect some such mention of the skeptical possibilities from automatically raising the standards, it is hard to see how the new contextualism could be correctly stated or so much as thought. (By "the new contextualism" here I mean not just a position in linguistics or in philosophy of language about the context-dependent ways in which uses of certain expressions acquire semantic value. I mean rather a position that, while perhaps using such a linguistic theory, also pronounces on who knows what when, despite the skeptic's arguments, or at least on who might know what when; and on what would be sufficient, or necessary, in somewhat general terms, for any such knowledge.)

It may be replied that the contextualist could just claim in the metalanguage that people sitting in ordinary contexts who say "I know I am sitting" are often enough right. This may be thought to capture enough of what is right in the Moorean stance. But the Moorean stance is not about what one might say with truth in an ordinary context using the verb 'knows'. It is rather a stance, adopted in a philosophical context, about what one then knows and, by extension, what people ordinarily know. At a minimum it is a stance about whether people are right in their ordinary claims to know, which is not quite the same as whether they are right in their ordinary utterances of the form "I know that p." Once we abandon the object language and ascend to the metalanguage, we abandon thereby the Moorean stance.

Of course, if the verb 'knows' allowed disquotation, then we could after all retain the Moorean claim even with ascent to the metalanguage. For our claim that "Paul says 'Mary knows that p' in an ordinary context and is right," would then still entail "Mary knows that p." But this would be to give up the response to skepticism via attributor contextualism, which is incompatible with such semantic descent. At least, it is far from clear that the two are consistently combinable. Just compare the move from the premise that A has correctly *uttered* "S is short" to the conclusion that A has *said* that S is short. Is *that* move legitimate? An NBA basketball coach complains of Tom Recruit that he "is short." Has he then *said* that Tom is short and has he thereby spoken truly? Plausibly he has, given Tom's height of six feet, yet when a passerby in the street considers Tom "not short" he has equally plausibly *said* of Tom that he is not short, and seems also right, with equal plausibility. Contradiction.

One might try to explain what is plausible in the various sides of the debate by attributing varying standards to the various attributors of knowledge.[8] We can then report that the ordinary subject believes he knows by ordinary standards that he sits. The skeptic believes the ordinary subject does *not* know by *absolute* standards that he sits. Each claim is not only plausible but correct. Even if this account is combined with some variety of contextualism, it is not now the contextualism that is most important for explaining what is plausible in the various sides of the debate. For, in explaining what is plausible in the Moorean stance we must attribute to ordinary subjects a *de re* belief concerning ordinary standards, and our own endorsement of what ordinary subjects thus believe must itself amount to a claim concerning ordinary standards. So our word 'knows' as thus used in a philosophical context amounts to 'knows by ordinary standards'. And this expression is no longer relevantly contextual.

2 Epistemic Justification: Internalism versus Externalism[9]

Reply to Richard Foley

Two issues stand out for me in this chapter. First is the issue whether epistemologists have failed properly to distinguish a kind of justification with its inherent importance quite apart from however it may or may not contribute to the attainment of knowledge. According to Foley, epistemologists too often focus on a conception of epistemic justification such that "the properties that make a belief justified must also be properties that turn true belief into a good candidate for knowledge." This, however, is in tension with the fact that justification is properly involved in "everyday assessments of the rationality and justifiedness of opinions, which tend to focus on whether individuals have been responsible in forming their opinions rather than on whether they have satisfied the prerequisites of knowledge."

It is hard to assess what makes something a "good candidate" for knowledge, however, especially if we restrict ourselves to factors *necessary* for knowledge. Accordingly, it seems better to focus directly on this latter question of whether epistemic justification is even necessary for knowledge. Foley appears to think that it is *neither* necessary nor (as Gettier showed) sufficient. He seems to believe that you can be so related externalistically to a fact as to know it to be so, even while lacking reasons sufficient to justify your belief. He wants therefore to keep justification quite separate from knowledge, and to focus on issues of justification, of epistemic responsibility, of "beliefs supported or supportable by reasons."

What Foley offers as an account of such epistemic justification is in the end Foley-rationality: *that your belief comport on appropriate reflection with your deepest epistemic standards*. Yes, I reply, it is a good thing epistemically to be thus Foley-rational, better to be thus coherent than incoherent. But there are other internal epistemic conditions that it is also good to satisfy. Thus, it is better not to engage in wishful thinking, and not to be epistemically negligent by rushing to judgment. It is also better *epistemically*, for example, to reject Kierkegaard's advice to believe Christian dogma precisely by virtue of its absurdity;[10] whatever his reasons in favor of this advice, they do not touch its epistemic shortcomings. In any case, such avoidance of bad policies and of negligence are only partial constituents of the internal epistemic good. And Foley-rationality falls short as well, or so I contend. That is to say, it is good to avoid beliefs incoherent with one's own deepest standards, but that can be of limited value at best, if the quality of the standards is low enough. I mean the *epistemic* quality of the standards, which presumably would involve some appropriate relation to the truth. If our deepest standards distance us far and systematically enough from the truth, then one's attainment of coherence may be good *as far as that goes*, but it would seem considerably better to attain such coherence *and* to have deepest standards that provide a closer approach to the truth.

So far the first issue: I have agreed that epistemic justification of at least one sort is independent of how reliably the agent forms his belief, given the environment in which that belief is formed, but have objected to Foley's account of what is involved in such justification, namely his proposed Foley-rationality. Next I turn to my own proposal, and to the objections raised against it.

First a preliminary point. Now and later, I downplay distinctions among intellectual or epistemic standards, principles, inference patterns, rules, and even faculties, or virtues, which I understand as bundles of commitments. These distinctions seem unimportant for the basic issues we are facing. The important things are (a) that they are all varieties of commitment, of commitment that has propositional content, and (b) how this bears on their respective varieties of normativity. These commitments would seem normatively assessable, epistemically normatively assessable; at a minimum, they would seem evaluable as correct or incorrect depending on the truth or falsity of their content. Furthermore, the full set of familiar epistemic issues seems in place. Such commitments are evaluable as apt or inapt, and as epistemically justified or not. Issues of external and internal evaluation seem naturally applicable across the varieties of commitment.

Having distinguished justification sharply from knowledge, Foley suggests that a belief is *justified* if and only if it is "internally defensible." The internalist project is "that of exploring what is required to put one's own internal, intellectual house in order." It aims to uncover "what is involved in having justified beliefs, that is, beliefs supported or supportable by reasons." The theory of justified belief concerns "everyday assessments of the rationality and justifiedness of opinions, which tend to focus on whether individuals have been responsible in forming their opinions."

That much seems right. But we need a further distinction, concerning reasons and justification, between the epistemic and the non-epistemic. The reasons one might have in favor of a certain belief need not all be relevant to the epistemic assessment of that belief. Athletes and patients have pragmatic reasons for confidence, reasons beyond those that constitute evidence. Reasons to trust one's spouse, for example, go beyond the balance of the evidence. Practical reasons for trust, for confident belief, often go beyond one's evidence, as Foley recognizes. If sources of epistemic justification outstrip "evidence" properly so called, moreover, then not all sources of one's epistemic justification for a belief need be sources of its *evidential* justification.

What then is the difference between epistemic and non-epistemic reasons (or, perhaps more generally, epistemic and non-epistemic sources of justification)? The epistemic would seem to involve truth rather than just expediency or morality or general success. What the athlete and the patient need for epistemic justification is evidence, i.e., reasons that render it likely that things will go well. And this must be distinguished from the practical justification deriving from the good consequences of such confidence. That a reason in one's possession renders an external state of affairs likely depends on the lay of one's external world, which would seem to make the relation *X is a reason for believing Y* depend on external circumstances. Justification and rationality would thus depend on the luck of your contingent situation.

Epistemic justification is widely regarded an internal matter, however, one isolated from any such brute, external luck. Compare the Kantian view that moral quality derives from how it is in the subject's mind and not from external circumstances that help yield causal consequences of his policies and decisions, figuring thus among the essential determinants of how well these turn out in the actual world. There is in epistemology an analogue of such Kantianism: epistemic worth should derive from qualities of the subject's mind and not from contingent externalia determining (a) the causal origins of the subject's beliefs and inference patterns, and (b) how reliably truth-conducive *such* causal determination of beliefs and inference patterns is generally in our actual world. Suppose epistemic justification properly depends only on such internal matters independent of the subject's contingent emplacement. How, more positively and fully, should we then conceive of such justification? Some have tried to understand it as a matter of being blameless or of avoiding any wrongful violation of epistemic norms required for right belief formation. But this way of understanding epistemic justification takes us only so far, and comes up short: if you are brainwashed or brought up epistemically in a superstitious community, you may bear no blame for beliefs and inference patterns that still fall short epistemically. You are not then "wrongfully violating" any norms, since how you proceed is then not "up to you," deriving as it does only from aspects of your psychology before which you are then helpless. Internal epistemic justification hence seems not fully explicable through mere blamelessness. How then *is* it to be understood?

It will be helpful to distinguish between two sorts of justification.

Aptness   (For all worlds w) [B is apt-justified in w *only if* B derives in w from the exercise of one or more intellectual virtues that *in that world w* virtuously produce a high ratio of true beliefs]

Adroitness (For all worlds w) [B is adroit-justified in w *only if* B derives in w from the exercise of intellectual virtues that *in our actual world* virtuously produce a high ratio of true beliefs]

Take a world where people, and even rational beings generally, would normally go astray in taking their experience at face value. In this especially hostile demon world, your beliefs plausibly *lack* warrant even if formed by taking experience at face value, or in some other way that is reliable in our actual world. It is this notion of warrant that is presumably invoked when we countenance the possibility of higher beings who gain knowledge by properly and reliably forming "warranted" beliefs, despite the fact that their epistemic ways, while successful in their world, would be miserably inadequate in ours.[11] Correlative to this is the intuition that the victim of the demon fails to be justified, an intuition in line with our Aptness account. The beliefs of such a victim would not qualify as apt-justified.

Nevertheless, in line with his internalism, Foley suggests a notion of epistemic justification, *also* intuitively gripping (however it may relate to knowledge, and however it may relate to the kind of warrant that is necessarily contained in knowledge), a notion according to which the victim of the demon *would* still be justified. This is perhaps the notion that the classical foundationalist explicates in terms of (i) a foundation where one takes the given, and (ii) a superstructure that one builds on that foundation through valid reasoning. Sometimes internalist epistemologists even claim that the traditional issues of epistemology concern only such rational justification, and see our Gettier-related focus on "knowledge" and reliability as an unfortunate diversion.[12] Answering the skeptic is traditionally a project of epistemology, perhaps its main project, which has been thought to require showing how, despite the skeptic, we still remain "justified" in the bulk of our commonsense beliefs. It is *this* kind of justification that, according to internalists, you might still have even if unlucky circumstances make your animal mechanisms unreliable.

Given this, the project for the reliabilist is to show how, within a broad reliabilism, within truth-connected epistemology, we can understand such a notion of justification. This is a project engaged by admitting not only the normative status of Aptness but also that of Adroitness.

Reply to Richard Fumerton

Fumerton grants that reflective knowledge is *better* than mere animal knowledge, but regards this as trivial since reflective knowledge involves having *more* knowledge, which is trivially better, epistemically, than having less. This fails to satisfy the internalist desire for enhanced philosophical assurance, however; nor will it help merely to layer meta-level knowledge or justified belief on a first, animal, level. Such layering is bound to fall short if "*the knowledge or justified belief at the meta-level is given the same externalist analysis as first-level knowledge or justified belief.*" This "does not really allow us to leave the realm of animal knowledge."[13] As for my compromise position between internalism and externalism, this is said to "require for reflective knowledge something more satisfying" than mere animal knowledge. Approvingly, he adds that

> the problem with leaving one's meta-epistemology with only the conceptual resources of epistemic concepts understood as the externalist understands them is that we realize that satisfying such concepts doesn't give us the kind of *assurance* of truth we seek as philosophers, or simply as cognitive agents who find ourselves reflectively worried about whether or not we really know what we think we know....
>
> How does one get the additional assurance...? Sosa's answer is that one gets oneself metabeliefs about the sources of one's beliefs where the metabeliefs cohere in important ways....
>
> But now one must insure that the account of *justification* that one employs in one's account of reflective knowledge does not *itself* leave one yearning for a more satisfying ascent to yet another sort of justification.

Fumerton then argues that mere coherence at the meta-level will not give us the desired sort of justification, absent awareness of that coherence. Here he is evidently thinking of coherence as a matter of abstract relations of logic, probability, etc., among the propositional contents of the thereby coherent beliefs. The mere fact that our beliefs cohere in this sense is insufficient to give us a satisfying level of justification, true enough, especially if we lack any awareness of that fact. Perhaps we must require "access" to such coherence at the meta-level. But if this access involves knowledge or justification, then we are in a vicious circle, for it is *knowledge* and *justification* that we are trying to explain.

One might alternatively require direct acquaintance with our beliefs and with the abstract relations among them constitutive of their cohering. But to involve direct acquaintance thus in the explanation of justification and knowledge is to go beyond coherentism, to a kind of foundationalism of direct acquaintance. It is in fact this option that Fumerton himself prefers.

The philosophically more satisfying justification dear to the internalist is located by Fumerton in one's taking of the given, as when one combines direct awareness of one's pain with belief that one is in pain, while one is also directly aware of the correspondence between the thought that one is in pain and the pain. According to him, this

> just is the epistemic state that satisfies philosophical curiosity, that constitutes philosophical assurance. When one represents the world a certain way and one has the relevant truth-maker for that representation unproblematically before consciousness, there is nothing more one could *want* by way of epistemic assurance.

This defense of the given requires a closer look, and we shall return to it in due course (in connection with Richard Feldman's paper). For now I would point out only that so demanding a philosophical assurance could not extend very far. Obviously we could then be assured only in our takings of the given. Is there then some more relaxed assurance that we could still hope to attain in our beliefs about the past, the world around us, neighboring minds, and so on and so forth?

What is required if one is to attain high *inferential* justification for believing P on the basis of E? One necessary condition would be that the subject "be aware of either a logical or probabilistic connection between E and P." But ordinary epistemic agents (or, for that matter, most epistemologists) will be able to meet *no* such requirement for the bulk of their beliefs about the past, the future, their physical surroundings, other people and their thoughts, to take only some obvious classes of beliefs. Fumerton seems quite prepared to accept the entailed skepticism about any realm that we could access only inferentially on the basis of our takings of the given.[14]

Let us now consider those demanding standards of high internalism. What binds them together? What is it about high *inferential* justification as understood by Fumerton that puts it together with high *non-inferential* justification, making them alternative ways to attain or at least approach the sort of epistemic assurance that we want as philosophers?

High non-inferential justification is what we enjoy in taking the given. Our belief is then justified by factors immediately present to our consciousness. For now let us not question exactly why or how this makes a crucial epistemic difference. Suppose it just does. How then are we to think of inferential justification? When we reach a certain conclusion, becoming thus justified in believing that conclusion, do we have immediately present to our consciousness the factors that yield our justification? What indeed *are* the factors that then yield our justification? What is it about our belief in that conclusion that renders it justified? Fumerton speaks of believing P on the basis of E, and points to the need for a supporting belief to the effect that E entails or probabilifies P, or the like. But even if these are necessary conditions for our justified belief in the conclusion, they will hardly suffice. The mere fact that I believe P and believe E and believe that E entails or probabilifies P will hardly suffice for me to be justified in believing P, if I do not *rest* my belief of P on those other beliefs.

Accordingly, let us add that further factor to those that in combination yield my being justified in believing the conclusion. Is this apparently causal fact present to my consciousness? Do I enjoy direct awareness of such causal facts? Pretty surely not, at least not awareness that has the sort of directness *in excelsis* dear to the radical foundationalist. So we may already be falling short of the high philosophical standards even in this first step from non-inferentially justified beliefs to those that are inferentially justified. What is more, many of our inferentially justified beliefs would seem to require not just an immediate inference from premises in view, but diachronic reasoning through lemmas and through premises brought in at different times in the course of one's reasoning. Thus are we pushed beyond mere *basings* or *restings* of a conclusion on certain premises, to mnemonic linkages of retained beliefs, to be brought in as needed later in the reasoning. The factors that justify our belief in the final conclusion must hence include the proper operation of memory in the course of the reasoning. At the time when the final conclusion is drawn, those are among the factors essentially involved in rendering justified our belief in that conclusion. Clearly these factors are not present to our consciousness at the time when we finally draw our conclusion. Here again, therefore, in a case of diachronic inference, it is evident that we cannot hope to satisfy the high standards laid down by the purist internalist. Note moreover that this pertains not only to inductive inference but even to deductive proof beyond the most elementary. Our problem does not derive simply from our lack of direct insight into the probabilifying relations requisite for inductive inference. On the contrary, it is a problem even for our knowledge through the most rigorous deduction that rises above the most trivial. Any such deduction will require a chain of steps of reasoning linked appropriately by memory, and no such chain will reveal itself to our direct gaze at any given time, in one unitary view.

It seems dubious, therefore, that any very interesting internalism is defined through insistence on such standards of direct presence to the mind. (And we shall see further reasons for doubt when, in response to Feldman, we assess the taking of the given as source of high-grade justification.)[15]

Reply to Richard Feldman

We need some account of how we acquire justification for the application of simple geometrical or arithmetical concepts (SGA concepts), how we get to apply them perceptually with adequate justification. How do we derive justification by using our eyes for the belief that we face a figure with a given simple shape, or a collection with a certain low cardinality? How, indeed, do we get justified in believing that a certain image in our visual field has a given geometrical or arithmetical property?

What is required, I suggest, is an ability to apply the relevant SGA concept reliably, whether to external objects or to internal images. According to my suggestion, our knowledgeable application of such a concept involves its safe and virtuous application. Explicating this would seem to require appeal to causal, tracking, or reliability concepts dear to externalists.

Feldman apparently demurs, but exactly how and why? He suggests that we can perhaps explain our justified application of theoretical SGA concepts as based inferentially on the application of phenomenal concepts. If SGA concepts are just simple geometrical or arithmetical concepts such as that of triangularity, however, or that of a collection with five members, then these are concepts of some of the very same properties of which we may also have phenomenal concepts. To say that we have a phenomenal concept of triangularity is to say that we can discriminate triangles reliably under a sensory mode of presentation. (Note that compatibly with this it may be added that in fact we have multiple phenomenal concepts of triangularity, one apiece for each relevant mode of presentation.) Of course, we may *also* know a lot about the geometry of triangles, thus involving a rich theoretical, SGA concept of that property.

How then do we get justified in believing we see a triangle, if we follow Feldman? Well, we might first apply some phenomenal concept of triangle to an image of ours or to a figure on a surface before us, and then infer that the thing fitting the phenomenal concept must also fall under the theoretical SGA concept of triangularity. And what justifies us in applying the phenomenal concept? Well, phenomenal concepts come with built-in epistemic justification, in virtue of the fact that they are guaranteed reliability. The possession of a phenomenal concept is *defined* in terms of a corresponding discriminative ability. We must be keyed to the mode of sensory presentation so as to be able to respond differentially to its presence, which means that we would have been able to detect its presence at least in practice, by differential responses, across some variety of possible alternatives that we might then have confronted. And this is to say that we are reliable detectors of its presence.

As the outlines of Feldman's proposal become increasingly clear, its difference from my proposal, to which it is ostensibly opposed, becomes increasingly obscure. Feldman uses one's possession of a phenomenal concept, presumably with its constitutive reliability of discrimination, to explain the foundational justification of one's application of that concept. Given a background belief that items falling under that phenomenal concept also fall under a certain theoretical SGA concept – that of being circular, say, or of having three members – we can now inferentially justify applications of this latter concept based on applications of its phenomenal partner.

You would seem to need a discriminative ability enabling you perceptually to apply a phenomenal concept reliably, if such applications of that concept are to be justified. A phenomenal concept can be a concept of the same property of which we also enjoy a theoretical concept. It is, let us say, a concept of a certain shape or of a certain cardinality. It is phenomenal only if the possessor has an ability to discriminate under some mode of presentation instances of that shape (to which he is suitably related) as so shaped. It is a theoretical SGA concept of that property only if it involves some minimal amount of theoretical understanding of its place in the geometrical scheme of concepts. If a perception-based application of an SGA concept is to be justified epistemically, it must manifest reliable discriminative abilities. If so, then it is in effect required that the subject who applies an SGA concept with such perceptual justification must have a corresponding phenomenal concept of that same geometrical or arithmetical property. That is to say, he must enjoy an ability to discriminate perceptually (or introspectively) instances of that shape or cardinality. This seems to be the essence of Feldman's relevant view, and it is and has been something essentially involved in my own view as well.

How does our application of such concepts acquire epistemic justification? What makes justified for us the proposition that we "see" a 48-speckle image, or a red-triangle image? I claim that this essentially involves our ability to discriminate reliably, but Feldman here has a different view. He introduces his idea of "attending," noting that we might experience a property only *peripherally*, in which case we do not properly "attend" to the property.[16] When a property is experienced in this sort of way, Feldman suggests, then we are justified in believing ourselves to experience it, at least if we do so by means of a proposition that picks out that property through a phenomenal or indexical concept. So, presumably, when red-triangularity is experienced consciously, vividly, and focally, then we are epistemically justified in believing that we experience it if this is something we believe through a phenomenal concept.

What does it mean to say that we believe this through a phenomenal concept? Perhaps it is to believe in part through our ability to discriminate red triangles thus presented (consciously, vividly, and focally) under one or more sensory modes of presentation. This requires reliability on our part in thus applying our sensory-mode-dependent red-triangle concept, which imports reliability in discriminating red triangles thus presented. Such causal, tracking, reliability considerations are thus once again at the heart of classical foundationalism. But is there an alternative? What could it be?

Shall we say that it is not constitutive of our possessing our phenomenal concept of red-triangle that we be thus able to discriminate reliably? How then do we explain our epistemic justification for believing we see a red-triangle, even if we are doing so through a phenomenal concept? Suppose someone happens to have the phenomenal concept of a 48-speckle image, but is terrible, like the rest of us, at reliably discriminating cases where he sees such an image from cases where he does not. Shall we say that he is then epistemically justified in taking himself to see it, when indeed he happens to do so?

It might be replied that we just do not *have* such a phenomenal concept. But the objection does not suppose that we *do*. It supposes only that we *might*. And if it is rejected that we even *might* have such a *phenomenal* concept, then we must press for an account of what makes a concept phenomenal and a concept of a certain property. Presumably it would not be just that the property in question makes an appearance in our experience, say in our visual experience, nor even that it does so consciously, vividly, and focally. After all, if I look at a pure white surface showing eleven fat, black dots in a horizontal array and I focus intently on that array, presumably that very pattern is one I am then attending to in a vividly focused way. Yet I may be far from justified in believing that I then see *an eleven-member array*. But what then is required beyond the property's appearing in our experience thus consciously, vividly, and focally? What is the requirement whose violation keeps us from having a phenomenal concept of 48-speckleness? How is it precluded that we have that concept despite being as unreliable in its application as humans normally are?

If on the other hand it is granted that what gives us a grasp of a phenomenal concept is, at least in part, our discriminative abilities, then we are back with tracking, causation, and reliability, to some requirement of the sort dear to the externalist and heretofore repugnant to the internalist.

3 Human Knowledge, Animal and Reflective

Reply to Robert Audi, John Greco, and Hilary Kornblith

These comments push me to be more clear and explicit about the content and basis of my two-level epistemology. Although the letter of my earlier statements still seems to me defensible, a detailed defense, with close attention to verbal nuance, would be tiresome all around. Besides, those statements do bear some blame for the ways in which they have been misinterpreted. So I will instead try to capture the spirit of my proposed position with a fuller and more specific formulation, which I claim to be compatible with the earlier, partial statements. And I will then try to explain how this position enables answers to the questions and objections posed against it.

In distinguishing between "animal" and "reflective" knowledge and justification, I do not mean to suggest that the former is restricted to lower animals, or brutes, and the latter to human beings. Compare the distinction between the animal excellence of a tennis player and his strategic excellence. Serena Williams's animal excellence would include her ability to run fast, jump high, react quickly, etc., along with the physical skills and abilities that enable her to hit a fast serve, her accurate, powerful groundstrokes, her quick reactions at the net, and so on and so forth. Her strategic excellence is what makes her not only a skilled and powerfully athletic player, but also a smart player, one who uses her abilities well, enabling her to win more matches, or at least by a wider margin, than might be possible otherwise. Alternatively, and to pretty much the same effect, we could distinguish between her unstrategic and her strategic excellence. Thus, Williams can and does combine her unstrategic excellence as a tennis player with her strategic excellence. By strategic excellence I mean not only the cerebral knowledge of a coach, but knowledge you embody as a player as to what are the shots to hit given your position, strengths, and weaknesses, and those of your opponent. Such subtle and complex knowledge is engaged repeatedly in the heat of a match, absent verbal formulation, or even fully conscious awareness. In any case such knowledge depends essentially on no such formulation. Yet it is surely something more cerebral, in some sense, than other, more "physical" abilities, something requiring intelligent selection from available alternatives, even if this is done neither verbally nor even consciously, certainly not through any conscious deliberation.

Brutes outstrip humans in the sorts of physical abilities that matter for athletic excellence. And they perform actions attributable to them as their doings, for which they are "credited." Take a great horse, and its wins on the racetrack. That horses are no "athletes" seems a relatively superficial linguistic fact. Do brutes have strategic excellence, or in any case any more "cerebral" excellence? If they do, it seems of a different order. Although cunning can determine the winner in a struggle for dominance among brutes, such cunning is still different, at least in degree, from the smart play of Williams over the course of a long match, let alone the smart play of a quarterback leading a complex drive in multiple stages. Note how a particular run or a particular throw by that quarterback acquires part of its justification through its place in a much broader plan in his mind, involving considerable temporal, spatial, and social complexity.

Compare now the distinction between two sorts of knowledge, the animal and the reflective. Animal, unreflective knowledge is largely dependent on cognitive modules and their deliverances. The visual deliverances of someone with 20/20 eyesight will differ in quality from those of someone nearly blind. Reflective knowledge manifests not just modular deliverances blindly accepted, but also the assignment of proper weights to conflicting deliverances, and the balance struck among them.

Is reflective knowledge different in *kind* from animal knowledge? Well, what kind of kind? It is, trivially, a different sort of knowledge, knowledge distinguishable in the respect of being reflective, from knowledge that is not reflective. But why focus on this particular respect in which one might sort cases of knowledge? What is so important, epistemologically, about this particular respect? Take consultative knowledge, which by definition derives from consultation. Why not say that this, too, is epistemologically relevant, and constitutes another sort of knowledge with its own epistemological relevance? Why not distinguish consultative knowledge as a sort with its own epistemological importance? Why should it not be considered along with perceptual knowledge, mnemonic knowledge, testimonial knowledge, and so on?

The importance of the social must of course be recognized in a true epistemology. Social roots yield a better tree of knowledge. Socially rooted knowledge (through consultation, or more broadly through testimony) is a distinctive and important category, over and above perception, memory, and reason, deductive and inductive. Once having admitted consultative knowledge, moreover, must we not wonder why reflective knowledge should deserve a higher profile, why not think of it as one more sort of knowledge alongside the consultative, the perceptual, and the mnemonic?

Yes, reflective knowledge is indeed one more sort of knowledge to be listed alongside these others. Among these it deserves a special place, however, or so I will now argue.

The special status of reflective knowledge involves in part its prominence as an intellectual desideratum, which derives from its perennial attraction for the reflective. It may be replied that those of us in seminars, who rely on discussion, as did Socrates and Plato already, also put a premium on consultative knowledge. Why not give this equal billing? Why the pride of place for reflective knowledge?

One answer is to be found in the special bearing of reflective knowledge on the understanding and coherence dear to intellectuals, and on the intellectual agency that we honor. We do prize discussion and interpersonal dialectic as well, however; so, why highlight reflection above consultation? Here is a further reason: No matter how much we value consultation, we are unwilling to yield our intellectual autonomy, which requires us to assess the place of consultation in the light of all our other relevant information and recognized desiderata. For, to assess it thus is to evaluate it in the light of reflection. Of course, reflection itself might benefit from consultative evaluation. So, why put reflection above consultation? Partly, it seems to me, because the deliverances of consultation need assessing in the light of reflection in a way that is different from how reflection is to be assessed through consultation. In the end reflection has properly a closer, more finally determinative influence on the beliefs we form, and the deliverances of consultation bear properly only through reflection's sifting and balancing. *Conscious* reflection on the spot is not required, however, since a second-order perspective can work beneath the surface of consciousness.

There is, nevertheless, a further way in which reflection is particularly important. It is the ideal of reflective knowledge that best explains the traditional attraction and importance of skepticism. The skeptic claims that vicious circularity will inevitably block our pursuit of reflective knowledge. Reflective knowledge requires that we believe our basic epistemic sources to be reliable (enough), and that we do so with rational justification. But how can we possibly attain such justification except by trusting those very sources. And this seems inevitably, and viciously, circular. Nothing like this affects consultative knowledge (or justification).

Finally, reflection aids agency, control of conduct by the whole person, not just by peripheral modules. When reasons are in conflict, as they so often are, not only in deliberation but in theorizing,[17] and not only in the higher reaches of theoretical science but in the most ordinary reasoning about matters of fact, we need a way holistically to strike a balance, which would seem to import an assessment of the respective weights of pros and cons, all of which evidently is played out through perspective on one's attitudes and the bearing of those various reasons.[18]

4 Safety, Bootstrapping, Circularity

Reply to Stewart Cohen and John Greco

Consider the Dretske/Nozick *sensitivity* requirement for S's knowing that p: the requirement that if it were false that p, then S would not believe that p. Compare what *safety* requires: that S would not believe that p without it being true that p. Such safety, a reversal of sensitivity, has important advantages, but still has serious problems. For instance, it runs against Kripke's example of a region wherein all red barn facades are facades of real barns, although nearly all barn facades are mere facades.[19] The belief that one faces a red barn will then seem both safe and sensitive, while the belief that one sees a barn is neither. This example seems to show that knowledge is not closed under deduction, regardless of whether we require sensitivity or safety. If by hypothesis, on whatever basis, in whatever way, we do know it's a red barn we see, and we deduce that we see a barn, this we should be able to know thereby, but if either safety or sensitivity is necessary for knowing, then we apparently know no such thing, despite having deduced it from what by hypothesis we know.

Some accept this failure of closure, thus joining Dretske and Nozick, who positively welcome it. The rest of us need to replace that simple condition of safety. However, we might still retain the following rather more complex condition, at least for knowledge based on a basis:

S's belief-that-p is safe iff S holds it on a basis that his belief would not have without being true.

Given this, the belief that one sees a real barn would seem safe after all, in the Kripke example, when deduced from one's safe belief that one sees a red barn. For one would not *on that deductive basis* then believe that one sees a barn without it being true that one does see a barn. But now we run against an objection urged by Cohen as follows.

> Though revised safety avoids closure failure, it does so only at the cost of producing strongly counterintuitive results. Kripke's red barn case is a variant of [the barns example, such that] . . . even if I see a barn, and so my belief that there is a barn before me is causally related to the fact of there being such a barn, I still fail to know there is a barn before me if unbeknown to me there are barn replicas in the vicinity. Most people share that intuition, especially if the case is specified so the barn replicas are abundant and very close by. In the Kripke version of the case, original safety produces closure failure by allowing that S knows he sees a red barn while failing to know he sees a barn. Revised safety avoids this problem by allowing that S can know there is a barn before him as well. But that result runs counter to the robust intuition that S fails to know in such cases. If S sees a barn in a region with perceptually indistinguishable barn replicas, he does not know there is a barn before him. So it looks as if revised safety avoids closure failure at the cost of producing a counterintuitive result for this case.

This last bit of reasoning is fallacious, however, since safety is advanced as nothing more than a necessary condition. A belief must be not only safe but also virtuous if it is to amount to knowledge, where the virtue of a belief derives largely from the reliability of its sources. The fact that the belief about the barns is safe does not automatically make it a case of knowledge, therefore, so it has not been shown after all that safety produces a counterintuitive result. Nevertheless, we can still learn something important from Cohen's reasoning.

Here's how. We start by comparing two examples: first the barns examples, including Kripke's variant, and, second, one due to Goldman, the dachshund example. You are in an area where wolves and huskies abound, and you are not good at telling these apart: you might easily believe you face a dog (a husky) even when you face not a dog but a wolf. Yet, even in that situation you know you see a dachshund, surely, when that is what you see. In that case you also know it's a dog you see, when you infer this from your belief that you see a dachshund.

Here we are pulled hard by conflicting intuitions. You can know you see a dog in a case with misleading wolves all around, when you infer this from your knowledge that you see a dachshund. But you cannot know you see a barn once misleading facades are all around, even when you infer that it's a barn you see from your belief that you see a red barn. How do we relieve this tension?

What's the true basis of our belief that we see a red barn? Here are two possibilities:

(a) There's a unified red-barn visual gestalt whose presence in our experience supports belief that we see a red barn, from which we can then infer that it's a barn we see, and something red.
(b) There's a unified barn visual character so present in our experience as to support belief that *here* we see a barn, and there's a red visual character so present in our experience as to support belief that *here* we see something red. And we rest on those two beliefs the further belief that *here* we see a red barn.

Compare the true basis of our belief that we see a dog in the dachshund case:

(c) There's a unified dachshund visual gestalt whose presence in our experience supports belief that we see a dachshund, from which we infer that it's a dog we see.

(d) There's a unified canine visual character so present in our experience as to support belief that *here* we see a dog, and there's a separate "dachshundish" visual character (also present in drawings, pictures, etc. of dachshunds) so present in our experience as to support belief that *here* we see something dachshund-like. We then draw from these two beliefs the belief that *here* we see a dachshund-like dog. And so on.

Even without the complete story before us in full detail, the following seems plausible. Whereas there is a barnish visual character *independent of color* that supports our belief that we see a barn, there is no doggish visual character *independent of the various more specific dog appearances* that similarly prompts our answer to the question whether we see a dog.

That is how I propose to explain the difference in our intuitions, relieving the tension. We know neither that it's a red barn we face, nor that it's a barn. We know both that it's a dachshund we face, and that it's a dog. In both cases closure is preserved. Why do we fail to know it's a red barn? Because we base that belief importantly on a belief that it's a barn, and this belief is not in that example safe. Why do we do know it's a dachshund? Because this belief, given how it is based in the example, is safe (and meets the other requirements for amounting to knowledge), and we can then infer from it, and thereby come to know, the conclusion that it's a dog we see.[20]

In giving that account of our examples, I have assumed that experience, by having a certain character, sometimes leads us to believe as we do about the scene before us. For example, we are so built that, in normal circumstances, *we do and would take experience at face value*: i.e., if things seemed to all appearances a certain way that is how we would take them to be. However, it has also emerged that there are different ways in which this could be so. If something appeared FG, one might on that account believe it to be FG, for example, thereby taking experience at face value. But this might happen "directly," or it might happen "indirectly," because one takes it to be F based on its appearing F, and takes it to be G based on its appearing G, and one bases on those takings one's belief that it is FG. However it happens, one will be relying on certain experience/belief ties, where one believes that things are thus and so based on one's experience as of things being thus and so.

We can adhere to a principle either consciously or subconsciously, explicitly or implicitly. Either way, we are required to satisfy the consequent when we satisfy the antecedent. What is more, this must derive from some psychological state of one's own. For our adherence to the principle, it will not suffice that it just happens to fit our conduct, in the sense that we do satisfy the consequent when we satisfy the antecedent. Adherence to the principle requires in addition that this not come about accidentally or because some external agency arranges for us to satisfy its consequent in cases where we satisfy its antecedent. No, our adherence to the principle requires that we act out of our own acceptance of the principle: i.e., there must be a state of our own with the propositional content of the principle, a state that is operative in leading us to fit the consequent when we fit the antecedent. This state of ours is not required to be a fully conscious state. It may never rise to consciousness. But it must at least be operative beneath the surface of consciousness if our conduct is to manifest our adherence to it and not the workings of some external agency, or simply accidental fitting.

Let us turn specifically to the case where the guiding principle concerns our intellectual conduct, and more specifically our belief formation. In cases where we immediately believe that Gx upon believing that Fx, we satisfy the principle that one is to believe Gx upon believing that Fx. Acceptance of this principle is a psychological state hosted by the subject. We have found it plausible to attribute propositional content to this state, a content whose falsity renders that attitude "incorrect" and whose truth comports well with it. This content is, plausibly, that if something were F it would be G.

What are we to call this state that guides us in fitting our conduct to its propositional content? We might call it "commitment" to the content; we need not call it "belief." What matters is, first, that it does have propositional content; second, that it need not be verbalizable, nor even conscious; and, third, that the way it bears on our conduct hence need not be through conscious deliberation.

The knowledge of normal, adult humans is thus meta-perspectival to some degree. The knowledge of lower animals or infants, and even some mature human knowledge, is graced with relatively little reflection. In any case, adult humans enjoy a rich epistemic perspective, even if its contained commitments remain implicit, mostly beyond our capacity to articulate. When explicit, moreover, such commitments tend to rise only to a Moorean commonsense level, below the sophistication of any Cartesian epistemology (fully) supernaturalized, or any Quinean epistemology (fully) naturalized. Learning can change our cognitive habits or commitments, moreover, as when diminishing acuity leads one to narrow the scope within which to trust one's senses, accepting their deliverances at face value. Such revision may be principled, through principles themselves evaluable epistemically as are beliefs. The point is that such states can powerfully affect one's cognitive dynamics, what one comes to believe in various circumstances given what else one already believes, what one gives up, and so on; and also one's psychological dynamics more broadly: what desires one acquires or relinquishes, and so on.

While unable to articulate a certain mode of belief acquisition or sustenance, we may yet grasp it well enough to enable appropriate responses as it starts to fail us through diminished powers or environmental change. Corrective responses may hence be driven by deeper-yet "beliefs" about how to respond. Just as inarticulate knowledge of a face can help guide our conduct, so inarticulate and even inarticulable knowledge can guide belief management. What is more, and moving up a level, such knowledge of how to acquire and sustain beliefs might guide corrective responses when faculties begin to falter.

A commitment that carried one from belief that Fx to belief that Gx might be ascribed the subjunctive-conditional content that generally $(Fx \rightarrow Gx)$, for example, with such commitment comprising, or at least yielding, the disposition to believe Gx when one believed Fx. Assigning it that content would seem appropriate, since our assessment of such a commitment would depend on whether the corresponding content was true. Thus a habit or even tendency of moving from the belief that some picked-out item is F to a belief that it is G might be criticized if items thus picked out (in the relevant circumstances) are *not* such that they would be G if F.

Much if not the whole of our epistemic structure of true, apt, justified "belief" that is non-accidentally true, un-Gettiered, etc., is thus applicable to these further psychological states – to these implicit commitments, including the innate – just as they are to the most explicit and central beliefs. Some implicit commitments are not verbalizable, nor, perhaps, are they even conscious, and they may even lie beyond our imagistic capacities. But this also applies to much ordinary belief, about faces and how they look, to dishes and how they taste, to sentences and whether they are grammatical, and to much of our most secure commonplace knowledge.

Our familiar epistemological framework is applicable to the underlying commitments – that is here the main point. We cannot depend just on habits that happen to be reliable no matter how they got there or stay in place. Once this is clear, it seems a harmless verbal simplification to view such commitments as "beliefs" of a sort, given how similar they are to ordinary beliefs that subconsciously guide our conduct.

Your cognitive structure might be mixed, however, containing elements that vary variously. Your epistemic perspective is included, containing both (a) articulable scientific or theological beliefs, as well as some that remain (b) implicit and even inarticulable. What is important is that the psychological states constitutive of that cognitive structure be evaluable epistemically in the usual ways, including both aptness and also justification or rationality. What is distinctive of the meta-perspectival component of any such cognitive structure is that its elements are "about" the body of beliefs upon which, at least in part, the perspective takes a "view."

Consider the clusters of commitments (habits, inference patterns) that constitute possession of a correlated subfaculty of perception – say, color perception, or shape perception, or combinations. Take, for example, a commitment to accept experience at face value with the following propositional content:

<When it looks as if I see something red, then (most probably) I see something red.>

Call this the R conditional. Commitment to this conditional might take any of at least four different forms:

(a) A disposition to respond to the look described in an instance of the antecedent with belief in the corresponding consequent.
(b) A disposition to assent to R on considering it.
(c) A conscious assenting to R.
(d) A belief, implicit or conscious, that one's faculty of redness perception would be reliable.

Why think of (d) as a form of commitment to R? Well, consider this sequence:

(i) When it looks as if I see something red, then (most probably) I see something red.
(ii) When it looks as if I see something red, then (most probably) my corresponding belief would be true.
(iii) Taking my redness experience at face value with a corresponding belief is (truth-) reliable, i.e., would (probably) lead me epistemically aright, not astray.
(iv) A disposition to believe I see something red upon its looking to me as if I see something red would be a reliable disposition.
(v) My faculty of redness perception would be reliable, i.e., would lead me epistemically aright, not astray.

Can't we move plausibly from either end to the other, either from (i) to (v) or from (v) to (i)? If so, then all five propositions stand in a kind of equivalence. In particular, propositions (i) and (v) stand in such equivalence: commitment to either would seem to bring with it at least implicit commitment to the other, as can be brought out by going through the (i)–(v) sequence, step by step, in each direction. But acceptance of (i) is just acceptance of R, and acceptance of (v) is tantamount to (d). So, commitment to R is, in the way explained, equivalent to commitment to (v), i.e., is equivalent to (d).

A general proposition might be accepted subconsciously even while denied consciously, as when someone is clearly prejudiced, his sincere protestations to the contrary notwithstanding. Does the subject then believe, all things considered, or not? Better just to distinguish the states, allowing conscious explicit affirmation – or even *conscious belief* – to co-exist with subconscious, implicit *dis*belief, detrimental as this may be to the unity of that mind. Do you really know that the members of the target race are your equals and not inferior, given your sincere, well-founded, conscious profession to that effect? Even if you are granted some grade of knowledge on that account, it will be knowledge at best degraded by your implicit and action-guiding "belief" to the contrary.

Whether the implicit states are called "beliefs" or not, they are in any case states of implicit adherence to "principles," or "commitments" that one holds. And some are presumably held *on the inferential basis* of others. Thus one may hold the implicit belief, about someone one perceives to be a member of the target race, that he in particular is inferior, based on a more general implicit prejudice that members of that race generally are inferior. So the epistemic status of some implicit commitments will depend on the epistemic status of other commitments whence they are validly derived. Accordingly, we might well inquire into the epistemic structure of our relevant body of psychological states, including not only our consciously explicit beliefs, but also our subconsciously implicit commitments, and even our sensory experiences.[21] And here looms the Pyrrhonian problematic, with its three familiar options: foundations, circle, and regress.

Suppose we opt for foundations. Can the foundations be exhausted by the taking of the given? What is thus taken would now include both necessary truths known by *a priori* intuition and contingent truths known through introspection of one's salient current states of consciousness, along with *cogito*-like propositions (*cogito* itself, for example, and also *sum*). How now can we know our cognitive faculties to be as reliable as we ordinarily take them to be?

It might be thought we could do so by appeal to the foundational inputs delivered by these very faculties. Consider the intuitive, perceptual, introspective, and mnemonic inputs that they deliver. These might now enable a picture of ourselves and the world around us, and of how the two are systematically related, one that underwrites the reliability of the very faculties that deliver those inputs.

However, in accepting those deliverances we already rely on a commitment to the reliability of those very faculties. *Arbitrarily* accepted inputs will yield no knowledge to underwrite the relevant picture. Faculties of perception in particular involve commitment to accept inputs of certain general sorts. Consider such a faculty or subfaculty: e.g., vision, or color vision, etc., beyond just perception in general. By entailing the delivery of certain sorts of beliefs in certain correlated general conditions, it may bundle built-in implicit commitments to accept certain beliefs based on awareness of certain circumstances.[22] That causes a problem for any foundationalism that would have us infer a belief in the reliability of a faculty such as perception from the deliverances of that very faculty (among others). After all, a commitment to the reliability of such deliverances is already required for the proper operation of the faculty. So the commitment must be there already and cannot without vicious circularity be supposed to obtain its epistemic status from any such inductive inference. Therefore, a question remains as to how such commitments could gain their required status. Absent such status, surely, the deliverances of the correlated "faculty" would be worth little, and could not provide inputs inductively yielding conclusions with derived epistemic worth.

There seems no alternative to granting foundational status to some such general commitments built into one's possession of a cognitive faculty. So these, some at least, must attain their epistemic worth independently of being inferred inductively. Just how, more specifically, can commitment to such principles be justified without vicious circularity? One possibility is that the principles be each a normative principle of evidence in its own right, a fundamental principle specifying conditions within which a belief would be justified, and from which it would derive justification. As a proposal in epistemology this has the drawback that the relevant principles would have to be a multitude with no apparent unity.[23]

One important concept of justification involves evaluation of the subject as someone separable from his contingently given environment. It is not only agents and subjects that we assess as justified or not, however; actions and beliefs are assessable, too. Indeed, when one is assessed as justified, one is assessed as justified *in acting or believing a certain way*. Nevertheless, the evaluation of particular acts might imply an indirect evaluation of the agent or subject himself. A tennis shot may count as accurate or not, which will imply only a minimal comment on the shot-maker. That same shot may also be assessed as skillful or not, however, which does substantially involve some evaluation of the agent by indirection.

Abstracting from the circumstances, anyhow, at least insofar as the agent does not bear responsibility for them, some evaluations of belief focus on the believer's relevant constitution and rational procedure. Such evaluations take into account only factors internal to the mind of the subject, not only beliefs but also experiences. Evaluations of a belief as justified or not thus take into account proceedings downstream from experience. Only if these manifest cognitive virtue are the outcome beliefs justified. And how do we assess whether such a procedure does or does not manifest the sort of virtue that helps make its output belief justified, and even a case of knowledge? No alternative seems more plausible for the determination of *epistemic* or *cognitive* virtue than that of truth-conduciveness. *Understanding* will matter too, however: knowing the whys and wherefores, especially on important issues pregnant with explanatory (and predictive) payoff. And such understanding is intimately connected with coherence, since the explanatory interrelationship among our beliefs is bound to function as a, or even *the*, main component of epistemically efficacious coherence.

One's commitment to a view that *when things look a certain way, one can expect a certain outcome*, may be revealed by repeated expectation of the outcome in situation after situation when things in fact do look that way. Our accepting that "When things look F they are likely to turn G" may be manifest not through conscious articulation, but only through a pattern of "inferences." Thus we come to the question "What might justify commitment to such an inference pattern?" Sundry things could do so: for one thing, the fact that the pattern fits one's experience and is accepted because of that. That's one way to block the regress. Another way is simpler: namely, that we be innately hard-wired for that inference pattern, by God or Nature, so that it may justifiedly guide our reasoning. And this it may do even independently of whether the environment jibes with our specific cognitive makeup when we make that inference. The inference is still "justified" in any case, since it is the sort of inference that it is appropriate for us to make downstream from experience, regardless of the aetiology of that experience or the nature of the environment, thus regardless of how "apt" the belief may be relative to the environment within which it is acquired or sustained. So long as in our world it is a normally successful pattern, and it is no accident that we sustain the commitment to its use (a gift perhaps of God, or Mother Nature) with sensitivity to its validity, we may evaluate ourselves individually as "justified" in the beliefs acquired or sustained by means of that pattern, and evaluate the beliefs (the believings) themselves as justified on that basis.[24]

Note finally how, compatibly with this approach, even victims of the demon might still enjoy such justification. For, in considering whether we are thus justified, we evaluate ourselves and our proceedings *downstream from experience*, and such proceedings are evaluable positively even if they unfold in a demonic world, so long as the basis for evaluation is how likely it is that their like would put us in touch with the truth *in the environment where we make the evaluation*. After all, the environment that provides the basis for the evaluation is not the demon world but the actual world inhabited by the evaluators who are considering, as a hypothetical case, the case of such a victim.[25]

Reasoning will yield animal knowledge only if it holds up with truth, aptness, and justification at every lemma on which it relies essentially in connecting its conclusion with relevant external reality. This is bound to depend on ultimate premises owed to some sort of perception, aided perhaps by memory. Of course, reasoning that is *merely* circular will fail properly to connect any conclusion with the world beyond the circle.

That is compatible with one's being subject to no such prohibition, however, when the objective is knowledge that is not just animal but reflective. Having grasped how it is around us through connections involving the perception/memory/reasoning required for animal knowledge, further reasoning on that basis may enhance our conscious integration and explanatory coherence, lending epistemic virtue to our beliefs. There is no more vice in this circular procedure than in a case of visually-apparent-sprinkling/circles-in-puddles/pitter-patter-on-the-window-panes/car-wipers-wiping/umbrellas-up/felt-drops-on-one's-bare-arms/recalled-forecast, etc. There is nothing wrong with accepting various sub-arguments in such a case concurrently, believing the conclusion of each partly on the basis of the other beliefs used as premises. It *would* of course be bad to hold those sub-arguments concurrently *absent any connection with the relevant externalia*. Even when one holds the lot of them concurrently interlocked, however, *this does not imply that one holds them so detached*.

A special, rational form of viciousness spoils attempts to reach conclusions about the contingent world around us through reasoning detached not only from the world beyond but even from those states and beliefs required as peripheral intermediaries for the desired connection with the world. Prominent among these states are the experiential states whose job it is precisely to mediate in that way between our contingent beliefs about the world around us and the world that they are about. Much purely circular reasoning would be defective in just that way.

By using our various faculties and subfaculties, including those constituted by certain habits or other inferential patterns, we may reach a consciously reflective world view distinguished by two features from the largely implicit framework that precedes it. Call that earlier framework of implicit commitments and other beliefs *framework FI*. Call the later explicit world-view *framework FE*. Two epistemically significant features may distinguish FE from FI: (a) that the earlier implicit "beliefs" are now explicit, and (b) that such consciousness-raising enables greater cognitive coherence. Explicitly considering our reliability encourages fuller, more sophisticated awareness of its sources, resulting in a tighter integration among member beliefs, now explicitly seen as interrelated.

It seems viciously circular to try to derive commitments through reasoning from those very commitments. This *is* viciously circular if we conceive of the commitments arrived at as identical with the commitments from which they are derived as conclusions. But we may now respond that the conclusions we reach are conscious, explicit beliefs, constitutive of an explicit, articulated world view; and these are not quite the same as our implicit intellectual-conduct-guiding commitments, no matter how closely related they may be, and indeed even should they turn out to share the very same contents.[26] Moreover, in fact the explicit perspective arrived at can far exceed the implicit commitments that enable reasoning to begin, for it can be far superior in its articulation of how it all happens, describing in vastly richer detail the causal structures operative in our reliable acquisition of beliefs, which would include explicit detail about the relevant features of our own constitution as well as those of our relevant context.

Still the question remains: How can those basic, originating commitments be justified? I mean the implicit ones engaged by our most basic observational knowledge. How can they be justified, if their contents are general, contingent propositions? How can such a proposition be acceptable foundationally or immediately, as a "self-evident" universal or probabilistic truth? How can we sensibly allow ourselves justification for commitment to such a truth from the armchair, absent proper empirical inquiry into our actual contingent surroundings?

Answer: What would make us justified is that we proceed in an epistemically appropriate and desirable way, given the aims of systematic acquisition and retention of truth (especially truth that gives understanding), and that we do so not by accident, but in a way that derives from our nature and the nature of things, which makes us non-accidentally sensitive precisely to the "validity" of the inferential patterns constitutive of those faculties, with their bundled implicit commitments. Now this last could be detailed more specifically in various ways, two main competing options involving respectively (a) Divine Providence, and (b) natural evolution; either one would serve present *epistemological* purposes. Descartes and Reid clearly took the first option. But, however the story is detailed at that level, the fact remains: humans are a certain way by nature, a way that, given our normal environment, furthers our epistemic aims of attaining both truth and understanding, and does so with non-accidental responsiveness to the truth, including the subjunctive truth required for the validity of our inferential patterns. So we can be assessed for whether our inbuilt mechanisms are operating correctly even if, unfortunately, we are in an abnormal environment relative to which those very mechanisms operate so as to take us away from truth and understanding. The main point is now straightforward: namely, that the mechanisms in question might include taking our sense experience at face value, and gaining access to the states of mind of our neighbors through beliefs instinctively prompted by the external, behavioral signs of such states. Et cetera.

Thus may we attain justification for the use of our basic faculties, for our "belief" in or implicit commitment to the various "principles" of belief formation adherence to which in practice is constitutive of such faculties. And this justification would remain even for victims of a Cartesian evil demon. Reasoning from such implicit commitments may eventually yield conscious awareness of your faculties and subfaculties, of their nature and how they fit you for cognitive success in your relevant normal environment. To a greater or lesser extent this would constitute a world view that underwrites, with coherent understanding, your use of those faculties. Moreover, such conscious awareness of your intellectual makeup (your nature and second nature) might also aid its gradual improvement, as when you no longer take the sun to be (strictly) rising, no longer take the oar to be bent, no longer take the Mueller-Lyer lines to be incongruent, and so on. You might no longer accept deliverances which earlier, however briefly or long, had been admitted without question.

Is that vicious? No more so here than it was for Descartes. Who could object to the use of our faculties resulting in such a world view with its attendant coherence and yield of understanding? How plausible that the individual component beliefs should also gain epistemically through integration in a more comprehensively coherent and explanatory establishment. When we judge them better justified, our assessment is relational, true enough, and indirectly dependent on intellectual surroundings involving the believer's operative cognitive virtue. But that is no more strange than is the evaluation of an archer's shot as skillful, which remains an evaluation of the shot itself, even if an indirect one dependent on factors involving the surroundings, and most of all the archer's operative skill.

In conclusion, let's focus more closely on a crucial part of Cohen's critique: his objection to the Moorean version of the Cartesian "small circle," and the problem of easy knowledge as it arises in two ways: (a) in connection with closure, and (b) in connection with bootstrapping.

Right after the cogito passage, Descartes reasons: "Now at last I have real certainty. What gives me this certainty? As far as I can see, only the clarity and distinctness (C&D) of the cogito proposition. But this could not be so if a proposition could ever have that degree of C&D while false." So, Descartes *concludes* that he can "already establish" that every proposition that is C&D (to that degree) is true. If we grant this to Descartes, could not Moore argue similarly like this: "Here's a hand. That's something I know for sure. What assures me of it if not the fact that I see it (while awake, etc.)? So I must be seeing it while awake, etc., and this is something we can now conclude and establish." In what way is this different from Descartes's reasoning? Cohen objects to the Moorean reasoning, and presumably he would object analogously to Descartes's reasoning as well. What is his objection?

Here is a form of the Moorean argument:

(1) Datum: I know with a high degree of certainty that here is a hand
(2) I can see and feel that here is a hand, and that is the only, or anyhow the best explanation of the source of my knowledge that here is a hand.

(3) So my perception that here is a hand is what explains why or how it is that I know (with certainty) that here is a hand.
(4) But my perception could not serve as a source of that degree of justified certainty if it were not a reliable faculty.
(5) So, finally, my perception must be a reliable faculty.

About this Cohen very reasonably wonders how it could possibly help to provide us with knowledge of the conclusion, given that the only way we could come to know the initial datum, premise (1), would require that we trust our faculty of perception. And this in turn would require that we accept principles of perceptual belief formation that, bundled together, *amount* to the reliability of our perceptual faculty.

First, in fairness to Moore it should be noted that he does not clearly advance this argument as a way to knowledge of the conclusion. Indeed, Moore himself never advances this very argument, though he does advance one that is closely related, even just a variant. I mean the argument put forward in his paper "Certainty"[27] to the effect that since he knows that here is a hand therefore he must not be dreaming. *This* argument may function for Moore only as a proof of the conclusion in the sense of being one that validly derives a conclusion distinct from any of the argument's premises, all of which are known to be true. (Moore grants in "Proof of an External World"[28] that perhaps other conditions would need to be satisfied for an argument to qualify as a proof, but he contends that his argument would satisfy those conditions as well.) Not every such "proof" is one that one can use to reason one's way to arrive at new knowledge of the conclusion. Of course, this leaves us with the question of how one *can* attain such new knowledge or at least new justification, and in particular how this could be done while avoiding vicious circularity.

Given our earlier reflections, we can now distinguish the implicit commitments that, bundled together, constitute our basic faculty of perception from the much richer perspective through which one might explain, by appeal to the workings of one's relevant faculties of perception, how it is that one knows oneself to see a hand. This richer, explicit perspective is attained through reasoning that does involve a kind of circularity, but it is hard to deplore the circularity as vicious when we compare it with all the conceivable alternatives, namely these:

(a) Abandoning any attempt to gain such perspectival knowledge of our own cognition, dismissing or ignoring all such questions.
(b) Attempting but *failing* to attain much of a perspective at all.
(c) Attempting to gain such a perspective and reaching only one that undermines, rather than endorses, the faculties by which it was attained, entailing that they are unreliable, and yield mostly error.

By comparison with these outcomes, how can the following be vicious?

(d) Attempting to gain such a perspective and reaching a rich perspective that endorses the faculties by which it was attained.

To think this vicious is to think that there is something bad or wrong about it, but how can that be if it is at least as good as any conceivable alternative? Will it be replied that alternative (a) is not clearly worse? Even if we grant this, it will not suffice to show that (d) is vicious. In order to accomplish this it would need to be shown that (a) is *better* than (d), *epistemically* better. But how might this be shown? How could it be shown that (a) puts us in better relation to the truth than does (d), in better relation so that it can be seen as epistemically better? I see no way of showing that (a) would inevitably fit better within a believer's world view than would the likes of (d).

That is a way to deal with the supposed problem of circularity. But we need to go beyond that if we are to engage more specifically the problem of easy knowledge, in its two forms. Here is Cohen's pithy formulation.

> The problem of easy knowledge arises in two ways. The first exploits the deductive closure principle. On Sosa's view, I can come to know, e.g., that the table is red simply on the basis of my belief being in fact safe. I do not need to know that the circumstances are not such that my color vision is unreliable. I do not need to know, e.g., it is not the case that the table is white with red lights shining on it. (It's enough for it to be unlikely in the context.) But once I know the table is red, it follows from closure (provided that I see the entailment) that I know it is not white with red lights shining on it. And similarly for any alternative to the table being red, I can come to know that alternative is false in this trivial way. But if one has no prior knowledge that there are no red lights shining on the table, it seems counter-intuitive that one could acquire it subsequently in this way.
>
> Imagine my 7-year-old son asks me: "Daddy but what if the (seemingly red) table is white with red lights shining on it?" I reply, "Well – look, the table is red." According to Sosa, this is something I can know provided my belief is safe. So I can appeal to it in reasoning. So I continue. "But since it's red, it can't be white with red lights shining on it. See?" I take it that this reasoning is unacceptable. But I don't see how Sosa can avoid sanctioning it without giving up closure.
>
> The second way the problem of easy knowledge arises has been pointed out by Jonathan Vogel and Richard Fumerton. Suppose my perceptual faculties produce the safe belief that there is a red table before me. Again, I can have this knowledge even if I do not know my perceptual faculties are reliable, or indeed even if I do not have any evidence for their reliability. Now suppose my introspective faculties produce the safe belief that it looks to me as if there is a table before me. Putting these two beliefs together, I would seem to have acquired some evidence that my perceptual faculties are reliable. But clearly if I did not have such evidence prior to my acquiring these beliefs, I cannot in this way acquire such evidence. Moreover, it is not clear why I could not in this way manage to produce enough evidence to come to know that my perceptual faculties are reliable. But intuitively, at least by my lights, one cannot, in this way, come to know one's perceptual faculties are reliable. But I do not see how, on Sosa's view, it can be prevented.

Two main ideas yield my proposed solution to this problem. First: If one's true belief is to amount to knowledge it must be not only safe but also virtuous. Second: Virtues bundle commitments, and perceptual virtues bundle commitments for taking varieties of experience at face value, as in our commitment to the conditional (R) <If it looks as if I see something red, then I do see something red>. One accepts the "deliverances" of such a perceptual subfaculty by adhering to such a principle in the instance involved. Now, if the conclusion to which one is said to reason is simply the conclusion that one's faculty is then reliable, and if this takes the form of acceptance of the very principle R, especially if the "conclusion" one "reasons" to is just an implicit commitment to that principle, then it is easy to see how and why this is questionable. Indeed, what is not so easy to see is how there could really be any such reasoning. How can one *base* one's implicit commitment on itself? How could one do so, whether rationally or irrationally?

Suppose, moreover, that I consciously pose to myself the question of whether red lights are shining on the scene before me. Can I properly answer that question in the negative by bringing to consciousness my knowledge that I see something really red, and noting that I could not enjoy such knowledge if there were red lights shining on the scene before me? This too seems clearly vicious. Is the view I defend committed to the validity and epistemic efficacy of any such reasoning as a provider of justification for belief in its conclusion? Not so. Knowledge is closed under deduction, true enough. But knowledge can be closed under a deduction *without* it being the deduction that provides the justification required for knowledge of the conclusion. The deduction may not be the *source* of that justification, as the example of the red lights brings out. In this case one must know the conclusion but not by deriving it from the premise that one sees something red. One must already have known the conclusion or something very close to it, at least in some implicit way, as a *prerequisite* for knowing that premise. Thus it was a prerequisite for knowing the premise perceptually (which by hypothesis is the only way one then knows it) that one could acquire that knowledge through adherence in that instance to principle R. But principle R requires that the lighting not be misleading, not in the way the presence of red lights would make it misleading, nor in any other way. This is hence something one must assume to be in place with epistemic priority (or at least without epistemic posteriority, even if this is not and need not be noted explicitly) to one's belief that one does see something red.

The main point is this. In adhering to principle R when one acquires perceptually the belief that one sees something red, the epistemic status enjoyed by one's commitment to R must be in place with priority (or non-posteriority) to the epistemic status of one's belief that one sees something red. And yet from R alone, without any help from the claim that one sees something red, one can derive the conclusion that no red lights are then shining on the scene before one. (This even if the derivation also relies on auxiliary premises about the misleading effects of red lights, premises access to which one gains with no help from the claim that one then sees something red.) Very well, but just how do we gain our implicit knowledge of R, how does commitment to R get justified, if it obviously requires that there be no red lights in place. What justifies our implicit trust in our color perception, given that we have no good reason to think that the lighting is good, and not spoiled by red lights?

We come into the world outfitted with sundry default commitments, our brains wired for cognitive and other success in the environment in which a human is normally born. We can turn to evolution or to Divine Providence hoping for a further explanation, but even in the absence of any such metanarrative, it is plausible that, innate to us, or soon naturally acquired, are default commitments that serve us well. So long as we exercise these cognitive or epistemic virtues, moreover, we do epistemically well, we gain non-accidental access to truths of interest and importance to us. This is not to say that the default justification thereby acquired cannot be defeated. It would be defeated if we gained further, specific information about the particular situation at hand, in the sorts of ways in which we might gain the information that the lights were indeed red. Absent such special reason, however, we have epistemic standing for our normal perceptual belief in a normal situation.

That is a response to the closure version of the problem of easy knowledge. A similar response is available for the bootstrapping version. Suppose we accept the deliverances of our gas gauge time after time. Can we thereby build up an inductive case in favor of the reliability of that gauge, or for the reliability of our method of trusting it for acquiring beliefs about the state of our gas tank? Surely not. Why not? Because in accepting the deliverances of the gauge in the first place we are adhering to the principle G <If the gauge reads X then the state of the tank is X>. Principle G is what we are concluding to, but if we had no independent basis for commitment to G, then how could adhering to that principle lend any status to the acceptance of G as a conclusion of any such inductive reasoning? This would be like accepting a *premise* with no epistemic status and hoping to give status to our belief in that premise by arguing from that premise to that very proposition as conclusion. My point is that this is no better when the proposition involved is the content of a commitment that takes the form of a pattern of reasoning, than when it is the content of a premise. (Well, maybe it's not *quite* as bad, but still bad enough, about as bad as in cases like that of the gauge.) Does this not reflect on the trust that we place in our perceptual faculties? Is that not also a case where we gain no epistemic support, where we therefore have no epistemic standing for commitments crucial for our ability to learn through perception. Is this not what makes the problem of the external world so hard?

Maybe so, but recall our proposed solution: We are born outfitted to trust our experiences implicitly, in a way that serves us well not only practically but also cognitively. This is a main, essential source of the epistemic standing of our animal beliefs, and what enables those beliefs to qualify as knowledge, animal and eventually reflective. The latter we *enhance* as we gain the ability to explain in richer and richer explicit detail just how it all works to our epistemic advantage.

Reply to Michael Williams

Michael Williams argues that I go wrong by attempting to extricate epistemological questions from semantic entanglement. What is his argument? For one thing, he targets my thumbnail sketch of Descartes's core epistemology, which runs as follows:

> First [Descartes] meditates along, with the kind of epistemic justification and even "certainty" that might be found in an atheist mathematician's reasonings, one deprived of a world view in which the universe may be seen as epistemically propitious. Descartes's reasoning at that stage *can* be evaluated, of course, just as can an atheist mathematician's reasoning.... Absent an appropriate world view, however, no such reasoning can rise above the level of *cognitio*. If we persist in such reasoning, nevertheless, enough pieces may come together into a view of ourselves and our place in the universe that is sufficiently comprehensive and coherent to raise us ... into the realm of a higher, reflective, enlightened knowledge, or *scientia*. There is in none of that any [vicious] circle.[29]

In direct response to this thumbnail sketch, Williams claims that Descartes allows "for an inference-independent kind of knowledge, *cognitio*," which allegedly dooms my approach. The problem derives from radical foundationalism's alleged commitment to a level of knowledge, radically foundational knowledge, with two important features. First, it functions as ultimate *epistemic* basis. Second, it is *semantically* self-standing, not dependent for its content or meaning on any non-basic commitments. The radical foundationalist is thus said to take seriously the possibility that one could start intellectual life with a foundation of such self-standing atomic, foundational beliefs, upon which one might then build the superstructure of one's knowledge.

> Clearly, Sosa fits this description, as is evident from his talk of our "piecing together" a system of reflective knowledge from beliefs that are instances of mere animal knowledge.

Having charged me with radical foundationalism, Williams goes on to compare my mistaken approach with the opposing views of a celebrated opponent of such foundationalism, adding that

> if Sosa thinks that Sellars is really just another coherentist, thus someone who has failed to escape the Pyrrhonian dialectic, Sellars can return the compliment. From Sellars's standpoint, Sosa is just another foundationalist.

Williams's critique of my alternative culminates by attributing to me a view of meaning that would allow animal beliefs unaccompanied by any reflective knowledge whatsoever. But this is said to be the nub of Sellars's critique of foundationalism.

> It is not hard to see where Sellars would take issue with Sosa's strategy for escaping the Pyrrhonian problematic. His point of attack would surely be Sosa's talk of our "piecing together" a system of reflective knowledge from elements of animal knowledge. If this piecing together involves inferring and hypothesis-testing, on the basis of defeasible evidence – and how else could it be understood? – then, Sellars would say, animal knowledge is already implicitly understood as subject to epistemic assessment, thus as no longer merely animal.

These objections rest on an unfortunate conflation. My thumbnail sketch should not suggest that *cognitio* is inference-independent. In it I speak of evaluating Descartes's *reasoning*, and of that reasoning's not rising above the level of *cognitio*. Let me now emphasize that, as he meditates along, in his ascent to the epistemic heights reached only at the end of the *Meditations*, Descartes does reason, he does infer. Moreover, the status of *cognitio* attained in the beliefs gained through such inferences is inference-*dependent*. But, at least in the earlier stages, before we are well within Meditation III, his beliefs still have a lower status, of mere *cognitio*, because he is still short of the perspective (the theological perspective, beyond the atheist) essential for the higher status of *scientia*. In none of this is it implied that one can attain beliefs that are basic in deriving from no inferences and in requiring not even the ability to infer. The *infra-scientia* atheist mathematician makes inferences aplenty, and is well endowed with abilities to infer, perhaps beyond the theologian. What he has not attained, according to Descartes, is the sort of endorsing perspective required for ascent to *scientia*.

And why should animal knowledge (*cognitio*) be ineligible for "epistemic" assessment? Despite its lack of endorsing perspective, it does involve belief that is *true*, well-supported, and the output of reliable cognitive virtue.

In my view, as in Descartes's, knowledge has two levels, the animal and the reflective, or *cognitio* and *scientia*. This requires no commitment to beliefs independent of the ability to infer, nor does it even require beliefs independent of actual inferences aplenty. It is especially easy to allow this when one downplays the epistemic importance of the distinction between conscious and subconscious inference (while of course recognizing the distinction itself). And it is easier yet if one downplays also the distinction between inferring and presupposing. Beliefs are psychologically based on, or dependent upon, other beliefs, and other psychological states, such as experiences – whether with propositional content, as in a visual experience of length incongruence; or without propositional content, as in a headache. That fact should not so much as suggest that there might be atomic beliefs entirely independent of any other beliefs. Beliefs come in packages, large packages, along with desires and a lot more, probably necessarily so. Nor is a particular belief's justification – its animal, epistemic justification – detachable from the support that the belief derives from other beliefs.

The confusion that concerns me is roughly one of *inference* with *reflective perspective*. Perhaps one conceives of inferring as the following of inferential rules, and one takes this to require adverting to beliefs held, those that constitute the premises, and to rules that will amount to reliability claims, that by inferring *such* a conclusion from *such* premises one proceeds truth-reliably. But this conception of inference seems viciously regressive. In any case, not all justification can be a matter of following such rules; nor can we obviously count on enough "non-inferential" justification to enable the grasp and application of enough of the rules thus required.

Ironically, downplaying the difference between conscious and subconscious inference, and also the difference between inferring and presupposing, as well as the difference between inferential patterns hosted and beliefs held, does smooth the way to a close association between inference and reflective perspective. Thus consider the clusters of commitments (habits, inference patterns) that constitute possession of a correlated subfaculty of perception – say, color perception, or shape perception, or combinations. Take, for example, a commitment to accept a certain sort of experience at face value, a commitment with the following propositional content:

<When it looks as if I see something red, then (most probably) I see something red.>

Call this, again, the R conditional. "Commitment" to this conditional, as has been argued above, might take various forms. It might take the form of a disposition to respond to the look described in an instance of the antecedent with belief in the corresponding consequent. But it might also take the form of a belief, implicit or conscious, that one's faculty of redness perception would be reliable. This last is constitutive of a reflective perspective on one's own cognition, and is equivalent to the disposition to respond systematically to the look with the belief. At least, it is equivalent to a disposition to assent to R,[30] and this is "equivalent" to the disposition to respond to the look with the belief, once this disposition, or the "commitment" that it constitutes has been made explicit.

Would that stance expose one to Williams's fire after all? No, but it does lead me to think of the difference between the two sorts of knowledge, the animal and the reflective, as a difference of degree. The higher brutes may be credited, along with small children, with some minimal degree of perspectival, reflective knowledge, of the implicit, subconscious sort, which largely resides in hosted inference patterns. In richness, explicitness, and explanatory power, that still falls short of the reflective knowledge to which a human can aspire, especially someone philosophically inclined, say René Descartes. (The three factors are of course not unrelated; thus explicitness may enable greater richness and explanatory power, whether through an epistemology theologically supernaturalized, or one scientifically naturalized.) Reflective knowledge that is thus richer, more explicit, and more powerful may well be thought superior, which might prompt the worry that any aspiration to attain it will be dashed, say by vicious circularity. Thus may the reflective ideal help explain the interest of the skeptical problematic, which gains urgency with the rejection (by Sellars, among many others) of inductive support as viciously circular.

And how indeed does the Cartesian strategy avoid vicious circularity, especially once we apply it beyond the armchair to cover also our empirical knowledge of the world around us? Unavoidably, as I see it, we must here rely on our animal endowment of implicit commitments that constitute our perceptual faculties; we need animal faith in our commitments constitutive of our engrained tendency to "take experience at face value." How can those basic implicit commitments be justified, if their contents are general, contingent propositions, at least about tendencies or the like? How can such a proposition be justified foundationally or immediately, as a "self-evident" universal or probabilistic truth? How can we sensibly allow ourselves justification for believing such a truth "*a priori*," absent proper empirical inquiry into our actual contingent surroundings?

At this fundamental (and foundational?) level, we proceed with epistemic adroitness, in an epistemically appropriate and desirable way, if we satisfy the distinctively epistemic value of systematic acquisition and retention of truth, and if we do so not by accident, but in a way that derives from our nature and the nature of things, which makes us non-accidentally sensitive precisely to the "validity" of the inferential patterns constitutive of those faculties and their bundled implicit commitments. It is not easy to specify the kinds of accident that will spoil epistemic justification. We are, in any case, a certain way by nature, a way that, given our normal environment, enables us to attain truth and understanding on questions of interest, and with non-accidental responsiveness to the truth, including the subjunctive truth constitutive of the validity of our inferential patterns. Our inbuilt mechanisms may still operate correctly even if, unfortunately, we are in an abnormal environment relative to which those very mechanisms distance us from both truth and understanding. The mechanisms include taking our sense experience at face value, and coming to know what others think or feel as we acquire beliefs prompted by the external, behavioral signs of their states of mind.

That is a way in which we can become justified by using our basic faculties, through implicit commitments to the inference patterns that constitute such faculties. Even victims of a Cartesian evil demon would retain such justification. By reasoning from such implicit commitments we may eventually gain conscious awareness of our faculties and subfaculties. We may thus gain conscious knowledge of their nature and of how they enable our cognitive success. And this can help provide a perspective that underwrites, with coherent understanding, our use of those faculties. Such conscious awareness of our intellectual makeup may also enable its gradual improvement, as when we are no longer taken in by familiar perceptual illusions.

Is that vicious? No more so here than it was for Descartes, or so I have argued.

5 Coherence

Reply to Robert Audi, Peter Klein, Alvin Goldman, and Allen Habib and Keith Lehrer

Audi's main reservations seem to concern whether reflective knowledge is "unitary" and whether we can respond to the skeptic by dispensing with my so-called principle of exclusion. He doubts that reflective knowledge "is constituted by a certain kind of well-grounded true belief." On the contrary, it appears to him

> that reflective knowledge "that p" is not thus unitary, but is better conceived as knowledge *regarding p*. It consists of knowledge that p, *together with* appropriate second-order capacities, including dispositional beliefs that themselves constitute knowledge.

Reflective knowledge is definitely in my view unitary in the way specified: in being constituted by a certain kind of well-grounded belief. That is how it is, anyhow, so long as to be "constituted" is to be "at least partially constituted," which seems compatible with requiring that the belief must also be accompanied by certain second-order capacities. However, it is not enough that the beliefs constitutive of the reflective knowledge just sit there loose from those capacities. Such second-order capacities need to *sustain* any first-order belief that is to constitute reflective knowledge, although the sustaining relations in play need involve no conscious thought, much less deliberation or cogitation. Still some such beliefs or commitments, even if only subsconscious or dispositional, must be operative, thus exercising the relevant second-order capacities, if the first-order belief is really to constitute reflective knowledge. More on this below.

In several places, I have defended a principle of exclusion as follows:

> IF one really knows that p and considers whether one does, AND one then justifiedly believes that for one to really know that p it must also be the case that q, THEN one must also be justified in believing that q.

Audi suggests that if we can find a way to rebut this principle of exclusion, then we can dispense with the requirement of an epistemic perspective, and can more easily resist skepticism. With this I agree, although I am left with two problems. Firstly, I see no way to reject the principle of exclusion, not at least for knowledge with the reflective status perennially attractive to philosophers, and to the reflective more generally. Secondly, if we reject the principle of exclusion, we may succeed too well, making it a mystery how skepticism could have had the attraction that it has had for so long. It is by way of the principle of exclusion that one can best explain the impressive power of skeptical reasoning.

Finally, the principle of exclusion need not just stand on its own. It gains support from two principles, that of Ascent and that of Transfer, which I will now state. Aided by plausible auxiliary hypotheses, Ascent and Transfer together entail Exclusion.

ASCENT

If one really knows that p and one considers whether one does, then one must be justified in thinking that one does.

TRANSFER

If one is justified in believing X and in believing that for X to be the case Y must also be the case, then one must also be justified in believing Y.

EXCLUSION

IF one really knows that p and considers whether one does, AND one then justifiedly believes that for one to really know that p it must also be the case that q, THEN one must also be justified in believing that q.

I can see no way to rebut this reasoning, whose conclusion, the exclusion principle, supports a skeptical position. While agreeing with Audi that, unless we can reject the exclusion principle, skepticism is attractive indeed, I doubt that the principle could ever be rejected plausibly enough, and would myself seek a response to skepticism along another avenue.

Klein by contrast joins Audi in seeking a way to reject the principle, and questions its supportive reasoning by rejecting the ascent principle. My use of "really" in that principle is meant to suggest that the sort of knowledge involved is of a higher level than the animal knowledge requiring only that one's belief track the truth, or be formed reliably, whether or not one appreciates any of this. Ascent therefore postulates a status of real knowledge requiring one's belief to be on a higher epistemic level, to which one is denied access if unable to affirm that one does know, not even when one consciously ponders the question.

I defend this stance by comparing the three pairs of attitudes that open up once one consciously ponders whether one knows in believing that p, provided one retains one's belief that p. The three are: affirmation, denial, and conscious suspension of belief. Which of these is most rationally coherent? The first, say I, but Klein demurs. Let's see why.

First we need to distinguish two questions: (a) Which of these three pairs enjoys the greatest internal coherence, the greatest coherence between the two members of the pair in abstraction from anything else in the mind of the believer? (b) Which of these three pairs enjoys the greatest coherence within the mind of the believer, as it now stands, with its total body of beliefs, experiences, and anything else that may bear on the coherence of a mind at a time?

Klein focuses on the second of these questions. His doubt that affirmation that one knows yields the most coherent pair amounts to a doubt that this pair will automatically fit most coherently in the overall mind of the believer. He reasons that the believer may have good reason to doubt that he is a reliable believer on the subject matter of the question whether p. Given this, it would seem most coherent for the believer to suspend judgment with regard to whether he knows in believing that p.

That point seems clearly right. However, my claim was not that the first pair (*believing that p*, and *believing that one knows in so believing*, upon consciously considering this question) is the pair that then fits most coherently within the overall mind of the believer. In other words, my claim concerned not question (b), of the two recently distinguished; my claim concerned rather question (a). That being so, how then does my claim bear on whether S's belief that p attains the status of real knowledge? If some other pair fits more coherently within S's mind at the time, despite its two members being in isolation less coherent with each other, how then can we draw any conclusion that S needs to endorse his own belief as knowledge if that belief is to attain the higher level of *real* knowledge?

Here is a way to draw that conclusion. Why might it now be more coherent for you to suspend judgment on whether you know that p than it would be to affirm that you do know? If the reason is that broached by Klein, namely that you might now have good reason to doubt your reliability on the question whether p, then it seems to me we can still conclude that you are falling short of real knowledge in believing that p. For consider your situation: there you are believing that p at the same time that upon consciously considering whether you know in so believing, your most coherent stance, if you are to retain your belief that p, would be to suspend judgment on whether you know. And the reason why this is your most coherent stance, within your overall body of beliefs and commitments at the time, is that you justifiedly, rationally believe yourself unreliable on the subject matter of whether p (you take your beliefs on that subject matter, given how they are formed, to have no better than an even chance of being right). Or, at a minimum, you have no rational basis for affirming your reliability, and must at best suspend judgment on the matter.

It seems to me that in such a situation your belief that p would itself fall short epistemically; it would not ascend to the epistemic heights required for reflective knowledge. Consider now an arbitrary case where you must settle for one of the *internally* less coherent pairs, those that pair your belief that p with either suspension or denial on whether you know in so believing. I suggest that in any such case you would fall short in your belief that p, and that this is so even in the cases where the pair that combines belief with suspension would fit more coherently within the overall mind of the believer at the time.

What, more generally, is the place of coherence in epistemology? What is its place in an account of human knowledge? How does coherence help us attain better-justified beliefs? We get two rather different takes on this from Goldman, on one side, and Allen Habib and Keith Lehrer, on the other. For Goldman coherence aids epistemic justification but only through its role in a reliable process of belief formation:

> It isn't coherence *per se* – a certain relationship between the contents of one's beliefs and/or perceptual experiences – that contributes toward justification and hence toward "superior" knowledge. The coherence in question must be detected by a reliable process or method. But that seems to suggest that even in the domain of coherence, what really does the epistemic work is reliable processes.

By contrast Habib and Lehrer suggest a *defeasibility constraint* on epistemically relevant *coherence*. This is a requirement "that a target belief that coheres with a system of beliefs can be defended by the system against [all] objections to the belief." This constraint, they argue, will make coherentism more defensible as a general account of knowledge, or at least of reflective knowledge.

On one hand, then, is the view that coherence does none of the epistemic work, reliability doing it all. On the other hand is the view that coherence does all, or nearly all, of the epistemic work, once supplemented with the defensibiity constraint and with the further requirement that the belief system be true.

Here I aim first to clarify the proper role of coherence in epistemology, hoping this will help us to resolve the disagreement before us.

Clearly, the mere fact that a set of propositions coheres logically does little to render justified one's belief in any of its member propositions. This seems obvious, and analogous to a closely related fact: namely, that even if a certain conclusion follows validly from certain premises, this might do little to render justified one's belief in that conclusion. At a minimum, one would need to believe the premises. But even this would not suffice, if one failed to discern how the conclusion follows logically from those premises. And even this may fall short, if one does not *draw* that conclusion from those premises, once having discerned how it follows. That is to say, one must not only believe the premises; one must also *deduce* the conclusion from those premises.

Something quite similar applies to coherence. It is not enough that a certain set of propositions cohere; this will not suffice to render justified one's belief in any of them. At a minimum one must also believe the other members of the coherent set. And, moreover, analogously to the case of deduction, one must also believe each member at least in part on the basis of the other beliefs in the coherent set.[31]

This last requirement shows the epistemically relevant coherence, the kind that helps enhance the epistemic status of the coherent beliefs, to be more than mere logical consistency. One would not believe the members of a logically consistent set on the basis of their mere logical consistency with each other. Compare the special case of just two propositions that one knows to be mutually logically consistent. Even if one had some independent reason to believe one of them, this enhanced status would not rub off on the second proposition merely through the fact, even the perceived fact, that it is logically consistent with the first. Coherence is more than just consistency, then, and seems more plausibly to involve relations of entailment, or at least probabilification. The importance of explanatory coherence in particular has been broadly recognized. And note how the explanatory coherence of a body of beliefs comports with its providing the subject a corresponding yield of understanding. The cement that binds beliefs Bp and Bq in that body coherently would be a further belief of the form B(p because q) or B(q because p). And such a belief would embody some measure of understanding as to why p or as to why q. Therefore, the value of such coherence, explanatory coherence, is allied to the value of understanding.

Consider, moreover, how explanatory induction, or inference to the best explanation, is thought to render a conclusion credible or at least to enhance its credibility. This fits nicely with a commitment to the reliability of such induction, i.e., with a belief that such inferences are to some degree epistemically reliable, or enhance the likelihood that we would get it right in believing the conclusion. Already Descartes argues in line with this idea that if we are able to make perfect sense of a theretofore indecipherable tome by interpreting it as in a one-off alphabet (each letter read as the one a slot forward except for Z, which is read as A), this makes it likely that in truth that is the code employed in the writing of that tome. And he then suggests that his scientific principles have a similar status *vis-à-vis* the book of nature, and gain correspondingly in credibility, in the credibility of the claim that they are not only explanatory but true.

Already Aristotle had said: "Men do not think they know a thing unless they have grasped the 'why' of it" (*Physics* II, ch. 3; compare *Metaphysics* V, ch. 2). This is hard to defend for sheer perceptual intake, and for animal knowledge, but comports with a more demanding sort of "reflective" knowledge. What is more, such reflective knowledge is also plausibly enhanced by the subject's ability to defend their belief in the "arena of reflection," particularly when the question arises as to why one should expect him to be right in the target belief, as to what might secure the truth of that belief. Note how answering this question with truth will require the believer to draw on certain perspectival resources as to the source of that belief and the reliability of that source in the circumstances.

The point transcends Aristotle's epistemology, being also deeply relevant to Descartes's, or so I would argue. Thus consider how the reasoning might go:

(1) I know that p if and only if I know myself to be right in thinking that p.
(2) In order to really know that I am indeed right in so thinking (that I think correctly in so thinking, that I think with truth in so thinking), I need some explanation of why I am right in so thinking, of what makes it more than just an accident that I am indeed right.
(3) I need therefore some account of how it is that I *would* get it right about the subject matter in question given my relevant constitution and circumstances.
(4) And this will require some account of how I am so constituted as to be truth-reliable about such subject matter in such circumstances.

A belief constitutes not just animal but reflective knowledge, then, only under a supporting perspective by the subject, who must have some awareness of the source of that belief and the reliability of that source. This will add a measure of epistemically relevant coherence to that subject's mind. And it will do so through a kind of distinctive explanatory coherence, as it comes in tandem with the subject's ability to explain how the relevant belief is bound to be true, given its source.

My view of reflective knowledge hence involves a distinctive requirement of epistemic perspective, allied to the belief's defensibility in the arena of reflection. This is of course a matter of degree, since one might be able to defend one's belief more or less well. A high degree of defensibility would require one to know that one knows in so believing. This would defend the belief along various epistemically relevant dimensions: truth, safety (how easily one might then go wrong in so believing), rational justification, and reliability of one's operative intellectual virtues (faculties, sources, methods). And note how if one is really to know that one knows, one must then be able to explain how it is that one gets it right in so believing, if we are to believe Aristotle's implicit suggestion that one knows (*really* knows? *best* knows? *reflectively* knows?) that such and such only if one grasps why it is that such and such.

Even if we claim such perspectival coherence to import an epistemic status distinctive of *reflective* and not just animal knowledge, this is compatible with the Cartesian view that basing a belief thus on explanatory coherence makes it more likely to be true. This I find the most attractive position, that there are two separable reasons why basing a belief in explanatory coherence enhances it epistemically: first, because this is a source with some measure of reliability; second, because coherence imports understanding, a source of epistemic value beyond mere truth, one that distinctively enhances the epistemic standing of the beliefs whose existence and correctness one thereby understands.

What I have said so far addresses at least partially the question raised by Goldman as to the place of coherence in epistemology, and whether it has any distinctive place at all, or whether all of the value that it imports is assignable simply to its inherent reliability as a source.

Why not join Habib and Lehrer at the opposite extreme, by agreeing that relevant coherence suffices on its own to explain all epistemic status, or at least all the epistemic status proper to a belief that constitutes reflective knowledge? Well, what is the coherence that for them is epistemically relevant? This turns out to be a coherence that satisfies their *defeasibility constraint* on epistemically relevant *coherence*: "that a target belief that coheres with a system of beliefs can be defended by the system against [all] objections to the belief."

I find these ideas congenial, and nothing commits me to rejecting every form that they might take. Once we understand what "objections" are and what is required for a proper "defense" against an objection, it may well be that there is a substantial overlap between these ideas and my own formulations. It all depends on how the key notions are understood. In order to see better into this issue, however, we do need to see what might figure as an "objection" to a particular belief, as held by a particular subject. In fact this concept is so understood by Habib and Lehrer as to raise some serious questions for their view.

Three things are suggested as potential "objections" against which a belief must be defensible if it is to constitute knowledge: first, that the belief is not formed in an appropriate way or derived from a reliable source; second, that the circumstances in which the belief is formed are not propitious to the formation of true beliefs; and, third, that the belief is not properly connected to experience. Accordingly, in order for the system to exhibit appropriate coherence, it must include the resources to defend against these objections. And this is said to involve its containing beliefs that counter the objections: beliefs in the respective negations of the three objections.[32]

Two questions come to mind. First of all, objections can apparently be framed in epistemically normative terms: thus, see "appropriate way," and "propitious circumstances," and "proper" connection with experience. So, presumably it would be an epistemic objection to a belief that it does not constitute knowledge. (Someone says "*p*," expressing thus the corresponding belief. We *object*: "You don't know that.") But this would seem to trivialize the proposed account, according to which in order to know that *p*, in so believing, you must have within your belief system true denials of all potential objections to that belief. If, as suggested, it is a potential objection that you do not know in so believing, then of course your system must contain the true belief that you do know, and this *will* guarantee that once you satisfy the requirements of this account you will know. But this trivializes the account. Indeed, one could then replace it with a much simpler view: *One knows that p iff one can thus defend against the objection that one does not know in believing that p.*

On the other hand, there is a curiously opposed sort of problem. What is required in order to know that *p*, let us suppose, is that one be able to answer potential objections to the belief that *p*. And consider now a belief whose presence and truth are required for such successful defense against a potential objection. Objections to *this* belief would themselves seem objections to the original belief, as held then by that believer. But this threatens a vicious regress. For the system must now contain not only true beliefs that defend against first-level objections to the original belief, but also true beliefs that defend against (second-level) potential objections against the first-level defensive beliefs. And so on. No belief will hence amount to knowledge unless it is embedded in an infinitely complex actual corpus. And this lies beyond human capabilities.

So my doubts about the proposal are (a) that it reduces to the trivial alternative that one knows that p iff one knows that p; and (b) that if in some non-*ad hoc* way Habib and Lehrer are able to rule out of consideration any such objection as "But you don't know that!", so as to avoid the triviality fate, they still face a potentially vicious regress. For consider one's defending beliefs against objections to one's belief that p, and call these "defenders." The problem is that objections to defenders would seem to count indirectly as objections to the original belief, so that a full defense of the original belief against all potential objections to it would require a mind housing an actual infinity of defending beliefs. None of our minds would seem spacious enough for that.

6 Philosophical Skepticism

Reply to Barry Stroud

Stroud doubts that we can attain a philosophically satisfying account of our knowledge of the external world if we think that our knowledge is based on but goes beyond what lies open to our direct awareness. If we view our perceptual knowledge as does the indirect realist, then we are hard put to see how we could gain any such philosophically satisfying understanding. This is brought home if we compare our situation with that of a crystal-ball gazer who thinks that what he can see in the ball enables him to tell about matters beyond. Such beliefs could be reliably acquired if their subject matter were suitably related to what can be seen in the ball. Similarly, on the indirect realist picture we can know about external reality if the experiential basis for such beliefs is suitably related to their subject matter. In each case, *if* there is a suitable relation between our basis and what we believe on that basis, then our beliefs repose truth-reliably on that basis. But if we do not know that there is such a relation between our basis and what we believe on that basis, then we attain no philosophically satisfying understanding of how we know on that basis.

It is hard to disagree with that analysis. If our acceptance of an account of a certain subject matter is to give us real understanding of that subject matter, then it must at a minimum be true, but more than that it must be something we know to be true. Mere beliefs about how people know what they do will not constitute understanding, will not give "a satisfactory explanation of human perceptual knowledge." Moreover,

> even knowing that people know things in that way would not be enough, if knowing is simply a matter of fulfilling the conditions Sosa's theory says are sufficient for knowledge. All the theorist can appeal to in accounting for his own knowledge as more than confident belief are the perceptual experiences he knows he has had, the beliefs he holds, which he believes to be the result of those experiences, and the theory of knowledge that he also believes. That theory says that *if* one further condition holds, then he does know what he thinks he knows. And he believes that that further condition holds. But still he remains in no better position for understanding himself as knowing what he thinks he knows than someone who reflects on his knowledge with equal confidence and in an equally satisfactory way and yet knows nothing at all.

Or so we are told; and here we have reached the distinctive core of Stroud's particular form of skeptical doubt. About his distinctive view, we must ask: Why might it be that even our knowledge that people know things in a certain way would still not yield philosophically satisfying understanding of how they know? Why is it that the theory we know to be true as to how it is that they know still fails to give us any such understanding?

> The question is whether holding such a theory leaves anyone in a position to gain a satisfactory understanding of knowledge of the world, even if he fulfills the conditions Sosa's theory says are sufficient for knowledge. Could someone in such a position come to recognize himself as knowing, and not merely confidently believing, perhaps even truly, that sense perception is a way of getting knowledge of the world and crystal-ball gazing is not?
>
> I think that, on the understanding of perception that appears to be involved in Sosa's question ..., the answer is "no." On that view, what we are aware of in perception is restricted to features of our perceptual experiences. The external facts we know as a result of those experiences are nothing we ever perceive to be so. What we get in sense perception therefore bears the same relation to the world we think we know by that means as what is seen in crystal-ball gazing bears to the world the gazers think it gives them knowledge of.

We do believe that our perceptual experiences are reliably connected with what we think we know on their basis.

> But anyone who thinks that all it takes to have satisfactory understanding of perceptual knowledge is to conclude by *modus ponens* that we know by perception that there are external things would have to concede that the crystal-ball gazers have a satisfactory understanding of crystal-ball gazing knowledge. They could draw the corresponding conclusion equally confidently from what they believe about themselves.

Remarkably, this is said to be so despite the fact that, while the contents of our experiences *are* reliably connected with the beliefs that they yield, the contents of the crystal balls have *no* reliable connection with the truth of their deliverances. Thus "there are no reliable connections between what people see in crystal balls and what goes on in the world beyond them. If the gazers could raise their eyes from their crystal balls and see what is so in the world around them, they could see that too." So, while we can know our perceptual beliefs to be reliably formed, the gazers cannot know their gaze-derived beliefs to be thus reliable, and cannot know that they know things about the world around them by basing them on any such reliable basis.

Stroud's reasoning now is hard to follow. He had explicitly granted, at least for the sake of argument, my externalist account of knowledge. So his doubts do not target that account. He is willing to assume that perceptual knowledge is a matter of perceptual beliefs prompted truth-reliably by perceptual experiences. How then can he coherently suppose that if we conclude by *modus ponens* that we know about the world around us through perception, given that our perceptual faculties are reliable, then we would be in the predicament he alleges? He alleges that we then "would have to concede that the crystal-ball gazers have a satisfactory understanding of crystal-ball gazing knowledge. They could draw the corresponding conclusion equally confidently from what they believe about themselves." But this is refuted by a crucial difference that Stroud and I both recognize: namely, that we know our perceptual faculties to be reliable whereas the gazers believe but do not know their gazing to be reliable. So, how can we be in an equally good epistemic position to understand how we know, if we *do* know but they *do not* know about the reliability of the faculties involved?

Stroud in any case rejects my appeal to a reliable sensory basis for understanding how our perceptual beliefs can constitute knowledge, and indeed traces to that particular feature of my account its failure as a philosophically satisfying account of our perceptual knowledge. His preferred account would explain rather that we can often enough just *directly see that we can see* some external fact to be so, and that we can in this way know how we know about the world around us. Circularity is here not a threat, since circularity occurs in reasoning, and here there is no reasoning, but only plain seeing.

I find three problems with this interesting approach. Let us grant, first, that some perceptual knowledge is direct in not depending on other perceptual knowledge or distinguishable perceptual experience. Even so, our knowledge that someone else knows something perceptually does not seem plausibly a case in point. Second, even if *sometimes* we know how others know the world around them because we *perceive*, for some external fact, *that they perceive it* (that they perceive that external fact), perception is not the only source of our knowledge of the external world. Unaided perception is, on the contrary, a very limited source of such knowledge, if we consider the vast bulk of our stored knowledge, and the dependence of this knowledge on the likes of inference, memory, and testimony. So it remains to be seen how we can know about our general possession of such knowledge, including our non-perceptual knowledge. We would hardly be able to perceive directly that we enjoy much of our mnemonic or inferential or testimonial knowledge.

That gives rise to a third problem for Stroud, whose reasoning culminates as follows.

> The conclusion I would draw from all this is that in order to achieve a satisfactory understanding of our knowledge of the world we must set aside or overcome the idea that the deliverances of perception even at its best are limited to the character of one's perceptual experiences alone. . . . Perceptual knowledge of external things is seen [in externalist accounts like Sosa's] as a combination of some prior knowledge which is not knowledge of external things plus something else. That is what I think leaves us in the plight I have described.

The further problem concerns the vast bulk of our knowledge that, while based on perceptual knowledge concurrent or past, is not itself perceptual knowledge. A lot of our knowledge *is* after all in some way a "combination" of some prior knowledge plus something else. Moreover, the supporting facts now or earlier perceived to be so and the knowledge supported at one or another remove by our perception of those facts, are not generally connected in ways that we can see or otherwise perceive. If we recall the main objection brought by Stroud against externalist reliabilism concerning perception, his own view seems now ironically subject to that same objection. For the vast bulk of our knowledge of the external world presumably goes beyond the perceptual knowledge on which at some depth it is based, and yet we cannot just perceive that the content of that knowledge is related appropriately to the perceptual knowledge that forms its basis. It remains to be seen how, despite that fact, we do know all those things about the world around us that we know non-perceptually, and how we can know in a philosophically satisfying way that we do have any such knowledge.[33]

7 Praxis and Epistemology

Reply to Paul Moser and Nicholas Rescher

Paul Moser and Nicholas Rescher both place praxis at the heart of epistemology:

> [What] . . . is it that justifies making presumptions, seeing that they are not established truths? The answer is that this is not so much a matter of evidentially *probative* considerations as of procedurally *practical* ones. Presumptions arise in contexts where we have questions and need answers. And when sufficient evidence for a *conclusive* answer is lacking, we must, in the circumstances, settle for a more or less *plausible* one. It is a matter of *faute de mieux*, of this or nothing (or at any rate nothing better). . . . And so presumption affords yet another instance where practical considerations play a leading role on the stage of our cognitive and communicative practice. (Rescher, "Sosa and Epistemic Justification," p. 152 paragraph of section 6)

> Suppose we form the settled intention to use "truth-indicator" and "epistemic reason" in such a way that a visual experience of an apparent X in a situation with no accessible defeaters is a (possibly defeasible) truth-indicator and thus an epistemic reason for a visual proposition or belief that X exists. This intention, given its meaning-conferring role for us, could then serve as a directly accessible semantic truth-maker for our ascription of an epistemic reason for a visual belief that X exists. It would then be *part of what we mean* by 'epistemic reason' that *such* an ascription captures an epistemic reason for a visual belief that X exists. . . . Our semantic intentions . . . thus serve as non-doxastic truth-makers for a claim that a certain kind of situation includes one's having an epistemic reason for a visual belief. (Moser, "Skepticism Undone?" p. 142)

For both thinkers, at bottom we *decide* what are good reasons for belief. For Moser we do so indirectly, by deciding to mean something by 'reason', for Rescher the decision is a matter of adopting a belief-forming policy. Let us explore these ideas, which are advanced as alternatives to my preferred objectivist, truth-involving, circularity-embracing epistemology.

Rarely if ever do we institute a non-linguistic fact by linguistic fiat. Even socially constituted facts normally go beyond sheer linguistic stipulations or conventions. Perhaps in a certain dialect of ours it can become true that someone is Skip simply because of the intentions of certain socially related folks. But that is a rare case. In the vast majority of cases, if it is true that p, this does not become so as a necessary outcome of anyone's intentions to use language a certain way, nor does the fact that p then depend on any such intentions. Thus, even if there had been no English speakers, apples would have been different from oranges, though there would not have been the English sentence, with its present meaning, in which to express that fact: namely, 'Apples are different from oranges.' English speakers and their intentions to use these words in certain ways are not determinative of that fact.

Nor does it seem much more plausible that through our linguistic intentions we determine the truth of epistemic normative facts as to what can serve as a reason for a given belief. That dark clouds truth-indicate impending rain, i.e., indicate that most likely it will soon rain, is not something we can stipulate into being. It depends on the objective facts as to how likely rain is, out there in the world, or in a certain region of its space-time, given dark clouds. And the same would seem to be so with regard to what our sensory experience truth-indicates.

Something similar holds even of normative vocabulary, such as 'epistemic reason'. Whether R is an epistemic reason for believing P lies beyond our individual or even collective power or authority to institute. We can of course institute, if only by brute and explicit stipulation, that 'epistemic reason' will mean *epistemic reason*. But it is a far cry from this to instituting that R in particular is an epistemic reason.

Nor does it seem much more plausible that we can just decide to follow a policy to believe certain things based on a certain basis, and expect *thereby* to have brought it about that believing those things on that basis is now epistemically justified. We lack the power and authority to dictate or even legislate what can provide good epistemic reason for what. Matters of logical necessity, for example, and the rational relations that they help induce, are not relevantly under our control.

Why should it be any different with regard to the epistemic relations between our sensory experiences and our perceptual beliefs? Whether a given sensory experience E gives reason to believe that p, however tentatively, is not up to us. If E does constitute an epistemic reason to so believe, this we must learn to accept, avoiding the futility of trying to change it. Whether it does constitute such a reason or not, moreover, cannot be wholly divorced from how likely the truth of <p> is given the fact of E, at least how likely that is in our normal or standard setting. Our question is, recall, whether E gives good *epistemic* reason for so believing, and this E could hardly do if, for example, it obviously entails that not-p, nor even, one would think, if (of course defeasibly) it renders <not-p> highly likely. But whether E makes <p> likely is not likely to be something we can stipulate by personal or collective fiat.

Accordingly, I cannot see the solution to deep skepticism in praxis. It is not only the world beyond us that lies mostly beyond the reach of our will. Even more thoroughly and obviously, surely, are the truths of logic discovered, not instituted or otherwise created. I am able to see no sufficient reason to suppose the structure of reasons to be malleable at will.

True, Moser argues explicitly if briefly for decoupling the standing of R as an epistemic reason for <p> from its so much as probabilifying <p>, even weakly. However, his reasoning overlooks a way for us to retain that coupling while still granting the internalist his intuitively persuasive claim that the demon's victim is epistemically justified despite the massive unreliability of his ways of forming beliefs.[34]

8 Epistemic Value

Reply to Linda Zagzebski

According to Zagzebski, I argue for the conclusion that there are the following four kinds of epistemic value:

(a) The value of the truth of a belief.
(b) The praxical, extrinsic value of true believing where the agent brings about the belief.

(c) The eudaimonist, intrinsic value of true believing when getting the truth is attributable to the agent as his own deed.
(d) The extrinsic value of one's intellectual performance, whether or not that performance leads to the truth, when that performance would produce the truth if properly installed in a suitable environment.

She thinks this is "more complicated than necessary," but takes my proposal to suggest very naturally another view, one that provides a more unified account with three components:

(a) The truth of a belief is valuable, perhaps intrinsically so.
(b) Virtuous intellectual performances are extrinsically valuable (derived from the value of truth). This is a value performances can have whether or not they lead to the truth on a given occasion.
(c) The organic unity of a true belief produced by a virtuous intellectual performance is better than the value of truth plus the value of the performance. That is why knowledge is better than mere true belief.

According to Zagzebski, finally, I must give up "epistemic value monism," *the thesis that any epistemic value other than the truth of a belief derives from the good of truth.*

However, it is impossible for me to "give up" this thesis, since I never held it, not if I understand it properly. The reason why I hesitate here, is that I am not sure what "the value of truth" or "the good of truth" amounts to. Would this be the thesis that all things true are thereby to some degree valuable or good? If so, then I never have believed in epistemic value monism. That thesis implies that true sentences have value, as do true inscriptions, as do true propositions. But there is no value resident in each true proposition simply in virtue of its truth. Supposing it is true that there are n motes of dust on my desktop now, the being true of this particular proposition seems devoid of value, especially when we consider its necessary equivalence with the proposition that there are indeed that many motes of dust there. The former would seem not to be able to exceed the latter in value, yet the latter has no value that I can appreciate.

When externalists and reliabilists insist on a truth connection in understanding epistemic value, then, they must steer clear of any notion that truth *per se*, wherever it may be found, imports intrinsic or fundamental epistemic value, value in terms of which other epistemic value can be defined or explained. What then is it that might involve truth and more plausibly have the role of fundamental epistemic value?

One possibility is true belief, and this is most likely what Zagzebski intended all along. Indeed true belief *per se* may well have fundamental epistemic value. It may well be that we prefer that our beliefs be true rather than not true, and no deeper reason may be required for that preference to be acceptably rational. Another way to possess the truth goes beyond merely believing it, however; more is now required, namely that the truth in question be believed aptly and virtuously (through intellectual virtue). A belief can be true through superstition, or brainwashing, or happenstance, and would then be an epistemically lesser belief, by comparison with a belief that is not only true but also apt through the exercise of cognitive virtue. This latter sort of belief is what I have focused on in the work under examination, and it is a sort of belief that seems to me plausibly possessed of epistemically intrinsic, fundamental value.

How, exactly, does Zagzebski disagree? She claims that such a belief, one that is true through virtue, is an organic unity, and that it need not be regarded as intrinsically valuable. I am not quite sure how to understand the term 'intrinsic value' as it is used here. In any case, on my own usage of that term, there is no incoherence in an organic unity's having intrinsic value. All I mean by intrinsic value is value that is fundamental and not wholly constituted through relation to something else that has value. Thus *efficiently instrumental* value is extrinsic, not intrinsic, since it is wholly constituted through its causal efficacy in bringing about something else with its own independent value.

To say that something is an organic unity is, as I understand it, to say that it has a value that is not just the sum of the values of its parts. Thus, it can be that the way in which the parts are related, temporally or causally, imports an extra boost of value for the whole, beyond the value contributed by the parts severally. And this fits exactly my proposal of the eudaimonist epistemically intrinsic value of true, apt, virtuous believing, as something with its own epistemically intrinsic value, beyond the value imported by the truth of that belief. When I suggest that such believing has its own epistemically intrinsic value, I mean that it has fundamental epistemic value not definable or explicable wholly in terms of other, independent epistemic values, such as the value, if any, of the mere truth of that believing. Here it is still possession of the *truth* that is fundamentally valuable, but it must be possession of a special sort: namely, apt, virtuous possession.

Such possession of the truth may be intrinsically, fundamentally valuable, compatibly with its being an organic unity. Indeed the latter would seem entailed by the former. If the value of such possession were reducible to the independent values of the parts severally, then the value of the whole could hardly be an intrinsic, fundamental value. On the contrary, it would reduce to a sum of the independent values of the parts severally.

Therefore, if I have understood her key terms properly, it seems to me that Zagzebski's proposal is in line with my own and indeed I am finding it hard to distinguish the two. Nor is hers distinguished by allowing that true, apt, virtuous believing may also have value through its place in the life of someone who fares well. For I have no need to deny this, and no inclination to do so. What I would deny is that the whole epistemic value of that true, apt, believing would be exhausted by its contribution to such a life. For such a believing would retain intrinsic, fundamental epistemic value even if it were part of a life that was overall quite unhappy, and even if its contribution to the happiness of that life were overall minimal or even negative. Of course, it may be that – having intrinsic, fundamental epistemic value – such apt, virtuous believings do constitutively contribute to the value of the hosting life, even if instrumentally they are deleterious to the overall happiness of that life.

Although I cannot here go into the matter in much depth, I would like to record some skepticism about that idea, limited and modest as it is. The skepticism sets in when I consider the sort of epistemic value that is constitutive of knowledge, the sort that is constitutive of the safety, aptness, and virtue of an instance of believing, and when I ask myself whether that sort of value is the sort of value that in ethics or value theory would be regarded as intrinsic. I must say I rather doubt it. When we evaluate a belief in respect of whether it is a good candidate for knowledge, we consider whether it satisfies certain conditions such that it is better that a belief satisfy those conditions than that it not do so, other things being equal. But from this it does not follow that it is a good thing that the belief exist, whether satisfying the conditions or not, nor does it even follow that it is good that there, then and there, be such a belief satisfying the conditions. From the fact that it is better that there be a belief that *p* satisfying the conditions than that there be a belief that *p* violating the conditions, it does not follow that it is better that there be a belief that *p* satisfying the conditions than that there fail to be such a belief altogether. And the latter would seem necessary for a conditions-satisfying belief that *p* to have intrinsic value *tout court*, as opposed to simply having fundamental *epistemic* value, i.e., epistemic value not wholly constituted by the relations of such a believing to other things with their own epistemic value.

Notes

1 Special thanks go to John Greco, both editor and critic, who contributed enormously every step of the way.
2 More bitter yet the outright refutations, though I don't happen to recall any at the moment.
3 Actually, a more complex condition is closer to the truth, one that refers to the basis for the belief, or the way or "method" through which it is formed, so that a belief is *safe* iff its actual basis is such that it would be held on that basis only if true. (This move is similar to Nozick's introduction of his "methods.") For simplicity, here I stick to the first approximation in the text.
4 This is an additional explanation for why we tend to require sensitivity, additional to the contraposition-confusion explanation suggested earlier. Of course there can be more than one reason why people are attracted to an erroneous belief.
5 I require that the sentence do its conditioning "expressively" in order to avoid having to declare the following a conditional: 'The match's being dry is a necessary condition of its lighting when struck'. This does after all condition something on something else, but it does so "referentially," not expressively.
6 Even if DeRose's way to construe safety is also acceptable, even if no more (and no less) straightforward as the English correlate of '$B(p) \rightarrow p$', I prefer to avoid it because it pragmatically implicates the falsity of its antecedent.
7 Moreover, according to my definition of 'conditional' above, the following is a conditional, since it expressively conditions something on something else as a sufficient condition (at least probabilistically): *It would not be so that p unless it were so that q*. Compare its sensitivity correlate (which by my definition counts as its contrapositive): *It would not be so that not-q unless it were so that not-p*. The whole discussion about tracking, sensitivity, safety, skepticism, and contextualism could be formulated in terms of these two conditionals, with the first defined as the safety conditional and the second as the sensitivity conditional. Thus might we avoid issues about pragmatics and contraposition raised in DeRose's discussion. It is, however, crucial to distinguish 'It would not be so that *p* unless it were so that *q*' in my preferred, safety, disambiguation, from 'If it were not so that *q*, then it would not be so that *p*', the sensitivity disambiguation. And, indeed, the hard-to-discern ambiguity of my suggested locution may help explain at least some of the skeptic's ill-earned plausibility. (My "Relevant Alternatives, Contextualism Included," forthcoming in *Philosophical Studies* (cited as RA), briefly explains how this can come about, with a case study as an appendix.
8 As does my RA.
9 This section counters a kind of broad internalism and Radical Foundationalism, as advocated by three representatives, the three Richards: Foley, Fumerton, and Feldman, RFs all.

10 Compare Tertullian's *Certum est, quia impossibile*, "It is certain because it is impossible." And there's more: *Et mortuus est dei filius; credibile prorsus est, quia ineptum est. Et sepultus resurrexit; certum est, quia impossibile.* "The Son of God died: it is *immediately* credible – because it is silly. He was buried, and rose again: it is certain – because it is impossible." All from *De carne Christi*, ch. 5, 4.

11 It seems to me that the folk would naturally understand such speculation, and would not hesitate to attribute knowledge and proper belief formation to the superbeings. So I doubt that one could plausibly cleave to Alvin Goldman's hardline anthropocentric epistemology, according to which folksily we recognize only homebound justification that rigidly binds virtue to our lists of what works in the actual world. Cf. "Epistemic Folkways and Scientific Epistemology," in his collection, *Liaisons: Philosophy Meets the Cognitive and Social Sciences* (Cambridge, MA: MIT/Bradford, 1991).

12 That there is the distinction, and that the internalist side of it is more important is claimed by Laurence BonJour in his contributions to Larry BonJour and Ernest Sosa, *Epistemic Justification* (Oxford: Blackwell, 2003).

13 This point may also be found in Alvin Goldman's chapter in this volume.

14 But he is also interested in a lesser epistemic status, to be defined by relaxing the demanding standards of high internalism. And he has some interesting ideas about how this might be done.

15 For a further critique of foundationalist internalism, along these same lines, see my reply to BonJour in BonJour and Sosa.

16 Such terminology can mislead, however; I myself find it less misleading to speak directly of *experiencing consciously, vividly, and focally*, though I suppose this is the same or very close to what Feldman means by *attending*.

17 Which then requires a sort of deliberation, a weighing of pros and cons, and a striking of a balance, in ways nicely brought out in Thomas Kuhn's "The Essential Tension," in his book so titled (University of Chicago Press, 1977).

18 Audi's distinction between epistemic powers and epistemic virtues is attractive in this connection. Powers might depend to a greater extent on peripheral modules than could virtues, since these latter would require assessment in the broader light of possibly conflicting considerations for and against.

19 Kripke's example figured in widely delivered but never published lectures critical of tracking accounts of knowledge.

20 But what of a case where we see a *small* dog and come to know thereby that we see a dog? Here again I would argue that there is no concept of *smallness* in play that is detachable from our concept of a dog. The smallness we see is *smallness-for-a-dog*. So here again, as in the dachshund case we believe it is a small dog based on a unified gestalt of *small dog*, and infer from this that it's a dog we see.

21 Sensory experiences may plausibly be assigned content even when they do not give rise to belief, as when it looks to one as if the oar in the water is bent. The visual experience is here correctly characterizable in terms of such propositional content, even when one has no temptation to believe, consciously or subconsciously, that the oar is really bent.

22 This can even be applied to Reid's faculty of introspection or reflection, whose deliverances would be states of being ostensibly conscious or aware that one is in such and such a mental state. But it is unclear to what extent it may apply to the case of memory. Reid unfortunately does not distinguish personal, experiential memory (which can be viewed as analogous to external perception) from retentive memory (which cannot be so viewed, in important respects). Reid fails to recognize epistemically relevant differences between these cognitive subfaculties. Thus, while perceptual belief can be viewed as derived from perceptual experience with corresponding content (from "it looks as if here's something white and round," as experiential

premise, to "here's something white and round," as belief conclusion), there is nothing like this in retentive memory, which simply preserves a belief across time.

23 Reid is aware of this sort of issue: "I confess that, although I have, as I think, a distinct notion of the different kinds of evidence . . . yet I am not able to find any common nature to which they may all be reduced" (*Essays on the Intellectual Powers of Man*, in Thomas Reid, *Philosophical Works*, ed. H. M. Bracken (Hildesheim: Georg Olms, 1983), 2.20, p. 291).

24 But "validity" here is broader than just formal, logical validity, and includes also the kind of subjunctive validity that underwrites inferring that x is G from the perceived fact that it is F, a subjunctive validity that amounts to it being the case that anything F (in the relevant environment) would also be G. Even if ours is not the only sense one could reasonably assign to philosophers' terminology of "epistemic justification," moreover, it does seem one such sense.

25 Consider our implicit belief in principles, or habits, or other implicit commitments that guide our intellectual conduct. These are perhaps not "downstream from experience," and seem exceptions to our claim that assessments of epistemic justification are indirectly assessments of cognitive structures, mechanisms, and proceedings downstream from experience; but in any case much the same reasoning as above would still apply also to the evaluation of such implicit, belief-guiding commitments, which would still be intrinsic to the subject, and separable from the vagaries of her environment.

26 The point here would survive even if one granted that the "beliefs" at the end of the reasoning are indeed the same as the "beliefs" that serve as inputs to that reasoning. One could still defend such reasoning, so long as it results in conclusion beliefs that are somehow significantly *changed* from how they were as premises of that reasoning: for example, if the result is an explicitly conscious and integrated system of beliefs, this may be a valuable result of such "reasoning" despite the fact that the inputs to it involved the very beliefs, in implicit subconscious mode, that are now consciously integrated. This may still reasonably be regarded as a cognitively valuable result, adding some measure of cognitive virtue to the resulting beliefs.

27 G. E. Moore, "Certainty," in *Philosophical Papers* (New York: Collier Books, 1962).

28 G. E. Moore, "Proof of an External World," in *Philosophical Papers* (New York: Collier Books, 1962).

29 Quoted from p. 282 of my "Mythology of the Given," *History of Philosophy Quarterly* (1997).

30 As was argued earlier, in the reply to Audi, Greco, and Kornblith.

31 Compare my "Virtue Perspectivism: A Response to Foley and Fumerton" (*Philosophical Issues* (1994): 29–50; at p. 45: "[Some] . . . sort of awareness of the coherence of one's beliefs is required for justification. But this awareness may be constituted by the sensitivity to such coherence that one manifests by accepting one's system of beliefs (or a large enough fragment thereof) *partly in virtue of its coherence*, and by adjusting one's degree of assurance partly to the degree of coherence involved."

32 What they postulate is "a kind of coherence that is sufficiently constraining so that it requires of coherence that a target belief which is justified by a coherent background system of beliefs, or which coheres with that system, must be so strongly supported by the system that all objections to the belief can be answered. Thus, if it is an objection to the belief that it was not formed in appropriate way or derived from a reliable source, then the system must contain the belief that the forming was appropriate . . . or the source reliable. Similarly, if it is an objection to the belief that the circumstances in which it is formed are not propitious for the truth of the belief, then the system, to be coherent with the belief, must contain the belief that the circumstances are propitious. Finally, if it is an objection to the belief that it is not properly connected to experience, then, if the belief coheres with the system, it must contain the belief that the belief is so connected to experience."

33 For perception-transcendent, reason-dependent knowledge, then, we would seem to face three choices. Either we deny that there is any, or we affirm that there is some but deny that we can ever attain any philosophically satisfying understanding of it; otherwise, we must after all face the issue of vicious circularity.

34 Elsewhere, in discussing Chisholm's epistemic principles, I take up two main responses to the correlated problematic: Chisholm's decoupling of truth from reliability, and Sellars's flirtations with epistemic pragmatism. See "Human Knowledge, Animal and Reflective: A Response to Michael Williams," in *Aristotelian Society Supplementary Volumes* (2003).

Index

abilities, conditional analysis of, 264–7, 269, 270
acquaintance, 43
adroitness, 284
Alston, W., 76, 135
anti-realism
   and conceptual relativity, 201, 202–5, 206–13, 224–5, 228–9, 234, 235, 237, 240, 242, 245, 256–9
   and existential relativity, 201, 207, 208, 224–7, 229, 231, 232
   and mereological sums, 202, 212, 237, 240–1, 243, 258–9
   and mind-independent objects, 202, 237, 238
   and truth, 236
aptness, xxiii, 6, 14, 66, 140, 284–5
Aristotle, 7, 8, 181, 312, 313
Armstrong, D. M., 59
A-series, 249–51
Audi, R., 290, 309, 310
Ayer, A. J., 74, 257

barn façade problem, 20–1, 70, 292–3
Berkeley, G., 220, 222n12
Bishop, M., 134n17
blindsight, 101–2
BonJour, L., 15n13, 80, 88
Brandom, R., 126, 133–4n9, 178
Brentano, F., 194, 195
Broad, C. D., 253
Burge, T., 263

Cantor, G., 261n29
Carnap, R., 234, 239, 241, 243
Case, J., 242, 243
causation
   perspectival character of, 201, 205
   and reference, 201, 235
Chisholm, R., xxi, 87, 175, 177, 182, 185, 252, 253, 325n34
circularity, 106–7, 114–16, 123n7, 135–40, 165, 167, 168, 174, 317
Cohen, S., 41n14, 292, 293, 301, 302, 303
coherence, 6, 87, 88, 107–9, 174, 175, 309–15
coherentism
   and defeasibility constraint, 110–11, 311
   and epistemic perspectivism, 108, 110–11
   and justification, xvi–xviii
   and skepticism, 174–5, 184, 276, 280–2
content
   and dispositions, 266
   and existential statements, 208
   of mental states, 263
   and twin-earth problem, 263–4, 269–70
content externalism, 263, 264, 268, 270
contextualism
   and sensitivity, 35
   and skepticism, 22, 35–8, 40n9, 280–2
   Sosa's response to, 276–82
Czyzewska, M., 102

Davidson, D., 126, 133–4n9, 154, 159, 163–4n8, 176, 233, 243, 248n26, 263
definite descriptions, 215

DeRose, K., 276–82
Derrida, J., 159
Descartes, R., xv, 6, 14, 61, 73, 86, 87, 90, 96, 103, 112, 113, 119, 125n20, 149, 154, 181, 182, 188, 300, 301, 305, 306, 307, 308, 312, 237
Devitt, M., 235
Dewey, J., 154
Dreben, B., 240
Dretske, F., 16n15, 20, 22, 24, 119, 276, 280, 292

empiricism, 183, 185–7
epistemology, the task of, 174, 187–8
essences
  nominal, 209
  real, 209, 212
eudaimonia, 193, 195, 196, 198n9
Evans, G., 221n1
evidentialism, 145
evil-demon problem, 10, 12, 64, 107
  and new evil-demon problem, xxii, xxiii, 65–6, 67, 108, 110, 111, 193, 276, 278, 280, 284, 299
evolution, 155–61, 162n15, 163n12
exemplification, 203, 211, 249, 250, 257, 258
experience *see* sensory experience
externalism *see also* content externalism appeal of, 73–5
  and foundationalism, 81
  and internalism, 61, 72, 79, 123n5, 282–90
  and justification, xviii, xxii, xxiii, 13–14, 73–6, 80, 81, 282–90
  and reliabilism, 6, 178, 179

Feldman, R., 287–90
Fodor, J., 235
Foley, R., 282–5
form, 209, 210, 211, 213, 256, 259
foundationalism
  classical, xv, xvi, 6, 42, 43, 46, 285
  doxastic ascent arguments against, xviii
  and justification, xvi, 42, 43, 45, 47–9, 53, 58n10, 176
  moderate, 178
  and propositional justification, 43–4
  and sensory experience, 145, 146
Fumerton, R., 19, 285–7, 303
functionalism, 186

Geach, P., 204
generality problem, xxiv, 8, 97, 98–9, 100, 103
Gettier, E., 59, 70, 197, 282
Gettier problems, 59–61, 66, 67, 69–71, 83, 196, 197
Gibbon, E., 148
Ginet, C., 21n3
Glymour, C., 235
Goldman, A., 20, 59, 60, 70, 293, 309, 311, 313, 323n11
Greco, J., 15n11, 15–16n14, 198n12, 290, 292

Haack, S., 83
Habib, A., 309, 311, 314, 315
haecceities, 221n4, 252
Haugeland, J., 126, 133–4n9
Hayek, F. A., 163n14
Heller, M., 41n14
Hempel, C., 175, 176, 177, 179, 185
Hill, T., 102
Hume, D., xvi, 75, 82

identity
  of indiscernibles, 221n5
  and mereology, 239
  numerical vs. qualitative, 217
  and persistence, 210, 255, 261n26
indexicals, 204, 253–4, 259, 264
individuation, 210–13
individuators, 215, 217, 218, 220, 221
infallibilism, 14
infinite regress, 15n12, 114, 116–18, 125n21, 174, 176
infinitism, 117–18, 124n12
internalism
  and coherentism, xix, 108, 110
  and externalism, 61, 72, 79, 123n5, 282–90
  and foundationalism, xix, xx
  and justification, xviii–xx, 6, 14, 80, 81, 282–90
  and skepticism, 113, 114, 116, 118, 168, 171
introspection, xx–xxii, 50
intuition, xx–xxi

James, W., 154, 161
justification
  argumentative account of, xvi–xvii
  and causality, 146–8, 176
  and evidence, 145, 146, 284

and externalism, xviii, xxii, xxiii, 13–14, 73–6, 80, 81, 282–90
and indefeasibility, 59, 71
inferential, 73, 82–4, 286–7
and intellectual virtue, xx–xxiii, 4, 9
internal, 103–4, 106
and internalism, xviii–xx, 6, 14, 80, 81, 282–90
prepositional and doxastic, 43, 47, 48
and reliabilism, xxii–xxiii, 60–1
strong vs. weak, 148–9
subjective, 103–4
supervenience of, xvii, xviii–xix, 48, 116

Kant, I., 154
Kepler, J., 158
Kierkegaard, S., 283
kinds, 207–12, 258, 264
Klein, P., 309, 310, 311
knowledge
  animal and reflective, xxiii, 4, 6, 8, 13, 15n12, 17–19, 66, 72, 73, 74–5, 77–8, 79, 82, 84–90, 96, 101, 102, 106–8, 126–33, 181, 285–7, 290–2, 306–9
  aretaic conception of, 4
  causal theory of, 11, 59, 60
  cognitio vs. scientia, 6, 17, 96, 117–18, 181, 305, 306
  and credit, 8, 11, 197
  and Gettier problems, 59, 60, 61, 66, 67, 69–71, 83, 196, 197
  and luck, 4, 5, 64, 65, 70, 108, 138
  naturalized, 60, 73
  and sense perception, 18, 19, 73, 166–8, 170, 177, 179, 180, 183, 184
  sociality of, 104, 291
  and species-relativity, 5
  value of, 130–2, 190–7, 319–22
Kornblith, H., 290
Kripke, S., 20, 21, 210, 247n24, 292, 293, 323n19
Kuhn, T., 261n23, 323n17

Lehrer, K., 108, 109, 110, 119, 124–5n19, 126, 133n8, 309, 311, 314, 315
Leibniz, G. W., 43
LePoidevin, R., 260n15
Lewicki, P., 102
Lewis, D., 41n14, 224, 225, 226, 227, 252, 253, 262n30

Locke, J., 209, 210, 222n121
lottery problem, 23

MacBeath, M., 260n15
matter, 211, 213, 255, 256, 259
McDowell, J., 163–4n18, 221n1
McTaggart, J. M. E., 249–50
memory, 99, 181
mental states, 263–4, 269–70
meta-incoherence problem, xxii, xxiii, 64–5, 77, 80–2, 97–100, 103, 285–6
Moore, G. E., 18–19, 36, 38–40, 40–1n12, 166, 194, 197–8n4, 301
Moser, P., 318, 319
myth of the given, 174, 178, 182, 185

Neurath, O., 175, 176, 183
new evil-demon problem *see* evil-demon problem
Newton, I., 261n23
Nozick, R., 20, 22, 24, 25, 30, 31, 36, 276, 280, 292

Peirce, C. S., 157
perception, 18, 19, 73, 165, 166–70, 171, 179, 180, 183, 184, 315–17
  and cognitive psychology, 105n8
  and reference, 218–20
  and reliability, 99–101, 140, 141, 149, 150, 152
  see also sensory experience
Perry, J., 252, 253
persistence, 203–4, 209–11, 255, 261n26
perspective, epistemic
  and circularity, 106–7, 114–16, 135–40, 165–8, 174, 317
  and coherence, 109–10, 111
  and the generality problem, xxiv, 8, 97–100, 103
  and intellectual virtue, 3, 8, 90, 91, 93, 94, 96, 97
  and internalism, 127
  and meta-incoherence problem, xxii, xxiii, 64–5, 77, 80–2, 97–100, 103, 285–6
  and new evil-demon problem, xxii, xxiii, 65–7, 108, 110, 111, 193, 276, 278, 280, 284, 299
  and psychological plausibility objection, 97–101

perspective, epistemic (*cont.*):
   and reliabilism, 90, 91, 93, 94, 97, 98, 103, 126
   and skepticism, xxiv, 112
phenomenalism, 222n11
Plantinga, A., 75, 76, 80
Plato, 291
Pollock, J., 142, 143
positivism, logical, 175
presentism, 250–1, 261n18
principle of ascent, 73, 120, 309–10
principle of exclusion, 12, 13, 309, 310
principle of transfer, 309, 310
Prio, A. N., 253
problem of easy knowledge, 19, 303–5
problem of narrow foundations, xvi, xx, xxii
problem of the specked hen, xxi, 45–6, 48–51, 57–8n9, 87, 88, 289
properties
   accidental vs. essential, 210–13
   intrinsic, 238
   of mind-independent objects, 219
propositional attitudes, 249, 252
propositions
   and conceptual relativism, 205, 206, 256–9
   existential, 249, 254–8
   and individuators, 215
   and self-attribution, 252
   tensed, 249, 252, 253, 259
Putnam, H., 163n8, 201, 202, 205, 206, 224, 228, 229, 263

Quine, W. V., 154, 156, 240, 247n24, 248n26, 261n22
Quinton, A., 261n23

rationalism, xv, xx
rationality, 128, 153
realism
   and absolutism/explosionism, 205, 207, 213, 224, 228, 231, 243–4, 245, 255–7
   direct, 149
   internal, 201, 233–6
   and mereological sums, 258–9
   metaphysical vs. scientific, 201
   pragmatic, 234, 247n7
reference
   Fregean, 215–18
   and mind-independent particulars, 218–21

   perspectival character of, 201, 205
   and subjectivity, 216–18, 222
   and truth, 230–1, 234
Reid, T., 20, 73, 300, 323–4n22
relativity
   conceptual, 201–13, 224–5, 228–9, 234, 235, 237, 240, 242, 245, 256–9
   existential, 201, 207, 208, 224–7, 229, 231, 232
reliabilism
   and animal knowledge, 126
   and aptness, 140
   evolutionary, 155
   and generality problem, xxiv, 97–9, 100, 103
   and justification, xvi, xxii–xxiii, 60–1
   and meta-incoherence problem, xxii, xxiii, 64–5, 77, 80–2, 97–100, 103, 285–6
   and new evil-demon problem, xxii, xxiii, 65–7, 108, 110, 111, 193, 276, 278, 280, 284, 299
   process, 90–4
   Sellar's objection to, 179–82
   and tracking account, 91
   two-stage, 94
   and value problem, 190–7, 319–22
Rescher, N., 318
Riggs, W., 198n12
Rorty, R., 176
Russell, B., 43, 161, 162n2, 222n10, 237, 253, 255, 260n14

safety, 20, 21, 26–7, 29–35, 276–9, 292, 293
Schlick, M., 175, 177
Searle, J., 218
Sellars, W., 174, 176–81, 182–6, 189n5, 306, 307
sense-datum theory, 257–8
sense perception *see* perception
sensitivity, 22–9, 35, 128–9, 276–9, 292
sensory experience, xvi, 145–7, 161
Sextus Empiricus, 135
Sider, T., 253, 260n14
skepticism
   academic, 113, 116–18, 120
   and brains in vats, 23, 26, 38–9, 40n5, 41n15, 41n16, 276, 278
   Cartesian, 119, 120–1
   and coherentism, 174, 276, 280–2

and contextualism, 22, 35–8, 40n9
about external things, 166–8, 315–17
and externalism, 73–5, 113, 168–73
and foundationalism, 42, 73, 174, 297–8
and infinitism, 117–18, 124n12
and intellectual virtue, 11, 12
and internalism, 113, 114, 116, 118, 168, 171
and non-question begging warrant, 135–40, 141
and principle of exclusion, 12, 13, 309, 310
Pyrrhonian, 113, 114, 116, 117, 119–20, 121, 174, 180–3, 297, 306
and safety, 33–4, 276–9
and sense perception, 18, 165–71, 315–17
and sensitivity, 22–7, 35, 276–9
and subjunctive conditionals account, 24–6, 27, 276, 277
about unobserved matters of fact, 168, 170, 317
Socrates, 291
Stine, G., 41n14
Stone, J., 260n8
Stroud, B., 315–17
supervenience, xvii, xviii–xix, 48, 116, 203, 253, 254–8, 263

time, 249–54
truth, correspondence theory of, 229–30

Twain, M., 160
twin-earth problem, 263–4, 269–70

Unger, P., 22

value, epistemic, 130–2, 190–7, 319–22
van Inwagen, P., 228
virtue, intellectual
  believing out of, 15n6, 92, 93
  as faculty, 101–2
  and luck, 4, 5, 64, 65, 70
  possession of, 5, 92, 93
  as power, 7–8
  as truth-conducive disposition, xxi, 62–3
  and value, 191, 192
  and virtue ethics, 3
  and wisdom, 15n5
Vogel, J., 19, 39n4, 303

Whitehead, A. N., 154, 237
Williams, B., 235, 236, 237, 238
Williams, M., 126, 305, 306, 307
Williamson, T., 22
Wittgenstein, L., 186
Wright, C., 246n6

Zagzebski, L., 319–31
'zebra-in-the-zoo' case, 23, 119
Zermelo, E., 262n29
Zimmerman, D., 260n13